Making the Most of your MICROWAVE

Making the Most of your MICROWAVE

BRIDGET JONES

HAMLYN

To Neill

To remind him not to turn our microwave oven
down to a lower power when I'm not looking!

The author and publishers would like to thank the following
for lending the crockery and cutlery shown in the
photographs: Corningware by Corning Limited; Divertimenti;
Lifestyle Department, Army and Navy; David Mellor;
Microwave Ovenware; The Reject Shop.

The microwave ovens used for testing these recipes were
supplied by Moulinex Limited and Toshiba (UK) Limited.

Line illustrations by Elaine Hill
Photography by Chris Crofton

Published 1985 by
Hamlyn Publishing,
Bridge House, London Road,
Twickenham, Middlesex

Reprinted 1985

Copyright © Hamlyn Publishing 1985,
a division of The Hamlyn Publishing Group Ltd

ISBN 0 600 32471 0

Set in Monophoto Gill Sans by Servis Filmsetting Ltd.

Printed in Spain

CONTENTS

USEFUL FACTS & FIGURES

Notes on Metrication

In this book quantities are given in metric and Imperial measures. Exact conversion from Imperial to metric measures does not usually give very convenient working quantities and so the metric measures have been rounded off into units of 25 grams.

Ounces	Approx g to nearest whole figure	Recommended conversion to nearest unit of 25
1	28	25
2	57	50
3	85	75
4	113	100
5	142	150
6	170	175
7	198	200
8	227	225
9	255	250
10	283	275
11	312	300
12	340	350
13	368	375
14	396	400
15	425	425
16 (1 lb)	454	450
17	482	475
18	510	500
19	539	550
20 (1¼ lb)	567	575

Note: When converting quantities over 20 oz first add the appropriate figures in the centre column, then adjust to the nearest unit of 25. As a general guide, 1 kg (1000 g) equals 2.2 lb or about 2 lb 3 oz. This method of conversion gives good results in nearly all cases, although in certain pastry and cake recipes a more accurate conversion is necessary to produce a balanced recipe.

Liquid measures The millilitre has been used in this book and the following table gives a few examples.

Imperial	Approx ml to nearest whole figure	Recommended ml
¼ pint	142	150 ml
½ pint	283	300 ml
¾ pint	425	450 ml
1 pint	567	600 ml
1¼ pints	851	900 ml
1¾ pints	992	1000 ml (1 litre)

Spoon measures All spoon measures given in this book are level unless otherwise stated.

Can sizes At present, cans are marked with the exact (usually to the nearest whole number) metric equivalent of the Imperial weight of the contents, so we have followed this practice when giving can sizes.

Oven temperatures

The table below gives recommended equivalents.

	°C	°F	Gas Mark
Very cool	110	225	¼
	120	250	½
Cool	140	275	1
	150	300	2
Moderate	160	325	3
	180	350	4
Moderately hot	190	375	5
	200	400	6
Hot	220	425	7
	230	450	8
Very hot	240	475	9

Notes for American and Australian users

In America the 8-oz measuring cup is used. In Australia metric measures are now used in conjunction with the standard 250-ml measuring cup. The Imperial pint, used in Britain and Australia, is 20 fl oz, while the American pint is 16 fl oz. It is important to remember that the Australian tablespoon differs from both the British and American tablespoons; the table below gives a comparison. The British standard tablespoon, which has been used throughout this book, holds 17.7 ml, the American 14.2 ml, and the Australian 20 ml. A teaspoon holds approximately 5 ml in all three countries.

British	American	Australian
1 teaspoon	1 teaspoon	1 teaspoon
1 tablespoon	1 tablespoon	1 tablespoon
2 tablespoons	3 tablespoons	2 tablespoons
3½ tablespoons	4 tablespoons	3 tablespoons
4 tablespoons	5 tablespoons	3½ tablespoons

An Imperial/American guide to solid and liquid measures

Solid measures

IMPERIAL	AMERICAN
1 lb butter or margerine	2 cups
1 lb flour	4 cups
1 lb granulated or caster sugar	2 cups
1 lb icing sugar	3 cups
8 oz rice	1 cup

Liquid measures

IMPERIAL	AMERICAN
¼ pint liquid	⅔ cup liquid
½ pint	1¼ cups
¾ pint	2 cups
1 pint	2½ cups
1½ pints	3¾ cups
2 pints	5 cups (2½ pints)

Note: When making any of the recipes in this book, only follow one set of measures as they are not interchangeable.

Comparison of Some Common Different Microwave Oven Settings

Settings	Approximate % Power Input	Use
1 Low Stay Warm Heat and Hold	25%	To keep cooked dishes hot for comparatively long periods of time.
2–3 Defrost Simmer Stew	30–40%	To defrost foods or for lengthy cooking of less tender foods.
4–5 Medium Bake	50%	Reheating foods or cooking delicate foods.
6–8 Medium/High	60–70%	Reheating foods or cooking delicate foods, or simply slowing down the cooking slightly.
9–10 Cook – High – Roast	100%	Cooking food.

Note: Most microwave ovens (other than catering appliances) have a maximum input of 600 or 650 watts but some are 500 watts or 700 watts.

All the recipes in this book were cooked on full power in 600 and 650 watt ovens. If the output of your appliance varies from these levels adjust the timing slightly according to whether it is more or less powerful (see page 12).

KEY TO SYMBOLS

To achieve the best results from microwave cooking many of the recipes in this book require limited use of a conventional cooker. The symbols below indicate which elements of the cooker are needed in the recipe.

 Denotes use of the hob   **Denotes use of the grill**   **Denotes use of the oven**

FOREWORD

It is often difficult to know what to expect of a new piece of kitchen equipment; will it live up to expectations and perform all the chores you had planned for it or will it become a little-used item of clutter in the corner of a cupboard? Advertisements and books will try to convince you that microwaves will revolutionise your cooking. Microwaves do cook food quickly and they will add a whole new dimension to your cooking methods but you must experiment with your new microwave oven to make it suit your eating habits, otherwise you could find that you change your eating habits to fit in with the microwave!

There is a great deal of controversy over which foods are cooked well in the microwave oven, indeed many people use their microwave ovens only to defrost and reheat convenience foods! I hope that these recipes and ideas will guide you towards achieving the best possible results, avoiding any disasters. Between the successes and disasters lots of foods can be cooked in the microwave with inferior results but these are not included in this book.

Read the manufacturer's instructions carefully and find out at what power output your oven operates. These recipes were tested in 600 and 650 watt ovens, so if your oven differs you will have to adjust the cooking time accordingly. Even similar ovens vary slightly, so read the instructions to find some of the times for basic cooking techniques. You will become accustomed to your oven's characteristics as you are with your conventional cooker.

Remember not to use metal containers, dishes trimmed with metal or those handy metal ties. The food will transmit heat to the container as it cooks – the longer the cooking time, the hotter the dish will be. If you are quickly heating or cooking a small amount of food, then the dish will still be cool; however, if a food requires fairly lengthy cooking the dish will become hot and you will have to use a tea-towel to hold it. Roasting bags also become very hot, so use a tea-towel to lift these. Take care when removing the cling film which is covering a dish. Always hold your arm over the covered side of the container to prevent scalding yourself on the steam which escapes.

On a positive note, once you are used to microwave cooking you will discover that meals can be prepared speedily without a great deal of forethought and that foods can be reheated more successfully than ever before. For hurriedly defrosting foods and preparing snacks or individual meals the microwave is wonderful. The kitchen does not become hot and steamy and there is no danger of burning yourself when you're dashing about the kitchen. Used properly, the microwave oven is one of the most invaluable pieces of kitchen equipment – once you have used one for some months you will wonder how you ever coped before!

Most important of all, I hope you will enjoy using your microwave oven and encourage all the family to acquaint themselves with it because it is most probable that future generations of cooks will take the microwave oven as much for granted as we do our conventional cookers.

To offer you guidance, many of the recipes are featured in the colour pictures. Thanks are due to Nicola Diggins who spent a couple of months working very hard both preparing and presenting all the food for these pictures. As always Neill, my husband, offered support throughout the many hours of testing recipes and he frequently prevented the washing-up from taking over the kitchen; so, thank you Neill!

Bridget Jones

INTRODUCTION

Microwaves & Molecules

What are microwaves, are they dangerous and how do they cook food? These wonder waves of the kitchen have received more publicity than almost any other culinary innovation in recent times. Some people report the fantastic advantages and space-age speed with which they cook; others warn of the bodily dangers of observing a working microwave oven at close range, or of the long-term ills of this type of cooking. In fact, since the domestic microwave oven was proven useful in the average household, there has been a wealth of confusing and conflicting information available. So what do we believe?

Microwave Facts

There are a few basic facts – not opinions, theories or hearsay – which are worth knowing. Microwaves are high-frequency, non-ionizing, electro-magnetic waves which are similar to radio waves but shorter. Unfortunately, whenever microwaves are mentioned many people mentally link them with the notorious X-rays or gamma rays and other high frequency waves. However, *microwaves do not resemble these rays in any way*. Microwaves do not have any effect on the cell structure of the body and therefore they do not have a cumulative effect on human tissue. The only harm they can do is thermal. If you want to compare microwaves with any other waves, then remember that they are most similar to harmless radio waves and infra-red waves.

Microwaves for Cooking

We are all familiar with the way in which foods cook by conventional methods but microwaves cook food by a completely new method. These waves react in different ways to various materials. For example, they pass straight through certain materials (in the same way as light passes through a window), they are absorbed by other substances and they can be reflected off metals.

Many conventional cooking containers – dishes, glassware and certain plastics – allow the microwave energy to pass through them and therefore they are useful for holding food in the microwave oven. Metals, and some highly glazed surfaces, reflect the microwaves and as a general rule these should not be used in the oven. Food of all types absorbs microwave energy and it is in this way that it cooks.

This is where the molecules begin to play their part. To outline the cooking process in simple terms, when microwaves cook food they excite the water molecules therein. Most foods contain quite a high percentage of water – fish, meat and vegetables, for example, all contain a lot of moisture even if we cannot actually see it.

The microwaves penetrate the food and the further they travel towards the centre, the less powerful they become. As they are absorbed by the food it is heated by the molecules which are jostling against each other. So the heating is from the inside rather from the outside. If there is a large quantity of food, or if the food is very dense, then the waves will not penetrate in as far as the centre but the heat will be greatest at about 2.5 to 5 cm/1 to 2 in. in from the surface.

The effect of this cooking method is basically very similar to steaming. Because the moisture molecules are excited, they evaporate and produce steam. Unlike baking and grilling, microwave is a moist, not dry, cooking method. Similarly to conventional cooking, fats melt in the microwave oven, so if there is a layer of fat on the food this will melt if the cooking time is long enough and the surface may begin to brown. However, usually, because microwave cooking is moist, then foods do not brown and they do not form a crisp crust.

Of what use is it, you may think, to know all this fascinating information? The point is that once you understand the way in which your microwave oven operates then you will be able to judge which foods cook best, which ones are likely to need a standing time after cooking and before eating and, most important of all, you will be able to put the oven to its best use in your kitchen.

It also follows that certain foods cannot be cooked successfully in a microwave oven. Microwave cooking is not magically quick, but in most cases it is significantly faster than conventional cooking methods. Foods which need lengthy, slow cooking cannot be prepared in the microwave, so forget about putting tough stewing cuts and less tender meats in the microwave and cook these as you always have done. Recipes which rely on a crust for good results should not be attempted in the microwave oven. These include items made from choux pastry, batters and soufflé-type mixtures. This is not, of course, true if you have an oven which combines microwave energy with conventional heat.

Utensils to Use

Common Kitchen Cookware

If you have a reasonably well equipped kitchen then the chances are that you really do not have to rush out and invest a small fortune in microwave cookware. Most kitchens have a selection of plain china bowls and basins, heatproof glass measuring jugs, plain heatproof or ovenproof serving dishes and casseroles, plates, quiche dishes, gratin dishes, mugs or sturdy cups. It may sound rather like a gathering of the jumble items from the back of the store, but you will find that all sorts of small dishes and basins are useful for microwave cooking.

First let's look at the utensils which you most definitely cannot use. Do not put metal dishes, saucepans, cutlery, metal-trimmed teapots or coffee jugs, jam pot lids, cooking foil, tins or whisks into the microwave. Remember not to put butter wrapped in foil-backed paper in the oven too!

Plastics are a border-line case: if they are strong and designed to withstand a fair amount of heat, then they can be used for short reheating or defrosting foods. Similarly, baskets and wooden containers are useful only for brief reheating, for example heating bread rolls to take to the table.

Plain, fairly deep, ovenproof casseroles or soufflé dishes can be useful for preparing moist dishes – not only casserole-type recipes, but sauces, rice dishes, and desserts. Avoid any which have metal trims or painted metallic patterns. The most basic kitchen equipment – mixing bowls and basins – are often the most important for microwave cooking. The only disadvantage of using these is that the food will have to be

transferred to a serving dish before it is taken to the table. Medium-sized basins (1.15-litre/2-pint capacity) are ideal for recipes which require whisking during cooking – sauces and scrambled eggs for example. Large containers have to be used for foods which are likely to froth up during cooking – generous quantities of rice for example.

For cooking fish fillets or steaks, or other foods that should be positioned as far apart as possible, plain white or heatproof glass quiche dishes are the best form of container. A 25-cm/10-in quiche dish will fit into most ovens, with or without a turntable. If you have an oven which has a turntable that can be turned upside down to stop it from turning, or an oven without a turntable, then you may find that a lasagne dish and oval gratin dish are also good candidates for microwave cooking. Similarly, roasting dishes can be utilised to arrange single items of food as far apart as possible or roasts which are to be pre-cooked in the microwave oven, then transferred to the conventional oven for browning and crisping can be cooked in these dishes. The roasting dish can also serve to make the gravy in the microwave.

Many of the recipes in this book follow this pattern of cooking first in the microwave, then browning under a hot grill or crisping in the conventional oven, so dishes which are ovenproof as well as microwaveproof are usually the best. These also have the added advantage of being

useful for all sorts of traditional cooking processes. If you are thinking of investing some money in a new set of saucepans or a frying pan, then it is a good idea to look at the heatproof glass range of pans which can be used on the hob, in the conventional oven or in the microwave. A point to remember is that if you have an oven with a turntable, then the larger saucepans will not be of any use because the handles will knock against the oven wall. The same caution applies to the frying pan, but if you have the room this is particularly useful for frying off some ingredients first, then putting in the microwave for final cooking – chicken joints, chops and sausages for example.

In addition to the main cooking dishes, you will find that some smaller vessels are a boon to microwave cooking. A heatproof glass measuring jug can be used for cooking small quantities of rice, for making small amounts of sauce or for melting chocolate. Plain mugs can also come in handy for melting small amounts of fat or for heating liquids. The jugs are also ideal containers for bread (see recipe on page 192), as too are earthenware flower pots if you remember to cover the holes with greaseproof paper. Wooden spoons and sturdy plastic utensils can be used to stir foods, then left in the microwave oven for a short time, but if they are left in there for too long they will begin to cook.

Covering It All Up

It can be very important to cover some foods when they are cooked in the microwave oven. When the water molecules are leaping about inside the food, they can produce a great deal of evaporation and certain foods can become quite dry on the surface if the cooking container is not covered. Casserole dishes with lids can be used, but if you are cooking in a basin or bowl, then you have to look at a new way of covering hot foods and cling film presents itself as the perfect answer.

It is well worth investing in a big roll of cling film. There are times when food is covered and cooked for just a few minutes, in which case the cling film will not balloon up. If the food is cooked for longer periods, then it is usually necessary to allow a small gap in the covering to allow the steam to escape. If the cling film is the thinner variety (and there is nothing wrong with using this kind) then you may well find that if you pierce a little hole in it the whole covering splits in two. That is very annoying! So, instead of making holes in the cling film, allow a small open gap at one side of the dish.

Other disposable kitchen stationery which you may find useful for microwave cooking includes roasting bags and absorbent kitchen paper. The bags can hold vegetables as well as meats and poultry, but remember not to secure them with metal ties; elastic bands can be used instead. Absorbent kitchen paper comes in useful for covering bacon rashers or other foods which are likely to spit during cooking but which should not be covered with cling film. A piece of kitchen paper also makes a good base for baked potatoes and hamburgers.

Microwave Ovens: Simple to Sophisticated

If you look round the shops you will soon become aware of the enormous range of microwave ovens that are available. Small ones, big ones, high-tech designs with flashing lights and sci-fi warning buzzers, or basic squarish models that look almost primitive by comparison. The choice is quite mind boggling and the task of deciding which one to put your money on is no mean feat. But how good are the elaborate appliances?

Microwave Oven Components

The fundamental components of microwave ovens are all the same. The oven is plugged in and the mains supply electricity is increased to high voltage energy which enters a magnetron. It is this part which actually produces the microwaves and these then flow into the oven. The way in which the waves are directed into the oven cavity may vary, but once inside they can be distributed evenly by a hidden stirrer. Some ovens do not have a stirrer but they have a turntable instead. Certain ovens have turntables as well as stirrers.

From this point onwards in the make-up of an oven the range expands and microwave-oven technology really is a fast-moving industry so the gadgets available are always increasing in number. The most basic oven has a timer and an on/off switch, but there are few of these models available. If you bought a microwave oven a few years ago you may have one of this type. Most cookers now offer at least a defrost setting in addition to the on/off switch.

When the oven is turned on it operates at full power output and this varies with the particular model of oven. The output is usually between 500 to 700 watts. Somewhere on your oven there will be a plate telling you what the output is, or your handbook will tell you. It is important to know this as the higher the power output, the quicker the oven will cook and vice-versa. *All these recipes were tested in 600 and 650 watt ovens.*

Defrost Setting

If an oven has a defrost setting, then for the length of time the oven is switched on the food will receive less energy than when full power is selected. This is achieved automatically by a device which pulsates the energy into the oven. In effect the oven switches itself on and off at regular intervals.

Variable Power

The next stage up in the microwave oven range is the variable power oven. The majority of microwave ovens offer a range of power settings. These may be presented in different ways because, unlike conventional cookers, there are no standard settings for microwave ovens. The simplest way in which the power levels can be presented is in the form of high, medium or low settings. Some ovens offer a range of setting on a scale from 1 to 10 while others present the different cooking levels as roast, simmer or heat. The settings are a total confusion of numbers, terms and comparisons with no way of telling how the different ovens compare. All you can be sure of is that when an oven is on its highest setting, then the food is cooked by the most power which enters the cavity at any time.

In most cases these different settings do not reflect different levels of power entering the oven all the way through the cooking process. They usually mean that, as for the defrost setting, while the appliance is switched on the power is pulsated into the oven, so that the energy level over a given length of time can be increased or decreased, with the power on all the time when the highest setting is selected.

There are a few ovens which actually offer two or more completely different power settings and these levels will be stated on the appliance. For example these ovens could be operated at a choice of 600 watts or 500 watts perhaps.

Reheat and stay-warm controls are also features of some ovens. These are settings at which the power is directed into the oven for very short periods so as to keep food hot rather than heat it up.

Knobs or Chips

The controls on the oven can be very simple, with a timer dial as the most basic. A touch control unit can be included for selecting the power level or cooking time. A digital display may be used to indicate the cooking time, the length of time for which the food has already cooked and the power level at which it is cooking. A built-in clock to tell the time of day may also be included.

Ovens which incorporate microprocessors in their controls can offer any number of functions. For example, some ovens have a memory facility so that different cooking levels can be selected for one operation. If, for example, you have a frozen food which you take out of the freezer to serve for dinner as soon as possible, this can be put into the oven and defrost power selected for a certain number of minutes. At the same time as tapping in the defrost setting you would instruct the oven to cook the food on the required power level for a given time, then, if necessary, the oven could be programmed to keep the food hot on a stay-warm setting for an indefinite length of time. This can now be done all in one simple operation, leaving you free to go away and do whatever you want.

The range of pre-select programmes is continually changing and increasing. It is possible to cook food by weight and type, or to select a pre-set programme for a precise recipe (supplied by the manufacturer) or food.

Temperature Probe

One of the more common features of newer microwave ovens is a temperature probe. This can be used to determine the temperature of the food in the oven. Before the food is put into the oven the temperature at which it will be cooked must be selected. The probe is put into the food, then when the required temperature is reached the oven will automatically switch itself off.

Built-in Grills

Some microwave ovens have built-in conventional grills or browning elements which can be used to brown or crisp the food once the microwave cooking is completed. This is a useful facility, which is exactly the same as using a conventional grill but nominally easier.

Combination Ovens

Probably the most exciting development in the way of microwave ovens is the combination oven – an oven which offers the facility for cooking with microwaves at the same time as cooking with conventional heat. This appliance offers an ideal way of cooking: the speed of microwaves with the crisp, brown results of conventional methods.

Three Categories of Ovens

To summarise the types of oven available: they can be grouped into single power ovens which usually offer a defrost setting, variable power ovens and combination ovens. Within each category the ovens may have a turntable. In the higher price bracket (variable power ovens) the range of gadgets offered can be quite broad. The combination ovens are all different and they are difficult to compare.

From the outside, the ovens vary in size, colour and finish. There are some very small ovens on the market and some which are quite large but microwave ovens are not as big as conventional ovens. The only exceptions are free-standing or built-in combination ovens. The exterior finish can be matt, in brown or black, shiny or enamelled. Some ovens can be built-in to standard kitchen units and some are designed to fit above or below a conventional oven in the one unit. Whichever type of oven you buy it is a good idea to take note of the dimensions before you decide where to put it in your kitchen.

Successful Experimenting

The only way you are going to get to know your own microwave oven and to get the best out of it is by experimenting. At first you may, very sensibly, want to stick to a recipe book or your manufacturer's recipe guidelines but after a while you really should make the effort to try out lots of different foods and techniques in your microwave oven. Reading about what you can and cannot cook is never the same as discovering for yourself exactly what happens when something is overcooked or if something is steamed instead of grilled. I am not suggesting that you set out with the sole intention of ruining that evening's dinner or watching a so-called boiled egg explode in a dreadful mess, but you can see how easy it is to overcook food just by putting a bread roll in the oven and cooking it for several minutes. When it is hot it will be very moist but as it cools it will become very hard indeed.

Remember that it is easy to overcook food in the microwave oven but you cannot spoil food by under cooking it. For example if you are making a steamed sponge pudding you will have to remember to use a large basin for a small amount of mixture because it rises more than usual. Put it in and observe what happens when it cooks. When it looks as though it may be cooked, open the door and take the pudding out. If it is not cooked, then put it back and continue the cooking process – unlike conventional cooking methods, this is quite acceptable.

When you are trying one of your own recipes in a microwave oven try to compare it with one of the recipes written for the microwave, then you will have some idea of how long it is likely to take to cook. Start by giving the food several minutes less than you expect it to take, then cook the food in short stages until it is just right. Make a mental note of how long the recipe took – or better still write it down – so that next time you will know how long it takes.

If you have a recipe which requires a lot of water, then remember that this will take some time to heat through in the microwave oven. Large quantities of liquid can require very lengthy cooking – soups for example. So, use boiling water from the kettle and add it in stages if possible. Taking a soup as an example, cook the flavouring ingredients in a small amount of liquid to make a very concentrated liquid, then add the water or stock to thin it down.

Made for the Microwave

There is now a large range of cookware especially designed and produced for microwave cooking. The quality varies as do the prices.

Basic Containers

There are all shapes and sizes of cooking dishes available. Some of these have lids which can often be turned upside down to serve as vessels themselves. Starting with the smaller dishes, individual cocottes or ramekin-type containers can be used for poaching eggs, making pâtés or preparing individual puddings. They can also be useful for reheating or preparing small amounts of baby foods.

Among the larger containers which are available, there are casserole dishes, shallow quiche dishes and gratin dishes. These containers usually come complete with a lid if they are in the more expensive ranges. There are some large cooking containers available which resemble very big casseroles or mixing bowls.

So, are these containers worth buying and how useful will they be? Before you buy them, look at the quality of the material. If the containers are made of thin plastic which can be flexed easily then the chances are that they will not be very durable. Here we are thinking about basic dishes which you may well use every day, so they need to stand up to lots of heat and washing-up without becoming mis-shapen or damaged. Compare what you see with other conventional dishes which you may already own or which can be purchased quite cheaply. Would you want to serve food from some of the microwave cookware range or would you use them purely to prepare the food, then transfer it to a serving dish? If this is the case why not use instead heatproof glass basins and bowls which you already have?

If you are looking at the more expensive cookware, then you really should look at it in terms of serving food as well as cooking it. There are some very pleasing designs but there are also some which really do belong only in the kitchen. This is where the price factor does become important; compare the less attractive containers with the useful traditional dishes, then decide.

Special-purpose Containers

If you want to make cakes, breads or meatloaves in your microwave oven then you will have to abandon your traditional metalware and look for new loaf dishes, cake dishes, ring dishes and bun dishes.

As with basic containers the quality varies enormously and the price differences are staggering. So, how often do you intend making breads or whatever food requires a special pan? If you want to experiment first to see if you like microwave baking or meatloaves, then buy a cheap dish which may only last for a few months. If you know that you will be using a certain container frequently then buy a good one. The following are a few of the common dish shapes which are available in the more expensive ranges and sometimes in the cheaper materials.

Cake Dish – usually a plain round dish without a lid. A soufflé dish will do just as well, also I have found that all cake mixtures cook far better in a ring container.

Ring Dish – either plain or fluted, available in a heavy material or in a cheaper and eventually disposable variety. This shape container is by far the best to use for baking cakes. Try a cheap one first in case you would prefer to make your cakes in the conventional oven.

Bun Dish or Muffin Pan – a useful container for cooking eggs as well as small cakes and bread rolls.

Racks – these come in many shapes and sizes to stand on their own in the oven or to put over a large plain dish. They are intended for keeping meats free of cooking fat and juices or for cooking bacon. Absorbent kitchen paper makes a good alternative for bacon. If you are going to make the best use of your microwave to pre-cook meat and then finish it off in the conventional oven, it is best to keep the meat in its juices while it is cooking by microwave energy. The joint can be put on a metal roasting rack when it is transferred to the conventional oven, this way the meat stays moist.

Browning Dishes and Skillets – these are dishes which have a special coating on the underside of the base. When heated in the microwave this coating absorbs the energy and becomes very hot. The food is put on the base and it browns and sears quickly. The dishes need preheating for 5 to 8 minutes before the food is added. They are usually expensive to buy and can be difficult to clean. I always feel that I might as well put the food under the grill or into a frying pan instead. If you want to cook large chops, steaks, sausages or a traditional breakfast in your oven then you will probably find these containers useful, but for the majority of dishes they are not necessary.

Independent Turntables – if you buy an oven without a turntable and find that you have a problem with uneven cooking, then all is not lost. (I must emphasise that I would not suggest that any ovens without a turntable may give uneven cooking – I own an oven without a turntable and it is one of the best cookers I have ever used.)

Battery operated turntables are useful for overcoming such a problem. Spring powered turntables are also available and these need to be wound up after a certain length of time (about 30 minutes).

Racks and Shelves – specially designed shelf units are available and these can be useful if you want to prepare two or three dishes, then put them all in the oven for a final heating through. Plate dividing racks are also useful if you want to reheat two or more prepared meals.

Coffee Maker – specially designed, all-plastic coffee percolators which can be put into the microwave oven.

As with all cookware, it is important to follow the manufacturer's instructions for the above items.

The only comment to make about utensils to use in the microwave oven is to adopt a common-sense attitude towards them. I was horrified when someone told me that they would have to buy a whole new range of cooking utensils when they bought a microwave oven! That struck me as being quite ridiculous – it may well be necessary to buy a few new items or you may well want to experiment with different shaped dishes, but it is unlikely that you have no dishes at all which you can use for microwave cooking. I went out and bought two heatproof glass basins and a loaf dish first, then I decided to buy a bun dish and a ring dish (but only a cheap one because I prefer to make cakes in my conventional oven). My husband decided he had to try a browning dish (to make toasted sandwiches) but I stick to my frying pan (not too literally!) and the conventional grill. I certainly would not want to tell anyone what to buy because cooking habits are all different. The only advice I would offer is to spend some time getting used to your microwave oven, then you will gradually find out what you need in the way of new utensils as you go along.

Which Model to Buy

There is no easy way of deciding which model to buy because they all have their own advantages and disadvantages. You will obviously have set yourself a price limit and this will give you a starting point – look at all the models which you can afford. Read as much information as you can and ask questions about the ovens. If there are any available, then it is a good idea to attend a microwave cooking demonstration. Splashing out on the most expensive microwave oven is not necessarily the answer and you could be just as disappointed as if you were to buy the cheapest one you can find. Price, however, is to a certain extent indicative of quality and cooking efficiency.

There are a few guidelines which you can draw up for yourself in trying to make a decision. Before you look at the ovens look at your kitchen – where are you going to put the microwave oven when it arrives? Remember that you will need to allow some space around the oven for ventilation.

Think about the sort of things you are likely to cook and the numbers you are going to be catering for. If you really do need a large oven cavity, remember that an oven with a turntable has less useable cooking space than one which does not. If the oven you like does have a turntable can it be switched off or turned upside down to prevent it from rotating?

Look at the controls and try all the different types before you decide which suits you best. Try

INTENDED OVEN USE	FACILITY TO CHOOSE
Defrosting	DEFROST SETTING/MEMORY FACILITY (If you intend to use your microwave oven for defrosting lots of frozen foods and prepared dishes, then look for an oven with a defrost setting. If you want an oven in the higher price range, then one with the facility for programming in defrost and cook at the same time may be useful.)
Cooking Fresh Foods	FULL POWER/TEMPERATURE PROBE (Full power is the most useful setting for cooking. The temperature probe would feature in the ovens in the higher price bracket. It is a useful facility for cooking joints of meat and casserole-type dishes.)
Reheating Foods	VARIABLE POWER/STAY-HOT CONTROL (The various power settings are most useful for reheating foods. If you have a hectic family life with various members wanting different meals at odd times, then you can prepare individual meals and put them on to plates. These can be reheated as required and on a lower setting the quick-heating foods will not overcook before the dense items are hot. The stay-hot control will enable you to heat the food, then keep it hot for some time until you are ready to serve.)
Speed Cooking	FULL POWER/COMBINATION OVEN (If you want your microwave oven to cook food quickly, select a good model and you will only need to use full power. If you have the money then invest in a combination oven, but remember if you are cooking for more than two people you are unlikely to want to be rid of your conventional oven because most combination ovens are comparatively quite small.)
Economy	FULL POWER/DEFROST (If you are looking to your microwave oven to save on fuel costs, then buy a basic model. The defrost setting can be used to cook tougher cuts of meat. The time will be as long as your conventional oven but the fuel costs are lower.)
Dinner-party Cooking/Coping with Family Meals	DEFROST/VARIABLE POWER/STAY HOT CONTROL/LARGE OVEN (For someone who does a great deal of entertaining, preparing meals at all times of the day for the family or lots of pre-freezing and menu planning, then a more sophisticated oven offers useful options. Look for an oven which will take a large dish or remember to make sure the turntable is one which can be turned upside down, if there is one in the oven at all.)

the bells or buzzers or whatever device is used for telling you that the food is cooked. You are going to have to live with the noise in your kitchen, so make sure it is one that you can stand hearing! As well as looking at these points, find an oven which has an accurate timer. Whether it is in the form of a knob or button, digital or otherwise, it is important that it offers the facility for timing seconds up as far as 5 minutes and minutes up to 15 minutes.

Once you are familiar with the different types, sit down and make a list of your requirements, then list those ovens which fulfil those criteria. Use the following ideas as a guide, adding any special requirements you may have.

The most important feature of any microwave oven is even heat distribution. Ask to see a bar of chocolate melted in a few microwave ovens and you will see how they can vary. Some will melt the chocolate evenly, others will be less even and some may burn the chocolate bar at one end before the other side is melted! You will of course have to go to the shop armed with your own chocolate bar (or bars)! It may seem a little eccentric, but you are, after all, going to be the one to part with your money. If you are polite, interested and explain why you want to see the ovens working in this way, then, depending on whether they have a demonstration model or not, most good retailers will oblige you.

Care of the Appliance

As with any other new appliance, it is most important to follow the manufacturer's instructions for installing the oven. First read all the user instructions so that you know how to operate the appliance successfully and safely.

Cleaning: Inside and Out

You will find that your microwave oven is easy to keep clean. Because the oven itself does not heat up – it may become warm from the food inside, but it does not get very hot – no small spillages or steam and splattered food stick on the inside surfaces of the cooker. For cleaning all you will need is a cloth with hot, soapy water. Do not use any scouring pads or cleaners which may damage the oven lining, as this will adversely affect the oven's performance.

Clean the outside of the oven in the same way, paying particular attention to the area surrounding the door. The surface can be polished with a clean cloth if you like.

If you have any unpleasant lingering smells in your oven, then boil water with plenty of lemon juice inside it daily for 15 minutes until the smell

disappears. This may take a few days, depending on how easily the odour is absorbed.

In using the oven there are a few obvious rules to follow. It is a good idea to make sure that all the family know how to operate the oven. Make sure that the oven is not operated when empty (in this case some of the microwaves may be reflected back to the magnetron and cause damage, or they can spark and burn within the cavity) and that no metals are put in the oven. Keep your oven serviced as suggested by the manufacturers and make sure that a qualified engineer does the job.

Do not slam the oven door or treat the controls roughly. Make sure that any dish you put on the turntable is small enough not to knock against the sides of the oven as it turns. When the oven is not in use turn off all the controls which keep the internal light and fan operating.

Some Important Points to Remember

1 The larger the quantities, the longer the cooking time.
2 Several small items of food should be positioned as far apart as possible for even cooking.
3 Microwaves penetrate the food to a maximum depth of 5 cm/2 in, therefore a large piece of food may require turning or standing during cooking. The point of standing time is to allow the heat to disperse by conduction within the food.
4 The shape of the cooking container may influence the cooking time. Deep containers which are not too broad give the maximum exposure for certain foods like casseroles, rice or other moist dishes. Mixing bowls and basins or heatproof jugs are the right shape.
5 Vegetables require a moist cooking environment, so they should be cooked in roasting bags or in closely covered containers. Do not sprinkle salt on vegetables or it will cause the surface to dehydrate and possibly discolour during cooking. Season foods such as this after cooking.
6 If you are unsure of the cooking time, aim to cook the food in short stages, rather than overcook it in one go.
7 If a dish or food looks as though it is cooking unevenly, then stir it or rearrange the pieces.

SOUPS & STARTERS

It is often the first course of a special meal that creates the greatest problems and for this reason so many people rely on one or two old favourites which are usually cold dishes. Once you have a microwave oven you have the facility for quickly cooking the small portions of food which are presented as a starter. Alternatively, you can make you own superb pâtés and terrines in a fraction of the time taken conventionally, or prepare an elaborate dish in advance and reheat it at the last moment without any deterioration in flavour or appearance.

In addition to light soups, which will whet the appetite for the main course, many of the soups in this chapter are quite hearty and could well be served as good lunch or supper dishes for cold days. Meatball Soup Pot (see page 23) and Seafood Chowder (see page 20) are two such satisfying recipes, so don't just refer to the chapter only when dinner party menus are being decided. If you are planning to make a great quantity of soup for dozens of people, then the microwave is not the best means to use because it does take quite a while to heat large quantities of liquid. For portions numbering four to six the microwave is ideal, but a certain amount of measured liquid should be kept out of the soup until the very end. This way, the other ingredients have a chance to cook quickly before the liquid is reheated and served. One of the best aids for the microwave oven when it comes to making soup is the kettle. Boiling water in a kettle is much quicker than messing about with vast bowls in the microwave.

The microwave oven is positively amazing for making pâtés. The first time I made a pâté in the microwave I really was only half-heartedly experimenting but the excellent result compelled me to try several different pâtés, all of which were ideal for storing in my freezer. The key to success is to lightly cook the roughly chopped ingredients first, then process them into the required consistency for the recipe. This way, when the pâté is put into its dish it is not a dense mass of totally raw food so it cooks quickly without requiring lengthy standing time.

This chapter includes light Chicken Liver Pâté and Turkey Pâté (see page 28) both ideal for starters, as well as a coarse, well-flavoured Rich Pork Pâté (see page 27) and a Fine Herb Pâté (see page 28) which could also pass as a light lunch served with bread and a salad.

If you are looking for an unusual, light starter, then why not try a hot dip for a change? Hot Anchovy Dip and Hot Bean Dip can be found on page 29. You could, of course, always serve a more traditional opening course straight from your microwave and offer Baked Avocado with Cucumber (see page 33) or Mushroom Croustades (see page 30).

As you can see, the chapter includes quite a mixture of ideas. When you're planning your menu, make sure that you select the main course first, then look through the following pages for something to complement, not clash with, whatever you have chosen.

Seafood Chowder

——— SERVES 4 ———

This recipe makes a fairly light chowder which is suitable for serving as a first course; however, it can also be served with plenty of hot crisp bread as a light lunch or you can add some cooked pasta shells and serve the soup for a hearty main dish.

1 onion, chopped	1 fish stock cube
25 g/1 oz butter	450 ml/¾ pint boiling
450 g/1 lb cod fillet	water
6 scallops, cleaned	225 g/8 oz peeled cooked
3 tablespoons plain flour	prawns (defrosted if
salt and freshly ground	frozen)
black pepper	2 tablespoons chopped
300 ml/½ pint milk	parsley
1 bay leaf	

Place the onion in a bowl with the butter and cook on full power for 4 minutes. Skin the fish (see below) and cut the flesh into chunks, removing any bones. Cut the scallops into quarters.

Stir the flour into the onions, add seasoning to taste and gradually stir in the milk, making sure there are no lumps in the mixture. Stir in the prepared cod and scallops then add the bay leaf. Cover with cling film, allowing a small gap for the steam to escape, then cook for 8 minutes. Stir once during cooking.

Meanwhile, dissolve the stock cube in the boiling water. You can, if you like, use home-made fish stock instead of the cube and water. If this stock is cold, then remember to allow extra cooking time to heat it through.

Pour the stock into the chowder and stir in the prawns, then cook for a further 2 minutes. Stir in the parsley and serve at once.

To skin fish fillets: place the fillet flat on a board. Using a sharp knife, and holding it at an acute angle to the board, carefully cut between the fish flesh and skin. Work from the tail towards the head end, holding the tail end firmly in place. Use a gentle sawing motion and try to avoid breaking the skin.

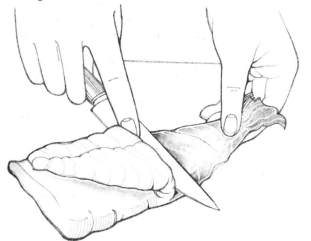

Chicken and Asparagus Soup

——— SERVES 4 ———

This is a rich creamy soup which is ideal for the first course of a dinner party. Offer thinly sliced Wholewheat Jug Bread (see page 192) as an accompaniment.

1 large chicken portion	1 (350-g/12-oz) can green
(about 350 g/12 oz in	asparagus, drained
weight)	300 ml/½ pint milk
1 onion, finely chopped	salt and freshly ground
1 large potato, diced	black pepper
300 ml/½ pint boiling	2 tablespoons dry sherry
water	150 ml/¼ pint single cream

Place the chicken portion in a large bowl with the onion and potato. Pour in the boiling water, cover with cling film and make a small hole in the top for the steam to escape. Cook on full power for 10 minutes.

Lift the chicken out of the liquid and cut all the meat off the bones (don't worry if it is not cooked through; it will be cooked again in the stock). Discard the skin and bones, then chop the meat.

Cut off and reserve the asparagus tips, then mix the stalks with the onion, potato and stock and blend in a liquidiser or food processor. When smooth return this purée to the bowl. Place the chicken meat in the milk and cook for 5 minutes, then stir it into the purée and add the seasoning to taste with the sherry. Cook for 5 minutes, swirl in the cream and add the asparagus tips. Serve at once.

As a general guide, whenever you need a fairly large quantity of boiling water for any dish, then boil it in a kettle instead of the microwave oven as large quantities of liquid require lengthy microwave cooking. This is particularly true of soup-making – start with a small amount of concentrated soup and add more liquid to it once the raw ingredients are thoroughly cooked.

Oriental Chicken Soup

—— SERVES 4 ——

1 chicken joint (about 350 g/12 oz in weight)	1 tablespoon soy sauce
2 carrots	a few drops of sesame oil
1 stick celery	3 tablespoons dry sherry
2 thin slices fresh root ginger	100 g/4 oz Chinese egg noodles
1 chicken stock cube	salt and freshly ground black pepper
900 ml/1½ pints boiling water	

Place the chicken joint in large bowl. Cut the carrots and celery into fine strips, then add both to the chicken. Peel and finely shred the ginger, then add it to the bowl and crumble in the stock cube. Pour in 300 ml/½ pint of the boiling water and cover the bowl with cling film, allowing a small gap for the steam to escape. Cook on full power for 10 minutes.

Remove the chicken and cut off all the meat. Discard the skin and bones, then cut the meat into fine strips. Add this to the soup with the remaining water, the soy sauce, sesame oil and sherry. Break up the noodles and stir them in, then cover and cook for 5 minutes. Taste and adjust the seasoning as necessary, then serve.

Cock a Leekie Soup

—— SERVES 4 ——

Serve this warming chicken and leek soup with plenty of hot crusty bread and some ripe cheese – a mature Cheddar or Stilton for example.

2 boneless chicken breasts	600 ml/1 pint milk
4 leeks, trimmed	salt and freshly ground black pepper
1 large potato, diced	4 tablespoons chopped parsley
300 ml/½ pint boiling water	
1 chicken stock cube	

Place the chicken in a large bowl. Cut the leeks into slices, then thoroughly wash them to remove any grit. Dry the slices on absorbent kitchen paper before adding them to the bowl. Add the potato and pour in the boiling water. Crumble the stock cube into the liquid with the chicken, then cover the bowl with cling film and cook on full power for 15 minutes.

Remove the chicken from the bowl and cut it into small dice. Blend about half the leek and potato mixture to a smooth purée with a little of the milk in a liquidiser or food processor. Pour the purée back into the bowl and stir in the remaining milk. Add seasoning to taste with the chicken and cook for 10 minutes.

To serve, sprinkle the parsley into the soup, give it a good stir and ladle it into individual bowls. Serve at once.

Spring Onion Soup

—— SERVES 4 ——

This is a thin, well-flavoured soup which makes an excellent first course, particularly for those who are counting the calories. Serve crisp melba toast as an accompaniment. For a soup which is low in fat content use a boneless chicken breast, with its skin removed, to make the stock.

1 chicken quarter (about 350 g/12 oz in weight)	900 ml/1½ pints boiling water
1 bunch spring onions	3 tablespoons dry sherry
1 stick celery	salt and freshly ground white pepper
1 chicken stock cube	

Place the chicken joint in a large bowl. Trim the roots and any damaged pieces off the spring onions, then cut the white part off. Shred the white onion very finely and cut the pieces into short strips – about 2.5 cm/1 in long. Add the shredded onion to the chicken. Shred the celery into similar sized pieces and put these in the bowl. Crumble in the stock cube and pour in 300 ml/½ pint of the boiling water, then cover with cling film, allowing a small gap for the steam to escape, and cook on full power for 10 minutes.

While the chicken is cooking, finely shred the green part of the spring onions and cut them into short lengths. Remove the chicken joint from the bowl and cut all the meat off the bones. Discard the bones and skin, then cut the meat into very fine, short strips. Add the shredded chicken to the stock and pour in the remaining boiling water. Stir in the sherry and seasoning to taste, then add the green part of the onions and cook for a further 10 minutes. Ladle the hot soup into individual bowls and serve at once.

Note: if you want to make a smaller quantity of soup, for example to serve two people, complete the first stage of the recipe using 300 ml/½ pint of boiling water. Use a small chicken joint; remember to reduce the quantities of spring onion and use half a stock cube. Pour in the required amount of boiling water and cook for a shorter time before serving – about 6 to 7 minutes. Use this technique for reducing the quantities of most soup recipes: keep the amounts of food or liquid used in the first cooking stage the same as stated in the recipe, then add the reduced portion of liquid at the heating up stage.

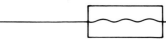

Bread rolls can be arranged in a napkin-lined basket ready for serving, then quickly heated in the microwave at the last minute.

Chicken Almond Soup

——— SERVES 4 ———

This is quite delectable – a delicate soup to serve with small pieces of fine melba toast.

1 large chicken breast (about 450 g/1 lb in weight)	600 ml/1 pint boiling water
100 g/4 oz blanched almonds	2 medium-thick slices white bread, crusts removed
1 small onion, finely chopped	150 ml/¼ pint double cream
1 blade mace	toasted flaked almonds to garnish
1 chicken stock cube, finely crumbled	

Place the chicken breast in a large bowl with the blanched almonds and onion. Add the mace and stock cube, then pour over half the boiling water. Cover with cling film and cook on full power for 10 minutes. Remove the chicken from the stock and cut all the meat off the bone. Discard the skin and finely chop the meat. Remove the blade of mace and discard.

Cut the bread into small pieces, then add it to the almonds and stock and pour on the remaining water.

When the bread has had plenty of time to soften, blend the mixture, until quite smooth, in a liquidiser or food processor. Pour this purée into a bowl, then add the chicken and cream and cook for 4 minutes.

Give the soup a good stir, then serve at once, topped with the toasted flaked almonds.

Chicken and Sweet Corn Soup

——— SERVES 4 ———

1 chicken joint	salt and freshly ground black pepper
1 chicken stock cube	1 medium-thick slice bread
1 bay leaf	
1 small onion, chopped	
600 ml/1 pint boiling water	300 ml/½ pint milk
225 g/8 oz frozen sweet corn	chopped chives to garnish

Place the chicken joint in a large bowl with the crumbled stock cube and the bay leaf. Add the onion and pour in the boiling water, then cover with cling film, allowing a small gap for the steam to escape, and cook on full power for 15 minutes.

Remove the chicken from the soup and add the sweet corn with seasoning to taste. Cook for a further 5 minutes. Meanwhile, cut all the chicken meat off the bones, discard the skin and cut the meat into small pieces. Cut the crusts off the bread and break the slice into the soup. Blend in a liquidiser or food processor until smooth.

Heat the chicken with the milk for 4 minutes. Stir this mixture into the soup and reheat for 5 minutes, then serve, topped with chopped chives.

Meatball Soup Pot

——— SERVES 4 ———

A good winter main-meal soup, this recipe can be served with lots of hot crusty bread and some matured Cheddar cheese.

225 g/8 oz turnips, cut into chunks
100 g/4 oz carrots, thinly sliced
1 large onion, chopped
225 g/8 oz potatoes, cut into chunks
50 g/2 oz butter
100 g/4 oz white cabbage, shredded
2 chicken stock cubes
1.15 litres/2 pints boiling water

salt and freshly ground black pepper
Meatballs:
450 / 1 lb good-quality pork sausagemeat
1 teaspoon dried mixed herbs
1 egg, beaten
1 tablespoon prepared English mustard
oil for deep frying
2 tablespoons chopped parsley

Place the turnips, carrots, onion and potatoes in a large bowl with the butter. Cover with cling film, allowing a small gap for the steam to escape, then cook on full power for 10 minutes, stirring once during the cooking time.

Add the cabbage, crumbled stock cubes and water, stirring to dissolve the cubes. Add seasoning to taste and cook for 15 minutes.

Mix all the ingredients for the meatballs, adding seasoning to taste. Heat the oil for deep frying to 190 C/375 F. Add the meatballs and deep fry until golden brown. Drain on absorbent kitchen paper.

To serve, ladle the soup into large individual bowls and float the meatballs in them. Sprinkle with the parsley, then serve at once.

Day-old French bread, which is very slightly stale, can be sprinkled with just a little water and heated in the microwave for 30 seconds, then placed under a hot grill until crisp. Use a clean plant spray to moisten the bread.

Spinach and Sausage Soup

—— SERVES 4 ——

1 onion, chopped
25 g/1 oz butter
salt and freshly ground
  black pepper
1 chicken stock cube
300 ml/½ pint boiling
  water

1 (250-g/8.82-oz) packet
  frozen chopped spinach
3 tablespoons plain flour
600 ml/1 pint milk
freshly grated nutmeg
1 (241-g/8-oz) smoked
  Dutch sausage

Place the onion in a large bowl with the butter and
seasoning to taste, then cook on full power for 4 minutes.

Dissolve the chicken stock cube in the boiling water,
then pour this over the spinach and break the block up
into small cubes. Stir the flour into the onion, then pour in
the stock and spinach and cook for 5 minutes.

Heat the milk for 4 minutes, then pour it into the soup,
stir well and cook for a further 6 minutes.

While the soup is cooking, brown the sausage under a
hot grill – it will take about 2 to 3 minutes on each side.
Cut it into thick slices and add these to the soup with a
little nutmeg. Taste and adjust the seasoning, then serve at
once.

Broccoli and Bacon Soup

—— SERVES 4 ——

A chunky, heart-warming soup, this recipe is ideal for the
opening course of a winter's evening dinner or for a light
lunch or supper. Serve hot bread rolls (make them in the
microwave: see page 193) as an accompaniment.

225 g/8 oz lean rindless
  bacon
1 large onion, chopped
2 tablespoons plain flour
salt and freshly ground
  black pepper
1 chicken stock cube

600 ml/1 pint boiling
  water
450 g/1 lb broccoli,
  chopped
300 ml/½ pint milk
freshly grated nutmeg

Finely chop the bacon, then place it in a large bowl with
the onion and cook on full power for 4 minutes. Stir in the
flour and seasoning to taste. Dissolve the stock cube in the
boiling water, then pour it into the onion mixture,
stirring all the time. Add the broccoli, then cook for 10
minutes, stirring once.

Heat the milk in a heatproof glass measuring jug for 3
minutes. Stir this into the soup and heat for 5 minutes.
Taste and adjust the seasoning, adding nutmeg to taste.
Serve at once.

Spiced Potato and Tomato Soup

—— SERVES 4 ——

1 onion, chopped
grated rind of 1 large
  orange
½ teaspoon fennel seeds
2 teaspoons ground
  coriander
1 large clove garlic,
  crushed
450 g/1 lb potatoes, finely
  diced
25 g/1 oz butter

salt and freshly ground
  black pepper
2 (400-g/14-oz) cans
  chopped tomatoes
1 beef stock cube
300 ml/½ pint boiling
  water
150 ml/¼ pint natural
  yogurt
2 tablespoons chopped
  fresh coriander

Place the onion, orange rind, fennel seeds, coriander and
garlic in a large bowl. Add the potatoes and butter and
cover with cling film, allowing a small gap for the steam to
escape. Cook on full power for 15 minutes.

Stir in seasoning to taste then add the tomatoes.
Dissolve the stock cube in the boiling water, then pour
this into the soup whilst stirring. Cook for a further 10
minutes, then taste and adjust the seasoning if necessary.
Serve with yogurt swirled into each portion and a little
chopped fresh coriander sprinkled over the top.

Chunky Corn Chowder

—— SERVES 4 ——

1 onion, chopped
25 g/1 oz butter
salt and freshly ground
  black pepper
350 g/12 oz frozen sweet
  corn
1 chicken stock cube

600 ml/1 pint boiling
  water
225 g/8 oz potatoes, diced
225 g/8 oz cooked ham,
  cut into chunks
2 tablespoons chopped
  parsley

Place the onion and butter in a large bowl with seasoning
to taste, then cook on full power for 4 minutes. Add the
sweet corn and cook for a further 2 minutes.

Dissolve the stock cube in the boiling water, then pour
150 ml/¼ pint of this into a liquidiser or food processor and
add about a quarter of the sweet corn mixture. Pour the
remaining stock into the bowl with the whole sweet corn.
Blend the small amount of corn and stock until smooth and
stir into the soup. Add the potatoes and cook for 10
minutes.

Stir the ham into the soup and cook for a final 5 minutes,
then taste and adjust the seasoning if necessary. Serve
topped with the chopped parsley.

Leek and Potato Soup

—— SERVES 4 ——

1 kg/2 lb potatoes
2 large leeks, sliced
50 g/2 oz butter
2 tablespoons plain flour
salt and freshly ground
    black pepper
1 chicken stock cube
300 ml/½ pint milk
600 ml/1 pint boiling
    water

4 tablespoons chopped
    parsley
Croûtons:
25 g/1 oz butter
2 tablespoons oil
2 slices bread, cut into
    small cubes

Cut the potatoes into small cubes and place them in a roasting bag. Thoroughly wash the leeks, then add them to the potatoes with half the butter. Cook on full power for 15 minutes, shaking the bag twice.

Transfer the cooked vegetables to a large bowl and stir in the remaining butter with the flour and seasoning to taste. Crumble in the stock cube, then pour in the milk. Cook for a further 5 minutes, stirring thoroughly once during cooking.

At the end of this cooking time whisk the mixture thoroughly and cook for a further 5 minutes.

Meanwhile, prepare the croûtons. Melt the butter with the oil in a frying pan. Add the bread cubes and cook, turning them frequently, until they are brown and crisp all over. Drain on absorbent kitchen paper.

To serve, stir the boiling water and parsley into the soup, then ladle it into individual bowls and top each portion with a sprinkling of the crunchy croûtons.

Cream of Celeriac Soup To make a deliciously creamy-flavoured soup, substitute 1 large celeriac root (about 1 kg/2 lb in weight) for the potatoes. Peel it thickly and cut the root into small cubes. Cook these in the same way as the potatoes, then continue preparing the soup following the recipe. Blend the cooked soup in a liquidiser until smooth, then reheat it for 3 to 5 minutes. Serve with a little single cream swirled into each portion. The croûtons are still a good accompaniment for the creamed soup.

Cardamom Cucumber Soup

—— SERVES 4 ——

This is a hot, clear soup spiced with cardamoms and garlic, and lightly flavoured with lemon. Serve crisp melba toast or popadums as an accompaniment.

1 large cucumber
6 green cardamoms
1 clove garlic, crushed
grated rind of 1 small
    lemon
1½ chicken stock cubes

600 ml/1 pint boiling
    water
salt and freshly ground
    black pepper
2 spring onions, finely
    chopped, to garnish

Thinly peel the cucumber, then dice it into small pieces and place these in a mixing bowl. Split the cardamoms and scrape out the tiny black seeds. Add these to the cucumber with the garlic and lemon rind. Cover the bowl with cling film, allowing a small gap for the steam to escape, then cook on full power for 15 minutes.

Meanwhile, dissolve the stock cubes in the boiling water. Pour the stock over the cucumber, add a little seasoning and stir well, then replace the bowl in the microwave and cook for a further 2 minutes.

Sprinkle the spring onions over the soup and serve at once. Alternatively, the soup can be cooled, chilled and served with an ice cube floating in each portion.

Somerset Soup

—— SERVES 4 ——

This is a rich cheese and cider soup. Serve plenty of warm crusty bread with it.

1 onion, finely chopped
25 g/1 oz butter
300 ml/½ pint dry cider
3 tablespoons creamed
    horseradish
225 g/8 oz matured
    Cheddar cheese, grated
3 tablespoons plain flour

1 chicken stock cube
salt and freshly ground
    black pepper
300 ml/½ pint boiling
    water
150 ml/¼ pint single cream
4 tablespoons chopped
    parsley

Place the onion in a large bowl with the butter and cook on full power for 3 minutes. Pour in the cider and creamed horseradish and heat for 4 minutes.

Meanwhile, mix the cheese thoroughly with the flour and plenty of seasoning. Gradually whisk this into the cider mixture, then cook for 5 minutes, whisking once during this time. Dissolve the stock cube in the boiling water, then whisk it into the soup and stir in the cream.

Heat the soup for 2 minutes, then serve at once, with a tablespoon of the parsley lightly stirred into each portion.

Borscht

——— SERVES 4 ———

225 g/8 oz lean minced beef
2 onions, 1 cut into chunks, 1 chopped
salt and black pepper
600 ml/1 pint boiling water
225 g/8 oz red cabbage
100 g/4 oz turnips
1 large carrot

350 g/12 oz uncooked beetroot
300 ml/½ pint dry red wine
50 g/2 oz butter
2 teaspoons red wine vinegar
150 ml/¼ pint soured cream
1 tablespoon chopped chives to garnish

Place the beef, chunks of onion and seasoning to taste in a basin with the water. Cover with cling film and cook on full power for 10 minutes.

Meanwhile, finely shred the cabbage, turnips and carrot. Peel and shred the beetroot, then place about a third of it in a basin with the wine and set aside. Place the butter in a large mixing bowl with the remaining prepared vegetables, then cook for 5 minutes.

Strain the beef stock over the vegetables, pressing the beef well to squeeze out all the liquid. Discard the beef and return the soup to the microwave then cook for a further 10 minutes, stirring once.

Cook the beetroot in the red wine for 5 minutes, then strain the wine over the soup, squeezing all the liquid out of the beetroot. Stir in the vinegar and add seasoning to taste. Heat through for 3 minutes, then serve with the soured cream swirled into each portion and the chives sprinkled on top.

Mulligatawny Soup

——— SERVES 6 ———

This soup is not too spicy – for its flavour it requires only 1 red chilli and a mixture of mild curry spices.

1 small white turnip
100 g/4 oz carrots
2 onions, finely chopped
2 cloves garlic, crushed
6 green cardamoms
4 cloves
1 dried red chilli
50 g/2 oz butter
1 beef stock cube
3 teaspoons ground fenugreek

1.15 litres/2 pints boiling water
225 g/8 oz red lentils
salt and freshly ground black pepper
3 tablespoons chopped fresh coriander to garnish

Dice the turnip and carrots, then place them in a bowl with the onions, garlic, cardamoms, cloves and chilli. Add the butter, cover the bowl with cling film, allowing a small gap for the steam to escape, then cook on full power for 10 minutes.

Meanwhile, dissolve the stock cube in 600 ml/1 pint of boiling water. Stir the fenugreek and lentils into the vegetables and pour in the stock. Stir well, re-cover and cook for a further 15 minutes.

Remove from the oven and beat the soup thoroughly, removing the chilli and as many of the spices as you can. Stir in the remaining boiling water and cook for a further 3 minutes. Serve hot, sprinkled with the chopped coriander.

Rich Pork Pâté

——— SERVES 6 ———

This is a coarse, well-flavoured pâté which would require lengthy cooking in a conventional oven. In the microwave it's quick to prepare, and it's a good meaty pâté; ideal to precede a light main course, or to serve for lunch.

675 g/1½ lb belly pork
225 g/8 oz lamb's liver
4 cloves garlic, crushed
2 small onions, finely chopped
4 tablespoons brandy
I egg, beaten
salt and freshly ground black pepper

50 g/2 oz fresh breadcrumbs
freshly grated nutmeg
Garnish:
a few bay leaves
a few juniper berries

Trim the rind off the pork and remove any bones, then cut it into cubes. Trim the liver and cut it into similar-sized pieces. Place the prepared meats in a large bowl or casserole with the garlic and onions. Cover and cook on full power for 20 minutes, stirring once.

Allow the meat mixture to cool slightly then mince it coarsely. If you have a food processor, then process the meat in one or two batches without making it smooth. Stir in the brandy, egg and plenty of seasoning, then add and thoroughly mix in the breadcrumbs with a generous seasoning of nutmeg. Transfer to 1.15-litre/2-pint dish – a soufflé dish or small ovenproof serving dish is ideal, but remember the no-metal rule.

Place the bay leaves decoratively on top of the pâté and add the juniper berries, then cover with cling film and cook for 5 minutes. Cover with a clean piece of cling film and weight down, then allow to cool completely and chill overnight or for several hours. Keep the weight on the pâté while it is chilling. Serve from the bowl and cut the pâté out in wedges, or scoop it with a large spoon.

In microwave cooking, the size and shape of food plays a part in determining the total cooking time. In recipes such as this one, where a significant amount of meat is pre-cooked, then cut the food into even-sized cubes which are not too large. This way the food will cook quickly and, with a quick stir halfway through the cooking time, the pieces will cook evenly.

Fine Herb Pâté

—— SERVES 8 ——

This is a delicious, smooth pâté which makes an excellent first course. Serve crisp toast or melba toast as an accompaniment.

450 g/1 lb lean boneless pork
1 large onion, finely chopped
350 g/12 oz pig's liver
4 cloves garlic, crushed
3 sprigs thyme
1 large sprig sage
3 or 4 sprigs marjoram
1 sprig mint
2 sprigs rosemary
1 egg, beaten
3 tablespoons brandy
salt and freshly ground black pepper
225 g/8 oz lean streaky bacon

Cut the pork into small cubes and place them in a large bowl with the onion. Cut the liver into cubes and add it to the meat with the garlic. Chop the herbs and add them to the meat with plenty of seasoning. Cover with cling film, allowing a small gap for the steam to escape, then cook on full power for 10 minutes.

Mince, liquidise or purée the meat mixture in a food processor until quite smooth. Stir in the egg and brandy. Trim the rinds off the bacon, then stretch the rashers out with the back of a knife until they are very thin.

Line a 1.5-litre/2¾-pint loaf dish with the bacon rashers, overlapping them neatly and making sure the ends come up to the top of the dish. Turn the puréed meat mixture into the dish and fold over the ends of the bacon. Cover with cling film and cook for 5 minutes. Turn the dish round and cook for a further 3 minutes. Cover the pâté with clean cling film, then weight it down and allow to cool completely. Chill thoroughly, preferably overnight, then turn out to serve.

Chicken Liver Pâté

—— SERVES 4 TO 6 ——

This pâté is incredibly quick and simple to prepare and delicious to eat. However, it is very rich, so if you are serving a substantial main course set all the pâté into one dish and spoon small portions on to the plates at the table. Serve crisp toast as an accompaniment.

450 g/1 lb chicken livers
2 large cloves garlic, crushed
salt and freshly ground black pepper
225 g/8 oz unsalted butter
2 tablespoons brandy
Garnish:
4 small bay leaves
juniper berries

Trim and roughly chop the chicken livers. Place them in a bowl with the garlic, plenty of seasoning and half the butter. Cover with cling film, allowing a small gap for the steam to escape, and cook on full power for 5 minutes. Give the livers a good stir, then replace them in the oven

and cook for a further 3 to 4 minutes, or until completely cooked.

Blend the livers in a liquidiser or food processor until smooth, then stir in the brandy and a further 50 g/2 oz of the butter. Spoon the pâté into the four ramekins or one large dish and smooth the top.

Melt the remaining butter in the microwave for 1 minute, then carefully pour a thin layer of it over the pâté. Arrange the bay leaves and juniper berries on top and chill thoroughly, preferably overnight, before serving.

Turkey Pâté

—— SERVES 6 ——

This is a delicious creamy pâté for those who are not so keen on pâtés which are rich in liver. Serve it as a starter or as a light meal, with French bread.

450 g/1 lb uncooked boneless turkey breast
225 g/8 oz turkey livers
1 onion, finely chopped
1 bay leaf
1 clove garlic, crushed
grated rind and juice of 1 orange
½ teaspoon ground mixed spice
salt and freshly ground black pepper
50 g/2 oz full fat soft cheese with herbs and garlic
Garnish:
orange slices
fresh herb sprigs, for example thyme, parsley or sage

Cut the turkey breast into small cubes. Trim and roughly chop the turkey livers, then mix both in a large basin. Add the onion, bay leaf, garlic, orange rind and juice, and mixed spice. Stir in seasoning to taste, then cover with cling film, allowing a small gap for the steam to escape. Cook on full power for 15 minutes, stirring once during cooking.

Remove the bay leaf, then purée the pâté in a liquidiser or food processor. Stir in the cheese and taste the pâté to adjust the seasoning if necessary. Turn into one large dish or six ramekins, then cool and chill thoroughly.

Before serving, garnish the pâté with orange slices and a few sprigs of herbs.

Liver of all types cooks well in the microwave, particularly the tender chicken livers or turkey livers. However, it is important to make sure that these ingredients are chopped, halved or cut up in some way before cooking otherwise they tend to pop and splatter over the oven as they cook. It is also a good idea to keep the container covered during cooking.

Lentil Pâté

—— SERVES 4 TO 6 ——

This creamy lentil mixture must be served well chilled, with some crisp toast, pumpernickel or crusty whole-wheat bread.

I onion, finely chopped	freshly grated nutmeg
25 g/1 oz butter	4 large sprigs fresh basil,
salt and freshly ground	chopped
black pepper	100 g/4 oz full fat soft
225 g/8 oz lentils	cheese (for example
600 ml/1 pint water	Philadelphia)
grated rind of 1 lemon	

Place the onion in a large basin (1.15-litre/2-pint) with the butter. Cook on full power for 3 minutes, then add seasoning to taste and the lentils. Pour in the water and cook for 15 minutes, stirring once.

Mash the cooked lentils thoroughly, then beat in the lemon rind and nutmeg to taste. Replace the basin in the microwave and cook for a further 5 minutes. Beat in the basil and cream cheese, then transfer the mixture to a serving dish, cool and chill thoroughly before serving.

Curried Lentil Pâté To make a deliciously spiced pâté or dip, add 2 crushed cloves garlic to the onion and butter. Stir in 2 tablespoons garam masala (this is available ready ground in tins, or you can prepare your own from a blend of ground roasted spices – cardamoms, cinnamon, cumin and coriander), then cook the onions and lentils as in the main recipe. Prepare the pâté as directed, omitting the basil but adding a generous sprinkling of chopped fresh coriander leaves instead. Serve popadums with the pâté.

Hot Anchovy Dip

—— SERVES 4 ——

Dips are generally thought of as being cold starters for hot days, but with a microwave oven you can whip up an unusual hot dip in minutes with no more effort than preparing a cold starter.

1 (50-g/1¾-oz) can	grated rind of 1 lemon
anchovy fillets	juice of ½ lemon
1 (85-g/3½-oz) packet	black pepper to taste
Philadelphia cream	150 ml/¼ pint soured
cheese	cream

Mash the anchovy fillets with the oil from the can. Gradually beat in the cream cheese, lemon rind and juice, and pepper to taste. Stir in the soured cream and transfer to a heatproof serving bowl (one which is suitable for putting in the microwave oven).

Heat the dip on full power for 4 minutes, stirring twice during cooking. Stir at the end of the heating time, then stand the bowl on a saucer and serve at once.

Stuffed Tomatoes

—— SERVES 4 ——

These tomatoes really are a quite substantial starter so bear this in mind when you are planning the menu. Offer crisp Italian breadstick rings to complement their soft texture.

4 beef tomatoes (about	2 tablespoons chopped
1.25-kg/2 lb 12 oz in	mixed fresh herbs, for
weight)	example parsley,
450 g/1 lb cooked ham,	thyme, tarragon and
minced	chives
50 g/2 oz fresh	1 egg, beaten
breadcrumbs	100 g/4 oz mozzarella
salt and freshly ground	cheese, sliced
black pepper	

Cut the tops off the tomatoes and scoop out all the seeds from inside. Turn the shells upside down on a double thickness of absorbent kitchen paper and allow them to drain completely.

Mix the ham, breadcrumbs and seasoning to taste – go easy on the salt in case the ham is salty. Stir in the herbs and egg and mix well. Spoon this filling into the tomatoes, pressing it well down into the fruit.

Arrange the tomatoes as far apart as possible in a large dish, then cook on full power for 5 minutes, turning the dish around once during cooking. Place a slice of mozzarella on each tomato and cook under a hot grill until melted and golden. Serve at once.

Hot Bacon Dip

—— SERVES 4 ——

Since testing recipes for this book I have become almost addicted to serving hot dips before the meal. Here is another hot dip and it is one that really does taste special. Serve crunchy bread sticks, corn chips, tortilla chips and fresh vegetables with it.

225 g/8 oz rindless lean	150 ml/¼ pint single cream
bacon rashers, chopped	freshly ground black
1 onion, chopped	pepper
100 g/4 oz Caerphilly or	
Lancashire cheese	

Place the bacon in a basin with the onion. Cover with cling film, allowing a small gap for the steam to escape, and cook on full power for 5 minutes.

Crumble the Caerphilly or Lancashire cheese into the bowl of a food processor or put it in a liquidiser. Add the cooked bacon mixture and a little of the cream. Blend until smooth, adding the remaining cream as the mixture blends. Stir in pepper to taste and transfer the dip to a microwave-proof serving bowl. Heat for 2 minutes, then serve at once.

Prawn-stuffed Mushrooms

——— SERVES 4 ———

Mushrooms cook particularly well in the microwave oven – the small button variety can be turned into any number of simple starters or side dishes and the large open types can be stuffed with substantial ingredients for a main course or, as in this recipe, with light mixtures for a delicious starter. If you would prefer to serve the stuffed mushrooms on a crisp salad they will taste just as good.

1 large red pepper	1 tablespoon chopped
100 g/4 oz butter	chives
1 clove garlic, crushed	4 medium-thick slices
salt and freshly ground	bread
black pepper	a few whole cooked
4 large open mushrooms	prawns to garnish
a little oil	
225 g/8 oz peeled cooked	
prawns, defrosted if	
frozen	

Cut the stalk end off the pepper and remove all the seeds and pith from inside, then finely chop the flesh. Place the chopped pepper in a basin with half the butter, the garlic and seasoning to taste. Cook in the microwave for 4 minutes on full power.

Meanwhile, wipe the mushrooms and remove their stalks, then brush their undersides with oil. Place them well apart on a large dish. Mix the prawns with the chives and set aside. Cut four circles from the bread – they should be slightly larger than the mushrooms.

Stir the prawn mixture into the pepper, toss well, then use a teaspoon to pile this filling into the mushrooms. Replace them in the microwave and cook for a further 3 minutes.

While the mushrooms are cooking, melt the remaining butter in a frying pan on the hob of the cooker. Add the bread circles and fry them turning once, until golden brown on both sides. Drain on absorbent kitchen paper and transfer to warmed individual serving plates.

To serve, arrange a mushroom on each bread croûte and add a garnish of whole prawns and lemon wedges. Serve immediately.

Defrosting prawns in the microwave oven is easy – place a double thickness of absorbent kitchen paper on a plate and spread the frozen prawns over it. Cover with a single sheet of paper and (for the 225 g/8 oz in the above recipe) cook on full power for 2 minutes. Rub the prawns gently with the kitchen paper to remove any ice, then dry them on a fresh piece and they should be ready for use; if they are still slightly frozen, then allow them to stand for a few minutes.

Pink and Green

——— SERVES 4 ———

In the microwave oven the fresh colour of vegetables is enhanced to the full, similarly the pink hue of peeled prawns.

450 g/1 lb young	350 g/12 oz peeled cooked
courgettes	prawns, defrosted if
grated rind and juice of	frozen
1 lemon	salt and black pepper

Trim and very thinly peel the courgettes – they should still retain a dark green colour when peeled. Cut them into small chunks, comparable in size to the prawns. Place the courgettes in a basin and sprinkle over the lemon rind and juice. Cook on full power for 3 minutes, then stir in the prawns and cook for a further 4 minutes.

Season the mixture to taste and serve at once, either from the bowl in which it was cooked or spooned on to individual plates or dishes.

Mushroom Croustades

——— SERVES 4 ———

This mushroom starter is neat to serve and quite light for the first course. The croustades can be prepared well in advance and filled just before serving.

4 (5-cm/2-in) thick slices	2 tablespoons brandy
bread	350 g/12 oz button
oil for deep frying	mushrooms, sliced
2 tablespoons plain flour	2 tablespoons chopped
25 g/1 oz butter	parsley
150 ml/¼ pint milk	lemon wedges to garnish
salt and black pepper	

Trim the bread into neat squares about 7.5 cm/3 in. in size or slightly larger. Hollow out the middle, leaving an even, neatly shaped case. The bread case must not be too thick or it will overpower the mushroom filling, however if it is too thin it may break up. Heat the oil for deep frying to 190 C/375 F, then fry the bread until golden brown. Drain thoroughly on absorbent kitchen paper, blotting the inside of each bread case to make sure they are not greasy.

Place the flour, butter and milk in a basin – not too small because you will have to stir in the mushrooms later – and whisk thoroughly. Cook on full power for 3 minutes, then again whisk the sauce to make sure there are no lumps in it. The sauce should be quite thick at this stage.

Whisk in the seasoning to taste and brandy, then stir in the mushrooms and cook for a further 3 minutes. Stir in the parsley.

Arrange the croustades on individual plates, then spoon the mushrooms into them. Add a garnish of lemon wedges – the juice can be squeezed over the filling to sharpen it if preferred – then serve at once.

Haricot and Bacon Salad

—— SERVES 4 ——

Serve hot Granary or wholemeal bread to accompany this starter. Served to two people, this dish is also satisfying enough for lunch or supper.

225 g/8 oz smoked streaky bacon
1 large clove garlic, crushed
½ teaspoon dried basil
salt and freshly ground black pepper

1 tablespoon olive oil
2 (425-g/15-oz) cans white kidney beans, drained
4 tablespoons chopped parsley

Cut the rinds off the bacon, then cut the rashers into thin strips. Place the bacon, garlic and basil in a basin, mix well and cook on full power for 5 minutes.

Stir in the seasoning, taking care not to overdo the salt as the bacon may be salty enough. Add the oil and beans, tossing them gently without breaking them up. Cover with cling film, allowing a small gap for the steam to escape, and cook for a further 3 minutes.

Sprinkle the chopped parsley over the beans and serve immediately.

Haricot Beans: *haricot* describes a wide variety of beans, however the name is most commonly used to describe the small, smooth, oval beans which are white in colour. Larger beans, sold as cannellini beans, are also part of the haricot family, as too are white kidney beans and flageolet. Canned canellini beans can be substituted for the white kidney beans in this recipe but red kidney beans are unsuitable.

Note: canned or freshly cooked chick peas or borlotti beans can be used instead of the haricot beans in this salad. Fresh basil makes a superior alternative to the dried variety and a few finely chopped spring onions will bring the whole mixture to life.

Bananas with Bacon

—— SERVES 4 ——

Using lean tender bacon, this old favourite of bananas wrapped in bacon can be cooked quite successfully in the microwave. The kebabs must be arranged on wooden skewers. Serve hot buttered toast as an accompaniment.

8 rashers lean bacon
prepared mustard with chives
4 bananas
lemon juice

To serve:
a few crisp lettuce leaves
¼ cucumber, sliced
a few radishes

Cut off and discard the rinds from the bacon, then stretch the rashers out as thinly as possible. To do this place the

rashers flat on a board and use the back of a knife to stretch them. Cut each rasher in half to give 16 pieces, then spread each piece with mustard to taste.

Peel and quarter the bananas, dipping each piece in a little lemon juice to prevent discoloration. Wrap the bacon around the pieces of banana, then thread these on to 4 wooden skewers. Place the kebabs on a double thickness of absorbent kitchen paper on a large plate, then cook on full power for 7 minutes, turning once during cooking.

To serve, arrange the salad ingredients on individual plates and place a kebab on each. You can vary the salad to suit your own taste, but try to keep the ingredients crisp.

Artichokes Dolcelatte

—— SERVES 4 ——

This is a delicious, well-flavoured starter with an interesting mixture of textures to offer; a good one to really arouse the appetite.

4 medium-thick slices bread, crusts removed
50 g/2 oz butter
50 g/2 oz ripe Dolcelatte cheese
50 g/2 oz cream cheese
1 small clove garlic, crushed
freshly ground black pepper

1 (396-g/14-oz) can artichoke hearts, drained
Garnish:
a few fine strips red pepper
4 black olives

Cut a circle from each slice of bread. Melt the butter in a frying pan and add the bread circles; turn them immediately so that both sides are coated with the butter. Cook until golden brown, then turn and cook the second sides in the same way.

Meanwhile, mash the Dolcelatte and beat in the cream cheese, garlic and pepper to taste. Drain the fried bread rounds on absorbent kitchen paper and arrange them on a large flat dish.

Cut the artichoke hearts in half and arrange them on the bread. Carefully spread a little of the cheese mixture over each portion and cook on full power for 4 minutes.

Top the portions with the garnishing ingredients and serve at once, on individual plates.

Note: there is a great deal of confusion between artichoke hearts and artichoke bottoms. The former are the un-formed central choke of the globe artichoke. Available canned, they resemble a large bud, surrounded by the unopened artichoke leaves.

Artichoke bottoms, on the other hand, are the tender white base of the fully grown artichoke. These are the central fleshy core on which the choke grows. To obtain them, the outer leaves and choke must first be removed. The stalk end is trimmed off and the artichoke bottoms, when fresh, must be liberally sprinkled with lemon juice to prevent discoloration.

Baked Avocado with Cucumber

SERVES 4

100 g/4 oz lean bacon
100 g/4 oz cucumber
25 g/1 oz full fat soft
   cheese with garlic and
   herbs

2 large ripe avocado pears
a little lemon juice

Cut the rinds off the bacon, then dice the rashers. Peel and dice the cucumber. Mix both together in a basin and cook on full power for 3 minutes. Stir in the cheese.

Halve the avocado pears and sprinkle the cut surfaces with a little lemon juice, then stand them in avocado pear dishes. Spoon the prepared mixture into the holes left by the stones, then cook on full power for 2 to 2½ minutes and serve at once. Eat with care – the avocado flesh becomes very hot!

Hot Bean Dip

SERVES 4

This dip is good to serve with drinks before a meal, or instead of a starter. I have used just one chilli and this gives a fairly hot dip. Be careful about adding any more because even though the dip may taste pleasantly spicy after just one mouthful, after several dippings you may find that your guests have their tongues hanging out!

1 small onion, chopped
1 pickled jalapeño chilli,
   chopped
2 cloves garlic, crushed
1 teaspoon ground
   coriander
about 50 g/2 oz butter
1 (425-g/15-oz) can red
   kidney beans, drained

salt and freshly ground
   black pepper
To serve:
tacos chips
crisps
crudités

Place the onion, chilli and garlic in a basin or heatproof serving bowl. Add the coriander and butter and cook on full power for 4 minutes.

Meanwhile, purée the beans in a liquidiser or food processor, then stir them into the cooked onion mixture and add seasoning to taste. Cook for a further 2 minutes, then give the dip a good stir before serving it.

Pepper Boats

SERVES 4

Whole stuffed peppers are often difficult to present in an attractive fashion without being terribly under cooked. These halved peppers are, on the other hand, easy to present and they make quite a filling starter. Offer some hot crusty bread with them.

4 eggs
2 large red peppers
100 g/4 oz button
   mushrooms
50 g/2 oz butter
2 tablespoons plain flour
salt and freshly ground
   black pepper

250 ml/8 fl oz milk
75 g/3 oz mature Cheddar
   cheese, grated
3 tablespoons chopped
   parsley

Cook the eggs in boiling water, on the hob of the conventional cooker, for 10 minutes. This cooking time is from the point at which the water comes to a rolling boil. Drain and place under cold water, then shell and quarter the hard-boiled eggs.

Cut the peppers in half horizontally, leaving their stalks in place. Remove all the seeds and pith from inside, then rinse and drain them. Cut the mushrooms into quarters.

Place the butter, flour and seasoning to taste in a basin (about 1.15 litres/2 pints in capacity), then gradually whisk in the milk. Cook on full power for 5 minutes, whisking thoroughly once during cooking. Whisk most of the cheese into the sauce at the end of the cooking time, reserving just a little to top the filled peppers.

Place the pepper shells in a roasting bag and secure the end loosely with an elastic band. Cook on full power for 5 minutes, then allow the peppers to remain in the bag for a further 5 minutes.

Meanwhile, stir the eggs, mushrooms and parsley into the sauce and reheat it for 1 minute. Arrange the peppers on a heatproof serving plate and spoon the sauce into them. Sprinkle the tops with the reserved cheese and brown under a hot grill for a few minutes. Serve immediately.

Dips are usually considered suitable only for hot summer days but many exciting warming dips can be prepared in the microwave. The added advantage for such dishes when you're entertaining is that they can be prepared in advance and even spooned into the serving dish (remember to make sure it's suitable for the microwave) then reheated just minutes before it is to be eaten. From cold, allow 4 minutes to make this dip piping hot.

FISH & SHELLFISH

Fish and shellfish, being tender and moist, cook particularly well in the microwave oven. Whole fish, fillets, steaks and chunks of fish can all be prepared very quickly with delicious results. Whether the main ingredient is poached in a sauce or cooked simply with just a few herbs and spices, the result is always a success.

In fact, cooking fish in the microwave is so successful that it makes sense to try some of these dishes if you are new to this type of cooking appliance. Rolled fillets of fish and small steaks are the best items to try first because they cook particularly evenly. Large fish fillets tend to cook slightly more quickly towards the tail, so they need a little more attention until you are quite familiar with the cooking pattern in your own oven. Small whole fish, for example trout and mackerel, can be cooked four at a time but if your oven is not large enough to take a large dish, then prepare the fish in pairs; the cooked pair will keep sufficiently hot while the others are cooking.

The short time needed to cook most fish and shellfish does mean that these items can be overcooked without great difficulty. So, check the fish a few seconds or a minute before you expect it to be cooked to make sure that the fish does not have time to dry out. When large pieces of fish – particularly tail pieces of cod or similar – are ready they should be slightly undercooked at the thickest part: that way a few minutes standing time – or even the time taken to add the garnish – will ensure a perfect result.

Although the microwave oven is not suitable for cooking large whole shellfish from raw, small ones (like mussels) cook very well. Because cooked foods can be reheated in the microwave without any loss of freshness, it is also ideal for

turning cooked lobsters and crabs into many delectable dishes. The chapter includes ideas for Lobster Thermidor (see page 52) and Crab Newburg (see page 53) among other shellfish recipes.

To inspire you to experiment with new ideas for familiar fish, there is a range of recipes to suit every occasion – from an inexpensive Fisherman's Crumble (see page 38) and ideas for mackerel to Moules à la Marinière (see page 51) and exotic Fish Plaki (see page 45). Using your conventional oven as well as the microwave, Haddie-corn Puff (see page 41) and Creamy Cod Flan (see page 39) can be prepared with ease and speed without forfeiting the traditional quality you would expect from baked goods.

For a special occasion you can cook a whole salmon in your microwave. Curled into a large quiche dish, a 2.25-kg/5-lb fish cooks perfectly. If you are feeding large numbers then you can always cook several and arrange them, decoratively garnished, on one or more serving platters. This is particularly useful if you don't own a fish kettle and the cooked salmon is much easier to handle curved than when it's lying flat.

Another characteristic of fish cooked in the microwave is its suitability for special diets. There is no need to add fat or seasoning to the fish and it still cooks well to give a full-flavoured result. So, if you're on a low-fat or low-sodium diet, or even if you're just counting the calories, then look through these recipes and adjust them to suit your needs.

Once you have become accustomed to the moist and delicate, yet full flavour of fish cooked in the microwave you will never again turn to your conventional oven or hob to cook fish unless you specifically want to fry it.

Cidered Cod Casserole

—— SERVES 4 ——

1 onion, chopped	1 fish stock cube
225 g/8 oz carrots, sliced	100 g/4 oz mushrooms,
25 g/1 oz butter	sliced
450 g/1 lb cod fillet	100 g/4 oz puff pastry
2 tablespoons plain flour	a little melted butter
salt and freshly ground	2 tablespoons chopped
black pepper	parsley
300 ml/½ pint medium dry	
cider	

Place the onion in a casserole dish with the carrots and butter. Cover with cling film and cook on full power for 5 minutes.

While the vegetables are cooking, skin the fish (see page 20) and remove any bones, then cut it into chunks. Stir the flour and plenty of seasoning into the vegetables, then pour in the cider and add the stock cube. Stir well, then add the fish. Cover and cook for 7 minutes. Give the fish a good stir and add the mushrooms, then continue to cook for a further 3 minutes.

Meanwhile, roll out the pastry on a floured surface to 3 mm/⅛ in thick. Use a pastry cutter to cut out neat circles. Brush these with the melted butter and place them on a foil-lined grill rack. Cook under a hot grill until puffed and golden. Turn them over and brush the second side with butter and grill until crisp and golden.

Sprinkle the parsley over the fish and stir it in very lightly, then arrange the pastry puffs on top. Serve at once.

Cod with Corn and Olives

—— SERVES 4 ——

The combination of colourful sweet corn, aromatic oregano and ripe olives makes this fish dish unusual and delicious. Serve it with a bowl of chilled Greek yogurt and some hot pitta bread.

450 g/1 lb cod fillet	1 (325-g/11½-oz) can sweet
1 clove garlic, crushed	corn
225 g/8 oz black olives,	2 tablespoons olive oil
stoned and roughly	salt and freshly ground
chopped	black pepper
1 teaspoon oregano	

Skin the fish (see page 20), then cut it into bite-sized pieces. Place these in a casserole and add the garlic, olives, oregano, the sweet corn with its liquid, the oil and plenty of seasoning. Stir well then cover with cling film, allowing a small gap for the steam to escape, and cook on full power for 10 to 12 minutes. Stir the mixture once during cooking. Allow to stand for 2 minutes before serving.

Fish Pie

—— SERVES 4 ——

This is a moist tasty dish which is good for family meals or for supper parties. If you want to make it rather special then you can add peeled cooked prawns, mussels or any other shellfish to the sauce with the white fish. Smoked haddock can be substituted for white fish or you can use half white fish and half smoked fish.

1.5 kg/3 lb potatoes	300 ml/½ pint milk
4 tablespoons water	1 bay leaf
1 onion, chopped	675 g/1½ lb white fish fillet,
75 g/3 oz butter	skinned (for example
100 g/4 oz carrots, diced	cod, haddock or coley)
3 tablespoons plain flour	25 g/1 oz cheese, grated
salt and freshly ground	
black pepper	

Cut the potatoes into small dice and place them in a large bowl with the water. Cover with cling film, allowing a small gap for the steam to escape, then cook on full power for 20 to 25 minutes. Allow these to stand in the bowl while you begin to prepare the filling.

Place the onion in a bowl with 25 g/1 oz of the butter and the carrots then cook for 5 minutes. While the onion and carrots are cooking add the remaining butter to the potatoes and mash them with seasoning to taste.

Stir the flour into the onion and carrot mixture, then add the milk and seasoning to taste. Stir in the bay leaf and fish and cook for a further 13 minutes, stirring once during cooking. Taste and adjust the seasoning.

Top the fish with the mashed potato, then sprinkle the grated cheese on top and cook under a hot grill until golden. Allow to stand for a minute before serving.

As you can see from the recipes on this page, fish casseroles cook particularly well in the microwave oven. When the fish is cut into neat, even-sized pieces there is no danger of it cooking unevenly. Remember this when you buy fish for microwave cooking and select even-sized steaks or neat, equally proportioned pieces of fish fillet from the thick end of the fish. If thin fish fillets are used – like plaice or whiting – then roll them up into an even shape for the very best results.

Mustard-crusted Cod

—— SERVES 4 ——

This is a very simple dish of fish in a lemon and parsley sauce, made more interesting (and filling) by the mustard-spread rounds of French bread which form the topping.

675 g/1½ lb cod fillet
25 g/1 oz butter
1 onion, chopped
40 g/1½ oz plain flour
grated rind of 1 large
  lemon
2 tablespoons capers,
  roughly chopped
600 ml/1 pint milk

1 fish stock cube
4 tablespoons chopped
  parsley
Topping:
50 g/2 oz butter
2 tablespoons Dijon
  mustard
8 slices French bread

Skin the fish following the instructions on page 20. Cut the flesh into cubes. Place the butter in a large basin or in a deep serving bowl. Add the onion and cook on full power for 5 minutes. Stir in the flour, then whisk in the lemon rind, capers and milk. Crumble the fish stock cube into the sauce, then add the fish and cover with cling film, allowing a small gap for the steam to escape. Cook for 17 minutes, stirring the mixture once during cooking.

Meanwhile, prepare the topping. Beat the butter with the mustard and spread the mixture over the bread slices. Cook these under a hot grill until golden just before the fish is ready.

Stir the parsley into the fish and taste for seasoning, adding pepper and a little salt if necessary. Transfer the fish to a serving bowl if it is not already in one. Top the fish with the mustard bread slice and serve at once.

When you are arranging pieces of fish in a dish, then place them as far apart as possible to allow plenty of room for even cooking. If you have any tail pieces of fish, then arrange them so that the thin ends are towards the centre of the dish. The food which is positioned in a ring round the outer edge of the dish will cook more quickly than the pieces in the middle, so the tail ends will not overcook before the thick portions are cooked.

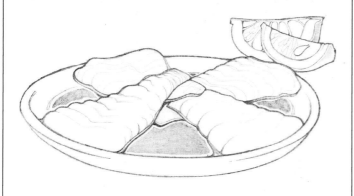

Machli Masala

—— SERVES 4 ——

Serve this fish curry with Pullao Rice (see page 129), popadums and a dish of Spiced Aubergines (see page 121).

1 large onion, chopped
25 g/1 oz fresh root
  ginger, grated
2 cloves garlic, crushed
2 green cardamoms
2 tablespoons ground
  coriander
1 teaspoon turmeric
½ teaspoon ground
  cinnamon
½ teaspoon chilli powder
3 tablespoons oil

salt and freshly ground
  black pepper
450 g/1 lb white fish fillet
  (for example cod or
  haddock)
1 fish stock cube
300 ml/½ pint boiling
  water
Garnish:
lemon wedges
2 tablespoons chopped
  fresh coriander

Place the onion in a bowl or casserole. Add the ginger, garlic and all the spices, then stir in the oil and seasoning to taste. Cook on full power for 5 minutes.

Meanwhile, skin the fish (see page 20) and cut it into bite-sized pieces. Add the fish to the cooked spices. Dissolve the stock cube in the boiling water and pour it into the dish, stir well but carefully to avoid breaking up the fish, then cook for 10 minutes, stirring once.

Taste and adjust the seasoning, then serve the curry garnished with lemon wedges and plenty of chopped fresh coriander.

Orange Capered Cod

—— SERVES 4 ——

These cod fillets are cooked with capers and the juice of only 1 large orange, so they are moist but not in a sauce. Other fish can be used, haddock or mackerel fillets are suitable. Serve Fantail Potatoes (see page 104) and Ratatouille (see page 123) as accompaniments.

450 /1 lb cod fillet
1 tablespoon finely
  chopped capers
grated rind and juice of 1
  large orange
50 g/2 oz butter

salt and freshly ground
  black pepper
Garnish:
orange slices
watercress sprigs

Skin the fish (see page 20) and cut the fillets into four equal portions. Remove any bones, then lay the fish in a shallow dish and sprinkle the capers over them. Add the orange rind and juice, season the cod to taste then dot the butter over the fish.

Cover with cling film, allowing a small gap for the steam to escape, then cook on full power for 8 minutes. Turn the dish once during cooking. Serve garnished with orange slices and watercress sprigs.

Fisherman's Crumble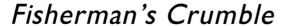

——— SERVES 4 ———

1 green pepper	*Topping:*
2 sticks celery	100 g/4 oz fresh
1 onion	breadcrumbs
25 g/1 oz butter	grated rind of 1 lemon
450 g/1 lb cod fillet	50 g/2 oz matured Cheddar
salt and freshly ground	cheese, grated
black pepper	2 tablespoons chopped
2 tablespoons chopped	parsley
parsley	lemon twists to garnish
1 (425-g/15-oz) can	
chopped tomatoes	

Cut the stalk end off the pepper, then remove all the seeds and pith from inside. Chop the green pepper shell. Dice the celery and chop the onion, then mix these prepared ingredients in a casserole dish or bowl. Add the butter and cover with cling film, allowing a small gap for the steam to escape. Cook on full power for 7 minutes.

Skin the fish fillets and cut them into chunks, removing any bones. Stir plenty of seasoning into the onion mixture, then add the fish, parsley and tomatoes. Stir well, re-cover the dish and continue to cook for a further 10 minutes.

Meanwhile, mix all the topping ingredients, adding seasoning to taste. Give the fish a good stir, being careful not to break up the chunks too much. Top with the breadcrumb mixture and continue to cook for 3 minutes. Brown the topping under a hot grill, then serve at once, garnished with lemon twists if you like.

Haddock Italienne

——— SERVES 4 ———

Fish cooked first in the microwave, then quickly browned under the grill retains far more natural moisture than fish which is cooked completely under the grill. And it's far easier to arrange the fish in a serving dish, cook it in the microwave, then simply brown it, than it is to turn the fish under a hot grill, add the topping and finish the cooking before arranging the pieces on a dish to serve.

1 large onion, chopped	450 g/1 lb haddock fillet
1 large green pepper	4 fresh plum tomatoes
1 tablespoon olive oil	100 g/4 oz mozzarella
salt and freshly ground	cheese, sliced
black pepper	

Place the onion in a shallow dish – an oval dish is ideal or use a quiche dish. Cut the stalk end off the pepper, then scoop out all the seeds and pith from inside. Chop the shell and add it to the onion with the oil and plenty of seasoning. Stir to make sure all the vegetable pieces are coated with oil, cover the dish and cook on full power for 5 minutes.

Meanwhile, skin the fish fillets, cut them into four portions and make sure there are no bones on the fish. Arrange the fish on top of the onion and peppers. Re-cover, allowing a gap for the steam to escape, then continue to cook for 6 minutes. Peel the tomatoes (see page 123), then slice them fairly thickly.

Top the fish with the sliced tomatoes and mozzarella cheese. Place under a hot grill until golden and bubbling, then serve at once.

Creamy Cod Flan

SERVES 4 TO 6

This flan makes a good family meal, serve it with baked potatoes and freshly cooked vegetables.

Shortcrust Pastry:
225 g/8 oz plain flour
50 g/2 oz lard or white fat
50 g/2 oz margarine
(or use 100 g/4 oz
    margarine or butter
    instead of the two
    different fats)
a little cold water
Filling:
1 small onion, chopped
25 g/1 oz butter

675 g/1½ lb pre-formed
    frozen cod steaks,
    partly defrosted
4 tablespoons plain flour
300 ml/½ pint milk
salt and freshly ground
    black pepper
100 g/4 oz cheese, grated
4 eggs
Garnish:
2 tomatoes, sliced
cucumber slices

First make the pastry (you can if you like buy frozen or chilled shortcrust pastry instead). Sift the flour into a bowl, then add the fat and cut it into pieces. Rub the fat into the flour until the mixture resembles fine breadcrumbs. Gradually stir in a little water (add it by the tablespoonful: you should need about three) and mix the crumbs together lightly to make a short dough.

Turn the pastry out on to a lightly floured surface, then knead it together very lightly and roll it out into a circle large enough to line a 23-cm/9-in flan dish. Lift the pastry over a rolling pin and press it into the flan dish. Roll the pin firmly over the top of the dish to press off any excess pastry. Prick the base all over with a fork and place a piece of greaseproof paper in the flan. Add dried peas or baking beans to cover the base and cook in a moderately hot oven (200 C, 400 F, gas 6) for 15 minutes. Remove the dried peas and greaseproof paper and cook for a further 15 to 20 minutes, or until the pastry is cooked through.

While the pastry is cooking prepare the filling. Place the onion in a large basin with the butter and cook on full power for 5 minutes. The fish steaks should be defrosted enough to cut into squares without too much difficulty. Stir the flour into the onion, then pour in the milk and add seasoning to taste. Stir in the fish and half the cheese. Replace in the microwave and cook for 15 minutes.

While the fish is cooking, boil the eggs for 10 minutes, then drain, shell and roughly chop them. Stir these into the fish mixture, taste and adjust the seasoning before you turn the filling into the flan case. Top the filling with the remaining cheese and brown it quickly under a hot grill. Add a garnish of tomato slices and cucumber slices before serving.

Seafood Terrine

——— SERVES 6 ———

Serve this terrine as a starter or as a light main course. It can be served hot, with Hollandaise Sauce (see page 201) or Tomato Sauce (see page 200), or chilled.

50 g/2 oz butter
1 clover garlic, crushed
2 tablespoons plain flour
salt and freshly ground black pepper
150 ml/¼ pint milk
450 g/1 lb cod fillet
50 g/2 oz fresh breadcrumbs
2 tablespoons chopped chives

1 tablespoon lemon juice
grated rind of 1 lemon
1 egg, beaten
175 g/6 oz peeled cooked prawns, defrosted if frozen
Garnish:
a few whole cooked prawns
lemon slices
parsley sprigs

Place the butter and garlic in a large basin or bowl and cook on full power for 1 minute. Stir in the flour and seasoning, then stir in the milk. Cook for 2 minutes.

Meanwhile, skin the cod fillet and remove any bones, then cut the fish into small cubes. Give the sauce a good whisk to make sure there are no lumps of flour, then stir in the fish and cook for 3 minutes. Stir in the breadcrumbs, chives, lemon juice and rind, and beaten egg. Make sure the mixture is thoroughly combined and that the fish is evenly distributed.

Grease a loaf dish – it needs to be a generous 900-ml/1½-pints container – then spoon in half the fish mixture and smooth the top. Lay the prawns on top, spreading them evenly, then spoon over the remaining fish mixture. Smooth the top and cover with cling film. Cook for 3 minutes, then turn the dish round and cook for a further 3 minutes.

Wrap the container completely in foil with the shiny side inwards, then leave in a warm place for 5 minutes. (Use this standing time to cook a sauce if you are going to serve the terrine hot.)

To serve, unwrap and turn out the terrine on to a warmed serving dish, then garnish and serve sliced. Alternatively, when the terrine has cooled, place it in the refrigerator and chill for several hours or overnight. If you are serving the terrine chilled you may like to offer either of the following sauces as an accompaniment.

Yogurt Seafood Sauce

· 1 tablespoon concentrated tomato purée
2 teaspoons anchovy essence
dash of Worcestershire sauce

1 tablespoon chopped chives
salt and freshly ground black pepper
150 ml/¼ pint natural yogurt

Mix all the ingredients into the yogurt, making sure there are no lumps. Serve lightly chilled.

Green Mayonnaise

2 tablespoons finely chopped parsley
1 bunch watercress
2 tablespoons chopped chives

300 ml/½ pint mayonnaise
salt and freshly ground black pepper

Mix all the ingredients in a liquidiser or food processor, having removed the stalks from the watercress. Blend until smooth, then add seasoning to taste and serve.

Skewered Haddock with Peanut Sauce

——— SERVES 4 ———

This is a recipe for those frozen preformed fish steaks. They are boneless and quick to prepare. Serve these kebabs on a bed of Lemon Rice (see page 128) and offer a tomato salad as an accompaniment.

450 g/1 lb haddock steaks, partially defrosted
salt and freshly ground black pepper
juice of ½ lemon
Sauce:
2 tablespoons crunchy peanut butter

2 tablespoons oil
1 tablespoon prepared mild mustard
1 large clove garlic, crushed
milk

Cut the fish into cubes, then thread these on to four wooden skewers. Sprinkle with seasoning to taste and put on a plate. Sprinkle the lemon juice over the fish, then cook on full power for 10 minutes. Turn the skewers once during cooking.

Meanwhile, mix all the ingredients for the sauce, adding enough milk to make the mixture up to 175 ml/6 fl oz. Cook the sauce on full power for 10 minutes, stirring once. Remove and set aside while the fish is cooked.

Cook the skewered haddock for 10 minutes, turning the skewers once during cooking. Remove them from the oven and cook the sauce for 30 seconds to reheat it slightly. Serve the skewers, garnished with lemon wedges and offer the sauce separately.

The microwave is ideal for cooking many types of kebab but always remember to use the wooden sticks, not metal ones. Arrange the skewers as far apart as possible on an oval plate or arrange them in a staggered circle round a large dinner plate, serving plate or shallow dish.

Scalloped Smokey

—— SERVES 4 ——

1.25 kg/2½ lb potatoes, cubed
4 tablespoons water
450 g/1 lb smoked haddock fillet
1 onion, chopped
75 g/3 oz butter
4 tablespoons plain flour

about 450 ml/¾ pint milk
salt and freshly ground black pepper
100 g/4 oz button mushrooms, sliced
2 tablespoons chopped parsley
4 eggs

Place the potatoes in a large mixing bowl with the water and cover with cling film, allowing a small gap for the steam to escape. Cook on full power for 22 minutes.

Skin the haddock fillet following the instructions on page 20 and cut the fish into chunks. Place the onion in a bowl with 25 g/1 oz of the butter. Cook for 5 minutes.

Mash the potatoes with remaining butter and a little milk. Pipe the potato round the edge of a gratin dish, making a neat edge to rise above the rim of the dish.

Stir the flour into the onion and pour in the remaining milk, stirring to prevent lumps from forming. Add seasoning to taste and the fish, then stir in the mushrooms. Cover with cling film, allowing a small gap for the steam to escape, and cook for 15 minutes. Stir once during cooking.

Boil the eggs for 10 minutes while the fish is cooking, then drain, shell and roughly chop them. Stir these into the cooked fish with the parsley, then transfer the mixture into the middle of the piped potato. Place under a hot grill until golden brown, then serve at once.

Smoked Haddock Mornay

—— SERVES 4 ——

675 g/1½ lb smoked haddock
Sauce:
40 g/1½ oz plain flour
600 ml/1 pint milk

salt and black pepper
150 g/5 oz cheese, grated
Garnish:
lemon wedges
watercress sprigs

Skin the haddock following the instructions on page 20. Cut the fillet into four portions and place these in a gratin dish. Cover with cling film and cook on full power for 10 minutes, turning the dish once.

Place the flour in a basin, then whisk in the milk and add seasoning to taste. Cook for 5 minutes, then whisk in most of the cheese and cook for a further 4 to 5 minutes. Whisk thoroughly to make sure the sauce is smooth, then pour it over the fish.

Sprinkle the remaining cheese over the top and cook the fish under a hot grill until golden brown and bubbling. Add a garnish of lemon wedges and watercrss sprigs, then serve immediately.

Haddie-corn Puff

—— SERVES 4 TO 6 ——

It is easy making filled pastry dishes, like pies and puffs, with a microwave oven in your kitchen because certain fillings can be cooked almost as quickly as you can roll out the pastry. This smoked haddock puff is made more interesting by the addition of sweet corn and potatoes, and it is seasoned with lemon and tarragon; it tastes as good cold as it does hot! Since it is quite filling, serve a couple of different simply cooked vegetables, like broccoli and carrots, as the only accompaniments. Alternatively, a salad would complement the cold puff.

350 g/12 oz frozen smoked haddock fillets with butter (boil-in-the-bag type)
225 g/8 oz frozen sweet corn
350 g/12 oz potatoes, diced
40 g/1½ oz butter
salt and freshly ground black pepper

350 g/12 oz frozen puff pastry, defrosted
2 tablespoons flour
150 ml/¼ pint milk
grated rind of 1 lemon
2 teaspoons tarragon
1 egg, beaten
To serve:
150 m/¼ pint soured cream
2 tablespoons chopped chives

Snip the bag containing the fish and lay it on a plate, then cook the haddock in the microwave for 8 minutes on full power. Meanwhile, mix the sweet corn and potatoes in a basin (about 1.15-litre/2-pint capacity) and add the butter. Season the vegetables very lightly and cover the basin with cling film. Cut a small hole in the top. Preheat the oven to hot (220 C, 425 F, gas 7).

Meanwhile, roll out the pastry on a lightly floured surface to give a square of about 35 cm/14 in. Trim off the edges to neaten them and transfer the pastry to a baking tray. Microwave the prepared vegetables for 5 minutes on full power, then stir in the flour and milk and cook for a further 5 minutes. While they are cooking, flake the fish off its skin and remove any bones. Reserve all the cooking juices.

Stir the lemon rind and tarragon into the sweet corn, then add the fish with all its juices. Mix well, taste and adjust the seasoning, then pile the mixture in the middle of the pastry. Brush the edges with beaten egg, then fold them up over the filling to form an envelope shape. Press the edges together to seal in the filling and trim off any excess. Roll out all the trimmings and cut out leaves to decorate the puff. Using a sharp pointed knife, make shallow cuts in a criss-cross pattern all over the pastry; do not cut right through it, just mark it. Brush with beaten egg and press on the leaves, then bake the puff in the hot oven for 25 minutes.

To serve, mix the soured cream with the chives in a small bowl and add plenty of pepper. Cut the puff into wedges and offer the sauce separately.

Halibut Mimosa

Remember it is not possible to hard boil eggs in the microwave oven as their shells explode and create an horrendous mess!

3 tablespoons plain flour
salt and freshly ground
 black pepper
300 ml/½ pint milk
25 g/1 oz butter
4 eggs

450 g/1 lb halibut fillet
100 g/4 oz button
 mushrooms, sliced
2 tablespoons chopped
 parsley

Place the flour and plenty of seasoning in a basin, then whisk in the milk. Add the butter and cook on full power for 5 minutes.

Meanwhile, place the eggs in a saucepan and add hot water to cover, then bring to the boil and cook for 10 minutes. Drain and rinse in cold water. Skin the fish fillet and cut it into four portions, then lay it in a shallow dish. Whisk the sauce thoroughly, then pour it over the fish and cover the dish with cling film, allowing a small gap for the steam to escape. Cook on full power for 10–12 minutes, depending on the thickness of the fish. Turn the fish round once during cooking.

While the fish is cooking, shell and chop the white part of the hard-boiled eggs. Sieve the yolks and keep them separate. Top the cooked fish first with the chopped egg white, then with neat rows of the yolk and chopped parsley. Serve at once.

Plain round quiche dishes make invaluable cooking vessels for the microwave oven. I have two 25-cm/10-in plain dishes, one white the other ovenproof glass, and they are used continually for cooking fish fillets and steaks, small whole fish or vegetables. Remember not to use one of these dishes if you are going to pour in a substantial quantity of sauce. I have made this most irritating mistake quite a few times!

Plaice Peperonata

—— SERVES 4 ——

Lively both in colour and flavour, this plaice dish is good served with pasta and a simple green salad; don't overdo the vegetables or the delicate flavour of the plaice could be lost completely.

1 red pepper	4 large plaice fillets
1 yellow pepper	150 ml/¼ pint soured
1 green pepper	cream
1 onion, chopped	2 tablespoons chopped
25 g/1 oz butter	parsley
salt and freshly ground	1 teaspoon chopped
black pepper	thyme

Cut the stalks off the peppers, then scoop out their seeds and pith and finely chop the shells. Mix these with the onion in a basin then add the butter and seasoning to taste. Cover with cling film, allowing a small gap for the steam to escape, then cook on full power for 8 minutes.

Arrange the plaice fillets in a dish, without overlapping them, then carefully spoon the pepper mixture on to each one keeping them as neat as possible. Cook for 5 minutes.

While the fish is cooking, mix the soured cream with the herbs and serve this with the fish.

Lemon Plaice Rolls

—— SERVES 4 ——

These stuffed plaice fillets make an excellent light main course, lunch or supper dish.

8 plaice fillets	salt and black pepper
75 g/3 oz fresh	1 tablespoon cornflour
breadcrumbs	1 fish stock cube
grated rind of 1 lemon	300 ml/½ pint dry white
½ teaspoon dried mixed	wine
herbs	*Garnish:*
2 tablespoons chopped	lemon wedges or slices
parsley	parsley sprigs
25 g/1 oz butter, melted	

Skin the fish fillets following the instructions on page 20. Mix the breadcrumbs with the lemon rind, herbs and butter. Add plenty of seasoning, then divide this stuffing between the fillets and roll them up neatly from the head end to enclose the mixture completely. Arrange the fish rolls in a large dish, as far apart as possible, with the end of each roll tucked underneath to prevent them from becoming untidy or unrolling during cooking.

Blend the cornflour with the crumbled stock cube and wine until smooth, then pour this sauce over the fish and cover with cling film, allowing a small gap for the steam to escape. Cook on full power for 10 minutes, turning the dish round once during cooking.

Give the sauce around the fish a good stir before serving, then add a garnish of lemon wedges or slices and some parsley sprigs. Serve at once.

Paupiettes Véronique

—— SERVES 4 ——

Serve these delicate plaice rolls, garnished with grapes, with Lemon Rice (see page 128).

8 plaice fillets
salt and freshly ground
  black pepper
a little lemon juice
1 small onion
25 g/1 oz butter
2 tablespoons plain flour

1 tablespoon chopped
  tarragon
300 ml/½ pint dry white
  wine
100 g/4 oz seedless white
  grapes

Skin the fish fillets following the instructions on page 20. Season the skinned side of the fillets with a little salt and pepper and sprinkle a little lemon juice over them. Roll up from the head end, then arrange these paupiettes in a shallow dish – a gratin or quiche dish works well.

Place the onion and butter in a basin and cook on full power for 6 minutes. Stir in the flour, tarragon and wine and add seasoning to taste, then cook for 2 minutes.

Reserve two small bunches of the grapes for garnish, then remove the rest of the grapes from their stalks. Add these to the sauce, give it a good whisk, then pour it over the fish. Cover with cling film, allowing a small gap for the steam to escape, and cook for 10 minutes. Turn the dish round once during cooking.

Before serving the paupiettes, gently stir the sauce around them and garnish with the reserved grapes.

Halibut in Tarragon Sauce

—— SERVES 4 ——

Halibut has a firm meaty flesh and delicate flavour which is complemented by the slight aniseed tang of tarragon. Serve new potatoes and mange-tout peas with this dish.

450 g/1 lb halibut fillet,
  cut into four equal
  portions
4 tarragon sprigs
juice of ½ lemon

50 g/2 oz butter
salt and freshly ground
  black pepper
lemon slices to garnish

Skin the halibut fillets (see page 20), then arrange the pieces neatly in a shallow dish. Top each portion with a large sprig of tarragon and sprinkle the lemon juice over. Dot with the butter and season to taste. Cover with cling film, allowing a small gap for the steam to escape, then cook on full power for 8 minutes, turning the dish once during cooking.

Allow the halibut to stand for 2 minutes, then add a garnish of lemon slices, leaving the tarragon sprigs in place. Serve at once.

Aromatic Fillets

—— SERVES 4 ——

This dish is both economical and delicious, and it's interesting enough to serve to guests if you know they are keen on both seafood and curries. Offer Spicy Peas (see page 121) and a bowl of Pullao Rice (see page 129) as accompaniments.

4 whiting fillets
4 cardamom pods
25 g/1 oz fresh
  breadcrumbs
2 teaspoons ground
  coriander
2 cloves garlic, finely
  chopped
salt and freshly ground
  black pepper

2 teaspoons celery seeds
grated rind of 1 lemon
50 g/2 oz butter
Garnish:
lemon wedges
cucumber slices
radish slices

Lay the fish fillets, overlapping very slightly, in an oval dish. Add the cardamom pods, placing them just to one side of the fillets.

Mix the breadcrumbs with the coriander, garlic and plenty of seasoning, then stir in the celery seeds and lemon rind. Sprinkle this mixture down the middle of the fish and dot with the butter. Cover the dish with cling film and cook on full power for 10 minutes, turning the dish once during cooking.

The cooked fish does not look particularly attractive so it is important that the garnish is colourful. Remove the cardamom pods from the dish, then arrange the lemon wedges, cucumber and radish slices attractively over the fish. Serve at once.

When you are arranging thin fillets of fish flat in a dish, then try not to overlap them too much as the thicker, double area of fillets will not cook as quickly as the rest of the fish. This in turn may result in the rest of the fish being slightly overcooked. To use the maximum amount of space available in the dish, arrange the fillets next to each other alternating the head and tail ends on one side of the dish. This way the fillets will double up only slightly.

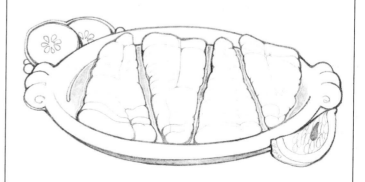

Fish Plaki

—— SERVES 4 ——

Although whiting is not the fish which would have been used in authentic Greek recipes for this dish, I think that the spicy tomato sauce makes the most of the otherwise rather bland fillets.

1 large onion, finely chopped	450 g/1 lb tomatoes
3 cloves garlic, crushed	salt and freshly ground black pepper
grated rind of 1 lemon	4 small whiting fillets
4 tablespoons olive oil	1 lemon, sliced, to garnish

Place the onion in a basin with the garlic and lemon rind. Stir in the oil and cook on full power for 5 minutes.

Meanwhile, peel the tomatoes (see page 123), halve them and remove all the seeds from inside, then chop the flesh. Stir the tomatoes into the onion and add seasoning to taste.

Skin the fish fillets following the instructions on page 20. Lay these in a large oval dish and spoon the tomato mixture over them. Cover with cling film and cook for 10 minutes, turning the dish once during cooking.

Arrange the lemon slices on top of the fish and serve at once.

Stuffed Mackerel

—— SERVES 4 ——

A Gooseberry Sauce (see page 205) would go very well with these mackerel.

4 (225-g/8-oz) mackerel, gutted with heads on	1 tablespoon capers, chopped
1 large onion, chopped	salt and freshly ground black pepper
25 g/1 oz butter	
75 g/3 oz fresh breadcrumbs	*Garnish:*
grated rind of 1 lemon	tomato wedges
	lemon wedges

Trim the fins off the mackerel and wash the body cavities, then pat them dry with absorbent kitchen paper.

Place the onion and butter in a basin and cook on full power for 5 minutes. Stir in the breadcrumbs, lemon rind, capers and seasoning to taste. Use a small spoon to press this stuffing into the body cavities of the fish, then arrange them in a large oval or oblong dish. Cover with cling film and cook for 7 minutes, turning the dish once during cooking.

Add the garnishing ingredients to the mackerel and serve at once.

Spinach-stuffed Trout

—— SERVES 4 ——

This is a delicious way of serving trout. The slightly spicy filling adds interest to the delicate trout. Serve with Lemon Rice (see page 128).

4 medium trout, gutted with their heads on	50 g/2 oz fresh breadcrumbs
1 small onion, finely chopped	salt and freshly ground black pepper
25 g/1 oz butter	a little grated nutmeg
1 small clove garlic, crushed	*Garnish:*
1 (227-g/8-oz) packet frozen spinach, defrosted (page 109)	twists of lemon watercress sprigs

Rinse and dry the body cavities of the fish, then trim off any fins.

Place the onion in a basin with the butter and garlic. Cook on full power for 4 minutes. Drain the spinach thoroughly, then add it to the onion with the breadcrumbs, seasoning and nutmeg. Mix thoroughly, then use a teaspoon to divide this stuffing between the trout. Press it into the body cavities, using your fingers if it is easier.

Arrange the fish in a large oval or oblong dish, two facing one way and the others facing in the opposite direction. Cover the dish with cling film, allowing a small gap for the steam to escape. Cook for 12 minutes, turning the dish round twice during cooking. Allow the fish to stand for 2 minutes, then remove the covering and garnish with twists of lemon and watercress sprigs. Serve at once.

Always arrange whole fish in a dish in a way which will make the best use of the whole area of the container, at the same time giving an even layer of food to cook. If all the thick areas of food are arranged at one end of the dish, then the cooking result will not be even.

Mustard Mackerel Fillets

——— SERVES 4 ———

Richly flavoured mackerel fillets are well balanced in this recipe – they are spread with hot English mustard and rolled up with fresh lemon thyme sprigs. A combination which goes to make a delicious fish dish. If fresh lemon thyme is not available (it's a herb well worth growing for its superb flavour and it can be cultivated in a pot on a light window sill), then use any lemon flavoured herb – balm or verbena – with a little fresh or dried thyme. At the very worst you can substitute grated lemon rind for the lemon flavoured herb. Serve Fantail Potatoes (see page 104) with this dish.

4 mackerel, gutted and filleted	salt and freshly ground black pepper
about 2 tablespoons prepared English mustard or to taste	50 g/2 oz butter *Garnish:*
bunch of fresh lemon thyme	lemon slices lemon thyme sprigs

Ask your fishmonger to fillet the mackerel for you unless you are adept with a filletting knife! Make sure there are no bones left on the fillets, then spread the flesh side of each with mustard to taste. Wash the herb thoroughly, then dry the sprigs and run your fingers down the stalk to press the leaves off on to the fish fillets. Add seasoning to taste. Roll up from the head end and arrange the fillets around the outside of a shallow round dish – a quiche dish is ideal. Dot with the butter and cover with cling film, then cook on full power for 5 to 6 minutes.

   Leave the fish to stand for 2 minutes before serving, garnished with the lemon slices and sprigs of lemon thyme.

If you do not have a dish large enough to accommodate four mackerel, or if you want to prepare two fish, then use half the ingredients and cook for 5 minutes.

Trout with Almonds

——— SERVES 4 ———

Small whole fish, like trout and mackerel, cook very well and retain all their flavour in the microwave oven. If your oven cavity is not large enough to take a shallow dish which holds four trout, then follow the timings given below and cook them two at a time.

4 medium trout, gutted with their heads on	4 bay leaves 50 g/2 oz flaked almonds
juice of ½ lemon	50 g/2 oz butter
salt and freshly ground black pepper	parsley sprigs to garnish (optional)

Rinse and dry the insides of the trout, then sprinkle the body cavities with lemon juice and seasoning. Place a bay leaf in each and arrange the fish in a shallow oval or large round dish. The fish should sit with two heads facing one way and two in the opposite direction. Cover the dish with cling film, allowing a small gap for the steam to escape, then cook on full power for 12 minutes, turning the dish round once during cooking.

   Leave the cooked fish covered and place the nuts in a small basin or mug then add the butter. Cover with cling film and cook for 4 minutes. By this time the almonds should be lightly browned. Give them a good stir, pour them over the fish with the butter and serve at once garnished with parsley sprigs if liked.

To cook two trout, or similar fish, in the microwave, arrange them in a dish and cover with cling film, then cook on full power for 7 minutes. Turn the dish once during cooking. If you are going to cook a second pair of fish, then cover the cooked first batch with foil, placing the shiny side inwards to reflect as much heat as possible back into the food. This way the fish should still be hot enough to serve as soon as the second pair are ready.

Poached Salmon

—— SERVES 6 TO 8 ——

The microwave is excellent for cooking fish of all types and it is particularly useful for poaching a large fish which would otherwise need to be cooked in a fish kettle or in the oven. To accomodate a large fish in the microwave oven, it should be curled in a quiche dish and a double thickness of cling film should be used, not only to retain the moisture during cooking but also to support the fish and prevent it from becoming mis-shapen.

The poached fish can be served either hot or cold, with a Hollandaise Sauce (see page 201) or with a Horseradish Mayonnaise (see below).

Judging by the fact that a 2.25-kg/5-lb salmon curled successfully into a 25-cm/10-in dish, but no smaller vessel would do, then this seems to be the largest fish which can be cooked in the microwave.

1 (2.25-kg/5-lb) salmon or	*Garnish:*
salmon trout	lemon and cucumber
2 bay leaves	slices
a few peppercorns	parsley sprigs
a few sprigs of parsley	1 (15-g/½-oz) packet fish
4 tablespoons water	aspic
juice of ½ lemon	a little white wine
	(optional)
	150 ml/¼ pint mayonnaise

Trim the fins off the salmon and descale the fish – do this by running the blade of a knife down the skin, working from tail to head. If you hold the fish in a sink under gently running water this is likely to make less mess. Thoroughly rinse the body cavity of the fish to make sure it is well cleaned. Tie the mouth shut so that it will look better at the table.

Put the bay leaves peppercorns and parsley into the body cavity of the salmon, then curl the fish into a 25-cm/10-in quiche dish, keeping the cut edges on the underside neatly tucked beneath the fish. Pour the water and lemon juice into the dish with the fish, then cover with a *double thickness* of cling film, wrapping tightly over the fish and right around the dish. This will keep the fish in shape during cooking, so use a lavish amount of cling film.

Make a small hole in the middle of the covering, then cook the salmon on full power for a total of 12 minutes. During cooking, turn the dish three times – a quarter to one-third turn of the dish is necessary so that the main bulk of the body does not end up in exactly the same position twice. Allow the cooked fish to stand, still covered, for 5 minutes.

If the fish is to be served cold, then allow it to cool covered in the dish, checking to make sure that it is thoroughly cooked first. To do this, carefully insert a pointed knife straight down into the top of the body so that you can see that the flesh is not opaque. This area will be garnished when the fish is cold, so the small slit will not show.

To serve the fish hot, carefully transfer it to a serving platter, removing the bay leaves, peppercorns and parsley first. Slit the skin around the body at the tail and head ends, then carefully peel it back from the tail towards the head. Add a garnish along the top of the fish and untie the mouth. Garnish the eyes if you like. Serve at once, with the Hollandaise Sauce. The salmon should be hot to warm when served; not mouth-burning hot or the flavour will be lost.

To serve cold: first make up a packet of fish aspic according to the packet instructions, adding a little white wine if you like. Transfer the salmon to a serving platter, removing the bay leaves, parsley and peppercorns from inside.

Slit the skin at the tail and head ends of the fish, then peel it back from tail to head. Untie the mouth and remove the eyes if you like. Prepare thin strips of cucumber peel and lemon rind, thin slices of cucumber, lemon and radish for the garnish. When the aspic is beginning to set, brush it carefully over the fish, then dip the garnishing ingredients in it and arrange these on the salmon. Add a little more aspic to glaze the salmon evenly, then chill until the aspic is firmly set. Pour any remaining aspic into a large shallow dish and chill it at the same time. This can be neatly chopped and added to the serving platter as a final garnish.

Just before serving, pipe neat rosettes of mayonnaise (make sure they are not too large and bulky as they should enhance the line of the fish) down the length of the body and to form a collar around the neck. Cover the eye cavities with mayonnaise. Add the chopped aspic to the dish, with more cucumber and lemon, then serve.

Horseradish Mayonnaise

300 ml/½ pint mayonnaise	4 tablespoons creamed
(home-made or good-	horseradish
quality bottled)	a little freshly ground
	white pepper

Do not use a mayonnaise which has a sharp tang of vinegar or the sauce will be too tart. Stir the horseradish and white pepper to taste into the mayonnaise and chill lightly before serving.

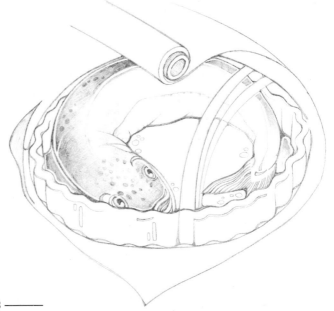

Salmon in Vermouth Sauce

——— SERVES 4 ———

Salmon steaks are rather special and best served in a simple, but special, sauce. Here dry white vermouth is used to flavour an otherwise plain sauce.

4 (175-g/6-oz) salmon steaks	a little milk
4 bay leaves	salt and freshly ground white pepper
a little freshly ground white pepper	50 ml/2 fl oz dry white vermouth
75 g/3 oz butter	2 egg yolks
Sauce:	lemon wedges to garnish
2 tablespoons plain flour	

Place the fish steaks as far apart as possible in a shallow dish – a plain white quiche dish is ideal. Add the bay leaves, one to each steak, then sprinkle a little pepper over the salmon and add 50 g/2 oz butter, dotted on each steak. Cover with cling film, allowing a small gap for the steam to escape, and cook on full power for 8 minutes, turning the dish twice during cooking.

While the salmon is cooking, put the flour for the sauce in a jug. Transfer the steaks to a warmed serving dish and keep hot. Reserve the bay leaves for garnishing the fish, then pour the cooking juices into the jug, stirring to make a smooth paste. Stir in enough milk to make the liquid up to 150 ml/¼ pint, then add seasoning to taste and the vermouth. If the jug is suitable for microwave cooking, then cook the sauce in it for 4 minutes.

Whisk in the egg yolks and remaining butter, then taste and adjust the seasoning. Cook for a further 30 seconds before pouring over the salmon steaks. Garnish with the bay leaves and lemon wedges and serve at once.

Seafood Delight

——— SERVES 4 ———

This really is a dish of sheer indulgence for all lovers of seafood. Save it for very special occasions – a birthday treat, as a Boxing Day alternative to cold roast turkey or for a wonderful mid-summer's lunch. Serve the cold salmon with a cucumber salad, dotted with a few thinly sliced fresh strawberries.

4 (175-g/6-oz) salmon steaks	2 teaspoons chopped chives
4 dill sprigs	1 tablespoon chopped fresh dill
50 g/2 oz butter	
2 tablespoons dry white wine	225 g/8 oz peeled cooked prawns (defrosted if frozen)
Stuffing:	
6 tablespoons mayonnaise	dill sprigs to garnish

Arrange the fish steaks as far apart as possible in a shallow dish. Top each one with a sprig of dill and add a knob of butter to each steak. Sprinkle over the wine and cover the dish with cling film, allowing a small gap for the steam to escape, then cook on full power for 8 minutes. Turn the dish round twice during cooking. Drain off and reserve all the juices from the fish, then set the steaks aside to cool.

Mix the cooking juices with the mayonnaise, chives and dill, then stir in the prawns to coat them completely. Arrange the fish steaks on individual plates, then carefully remove the skin and central bone from each one. Pile a little of the prawn mixture into each steak and top with a delicate garnish of dill. Serve unchilled so as to bring out the full flavour of the salmon.

Crunchy Creamed Seafood

——— SERVES 4 ———

Arranged on a bed of cooked rice or noodles, this creamy seafood mixture makes a delicious dinner which is easy to prepare. Serve with just a green salad. Alternatively, the seafood can be served in individual pots and baked potatoes can be offered as an accompaniment. For a light luncheon dish serve the seafood on its own with some hot crusty or Granary bread.

1 onion, finely chopped	100 g/4 oz button mushrooms, sliced
75 g/3 oz butter	4 tablespoons double cream
4 scallops, cleaned	
3 tablespoons plain flour	4 medium-thick slices bread
salt and freshly ground black pepper	2 tablespoons oil
150 ml/¼ pint milk	4 tablespoons chopped parsley
225 g/8 oz frozen peeled cooked prawns	
225 g/8 oz frozen cooked mussels	

Place the onion in a basin or bowl with 25 g/1 oz of the butter. Cook on full power for 4 minutes.

Meanwhile, slice the scallops. Stir the flour and plenty of seasoning into the onion and pour in the milk, stirring continuously. Add the prawns, scallops and mussels, then stir in the mushrooms. Cover the bowl with cling film, allowing a small gap for the steam to escape, and cook for 4 minutes, stirring once. Stir in the cream and continue to cook for 5 minutes.

While the seafood is cooking, cut the crusts off the bread and cut each slice into four neat triangles. Heat the remaining butter with the oil in a frying pan. Add the bread triangles and fry them until they are golden brown, turn and cook the second side. Drain the croûtons on absorbent kitchen paper and set aside.

Stir the chopped parsley into the cooked seafood and pour into individual dishes or over cooked rice or noodles. Top with the croûtons, arranged attractively then serve at once.

Lobster Maître d'Hôtel

──── SERVES 2 ────

This is particularly speedy and a delicious dish to serve for a special lunch party or for dinner. Keep the accompaniment delicate – Courgette Parcels (see page 117), Asparagus Hollandaise (see page 114) and Minted New Potatoes (see page 102) are suitable. Otherwise a salad would be an excellent alternative.

1 small cooked lobster (about 450 g/1 lb in weight)	50 g/2 oz butter
25 g/1 oz fresh white breadcrumbs	2 tablespoons chopped parsley
grated rind of $\frac{1}{2}$ lemon	a little lemon juice
freshly ground black pepper	lemon twists to garnish

Pull the legs and claws off the lobster and set these aside. Turn the lobster on its back on a board, then cut it in half down the middle and right through the shell. Use a heavy knife for this and have a steak mallet ready to tap the back of the blade if the shell is difficult to break.

When the lobster is cut in half, remove all the tail meat that runs down the length of the body. Carefully lift out any coral (the roe of the female lobster) and reserve this for the garnish. Remove and discard the gravel sac which is found at the head end of the lobster, between the eyes. Scrape out the shell and set it aside to serve.

Crack the claws of the lobster (use a mallet or nut crackers) and remove all meat from inside, then use a skewer to poke all the meat out of the legs. Mix all the lobster meat in a basin and break it up slightly. Stir in the breadcrumbs, lemon rind and pepper to taste. Spoon this mixture back into the shells.

Beat the butter with the parsley and lemon juice, then dot this butter (maître d'hôtel butter) over the lobster halves. Sit these in a large gratin dish and cook on full power for 2 minutes. Garnish with the reserved coral and the lemon twists. It is then ready to serve.

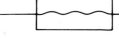

If you are preparing lobster for four, split and mix the meat from two lobsters following the recipe. Spoon it back into the shells and cook the halves two at a time; the cooking time is so quick that there is no danger of the first pair becoming cold while the second batch is cooked. Indeed you will have time only to garnish the first two before the second pair are ready.

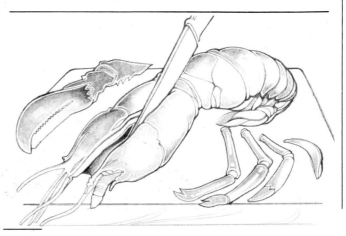

Moules à la Marinière

—— SERVES 2 TO 4 ——

Mussels cook really well in the microwave. If you have a large attractive bowl that is suitable for putting in the microwave and also for serving then that is ideal. Serve the mussels with plenty of hot French bread. Make sure you have spoons available to make the most of all the cooking juices.

1 kg/2 lb mussels
oatmeal
300 ml/½ pint dry white
   wine
1 bay leaf
salt and freshly ground
   black pepper

4 spring onions, chopped
25 g/1 oz butter
2 tablespoons plain flour
4 tablespoons chopped
   parsley to garnish

Place the mussels in a bucket of cold water and add a handful of oatmeal. Leave the bucket in a cool place overnight or for several hours. This process will clean the mussels of any sand and grit.

Drain and wash the mussels, then scrape them clean with a small sharp knife. Pull away the black hairs known as the beard; a firm tug should remove these. Discard any mussels that are not tightly shut and which do not shut quickly when tapped firmly.

Pour the wine into a large mixing bowl, then add the bay leaf and seasoning to taste. Stir in the spring onions and cook on full power for 5 minutes.

Add the mussels to the hot wine and cover with cling film. Cook for 5 minutes. While the mussels are cooking, beat the butter and flour together until smooth. Remove any mussels that have not opened and discard these. If you like remove the shell halves which do not contain the mussels, but this is not essential. Transfer the shellfish to individual serving bowls or 1 large bowl, or, if they have been cooked in their serving bowl, then strain most of the cooking liquid into a microwave-proof measuring jug or basin.

Whisk all of the butter and flour paste into the juices until the butter has dissolved and cook for 3 minutes. Pour this sauce over the mussels and sprinkle with lots of chopped parsley. Serve at once.

Gratin of Mussels

——— SERVES 4 ———

This really is a good way of serving mussels for a light main course or starter. If you want to prepare them for the main course of a dinner then cook double the quantity of mussels in two batches.

1 kg/2 lb mussels oatmeal	salt and freshly ground black pepper
450 g/1 lb ripe tomatoes	100 g/4 oz fresh
1 small onion, finely chopped	breadcrumbs
2 cloves garlic, crushed	2 tablespoons chopped parsley
50 g/2 oz butter	2 tablespoons freshly
300 ml/½ pint red wine	grated Parmesan cheese
2 teaspoons oregano	

Prepare the mussels as for Moules à la Marinière, leaving them in a bucket of water with oatmeal for several hours, then scrub them thoroughly and remove the black hairs known as the beard. Pull these off firmly to remove them in one piece.

Peel the tomatoes (see page 123), then cut them in half and remove all their seeds. Chop the tomato flesh and place it in a large mixing bowl. Add the onion, garlic, butter, wine and oregano. Stir well, adding seasoning to taste, then cook on full power for 8 minutes.

Add the mussels to the bowl and cover with cling film, then cook for 5 minutes. At the end of this cooking time discard any unopened shells and all the empty shell halves. Put the mussels in their shells, arranging them so that they stand neatly, in individual shallow dishes. Spoon the cooking juices over them.

Mix the breadcrumbs with the parsley and cheese, add a little seasoning and sprinkle this topping over the mussels. Cook under a hot grill until well browned and crisp on top. Serve at once.

Lobster Thermidor

——— SERVES 2 ———

1 small cooked lobster (about 450 g/1 lb in weight)	salt and freshly ground black pepper
1 small onion, finely chopped	4 tablespoons double cream
25 g/1 oz butter	2 tablespoons grated Parmesan cheese
3 tablespoons plain flour	2 tablespoons fresh
150 ml/¼ pint fish stock	breadcrumbs
150 ml/¼ pint dry white wine	a little chopped parsley to garnish

Prepare the lobster as for Lobster Maître d'Hôtel (see page 50), reserving the coral (if any) for garnish. Cut the lobster meat into chunks and set aside.

Place the onion and butter in a large basin and cook on full power for 5 minutes. Stir in the flour and gradually pour in the fish stock, stirring all the time to prevent lumps from forming. Cook on full power for 12 minutes, then whisk the sauce thoroughly. Stir in a little salt and plenty of pepper, then add the cream and lobster meat and heat for 1 minute.

Arrange the shells on a serving dish (one which can be put under the grill) then spoon the lobster into them. Mix the Parmesan cheese and breadcrumbs and sprinkle this over the lobster. Cook under a hot grill until golden brown, then serve garnished with the reserved coral and chopped parsley.

Coquilles St-Jacques

——— SERVES 4 ———

Coquilles St-Jacques is the French name for scallops and here they are cooked very simply in a wine sauce. Serve them for a light lunch or supper dish, with a green salad and thinly sliced bread and butter. They also make a very good first course.

8 scallops	wine is essential for a good sauce)
1 very small onion or 2 shallots	salt and freshly ground white pepper
25 g/1 oz butter	2 tablespoons chopped parsley
1 tablespoon plain flour	
150 ml/¼ pint dry white wine (a good quality	

Ask your fishmonger to remove the scallops from their shells and clean them for you if they are not already prepared. Otherwise follow the directions given below. Save four of the deep scallop shells for serving. Wash and thoroughly scrub these, dry them and set aside for later use.

Finely chop the onion or shallots and place in a bowl with the butter. Cook on full power for 5 minutes. Meanwhile, slice the scallops and set aside. Stir the flour into the onion, then gradually pour in the wine, stirring all the time. Add seasoning to taste then the sliced scallops. Cover with cling film and cook for 4 minutes. Gently stir the scallops in the sauce, then cook for a further 4 minutes.

Stir in the chopped parsley and spoon the scallops into the prepared shells or into individual dishes. Serve immediately.

To clean scallops: if the shells are not already open, then hold the flat shell up and prize the scallop open with a strong knife. The part of the scallop which is required is the white mussel and the red coral. Cut the scallop away from the shell using either a sharp knife or a pair of scissors. Discard the grey outer flesh and all the other parts except the white and red flesh. Rinse these thoroughly under cold water, being careful not to damage the scallop. They are now ready to use as required.

Tuna Fish Florentine

—— SERVES 4 ——

This is a good dish to rely on when there is little else in the cupboard.

I large onion, chopped	3 tablespoons plain flour
50 g/2 oz butter	300 ml/½ pint milk
2 (225-g/8-oz) packets frozen spinach, defrosted (page 109)	salt and freshly ground black pepper
I (198-g/7-oz) can tuna in oil	50 g/2 oz Cheddar cheese, grated

Place the onion in a basin with the butter and cook on full power for 5 minutes. Thoroughly drain the spinach, then add it to the onion and mix thoroughly.

Pour the oil from the tuna into a basin, then whisk in the flour, milk and seasoning to taste. Cook this sauce on full power for 5 minutes, whisking once during cooking and again at the end of the cooking time.

Flake the fish and stir it into the sauce. Season the spinach and put it in a gratin dish. Cook for 4 minutes. Pour the fish in sauce over the spinach and top with the cheese. Cook under a hot grill until golden brown and bubbling. Serve at once.

Devilled Tuna

—— SERVES 4 ——

This spicy tuna mixture is very good served with small boiled pasta shells coated in Béchamel Sauce (see page 200). If you would prefer something slightly less substantial then offer hot French bread and a salad.

2 (198-g/7-oz) cans tuna in oil	grated rind of I lemon
2 cloves garlic, crushed	salt and freshly ground black pepper
2 tablespoons chopped capers	dash of Worcestershire sauce
I pickled gherkin, chopped	4 spring onions, chopped cayenne pepper to taste
I tablespoon wholegrain mustard	I tablespoon paprika lemon slices to garnish

Drain the oil from the tuna into a large bowl or basin. Add the garlic, capers and gherkin and cook on full power for 2 minutes. Stir in the roughly flaked fish, the mustard, lemon rind, seasoning and Worcestershire sauce. Cover with cling film and cook on full power for 5 minutes. Stir in the spring onions and a little cayenne (be careful – it's very hot). Mix thoroughly, then arrange the fish on the serving dish. It can be spooned over pasta in a plain sauce, over a simple (finely shredded) green salad or into attractive individual bowls.

To serve, sprinkle the paprika over the tuna and add a garnish of lemon slices. Serve at once.

Crab Newburg

—— SERVES 4 ——

Lobster Newburg, a well-known American dish, consists of the seafood in a rich sauce of cream, eggs, Madeira and brandy. Here, that rich sauce is used to coat cooked crab meat. Serve the dish with plain boiled rice.

I (1.25–1.5-kg/2½–3-lb) cooked crab	2 tablespoons brandy
2 tablespoons plain flour	150 ml/¼ pint double cream
50 g/2 oz butter	2 egg yolks
150 ml/¼ pint dry white wine	*Garnish:*
2 tablespoons Madeira	croûtons (see below) chopped parsley

First prepare the crab. Loosen the body from the shell, by slipping a knife in at the tail end. Hold the body firmly in one hand, then pull away the shell with the other. Remove the legs and claws and set these aside for a while.

Scoop out all the soft brown meat from the shell. Remove and discard the stomach bag and the entrails which surround it; these are located behind the mouth end of the shell. Carefully poke all the white meat out from every crevice of the body, then discard all the inedible bits.

Now crack the claws and legs and remove all the meat from these. Place all the prepared white meat in a serving dish (one which is suitable for putting in the microwave oven).

Place the flour in a basin and beat in half the butter. Gradually beat in the wine, Madeira and brandy, then cook on full power for 4 minutes. Whisk thoroughly, then gradually pour in the cream, still whisking. Cook for 4 minutes, then whisk in the egg yolks and the brown crab meat.

Dot the remaining butter over the crab in the serving bowl. Cover with cling film, allowing a small gap for the steam to escape, then cook for 3 minutes. Pour the sauce over the crab and heat through for I minute, then serve topped with croûtons and chopped parsley.

To make croûtons: make these on the conventional hob. Cut the crusts off 3 thin slices bread, then cut the rest into small cubes, triangles or any shape you wish. Heat 2 tablespoons oil and 25 g/I oz butter in a frying pan. Add the bread cubes and toss them in the fat so that they are evenly coated. Cook, turning the bread occasionally, until golden brown all over. Drain on absorbent kitchen paper and use as required.

To defrost a frozen lobster: if you buy a lobster frozen in water, then make a small hole at one end of the packet and place the lobster in a large dish. Cook on full power for 10 minutes, turning the dish once. Rinse the lobster under hand-hot water to remove any bits of ice. Now it should be ready for splitting and using.

POULTRY DISHES

Chicken and turkey meat is lean and tender, therefore ideal for microwave cooking. Cut into cubes or shredded, in the form of boneless breasts or chicken thighs, these poultry cook evenly and quickly. Chicken joints can also be cooked successfully, but with greater care to prevent the joint ends from overcooking. Whole birds are not at their best when cooked totally in the microwave oven. However, by cooking a whole chicken partly in the microwave oven, then in the conventional oven, the result is both moist and exceptionally full flavoured with a crisp, golden skin. Similarly, whole turkeys can be cooked first in the microwave but the largest bird which cooks well is one weighing 4.75-kg/10-lb. A whole turkey needs a short period of standing time halfway through cooking to disperse the heat evenly.

Duck can also be cooked by this method and the result is very good, with the breast meat tasting moist and well flavoured. The skin is seasoned before the bird is put into the conventional oven and this gives a very crisp and golden crust.

As a general guide for cooking whole chickens and turkey in the microwave, then in the conventional oven, for chickens allow 5 to 6 minutes to the 450 g/1 lb in the microwave oven followed by 15 to 30 minutes in the conventional oven on very hot (240 C, 475 F, gas 9). Check to make sure that the bird is cooked through by piercing it at the thickest point of the thigh: when cooked the juices should be free of blood. For turkeys, allow 6 to 7 minutes in the microwave per 450 g/1 lb followed by a further 45 to 60 minutes in the conventional oven on moderately hot (200 C, 400 F, gas 6). Again make sure the bird is cooked. It is a good idea to check these cooking times against the instructions given with your

own oven because every model varies. Remember that you are going to finish the cooking in the conventional oven so do not allow the full timing recommended. If you want to cook the bird totally in the microwave then follow the timings given by the manufacturer.

If you are in a hurry it is possible to defrost a bird in the microwave. Again it is best to follow the specific instructions for your oven but as a guide, allow 5 minutes to the 450 g/1 lb on defrost setting. Cook the poultry for periods of 10 and 5 minutes and allow at least 30 minutes standing time halfway through and at the end of defrosting. It is most important that the bird is thoroughly defrosted, so rinse the inside with boiling water to defrost any icy bits and to help release the giblets if necessary.

The recipes in this chapter cover a range of international dishes. As well as roast chicken, there is a recipe for a galantine of chicken; a boned chicken is even in shape and ideal for microwave cooking. An idea for wrapping the galantine in a pastry crust is also included to make the result even more splendid.

Not forgetting day-to-day meals, there are recipes for Chicken and Parsnip Stew (see page 60), Peanut Chicken Pot (see page 65) and Turkey Charlotte (see page 70). For cook-ahead entertaining try Coq au Vin (see page 61), Lemon Spiced Chicken (see page 64) or Turkey Paupiettes and when you feel like preparing a splendid oriental feast have a go at Peking Duck (see page 72).

When you are quite familiar with using your microwave oven, then poultry is another of those foods that you will find cooks very successfully by this method but remember to bring the conventional oven or grill into play to give a perfect result.

Roast Chicken

—— SERVES 4 TO 6 ——

It is quite possible to cook a whole chicken in the microwave oven; however the result is steamed chicken which can be slightly unevenly cooked if the bird is not turned over and around several times during cooking. This is acceptable if the chicken is to be skinned and served coated in a chaud froid sauce, or if the meat is to be cut off the bones and used in some other dish such as a pie, flan or salad. Indeed the microwave oven is invaluable if you want to cook a whole chicken so as to use the meat in any of these ways.

Generally speaking, a roast chicken is expected to be thoroughly cooked, yet still moist, crisp and brown. If you own an oven which combines microwave energy with the facility for conventional cooking, then this appliance is perfect to achieve such a result; otherwise, by using both your microwave oven and your conventional oven you can turn out a chicken which is as good, if not better, than one cooked conventionally.

The secret is to three-quarters (or more) cook the bird in the microwave oven, so that it is moist and not overcooked at all (even the breast meat), then transfer it to a very hot conventional oven. This way the chicken is cooked quickly, the skin is particularly crisp and brown (but not overbrowned) and the result is delicious. If you are in a particular rush then you can cook the chicken completely in the microwave and brown it off under the grill, but it is not as good.

1 (1.5-kg/3½-lb) chicken	1 chicken stock cube
stuffing (see below)	450 ml/¾ pint boiling
oil for brushing	water
salt	salt and freshly ground
Gravy:	black pepper
3 tablespoons plain flour	

Remove the giblets from the chicken, then trim any excess fat from inside the bird and scald the body cavity with plenty of boiling water. Thoroughly drain the chicken and dry the inside with absorbent kitchen paper. Make sure that the body cavity is thoroughly clean before stuffing it.

Prepare the stuffing of your choice according to the instructions then use a spoon to press it into the chicken. Make sure the stuffing is pressed well into the bird, then truss the chicken neatly with clean string. Start by tying the legs together, binding the string around them twice, then take it under the bird and around the ends of the wings to tie them firmly in place.

Brush the chicken all over with oil and place it, breast side uppermost, in a large ovenproof dish. Cover with cling film, allowing a very small gap for the steam to escape, then cook on full power for 5 minutes. Turn the bird over so that the breast meat is downwards, turn the dish round in the oven and cook for a further 15 minutes.

Uncover the chicken, turn it breast upwards, season the top with salt, and transfer it to the top of a very hot oven (240C, 475F, gas 9) for about 15 minutes. The chicken should now be golden brown and thoroughly cooked.

To make gravy, transfer the chicken to a warmed serving dish and keep hot. Drain most of the fat from the cooking dish but retain the chicken juices. Stir in the flour. Dissolve the stock cube in the boiling water and gradually stir this into the flour mixture, making sure there are no lumps. Season to taste. Cook on full power for 8 minutes, whisk thoroughly and pour into a sauceboat to serve.

Apple and Orange Stuffing

(enough to stuff a 1.5-kg/3½-lb bird)

1 large onion, finely chopped	grated rind and juice of 1 large orange
25 g/1 oz butter	100 g/4 oz fresh breadcrumbs
2 cloves	salt and freshly ground black pepper
225 g/8 oz cooking apples, peel, cored and finely chopped	
2 tablespoons demerara sugar	

Place the onion in a fairly large bowl with the butter and cloves. Cover with cling film and cook on full power for 5 minutes. Stir in the apples and sugar – you may need slightly more or less sugar depending on how tart the apples are. Add the remaining ingredients making sure the stuffing is well seasoned, then mix thoroughly and use as required.

Spicy Rice and Raisin Stuffing

(enough to stuff a 1.5-kg/3½-lb bird)

1 large onion, finely chopped	50 g/2 oz raisins
25 g/1 oz butter	4 tablespoons chopped parsley
2 cloves garlic, crushed	salt and freshly ground black pepper
100 g/4 oz easy-cook rice	
1 chicken stock cube	
300 ml/½ pint boiling water	

Place the onion in a bowl with the butter and garlic, cover with cling film and cook on full power for 5 minutes. Stir in the rice.

Dissolve the stock cube in the boiling water, then pour this over the rice and cover with cling film, allowing a small gap for the steam to escape. Cook for 15 minutes, then stir in the raisins, parsley and plenty of black pepper, but go easy on the salt; its best to allow the stuffing to cool enough to be able to taste it, then stir in the salt. Use as required.

Galantine of Chicken

— SERVES 6 —

If you have a tame butcher and ask him very nicely, then he may just bone out a chicken for you (while you've got him in the mood ask for half-a-dozen and pop them in the freezer!). If you are not this lucky, then sharpen your knife and attack the task following the instructions at the end of this recipe.

1 (1.5-kg/3½-lb) chicken
350 g/12 oz lean bacon
1 large onion, finely chopped
2 sprigs thyme
2 sprigs sage
small bunch of parsley
100 g/4 oz fresh breadcrumbs
prepared mustard of your choice (wholegrain, with chives, or Dijon)
6 slices pressed tongue
a little oil
salt and freshly ground black pepper

First bone the chicken (see below). If you are not too keen on this task it is best to do it on the day before you intend to eat the bird.

Cut off and discard the rinds from the bacon, then chop the rashers and place them in a large basin with the onion. Cook on full power for 5 minutes.

Chop all the herbs together, then add them to the bacon with the breadcrumbs. Spread the mustard over the tongue, allowing enough to suit your own taste. Roll up the slices quite tightly.

Lay the chicken flat on a clean surface, with the skin side down. Place half the stuffing mixture over the breast meat, then top with slices of tongue, neatly arranged. Add the remaining stuffing and fold the chicken around it. Sew up the chicken into a neat shape using a trussing or darning needle and buttonhole thread, then brush it all over with a little oil and seasoning. Slide the galantine into a roasting bag. Secure the end loosely with an elastic band, allowing room for some of the steam to escape. Cook on full power for 15 to 18 minutes, turning the bird twice during cooking.

If you intend serving the chicken cold, then leave it to cool in the bag. Coat the cold chicken with a suitable sauce or mayonnaise and add a garnish of fresh salad ingredients. If you are going to serve the chicken hot, then brown it off under the grill first. Cut the galantine into slices to serve, removing the string as you do so.

To bone a chicken: turn the bird with the breast down on a clean surface. Use a sharp knife to cut down the length of the back, then cut under the skin, working as close to the bone as possible and remove all the meat. Keep the skin in one piece and scrape the meat downwards off the bones or out of all the crannies. Take particular care when you reach the soft breast bone not to break the skin. Cut a very fine sliver of bone off to avoid this. Turn the chicken round and work the other side free from the bones.

Galantine en Croûte

— SERVES 6 —

1 (1.5-kg/3½-lb) chicken
225 g/8 oz dried apricots (the type which do not need pre-soaking)
2 tablespoons dry sherry
1 red pepper
1 green pepper
4 spring onions
450 g/1 lb garlic pâté
3 cabanos
a little oil
450-g/1-lb frozen puff pastry, defrosted
1 egg, beaten
300 ml/½ pint mixed dry white wine and chicken stock
mixed salad ingredients to garnish

Bone the chicken. Place the apricots in a basin and pour in the sherry. Cover with cling film and cook on full power for 2 minutes. Shake the basin to coat the fruit in liquor, then set aside.

Cut the stalk ends off the peppers and remove all their seeds, then chop the flesh. Trim and chop the spring onions, then mix them with the peppers. Open out the chicken and lay it skin side down on a flat surface. Spread the pâté evenly all over the flesh. Press the pepper mixture evenly over the pâté and lay half the apricots down the middle. Arrange the cabanos on the fruit and lay the remaining apricots on top, sprinkling any juices over the filling. Fold over the pâté-coated edges of the chicken to enclose the stuffing completely in neat layers.

Using a trussing needle, or large darning needle, and buttonhole thread, sew up the chicken keeping it in a neat even shape. Brush the outside all over with a little oil and place the galantine in a roasting bag. Secure the bag loosely with a microwave-proof plastic tie or elastic band and lay the bird breast side uppermost in a large dish.

Cook on full power for 15 minutes, turning the chicken over and around after 7½ minutes. Turn the chicken over so that the breast meat sits in the juices and seal the cooking bag tightly. Leave to cool completely if you intend serving the galantine cold, otherwise set aside while you roll out the pastry.

On a lightly floured surface, roll out the pastry fairly thickly to make an oblong large enough to enclose the bird completely. Transfer to a baking tray or roasting tin. Lay the chicken in the middle of the pastry breast side down and carefully pull out the thread. Fold one side of the pastry over to half cover the chicken, then brush the edge with beaten egg. Fold the other side over to enclose the bird completely and press it down well to seal the edge. Trim the edges and reserve for decoration. Brush the ends of the pastry with beaten egg and seal well. Turn the galantine over so that the sealed edge is underneath.

Roll out any trimmings and cut out pastry leaves; brush with a little beaten egg and press on to the gelatine. Brush the pastry all over with beaten egg.

Cook the galantine in a hot oven (220C, 425F, gas 7) for about 20 minutes or until the pastry is well puffed and golden brown. If the cooking juices are to be served, then add the wine mixture to them and heat for 5 minutes.

Serve straightaway, or leave to cool completely before serving lightly chilled. If the chicken is served cold add a garnish of mixed salad ingredients to the platter.

Citrus Chicken

SERVES 4

Boneless chicken breasts can be poached most successfully in the microwave oven. This dish, well flavoured with lemon, benefits from an attractive garnish otherwise it can look rather insipid. Offer crisp vegetables – lightly cooked courgettes or French beans and some baby carrots – to complement the colour and texture of the chicken.

4 boneless chicken breasts (about 100 g/4 oz each)
grated rind of 1 large lemon
juice of ½ lemon
1 bay leaf
2 teaspoons chopped lemon thyme
1 chicken stock cube

450 ml/¾ pint boiling water
1 tablespoon cornflour
2 tablespoons water
Garnish:
lemon slices
lemon thyme sprigs (optional)

Skin the chicken breasts and place them in a dish without overlapping the joints. Sprinkle over the lemon rind and juice, add the bay leaf and lemon thyme. If you do not have any lemon thyme use any other lemon flavoured herb – for example, lemon balm or verbena – and some fresh or dried thyme. Dissolve the stock cube in the boiling water and pour the stock over the chicken. Cover with cling film, allowing a small gap for the steam to escape, then cook on full power for 5 minutes.

Blend the cornflour with the water, then carefully stir the solution into the sauce and rearrange the chicken breasts in the dish, turning them over too. Re-cover and continue to cook for a further 5 minutes.

Thoroughly stir the sauce before serving the chicken, garnished with the lemon slices and herbs.

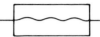

Frozen puff pastry can be thawed quickly in the micro-wave oven. Place the packet in the microwave and cook on full power for 1 minute, turning the pastry over and around once during cooking. Leave the pastry to rest at room temperature for 5–10 minutes before rolling it out.

Chicken and Asparagus ☐ Jalousie

-------- SERVES 4 --------

This attractive dish comprises a crisp pastry case, cooked conventionally, filled with a creamy chicken mixture and topped with asparagus. It can be served hot or cold, in which case the canned asparagus need only be drained before arranging it on the chicken.

1 (368-g/13-oz) packet frozen puff pastry, defrosted	2 tablespoons dry sherry salt and freshly ground black pepper
1 beaten egg to glaze	1 (295-g/10.4-oz) can white asparagus
2 chicken breast joints	
1 onion, chopped	1 (295-g/10.4-oz) can green asparagus
25 g/1 oz butter	
3 tablespoons plain flour	2 tablespoons double cream
½ chicken stock cube	
150 ml/¼ pint boiling water	

Roll out the pastry to give an oblong measuring about 20 × 28 cm/8 × 11 in. Trim the edges of the pastry to give a neat oblong shape which is 18 × 25 cm/7 × 10 in. Mark all round the oblong 2.5 cm/1 in in from the edge. Using a sharp pointed knife, cut all round this border, then lift off the strip in one piece and set it aside. Roll out the remaining oblong of pastry to the size it was before the strip was removed. Dampen the oblong strip of pastry and

carefully lift out on to the re-rolled oblong to form a neat rim. Press it on firmly, then trim the edges of the base.

Prick the base all over with a fork to prevent it from bubbling up during cooking. Carefully glaze just the top of the oblong rim with egg – do not allow any to run down the sides of the pastry as this will prevent it from rising evenly. Chill the pastry if you have time, then bake the case in a hot oven (220C, 425F, gas 7) for 20 minutes.

Meanwhile, cook the filling. Place the chicken joints in a casserole dish, cover them with cling film, allowing a small gap for the steam to escape, then cook on full power for 10 minutes. Allow to cool slightly, then remove all the meat from the bones and cut it into small pieces. Reserve the cooking juices from the chicken.

Place the onion in a bowl with the butter and cook on full power for 4 minutes. Stir in the flour, stock cube, reserved juices and boiling water, then add the chicken. Stir in the sherry and seasoning, cover the dish and cook for 5 minutes. Heat the asparagus separately with the liquid from the cans, for 5 minutes each, then drain.

Transfer the cooked pastry shell to a large, flat serving platter or board. Stir the cream into the chicken mixture, then spoon it into the jalousie. Arrange the green and white asparagus neatly on top and serve at once.

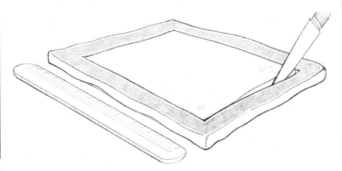

Chicken Suprême

—— SERVES 4 ——

Chicken suprêmes are the boneless chicken breasts. Here they are cooked in a cream sauce with mushrooms added – a very simple but quite rich dish which goes well with sautéed potatoes and colourful vegetables. For example, serve Broccoli with Bacon (see page 110), Julienne of Carrots (see page 109) or Courgette Parcels (see page 117) as side dishes.

1 small onion, chopped	3 tablespoons plain flour
25 g/1 oz butter	175 g/6 oz small button
4 boneless chicken breasts	mushrooms, halved
(about 100 g/4 oz each)	150 ml/¼ pint double
1 chicken stock cube	cream
300 ml/½ pint boiling	2 tablespoons chopped
water	parsley to garnish

Place the onion and butter in a casserole. Cover and cook on full power for 4 minutes.

Meanwhile, skin the chicken breasts and dissolve the stock cube in the boiling water. Stir the flour into the onion, then pour in the stock. Arrange the chicken in the casserole so that the pieces do not overlap. Turn them in the sauce to coat them completely. Re-cover the dish, allowing a small gap for the steam to escape, and cook for a further 5 minutes.

Stir the mushrooms into the sauce with the chicken and rearrange the chicken pieces. Re-cover and cook for 5 minutes. Stir in the cream, heat for 2 minutes and serve, sprinkled with the chopped parsley.

Chicken and Ham Pie

—— SERVES 4 ——

2 chicken breast joints	½ chicken stock cube
225 g/8 oz cooked ham	300 ml/½ pint milk
3 tablespoons plain flour	225 g/8 oz frozen puff
salt and freshly ground	pastry, defrosted
black pepper	beaten egg to glaze

Place the chicken joints in a casserole. Cover with cling film and cook on full power for 10 minutes. Allow to cool slightly, then take all the meat off the bones – don't worry if it is not quite cooked through at this stage. Cut the chicken and ham into bite-sized pieces, then set aside.

Place the flour, seasoning and stock cube in a basin. Whisk in the milk, then cook for 4 minutes and whisk the sauce thoroughly to make sure there are no lumps in it. Mix the ham and chicken into the sauce.

Roll out the pastry to give a piece about 5 cm/2 in larger than the top of a 900-ml/1½-pint pie dish. Cut a strip from the edge of the pastry and dampen the rim of the dish. Press the pastry strip on to the dish, then spoon the filling in the middle. Cover with the pastry lid, pressing the edges down well to seal in the filling. Trim and flute the edge of the pie, then re-roll any trimmings and cut out leaves to decorate the top. Lightly score the top of the pastry, attach the leaves and glaze the top with beaten egg.

Cook the pastry in a very hot oven (240 C, 475 F, gas 9) for 15 minutes, or until risen and golden brown. Serve immediately.

Christmas Pie Substitute 450 g/1 lb cooked turkey for the chicken. Make the sauce according to the recipe instructions, then add the cubed turkey and cook for a further 4 minutes. Stir in the ham and, if you like, add about 225 g/8 oz cocktail sausages (cooked under the conventional grill so that they are browned). Stir in a generous pinch of ground sage and continue making the pie following the recipe.

Chicken and Parsnip Stew

—— SERVES 4 ——

This is a hearty family casserole, serve creamed or baked potatoes as the only accompaniment.

450 g/1 lb parsnips	2 tablespoons plain flour
225 g/8 oz carrots	50 g/2 oz butter or
1 large onion, chopped	margarine
1 sprig sage	salt and freshly ground
1 bay leaf	black pepper
4 chicken joints	2 tablespoons chopped
1 chicken stock cube	parsley
450 ml/¾ pint boiling	
water	

Halve the parsnips lengthways, then cut them into chunks. Cut the carrots into similar-sized pieces. Place these vegetables in a roasting bag with the onion, herbs and chicken joints. Secure the bag loosely with an elastic band and place it in a dish to catch any juices which may escape during cooking. Cook on full power for 10 minutes, then give the bag a good shake. Take great care not to burn yourself – the bag will be very hot, so protect your hands with a tea-towel. Try to make sure that the chicken joints do not puncture the bag as you rearrange them.

Replace the bag in the oven and cook for a further 10 minutes. Carefully open the roasting bag – there will be an escape of hot steam so again protect your hands with a tea-towel. Remove the chicken joints and place on a grill pan.

Cook the chicken under a moderately hot grill until golden brown on top. Meanwhile, turn the vegetables into a fairly deep, heatproof serving dish and cook in the microwave oven for a further 2 minutes. Dissolve the stock cube in the boiling water. Beat the flour into the butter or margarine until smooth, then gradually stir this into the stock until dissolved. Pour the stock over the vegetables, add seasoning to taste and cook for 5 minutes, until thickened.

To serve, stir the parsley into the vegetables and arrange the chicken joints on top.

Chicken with Almonds

SERVES 4

1 onion, finely chopped	300 ml/½ pint boiling
2 sticks celery, finely	water
chopped	salt and freshly ground
50 g/2 oz butter	black pepper
2 tablespoons plain flour	4 chicken thighs
½ chicken stock cube	50 g/2 oz flaked almonds

Place the onion, celery and half the butter in casserole. Cover with cling film, allowing a small gap for the steam to escape, and cook on full power for 5 minutes.

Stir in the flour, crumbled stock cube and boiling water, making sure there are no lumps and that the cube has dissolved. Add seasoning to taste and the chicken joints, turning them in the sauce to make sure they are coated, then arranging them neatly in the dish with the meaty sides downwards. Re-cover and continue to cook on full power for 15 minutes, turning the joints over once during cooking.

Place the almonds in a small basin with the remaining butter. Cover with cling film, allowing a small gap for the steam to escape, then cook, for 4 minutes, by which time the almonds should have browned. Stir and immediately pour the nuts over the chicken. Serve at once.

Coq au Vin

SERVES 4

To achieve the deep red colour and to give the chicken the best flavour, this dish must be marinated overnight or for several hours. Serve a good mixed green salad and buttered rice as accompaniments.

4 chicken joints	12 pickling onions
1 large clove garlic,	1 bottle good red wine
crushed	25 g/1 oz plain flour
salt and freshly ground	50 g/2 oz butter
black pepper	225 g/8 oz small button
1 bay leaf	mushrooms
3 sprigs thyme	2 tablespoons chopped
3 sprigs parsley	parsley
2 sprigs sage	
100 g/4 oz lean smoked	
bacon	

Skin the chicken joints and place them in a large bowl. Add the garlic and plenty of seasoning. Tie the bay leaf with the other herbs to make a bouquet garni, then place it among the joints and pour in the red wine. Make sure that the chicken is immersed in the wine, then cover the bowl and chill for at least 12 hours. If you have the time to leave the chicken for a whole day or overnight then the flavour will be even better.

When you are ready to cook the chicken, trim the rinds off the bacon and chop the rashers, then place them in a casserole with the onions. Cover and cook on full power for 5 minutes.

Drain the chicken of its marinade – reserve the marinade of course – then place the joints in the casserole with the onions and bacon. Cover with cling film, allowing a small gap for the steam to escape, then cook for a further 5 minutes. Pour in the marinade with the bouquet garni, rearrange the joints and cook covered for 15 minutes.

Meanwhile, beat the flour with the butter until smooth. Gradually stir this into the sauce surrounding the chicken. When this had melted stir in the mushrooms and cook for a final 5 minutes.

Remove the bouquet garni, stir in the parsley and serve the coq au vin at once.

Chicken Boulangère

SERVES 4

Boulangère **is a name used for dishes cooked with potatoes and onions, usually sliced and cooked in the oven. Often joints of meat are cooked on a bed of sliced potatoes and onions with a little stock added. This dish of chicken in sauce topped with potatoes and onions is moist and crunchy on top. Serve an interesting mixed salad as an accompaniment.**

675 g/1½ lb potatoes	300 ml/½ pint boiling
2 large onions, finely	water
chopped	300 ml/½ pint milk
50 g/2 oz butter	100 g/4 oz button
100 g/4 oz carrots, diced	mushrooms sliced
350 g/12 oz boneless	2 tablespoons chopped
uncooked chicken	parsley
25 g/1 oz plain flour	
salt and freshly ground	
black pepper	
1 chicken stock cube	

Cut the potatoes into small cubes, then place them in a roasting bag with one of the onions and 2 tablespoons water. Secure the end loosely with an elastic band, then cook on full power for 10 minutes. Taking great care not to scald your hand, add half the butter to the potatoes, close the bag tightly and set aside.

Place the remaining onion, butter and carrots in a large bowl or casserole, cover with cling film, allowing a small gap for the steam to escape, then cook on full power for 5 minutes.

Meanwhile, cut the chicken into small cubes, then add these to the onion mixture with the flour and seasoning to taste. Dissolve the stock cube in the boiling water, then stir this stock into the chicken. Cover and cook for 5 minutes, then stir in the milk and mushrooms and continue to cook for a further 5 minutes. Stir in the parsley and transfer the mixure to an ovenproof serving dish if it is not already in one.

Top the chicken with the potatoes, place the dish under a hot grill and cook for just a few minutes or until golden brown on top. Serve at once.

Walnut Chicken

—— SERVES 4 ——

Serve either plain baked potatoes or rice to accompany this dish.

1 onion, chopped	1 chicken stock cube
100 g/4 oz walnut pieces, roughly chopped	300 ml/½ pint boiling water
2 tablespoons oil	2 tablespoons plain flour
salt and freshly ground black pepper	*Garnish:* walnut halves
1 red pepper	sprigs of parsley
4 chicken thighs	

Place the onion, walnuts and oil in a casserole with seasoning to taste. Trim the stalk end off the pepper, then remove all the seeds and pith from inside. Chop the flesh and add it to the onion mixture. Stir well, cover with cling film and cook on full power for 5 minutes.

Meanwhile, skin the chicken joints and dissolve the stock cube in the boiling water. Stir the flour into the onion mixture, then pour in the stock, stirring all the time. Add the chicken joints to the casserole, turning them in the sauce to coat them completely, and placing the meaty side down. Cover with cling film, allowing a small gap for the steam to escape, then cook for 12 minutes. Turn and rearrange the joints once during cooking. Serve the chicken straight from the casserole or transferred on to individual plates then garnish.

Spiced Walnut Chicken The combination of warm curry spices and walnuts go together to make a delicious dish. Add 1 cinnamon stick, 2 cloves garlic (crushed), 4 green cardamoms, 2 cloves and 1 teaspoon cumin seeds to the onion and walnuts. Cook for 5 minutes, omitting the red pepper. Reduce the quantity of liquid to 150 ml/¼ pint and cook for 10 to 12 minutes. Stir 150 ml/¼ pint natural yogurt into the sauce and heat for 2 minutes before serving. Sprinkle a little chopped fresh coriander leaves over the finished dish.

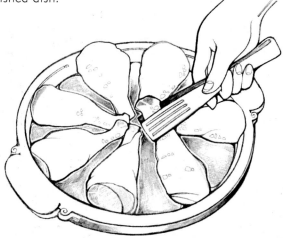

Remember to arrange chicken pieces with their thinnest part in the centre of the dish. The pieces should be turned over once during cooking to ensure more even penetration of the microwaves.

Fennel-flavoured Chicken

—— SERVES 4 ——

This recipe is quite rich – the chicken joints are in a cream sauce which is delicately flavoured with finely chopped fennel. When in season serve small, new potatoes and mange-tout peas to complement the dish.

1 small bulb fennel	150 ml/¼ pint double cream
1 small onion	
50 g/2 oz butter	*Garnish:*
2 tablespoons plain flour	2 tomatoes, peeled (see page 123)
1 chicken stock cube	
300 ml/½ pint boiling water	a few sprigs of fennel or dill
4 chicken thighs	

Trim the fennel reserving any of the feathery leaves for garnish, then finely chop the rest. Finely chop the onion. If you have a food processor, then it is ideal for chopping these vegetables. Place the fennel and onion in a casserole with the butter. Cover with cling film, allowing a small gap for the steam to escape, then cook on full power for 5 minutes.

Stir the flour into the vegetables and dissolve the stock cube in the boiling water, then pour this into the casserole, stirring continuously. Skin the chicken thighs, then add them to the sauce, turning them so that they are completely coated and placing the meaty side downwards.

Cover with cling film, allowing a gap for the steam to escape, and continue to cook for 12 minutes. Turn the chicken pieces over half way through the cooking time.

While the chicken is cooking, prepare the garnish. Peel the tomatoes according to the instructions, then halve them and remove all the seeds. Chop the flesh fairly finely. Stir the cream into the sauce surrounding the chicken and heat for a further 1 minute. Arrange the tomatoes and feathery fennel or dill leaves on each chicken portion and serve.

Chicken in Celery Sauce To make a delicious, rich celery sauce, substitute 4 celery sticks for the fennel. Chop them very finely – if the celery is coarsely chopped it will be tough and unpleasantly stringy to eat. Cook the chopped celery in the same way as the chicken and sprinkle a few celery seeds over the finished dish. Add a garnish of fresh celery leaves.

If you want to make fine, dry breadcrumbs for coating foods which are to be deep fried, then dry the bread out in the microwave before you make the crumbs. This way the bread will yield finer crumbs, and they will be pale enough to give a good golden colour when fried.

Curried Chicken

SERVES 4

This chicken curry, cooked with vegetables and butter beans, can be served as a complete meal. If you do want to offer any side dishes, mango chutney, popadums and Pullao rice (see page 129) are all suitable.

50 g/2 oz desiccated coconut
600 ml/1 pint boiling water
1 onion, chopped
50 g/2 oz fresh root ginger, grated
2 cloves garlic, crushed
2 tablespoons ground coriander
1 teaspoon chilli powder or to taste
1 tablespoon garam masala
4 tablespoons oil
4 chicken quarters
225 g/8 oz frozen mixed vegetables
1 (425-g/15-oz) can butter beans, drained
fresh coriander leaves to garnish

Place the coconut in a basin, pour in the boiling water and set aside for 30 minutes. Blend the onion in a liquidiser or food processor with the ginger, garlic, spices and oil to make a smooth paste.

Skin the chicken joints, spread the paste over the joints to cover them completely, then place them in a casserole, breasts down. Strain the coconut milk, squeezing all the liquid from the coconut, and pour it over the chicken. Cover with cling film, allowing a small gap for the steam to escape, and cook on full power for 10 minutes.

Turn the chicken joints over and around, then cook for a further 10 minutes. Stir in the frozen vegetables and butter beans and continue to cook, uncovered, for 5 minutes. If you like, grill the chicken portions before serving, otherwise allow the curry to stand for about 3 minutes before serving garnished with fresh coriander.

Lemon Spiced Chicken

SERVES 4

The combination of gentle spices and zesty lemon makes this a chicken dish to remember. Serve with Basmati Rice (see page 129) and the Hot Cucumber Salad (see below) to make a memorable menu.

1 teaspoon fennel seeds
3 teaspoons cumin seeds
½ teaspoon mustard seeds
4 green cardamoms
1 small onion, finely chopped
2 cloves garlic, crushed
2 tablespoons oil
grated rind of 1 large lemon
salt and freshly ground black pepper
4 boneless chicken breasts

Grind the seeds and cardamoms to a fine powder – a food processor or small liquidiser is useful for this. Blend in the

onion and garlic with the oil to make a paste. Stir in the lemon rind and seasoning to taste.

Skin the chicken breasts, then spread this paste over the flesh and leave them covered, in the refrigerator for several hours or overnight.

Cook the chicken pieces in a shallow dish, placing them as far apart as possible, on full power for 15 minutes. Turn the chicken twice during cooking.

Arrange the Hot Cucumber Salad (see below) on a serving platter and top with the chicken. Serve at once.

ACCOMPANIMENTS FOR SPICED DISHES

With any spiced dishes offer a selection of accompaniments both hot and mild, to complement the main dish. Rice, cooked very simply or in the form of a pullao, is essential if the main dish is quite hot.

Hot Cucumber Salad

Make this before you cook the chicken.

1 cucumber
2 sticks celery
2 green chillies
1 spring onion
1 tablespoon oil
juice of ½ large lemon

Peel the cucumber and cut it into 5-cm/2-in lengths. Slice these lengthways, then cut the slices into fine strips. Cut the celery into similar strips. Place both in a large bowl of iced water and leave for 1 hour.

Slit the chillies, remove all the seeds from inside and cut off the stalk end. Slice the green part into very fine strips, not more than 2.5 cm/1 in. in length. Cut the spring onion into fine strips.

Drain the cucumber and celery, then dry the strips on absorbent kitchen paper and toss the oil into them. Add the chillies, spring onion and lemon juice and mix well, then place the salad on to the dish ready for the chicken.

Cucumber Raita

A cooling dish to serve with very spicy food.

½ cucumber
salt
150 ml/¼ pint natural yogurt, thoroughly chilled
2 teaspoons chopped fresh mint
1 tablespoon chopped fresh coriander leaves (optional)

Very lightly peel the cucumber, then cut it into small dice. Place the vegetable in a colander or strainer and sprinkle with salt. Leave for 3 or 4 hours, then drain thoroughly and pat the cucumber dry on absorbent kitchen paper.

Place the cucumber in a bowl and pour over the yogurt. Sprinkle in the mint and coriander, if used, then toss the vegetable lightly and serve immediately, or within an hour before the cucumber has a chance to weep and thin the yogurt.

Tomato and Onion Sambal

This is quite spicy, so it should be eaten in small quantities with fairly mild main dishes.

225 g/8 oz ripe tomatoes
1 large onion, finely chopped
$\frac{1}{2}$ teaspoon ground cumin
$\frac{1}{2}$ teaspoon ground coriander
$\frac{1}{4}$ teaspon chilli powder
2 tablespoons chopped fresh coriander leaves
salt and freshly ground black pepper
1 tablespoon lemon juice

Peel and chop the tomatoes, then place them in a bowl with the onion and mix lightly. Mix the spices with the coriander leaves and seasoning. Sprinkle the lemon juice over the tomato mixture, then top with the spice mixture. Toss the ingredients together at the table.

Mexican Drumsticks

—— SERVES 4 ——

Pickled jalapeño chillies are available canned or in jars from many large supermarkets or delicatessens. Once opened, the canned chillies can be transferred (with their liquid) to a screw-topped jar and stored for several weeks in a cool place. This recipe requires two to four chillies depending on how hot you like your food. These chillies are hot so if you are unused to very spicy dishes add just two. Serve plenty of plain rice as an accompaniment.

1 small red pepper
1 small green pepper
2 onions, chopped
2 cloves garlic, crushed
1 tablespoon cumin seeds
3 tablespoons oil
salt and freshly ground black pepper
1 (795-g/1 lb 12-oz) can tomatoes
2–4 pickled jalapeño chillies, sliced
8 chicken drumsticks
2 tablespoons chopped parsley (optional)

Trim the stalks off the peppers, then remove the seeds and pith from inside and chop the flesh. Mix the chopped peppers with the onions and garlic in a large casserole or bowl. Add the cumin seeds and stir in the oil, then cover with cling film, allowing a small gap for the steam to escape, and cook on full power for 5 minutes.

Stir in plenty of seasoning, the tomatoes and chillies. Skin the drumsticks, then arrange them in the sauce, turning them to coat all sides with juice. Cover with cling film, allowing a small gap for the steam to escape, and cook for a further 10 minutes. Turn the drumsticks over and around, then cook for 15 minutes more.

Serve the drumsticks, lifted out of the sauce and arrange on a plate, then pour the sauce over to coat them neatly. Sprinkle with chopped parsley if you like.

Peanut Chicken Pot

—— SERVES 4 ——

4 large chicken drumsticks
1 (241-g/8$\frac{1}{2}$-oz) smoked pork sausage
4 tablespoons crunchy peanut butter
1 clove garlic, crushed
dash of Worcestershire sauce
salt and freshly ground black pepper
1 chicken stock cube
300 ml/$\frac{1}{2}$ pint boiling water

Skin the chicken drumsticks and cut the sausage into four large chunks. Mix the peanut butter with the garlic, Worcestershire sauce and seasoning to taste. Spread this over the chicken and place the drumsticks in a large casserole with the sausage. Cover with cling film, allowing a small gap for the steam to escape, then cook on full power for 5 minutes.

Dissolve the stock cube in the boiling water, then pour this over the chicken and sausage. Rearrange the meats, re-cover the casserole and cook for a further 15 minutes, stirring the sauce once during cooking. Allow to stand for a few minutes before serving.

Greek Parcels

—— SERVES 4 ——

These little packages of chicken and feta cheese, wrapped in delicate vine leaves, are deliciously different. Serve with cooked rice or fresh pasta.

16 vine leaves (from a packet not a can)
salt and freshly ground black pepper
4 boneless chicken breasts (450 g/1 lb in weight)
225 g/8 oz feta cheese
2 teaspoons oregano
1 clove garlic, crushed
4 tablespoons olive oil
2 teaspoons arrowroot
$\frac{1}{2}$ chicken stock cube
150 ml/$\frac{1}{4}$ pint boiling water
150 ml/$\frac{1}{4}$ pint dry vermouth

Cook the vine leaves in boiling, salted water for 5 minutes. While they are cooking, cut each chicken breast into four equal-sized pieces. Crumble the feta in a bowl and add the oregano, garlic and oil. Mix thoroughly to blend the ingredients into a coarse paste.

Thoroughly drain the cooked vine leaves and separate them. Place a little of the feta mixture on each leaf and add a piece of chicken. Wrap the leaf neatly around this filling, then place the packages in a dish – a quiche dish is ideal.

Blend the arrowroot with a little water to make a smooth paste. Dissolve the stock cube in the boiling water, then stir in the vermouth. Pour this mixture over the arrowroot paste, stirring all the time. Pour the sauce over the vine-leaf packages, then cover the dish closely with cling film. Cook on full power for 10 minutes. Turn the dish round before cooking for a further 10 minutes. Carefully spoon the sauce over the leaves and serve.

Turkey Paupiettes

—— SERVES 4 ——

4 turkey fillets (about
  100 g/4 oz each)
225 g/8 oz pork
  sausagemeat
50 g/2 oz fresh
  breadcrumbs
1 teaspoon dried mixed
  herbs
salt and freshly ground
  black pepper

½ chicken stock cube
300 ml/½ pint boiling
  water *or* 150 ml/¼ pint
  boiling water and
  150 ml/¼ pint red wine
25 g/1 oz butter
2 tablespoons plain flour
watercress sprigs to
  garnish

Place the turkey fillets between two sheets of greaseproof paper and beat them out until quite thin. Mix the sausagemeat with the breadcrumbs and herbs. Add plenty of seasoning and divide the mixture into four equal portions. Roll each into a small cylinder shape then wrap a thin turkey fillet around each one. Tie neatly in shape with string.

Dissolve the stock cube in the boiling water and add the wine if you are using any. Place the butter in a jug and cook on full power for 30 seconds then stir in the flour and stock. Replace in the oven and cook for 2 minutes.

Arrange the turkey paupiettes as far apart as possible in a casserole. Pour over the sauce, cover and cook on full power for 5 minutes. Turn the turkey and continue to cook for a further 5 minutes. Allow the paupiettes to stand for a few minutes, then add a few watercress sprigs to garnish.

Chicken with Okra

—— SERVES 4 TO 6 ——

Okra is quite difficult to cook conventionally because it can be easily overdone and so become slimy and unpalatable. Left whole, there is less likelihood of this happening, so trim just the very end off each vegetable.

1 small onion, chopped
1 small red pepper
2 cloves garlic, crushed
2 tablespoons oil
450 g/1 lb uncooked
  boneless chicken
salt and freshly ground
  black pepper

225 g/8 oz okra
1 (325-g/11½-oz) can sweet
  corn, drained
Horseradish Cream:
1 tablespoon horseradish
  sauce
150 ml/¼ pint soured
  cream

Place the onion in a large bowl or casserole. Trim the stalk end off the pepper, then scoop out all the seeds and pith. Chop the flesh and add it to the onion with the garlic and oil. Cook on full power for 5 minutes.

Cut the chicken into small cubes – less than 2.5 cm/1 in. in size. Add these to the onion and pepper with plenty of seasoning then cook for a further 5 minutes. Meanwhile, trim just the very ends off the okra and make sure that each piece is clean; discard any bruised vegetables.

Stir the vegetables into the chicken, cover the bowl with cling film, allowing a small gap for the steam to escape, then cook for a further 6 minutes. Stir once during cooking to ensure that the ingredients cook evenly.

Stir the horseradish into the soured cream, pour into a small bowl and serve.

Sweet and Sour Turkey

—— SERVES 4 ——

Serve this dish with plenty of plain cooked rice.

I green pepper	I tablespoon cider vinegar
I large onion	3 tablespoons peach
2 tablespons oil	chutney
I clove garlic, crushed	I tablespoon concentrated
450 g/I lb uncooked	tomato purée
boneless turkey	I (432-g/15¼-oz) can
2 tablespoons cornflour	pineapple bits
2 tablespoons soy sauce	

Cut the stalk end off the pepper and scoop out all the seeds and pith from inside, then chop the flesh. Chop the onion and mix both together with the oil and garlic in a casserole or large bowl. Cook on full power for 5 minutes.

Meanwhile, cut the turkey into bite-sized pieces, add these to the onion mixture and continue to cook for a further 5 minutes. Blend the cornflour with the remaining ingredients, including the pineapple and its juice. Pour this mixture into the casserole and cook for 5 minutes. Stir thoroughly and serve.

Lancashire-style Turkey

—— SERVES 4 ——

4 medium to large	600 ml/I pint boiling
potatoes	water
2 leeks, sliced	I chicken stock cube
2 carrots, sliced	350 g/12 oz cooked
50 g/2 oz butter	turkey, cubed
salt and black pepper	4 tablespoons chopped
40 g/1½ oz plain flour	parsley

Scrub the potatoes, then cook them in their skins on full power for 25 minutes. Remove from the oven and set aside. The potatoes should be tender but not too soft.

Thoroughly wash and drain the leeks, then place them in a large bowl with the carrots and half the butter. Cover with cling film and cook on full power for 10 minutes. Stir in the seasoning to taste, flour and boiling water. Crumble in the stock cube and stir until it dissolves. Add the turkey and cook for 15 to 16 minutes, or until the sauce has thickened and the turkey is thoroughly reheated. Stir the parsley into the turkey.

While the turkey is cooking, peel and slice the potatoes. Pour the turkey mixture into an ovenproof dish and top with the potatoes, overlapping the slices neatly. Dot with the remaining butter and cook under a hot grill until thoroughly browned all over. As the butter begins to melt, quickly brush it evenly over the potato slices. Serve at once.

Peking Duck

This is a traditional Chinese dish but I would not dare to suggest that this is an authentic recipe. However, I find that it is a good home-made version of the duck which is served in Chinese restaurants. The pancakes can be made well in advance (the day before if you like) and reheated in the microwave, rather than steaming them over boiling water which is the conventional cooking method.

1 (2–2.5-kg/4–4½-lb) duck	a little sesame oil
4 slices fresh root ginger	oil for cooking
1 teaspoon five spice powder	*Accompaniments:*
1 tablespoon honey	1 bunch spring onions, shredded
2 tablespoons soy sauce	½ cucumber, cut into fine strips
Pancakes:	plum sauce or Quick Plum Dip
225 g/8 oz plain flour	
generous pinch of salt	
150 ml/¼ pint boiling water	

Remove the giblets from the body cavity. Lift the skin away from the meat, do not cut it, but use your hand to separate the skin from the flesh. Use a hair dryer on a warm or cool setting to blow between the skin and the flesh. Put the ginger inside the duck. Rub the five spice powder all over the skin of the duck and set it aside in the refrigerator for a few hours, or overnight. Cover the duck with greaseproof paper during this standing time, but do not wrap it in cling film or any other material which will keep the skin moist.

Mix the honey with the soy sauce, then brush about half of this mixture over the duck and place the bird in a roasting bag, breast side uppermost. Stand the bag on a plate or dish and cook on full power for 5 minutes. Turn the duck so that the breast is down and cook for a further 20 minutes, turning the bird round once during cooking.

Remove the duck from the bag and place it on a roasting rack in a roasting tin. Brush the remaining honey mixture over and cook in a very hot oven (240 C, 475 F, gas 9) for 15 to 20 minutes.

If you do not want to make the pancakes well in advance, there should be plenty of time to prepare them as the duck is cooking. Sift the flour into a bowl and add the salt. Mix in the boiling water, then gather the pieces of dough together and knead the mixture lightly to give a smooth ball. Place this in the bowl and cover with a tea-towel, then set aside for 10 minutes. Do not cover the dough tightly in cling film or it will become soggy.

Cut the dough in half, then cut each piece into six small portions. Roll these out on a floured surface to give small pancakes measuring about 15 cm/6 in. in diameter. Brush six pancakes lightly with sesame oil and place the remainder on top so that they are sandwiched in pairs.

Heat a little oil in a frying pan, then add a pair of pancakes and cook over a medium heat until lightly browned on the under side. Turn and cook the second side until it too is lightly browned. Do not cook the pancakes over too high a heat or they will not separate. Remove the pancakes from the pan and separate them. Place them on a plate and continue until all the pancakes are cooked.

Arrange the spring onions and cucumber on small plates to serve with the duck. When the duck is cooked, remove it from the oven and carefully cut off all the crisp skin. Cut this into small neat pieces and arrange them on a warmed serving plate. Cut all the meat off the bones and slice it into small pieces, then place these on the plate next to the skin.

Cover the pancakes with cling film and cook them in the microwave oven for 2 minutes, so that they are heated through. They should be soft and warm when served so leave them covered for 2 minutes before they are taken to the table.

The pieces of duck are placed in a pancake, with a little of the plum sauce, spring onions and the cucumber. The pancake is folded and eaten with the fingers. The crisp skin is the delicacy.

Quick Plum Dip

Plum sauce is available in bottles or jars but if you cannot find any, then try this dip which tastes almost as good.

225 g/8 oz plum jam
2 cloves garlic, crushed
2 tablespoons soy sauce
1 tablespoon vinegar

Sieve the jam then mix it with the remaining ingredients and pour into a small bowl.

Duck à l'Orange

———— SERVES 4 ————

I was most pleasantly surprised with the result achieved by cooking a duck for half the time in the microwave oven and half in the conventional oven. The skin was particularly crisp and the meat was tender, very moist and full flavoured. To obtain a well-crisped duck by conventional methods often leads to the meat being rather overcooked.

1 (2–2.5-kg/4–4½-lb) duck	300 ml/½ pint boiling
2 large oranges	water
1 bay leaf	2 tablespoons plain flour
salt and freshly ground	1 chicken stock cube
black pepper	orange slices to garnish

Remove the giblets from the duck and set them aside to make the sauce. Prick the skin of the bird all over. Prick one of the oranges all over, then place it inside the duck with the bay leaf. Place the duck, breast side down, in a dish and cover it with cling film, allowing a small gap for the steam to escape. Cook on full power for 5 minutes, then turn the duck over so that the breast meat is up and continue to cook for a further 20 minutes, turning the dish round once during cooking.

Remove the duck from the dish and place it, breast side uppermost, on a roasting rack in a roasting tin. Rub salt into the skin and cook in a very hot oven (240C, 475F, gas 9) for 15 to 20 minutes. At the end of the cooking time the duck should be golden brown and crisp.

While the duck is cooking, place the reserved giblets with the pared rind from the remaining orange in a basin. Pour in the boiling water and cook in the microwave oven on full power for 15 minutes. Remove and strain the stock.

Place a couple of spoonfuls of the duck juices in a basin or large jug and stir in the flour, then pour in the hot stock, stirring continuously to prevent lumps from forming. Crumble in the stock cube. Squeeze the juice from the orange and pour it into the sauce, then cook for 5 minutes.

Transfer the duck to a heated serving platter, or cut it into four joints and arrange these on a serving dish. Add a garnish of orange slices, then serve accompanied by the prepared sauce.

DIFFERENT WAYS WITH DUCK:

Duck in Cherry Sauce Roast the duck as in the main recipe, omitting the oranges but using the bay leaf. Prepare the giblet stock and add the juice from a can of morello cherries. Stir in the crumbled stock cube and 4 tablespoons brandy, then use this liquid to prepare the sauce, cooking it for 8 minutes instead of 5 minutes.

Flaming Duck Roast the duck according to the main recipe, omitting the oranges but adding the bay leaf. Peel, core and thickly slice 4 full-flavoured dessert apples (for example Cox's Orange Pippins) and sprinkle them with a little lemon juice. Place these in an ovenproof dish and sprinkle with a little demerara sugar. Cook the apples in the conventional oven at the same time as the duck. Prepare the sauce from the giblet stock, adding a little extra boiling water instead of the orange juice. When you are ready to serve the duck, put the bird on a serving platter with the apples arranged round the edge. Heat 3 to 4 tablespoons of Calvados in a mug in the microwave for 30 seconds, then pour this over the duck and ignite it immediately. Serve still flaming.

Spiced Duck Place the bay leaf and two cinnamon sticks in the body cavity of the duck. Crush two cloves of garlic and mix them with 2 tablespoons ground coriander. Stir in a little lemon juice, a generous pinch of thyme, ½ teaspoon ground ginger and enough water to make a thick paste. Spread this over the duck and cook the bird following the instructions in the main recipe. Serve with soured cream or natural yogurt.

Duck with Peas

———— SERVES 4 ————

This is a quick way of preparing a duck, without turning on the conventional oven. Serve minted new potatoes and baby carrots as accompaniments.

1 (2–2.5-kg/4–4½-lb) duck	150 ml/¼ pint dry white
1 onion, finely chopped	wine
25 g/1 oz butter	150 ml/¼ pint boiling
225 g/8 oz frozen petit	water
pois	large sprig of sage
2 tablespoons plain flour	salt and freshly ground
1 chicken stock cube	black pepper

Remove the giblets from the duck, they are not required for this recipe. Prick the skin of the bird all over, then place it in a roasting bag and secure the end loosely with an elastic band. Place the bird in a dish, breast uppermost, and cook on full power for 5 minutes. Turn the duck over so that the breast is downwards and cook for a further 25 minutes, turning the dish round once during cooking.

Remove the duck from the bag and separate it into four joints. Place these on a rack in a grill pan and cook them under a moderately hot grill until they are thoroughly browned and crisp.

Meanwhile, place the onion and butter in a basin and cook for 4 minutes. Stir in the petit pois and the flour. Crumble in the stock cube, then pour in the boiling water and wine (in that order), stirring all the time. Add the sprig of sage and cover the bowl with cling film, allowing a small gap for the steam to escape. Cook for 15 minutes, stirring once during cooking and again at the end of the cooking time. Taste and adjust the seasoning as necessary.

To serve, arrange the duck joints in a serving dish, then pour over the peas and sauce. Serve at once, before the duck skin looses its crisp texture.

MEAT DISHES

It has to be said that not all meats cook well in the microwave oven. Stewing cuts and other similar pieces of meat do not come out on top, so save them for your conventional oven. It is, in fact, possible to cook the tougher cuts on defrost power for many hours (and many manufacturers suggest this) but I prefer to make stews in the old-fashioned way so I have not included any such ideas in this chapter. Here I am trying to give a selection of dishes which really do cook very well, with the advantages far outweighing any possibilities of lower standards.

So, what meats do we microwave? Pork is a tender meat and it does cook well in the microwave. As with all types of meat, it is important to trim off the excess fat as this becomes rather unpleasant when cooked. Veal and tender cuts of beef turn out well but certain lamb dishes do not taste their best. Minced meats of every variety are excellent and I have included several ideas for these.

It is possible to cook joints of meat in the microwave but the result is steamed and not ideal when you consider that the roasting cuts are so expensive to buy in the first place. So, here again you can use the microwave to full advantage to reduce cooking time for roasts quite considerably without any loss of quality if you link it with the conventional oven. Roast lamb and pork cook particularly well in this way; I admit that I prefer the old-fashioned way of cooking roast beef but the result achieved by half cooking it in the microwave, then transferring the joint to the conventional oven is acceptable and it does depend on individual taste.

The expensive fillet of beef cooks well by microwave energy but I include only one recipe for this as I always feel that if I have spent the money on something rather special, then I would prefer to cook it in the very best way.

To be positive, gammon and rabbit cook particularly well in sauces, or gammon steaks are excellent on their own. Tender offal, like liver and kidneys, can be conjured into all sorts of exciting dishes with great speed, so do experiment with your favourite ideas for these foods.

Ranging from traditional dishes like Beef Olives and Cottage Pie (see pages 76 and 80) to favourite ideas like Chilli con Carne and Moussaka (see pages 82 and 87), there really is no shortage of meat recipes which can be prepared in a microwave. Meatloaves can be cooked speedily and turned out for browning under the grill. Pies and other pastry items can be part cooked in the microwave, then finished in the conventional oven. Suet pastry dumplings are delicious cooked in the microwave and there's no danger of them disintegrating once they are added to the stew. In this chapter they are combined with cheap gammon offcuts in a satisfying family stew.

For entertaining you could try Lamb and Leeks in Orange Sauce or Rich Redcurrant Lamb (see pages 86 and 83) or a pork recipe, such as Pork with Oregano and Olives and Spanish Pork (see pages 90 and 91), may be more suited to your menu. The Stuffed Lamb (see page 84) is very successful and this is because the boned shoulder cut gives a good even shape. Transferred to the conventional cooker to complete its cooking, the joint is flavoursome and moist as well as brown and crisp. If you have a combination oven which offers the facility for conventional heat along with the microwaves, then you will find that roasts present no problem at all.

Roast Beef

—— SERVES 4 TO 6 ——

The extent to which you find beef cooked in the microwave oven acceptable will depend on how particular you are about your roast beef. If you know *precisely* the time you like your joint cooked in the conventional oven and find any variations on that timing are not as good, then you are best advised to cook beef in the microwave only when you are very short of time. If, on the other hand you hold an open mind about roast beef, or if you like it thoroughly cooked, then try roasting a joint both in the microwave oven and the conventional oven allowing about two-thirds of the cooking to be completed in the microwave, the rest traditionally.

1.5-kg/3-lb joint boned and rolled rib of beef or a similar joint	salt and freshly ground black pepper

Place the beef in a roasting bag and secure the end loosely with an elastic band. Cook on full power for 20 minutes, turning the joint once during cooking. Allow the beef to stand for 10 minutes before opening the bag.

Transfer the beef to a roasting tin and sprinkle the joint with salt and pepper. Cook in a hot oven (220C, 425F, gas 7) for 10 to 15 minutes if you like beef pink in the middle or for 20 to 30 minutes if you like your beef cooked through. Use the juices from the roasting bag to prepare gravy according to the instructions given on page 204.

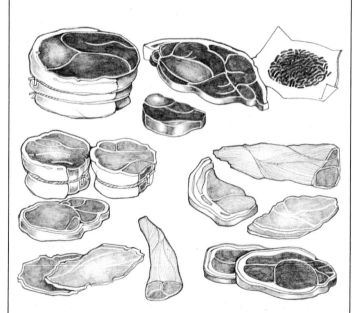

Select a neatly shaped joint of beef (or any other meat) to cook in the microwave oven. For example, rolled rib joints, topside or sirloin are suitable. Avoid joints which are unevenly shaped with large protruding bones. Make sure the meat is securely tied into shape or it will become mis-shapen during cooking.

Beef Olives

—— SERVES 4 ——

These make a good dinner party dish. Prepare the beef rolls well in advance ready for cooking at the last minute. Serve with Potatoes Anna (see page 105), Mushrooms à la Grecque (see page 124) and Julienne of Carrots (see page 109).

350 g/12 oz frying steak (two or four pieces)	salt and freshly ground black pepper
1 onion, chopped	1 beef stock cube
50 g/2 oz butter	150 ml/¼ pint boiling water
100 g/4 oz cooked ham, finely chopped	300 ml/½ pint full-bodied red wine
25 g/1 oz fresh breadcrumbs	2 tablespoons plain flour
50 g/2 oz mushrooms, chopped	**Garnish:**
1 tablespoon horseradish sauce	watercress sprigs tomato wedges

Cut the steak into four equal-sized pieces (if necessary) then place them between two pieces of greaseproof paper and beat out until very thin.

Place the onion in a basin with half the butter and cook on full power for 4 minutes. Stir in the ham, breadcrumbs, mushrooms and horseradish sauce. Add plenty of seasoning and mix thoroughly. Divide this mixture between the beef slices and roll them up neatly. Tie the rolls with cotton, to keep them tidy during cooking, then arrange them as far apart as possible in a dish.

Dissolve the stock cube in the boiling water, mix in the wine, then pour this liquid over the beef rolls and cover with cling film, allowing a small gap for the steam to escape. Cook for 5 minutes.

Beat the flour into the remaining butter, making sure it is quite smooth, then stir small knobs of this into the sauce surrounding the beef rolls until the butter has melted. Return the dish to the microwave and cook for a further 5 minutes.

The rolls look at their best if they are arranged on individual plates, with the sauce poured over and a garnish of watercress sprigs and tomato wedges added.

VARIATION

The beef rolls can be served on individual bread croûtes. Fry small circles of bread in a mixture of butter and oil until golden on both sides. Drain on absorbent kitchen paper and arrange one roll on each croûte. Serve at once, before the croûte becomes soggy from the sauce.

If you own an oven which combines conventional cooking means with microwave cooking then this is ideal for achieving a perfect roast joint. However it is most important to follow the manufacturer's instructions as these ovens vary considerably.

Steak and Kidney Ragoût

—— SERVES 4 ——

Even though it is not a good idea to cook the tougher cuts of meat in the microwave oven you can make a delicious steak and kidney by using frying steak; it may be more expensive but it is incredibly quick and absolutely scrumptious.

I large onion, chopped	225 g/8 oz lambs' kidneys
2 tablespoons oil	575 g/1¼ lb frying steak
2 tablespoons plain flour	salt and freshly ground
I beef stock cube	black pepper
300 ml/½ pint boiling water	

Place the onion in a casserole or other dish with the oil. Cook on full power for 3 minutes, then stir in the flour, stock cube and boiling water.

Halve the kidneys and remove their cores, then cut them into small pieces. Add these to the gravy. Trim all the fat off the steak and cut the meat across the grain into small thin slices. Add the meat to the kidneys and stir in plenty of seasoning.

Cover the dish and cook for 15 minutes, stirring once during this time. Give the ragoût a good stir and allow it to stand for a few minutes before serving, or use it for any of the ideas below.

Steak and Kidney Pie Use 225 g/8 oz puff pastry to make a lid for a 1.15-litre/2-pint pie dish. Line the rim of the dish with pastry, then put in the filling. Top with a pastry lid, make a small hole for the steam to escape and decorate with any pastry trimmings. Glaze with beaten egg and bake in a hot oven (230C, 450F, gas 8) for 15 minutes.

Steak and Kidney Thatch (This is my husband's idea – he felt like making a steak and kidney pie one day but didn't feel inclined to tackle the technique of rolling pastry.)

Top the cooked steak and kidney with freshly prepared mashed potatoes, seasoned with plenty of ground white pepper. Cook the potatoes in the microwave oven following the instructions for Cottage Pie (see page 80) or boil them conventionally, whichever is most convenient. Grill the top of the potatoes to give a good browned crust, then serve at once.

Steak and Kidney with Dumplings Prepare suet dumplings according to the instructions for Gammon Stew with Herb Dumplings (see page 94). Place the dumplings on the ragoût for the final 4 minutes of the cooking time. Serve at once.

Tender kidneys cook very well in the microwave oven, however, it is important to remember to split or dice them first. If the whole kidneys are threaded on to wooden skewers or cooked in a dish, then they will burst during cooking, causing extensive splattering and making the finished dish look unpleasant.

Steak and Oyster Pie

—— SERVES 4 ——

This is not a traditional recipe: it uses frying steak and canned smoked oysters in a pie filling which is delicious and worthy of any informal supper party. Serve Potatoes Lyonnaise (see page 102) and a simple green vegetable as accompaniments.

I large onion, finely chopped	salt and freshly ground black pepper
25 g/1 oz butter	300 ml/½ pint full bodied red wine
I (105-g/3.66-oz) can smoked oysters	225 g/8 oz puff pastry
450 g/1 lb frying steak	beaten egg to glaze
2 tablespoons plain flour	

Place the onion in a bowl with the butter and the oil from the can of oysters. Cover with cling film, allowing a small gap for the steam to escape, then cook on full power for 5 minutes.

Meanwhile, cut the steak into small thin slices across the grain. Stir the flour and plenty of seasoning into the onions and pour in the wine, stirring continuously. Add the meat, stir well and cook for 10 minutes.

While the meat is cooking, roll out the pastry to give a piece large enough to cover the top of a 900-ml/1½-pint pie dish with 5 cm/2 in to spare all round. Cut off a 2.5-cm/1-in strip from the edge and press this on to the dampened rim of the dish.

Stir the oysters into the pie filling and pour the mixture into the prepared dish. Dampen the pastry rim and lift the pastry over the top, pressing the edges well to seal in the filling. Trim the edges and pinch them into a neat fluted edge. Use the trimming to roll out pastry leaves to decorate the top of the pie and dampen these to stick them in place.

Glaze the top of the pie with a little beaten egg and make a small hole in the top to allow the steam to escape during cooking. Cook in a very hot oven (240C, 475F, gas 9) for 15 minutes, then serve at once.

If you are planning on buying new cookware at all, then consider investing in a range of pans which are made of heatproof glass. These can be used on top of the hob, put into the freezer, used in the conventional oven or they can be used in the microwave oven. This is particularly useful if you want to brown off some chicken joints or meat, then complete the cooking in the microwave.

Beef Satay

———— SERVES 4 ————

Beef fillet is expensive so these portions are small, however it is traditional to serve satay dishes in small quantities and the quality is worth it. These little kebabs are ideal to serve for a very special starter; alternatively arrange them on an attractive cucumber and Iceberg lettuce salad with one or two spring onions added. Serve plain rice mixed with 2 tablespoons chopped parsley to accompany them and to mop up all the delicious peanut sauce.

450 g/1 lb fillet steak
1 teaspoon ground ginger
1 tablespoon peanut oil or sunflower oil
2 teaspoons ground coriander
freshly ground black pepper
Satay Sauce:
1 small onion

50 g/2 oz unsalted peanuts
½ teaspoon chilli powder
1 tablespoon soy sauce
a few drops of sesame oil
1 tablespoon lemon juice
2 cloves garlic, crushed
2 tablespoons peanut oil or sunflower oil
100 ml/4 fl oz boiling water

Cut the steak into small cubes. Mix the ground ginger with the peanut or sunflower oil, coriander and plenty of pepper. Spread this mixture over the meat and use your fingertips to rub the marinade well into the pieces of meat, making sure they are completely coated. Cover and set aside to marinate for at least an hour or preferably overnight, if you have the time.

Chop the onion for the sauce, then place it in a liquidiser or food processor and add all the remaining ingredients apart from the water. Blend the mixture until it is almost smooth, but do not overprocess it as the sauce benefits from having a very slightly crunchy, nut texture. The sauce can be prepared as far as this stage up to a day in advance.

Thread the marinated meat on to eight wooden skewers, then place them on a double thickness of absorbent kitchen paper around the rim of a large plate or dish. Cook on full power for 6 to 8 minutes depending on whether you like your meat slightly pink in the centre or well cooked all the way through.

While the meat is cooking arrange the salad ingredients on individual plates. Lay the skewers on top. Pour the boiling water into the sauce and heat it for 2 minutes then serve at once, with the satay steak.

Note: other ingredients can be cooked with a satay sauce. Try, for example, preparing pieces of chicken or pork in this way. Cubes of skinned cod or small neat rolls of plaice fillet can also be threaded on to wooden skewers and cooked to serve with the spicy sauce. Remember to avoid any tougher cuts of beef or lamb as these would be most unpleasant to eat.

Minced Beef with Beetroot

———— SERVES 4 ————

This is a good, inexpensive family supper dish. It goes very well with pasta shapes, serve them boiled and buttered, or cooked rice – try Spanish Rice on page 136.

2 onions, chopped
1 clove garlic, crushed
2 tablespoons oil
1 teaspoon thyme
1 tablespoon concentrated tomato purée
450 g/1 lb lean minced beef
salt and freshly ground black pepper

pinch of ground mace
1 tablespoon plain flour
150 ml/¼ pint boiling water
1 beef stock cube
450 g/1 lb cooked beetroot (page 106)
150 ml/¼ pint soured cream to serve (optional)
chopped chives to garnish

Place the onions in a bowl with the garlic and oil. Cook on full power for 6 minutes. Stir in the thyme and tomato purée, then add the beef and break up the minced meat. Add seasoning to taste, the mace and flour, then stir in the water and crumbled stock cube. Cover with cling film, allowing a small gap for the steam to escape, and cook for 10 minutes, stirring once.

Cube the cooked beetroot, then add it to the beef and stir it in. Re-cover and cook for a further 5 minutes. Transfer the cooked meat mixture to a serving dish if necessary, then swirl in the soured cream (if used) and sprinkle the chives on top. Serve at once.

When you are cooking minced meats in the microwave oven the same rule applies as for pieces of meat: the better the mince, then the better the result. Tough, coarse minced beef will result in a tough chewy dish. Look out for finely minced or ground steak or, better still, buy lean chuck steak or braising steak and mince it once or twice yourself.

Steak Bourguignonne

——— SERVES 4 ———

Tougher cuts of meat cannot be cooked successfully in the microwave oven. Even if they are cooked for fairly lengthy periods on a low or defrost setting the result is not as good as by traditional stewing methods. Frying steak can be used to make a variety of dishes such as this slight variation on an old favourite.

100 g/4 oz pickling onions	salt and freshly ground
25 g/1 oz butter	black pepper
3 tablespoons plain flour	100 g/4 oz small button
350 g/12 oz frying steak	mushrooms
300 ml/½ pint red wine	2 tablespoons chopped
150 ml/¼ pint beef stock	parsley to garnish

Place the onions and butter in a bowl or casserole. Cover with cling film, allowing a small gap for the steam to escape, then cook on full power for 5 minutes. Stir in the flour.

Cut the steak across the grain into small thin slices, then stir these into the onion mixture with the wine and stock. Add seasoning to taste and cook for 10 minutes, stirring once during cooking.

Stir the mushrooms into the beef and taste for seasoning, then cook for 3 minutes and allow to stand for 2 minutes before serving. Add a generous sprinkling of chopped parsley.

Veal Rolls

——— SERVES 4 ———

Tender veal escalopes cook very well in the microwave oven. Serve with plenty of freshly cooked buttered pasta and a simple green salad.

4 veal escalopes (about	2 sprigs thyme, chopped
100 g/4 oz each)	salt and freshly ground
12 slices garlic sausage	black pepper
50 g/2 oz stuffed olives,	300 ml/½ pint dry white
chopped	wine
2 tablespoons chopped	50 g/2 oz butter
parsley	3 tablespoons plain flour

Place the veal, one piece at a time, between two sheets of greaseproof paper and beat out until very thin. Lay three slices of garlic sausage on each and roll up neatly. Tie with string and place well apart in a casserole.

Sprinkle the olives and herbs over the rolls, add seasoning to taste then pour in the wine. Cover and cook on full power for 3 minutes.

Beat the butter with the flour until smooth, then gradually stir the mixture into the sauce surrounding the veal, until the butter has dissolved. Continue to cook for a further 3 to 4 minutes, until the sauce is thickened and the veal is cooked through. Allow to stand for 2 minutes before serving.

Cottage Pie

——— SERVES 4 ———

In this recipe I have cooked the potatoes in a bowl in the microwave oven but you can boil them conventionally on the top of the cooker while the meat is cooking in the microwave if preferred. There is no time saved by cooking the potatoes in the microwave, but it does save washing up the saucepan!

1.5 kg/3 lb potatoes, cut	450 g/1 lb minced beef
into small chunks	2 tablespoons plain flour
4 tablespoons water	1 teaspoon dried mixed
1 large onion, chopped	herbs
100 g/4 oz carrots, diced	450 ml/¾ pint beef stock
2 tablespoons oil	100 g/4 oz button
50 g/2 oz butter	mushrooms, sliced
about 50 ml/2 fl oz milk	
salt and freshly ground	
black pepper	

Place the potatoes in a large bowl with the water. Cover with cling film, allowing a small gap for the steam to escape, then cook on full power for 22 minutes.

Put the onion in a large casserole dish or suitable heatproof serving dish. Add the carrots and oil, toss the ingredients well and cook in the microwave for 6 minutes.

Meanwhile, mash the potatoes thoroughly with the butter and milk, adding plenty of pepper and salt to taste. Stir the beef into the onion and carrots, breaking the meat well and adding seasoning to taste. Stir in the flour and herbs, then pour in the stock. Cook for a further 10 minutes before stirring in the mushrooms, then cook for a final 3 minutes.

Cover the top of the meat with the mashed potatoes, marking the surface with a fork. Cook under a hot grill until golden brown, then serve immediately.

Cheese Thatch Beat 100 g/4 oz finely grated mature Cheddar cheese and 1 tablespoon mild mustard into the creamed potatoes. Top the cooked mince mixture with the cheesy potato and sprinkle with a little extra grated cheese before browning under a hot grill.

Porky Pie Use lean, finely minced pork instead of the minced beef. Add a generous sprinkling of chopped fresh sage or ground sage to the meat mixture, then continue cooking the pie as above.

Beany Thatch Add 1 (425-g/15-oz) can baked beans to the beef and reduce the quantity of stock to a generous 150 ml/¼ pint.

Hungarian Mince

—— SERVES 4 ——

Spiced with paprika and flavoured with colourful peppers, this minced dish looks quite special if it is neatly presented in a ring of cooked rice or pasta. Make a good green salad, with lots of interesting vegetables and some ripe avocado pears as an accompaniment.

2 onions, chopped
1 red pepper
1 green pepper
2 cloves garlic, crushed
2 tablespoons oil
2 tablespoons plain flour
2 tablespoons paprika
salt and freshly ground
   black pepper
4 tablespoons
   concentrated tomato
   purée

300 ml/½ pint boiling
   water
300 ml/½ pint red wine
1 beef stock cube
350 g/12 oz minced beef
350 g/12 oz lean minced
   pork
150 ml/¼ pint natural
   yogurt
chopped parsley to
   garnish

Place the onions in a large bowl. Cut the stalk end off the peppers, then scoop all the seeds and the pith from inside. Wash, dry and chop the pepper shells, then add them to the onions. Stir in the garlic and oil then cook on full power for 6 minutes.

Stir in the flour, paprika and seasoning to taste. Add the tomato purée and gradually pour in the boiling water. Stir in the wine and crumbled stock cube, then add the beef and pork, breaking up the meat to mix it thoroughly with the sauce. Cook for a total of 20 minutes, stirring twice during this cooking time.

At the end of cooking, mix together thoroughly and serve the yogurt swirled into it. Sprinkle the parsley over and serve at once.

It is well worth investing in a few fairly large attractive bowls which can be used for cooking dishes such as this one. Many rice dishes can also be cooked in a large bowl and served straight from it if presentable.

Stuffed Cabbage Leaves

—— SERVES 4 ——

It is easier to blanch the cabbage leaves in a saucepan of boiling water on the hob than it is to cook them in the microwave oven. While these are cooking the stuffing can be prepared in the microwave, also the creamy sauce topping. To finish the dish, the sauce is browned under a hot grill.

1 large onion, chopped
2 tablespoons oil
450 g/1 lb minced beef
2 tablespoons
   concentrated tomato
   purée
1 tablespoon plain flour
salt and freshly ground
   black pepper
150 ml/¼ pint boiling
   water

1 beef stock cube
8 large cabbage leaves
100 g/4 oz button
   mushrooms, chopped
1 teaspoon dried mixed
   herbs
1 quantity Cheese Sauce
   (page 200)
2 tablespoons grated
   Parmesan cheese

Place the onion in a basin with the oil and cook on full power for 5 minutes. Add the minced beef, tomato purée and flour. Stir well, breaking up the beef as you do so, then add plenty of pepper and a little salt. Pour in the boiling water and stir in the crumbled stock cube. Cover the basin with cling film, allowing a small gap for the steam to escape, and cook on full power for 10 minutes.

Use this time to cook the cabbage leaves in a saucepan of boiling salted water until they are just tender. They should take about 3 to 5 mintues. Drain the leaves thoroughly and dry them on absorbent kitchen paper.

Stir the mushrooms and herbs into the meat and re-cover the basin, then cook for 5 minutes. When the meat is cooked, prepare the cheese sauce according to the recipe instructions. Open out the cabbage leaves and divide the stuffing between them, then carefully fold them up to make neat packages. Lay these in a shallow serving dish. Heat them for 2 minutes in the microwave and pour the sauce on top. Sprinkle the Parmesan cheese over the sauce and brown the top under a hot grill. Serve at once.

VARIATIONS
Instead of the creamy sauce, the leaves can be coated with a Tomato Sauce (see page 200), then reheated and sprinkled with a little Parmesan cheese before putting under a hot grill.

Minced pork or sausagemeat can be used instead of the minced beef and cooked long-grain rice can be added to the filling. Try varying the herbs – marjoram or basil are excellent (the latter is particularly good with a tomato sauce topping).

Chilli Tacos

—— SERVES 4 ——

Serve these tasty, meat filled corn pancakes with Creamed Corn (see page 120) and Spanish Rice (see page 136).

1 onion, chopped	2 ripe avocado pears
2 pickled jalapeño chillies	a little lemon juice
3 tablespoons oil	$\frac{1}{4}$ cucumber, chopped
3 cloves garlic, crushed	2 tomatoes, peeled and
3 teaspoons ground	chopped
coriander	2 tablespoons peanut
450 g/1 lb lean minced	butter
beef	150 ml/$\frac{1}{4}$ pint mayonnaise
8 tacos shells	

Place the onion in a basin. Chop the chillies, add them to the onion with the oil and stir well. Cook on full power for 5 minutes.

Stir in the garlic, coriander and beef, breaking the meat up well. Continue to cook for a further 8 minutes, stirring once during cooking. Spoon this meat mixture into the tacos shells, making sure they are neat and not too full. Lay them in a serving dish, so that they support each other.

Halve the avocados, remove their stones and peel the flesh, then chop it into pieces. Dip these in lemon juice to prevent discoloration. Mix in the cucumber and tomatoes and set this salad aside. Cook the filled tacos for 3 minutes, then top with the prepared salad.

Mix the peanut butter into the mayonnaise, then serve this nutty sauce with the tacos.

Chilli con Carne

—— SERVES 4 ——

1 large onion, chopped	1–2 tablespoons chilli
1 large carrot, diced	powder
1 large green pepper	salt and freshly ground
3 tablespoons oil	black pepper
2 large cloves garlic,	1 (795-g/1-lb 12-oz) can
crushed	tomatoes
1 tablespoon ground	2 (425-g/15-oz) cans red
cumin	kidney beans
450 g/1 lb lean minced	2 tablespoons chopped
beef	parsley

Place the onion in a large bowl with the carrot. Cut the stalk end off the pepper, remove all the seeds and pith from inside, then chop the flesh and add it to the onion and carrot. Stir in the oil and garlic, then add the cumin. Cover with cling film, allowing a small gap for the steam to escape, and cook on full power for 7 minutes.

Stir the minced beef into the onion mixture, making sure it is well broken up. Add the chilli powder to taste, plenty of seasoning and the tomatoes. Stir well, then re-cover the bowl and cook the chilli for a further 10 minutes. Give the meat a good stir, then gently mix in the drained kidney beans. Cook for a final 5 minutes, then stir in the parsley and serve the chilli at once, with plenty of hot French bread or buttered rice.

Rich Redcurrant Lamb ◎

—— SERVES 4 ——

Only tender, lean cuts of meat can be cooked in the microwave if you want results which are comparable to those achieved by conventional methods. It is not essential to brown the meat first for this recipe – I tested the recipe by placing the meat straight in the sauce and it tasted quite acceptable. However the finished flavour and appearance *is* improved if the meat is seared first.

675 g/1½ lb lean lamb fillet	2 teaspoons concentrated
2 tablespoons plain flour	tomato purée
salt and freshly ground	150 ml/¼ pint port
black pepper	225 g/8 oz redcurrants
2 tablespoons oil	1–2 tablespoons sugar
1 onion, chopped	watercress sprigs to
1 lamb or beef stock cube	garnish *or* a bouquet
300 ml/½ pint boiling	garni (optional)
water	

Cut the lamb into bite-sized pieces, then coat them in the flour and plenty of seasoning. Heat half the oil in a frying pan on the hob. It should be very hot when you add the meat so that the pieces brown very quickly without losing any of their juices. Toss the pieces of meat in the pan until they are browned all over.

Meanwhile, place the onion in a casserole dish or bowl and add the remaining oil. Stir the onion so that the pieces are coated, then cook in the microwave oven, on full power for 4 minutes. Stir the browned meat into the onion with any pan juices. Dissolve the stock cube in the boiling water and stir in the tomato purée, then pour the liquid into the dish. Add the port and cook on full power for 15 minutes

String the redcurrants, reserving a few sprigs for garnish if you wish, then add them to the lamb with sugar to taste. Cook for a further 10 minutes and allow to stand for 5 minutes before serving. Arrange the reserved currants on the side with a few sprigs of watercress if you like. Alternatively you can garnish with a bunch of fresh herbs tied into a bouquet garni.

Roast Leg of Lamb

———— SERVES 6 TO 8 ————

The quality of meat which you choose to cook in the microwave oven is important – good quality meat gives good results, poor quality meat has its lesser characteristics emphasised to the full. So make sure the leg of lamb is not too fatty and not a tough, old joint. This is a recipe for a plain roast but there are a few suggestions below for making the lamb more special or unusual if you wish.

1 (1.75-kg/4-lb) leg of lamb   salt and freshly ground
black pepper

Place the joint in a roasting bag and secure the end loosely with an elastic band. Cook on full power for 25 minutes, turning the joint over and around once during this time.

Heat the oven to moderately hot (200 C, 400 F, gas 6). Transfer the lamb to a roasting tin, removing the roasting bag. Sprinkle the joint with plenty of seasoning, then put in the hot oven for 30 minutes.

Make gravy following the instructions on page 204 and serve this with the carved lamb.

TO MAKE THE JOINT MORE INTERESTING

Garlic Peel 8 cloves garlic. Make very small slits into the skin of the lamb, without cutting into the meat. Press a clove of garlic into each slit and cook as in the main recipe.

Herbs Rosemary sprigs can be stuck into the skin of the lamb to flavour the joint. Sprigs of mint can be tied into a bunch and put into the roasting bag with the lamb. A bouquet garni of mint sprigs, rosemary, parsley, a bay leaf, a few sprigs of thyme and a bunch of marjoram can be tied and put into the roasting bag with the lamb. This should also be cooked in the gravy to give extra flavour.

Oranges A quartered orange can be placed in the roasting bag with the lamb. Pour the juice of 1 orange over the joint in the roasting tin before adding seasoning. Add the grated rind of 1 orange and the orange quarters from the bag. Cook as in the main recipe and use red wine to make the sauce instead of gravy.

Redcurrant Lamb Warm 2 or 3 tablespoons redcurrant jelly in the microwave for 1 minute. Brush this over the lamb for the last 10 minutes cooking in the conventional oven. Add a few tablespoons of port to the gravy.

If you want to cook roast potatoes with the lamb, then parboil them before you turn the conventional oven on. Put them in the roasting tin and brush them with a little oil, then place the tin in the oven as soon as it is switched on. Add the lamb and finish cooking as above.

Stuffed Lamb

———— SERVES 6 ————

Boned joints of meat, tied into a neat shape, can be cooked most successfully in the microwave oven, with a period in the conventional oven to give them the true flavour of a roast. Boned stuffed shoulders of lamb are particularly suitable for microwave cooking because of their even shape. Make sure that any excess fat is trimmed from the meat before it is stuffed and cooked and do allow at least 20 minutes cooking time in the conventional oven to avoid having a steamed result.

1.75-kg/4-lb shoulder of
lamb, boned
1 large onion, finely
chopped
75 g/3 oz fresh
breadcrumbs
225 g/8 oz pork
sausagemeat

1 clove garlic, crushed
2 teaspoons chopped fresh
rosemary
4 tablespoons redcurrant
jelly (optional)

Make sure that the lamb is boned out to give a neat pocket – ask your butcher to do this for you, or arm yourself with a very sharp, pointed knife and remove the bone yourself without making any slashes through the main part of the meat.

Mix the onion with the breadcrumbs, sausagemeat and garlic. Add the rosemary and mix the ingredients thoroughly to make sure they are all evenly distributed. Add plenty of seasoning and spoon this stuffing into the pocket in the lamb. Use a trussing needle or very large darning needle and heavy cotton to sew up the meat to enclose the stuffing completely. Prick the skin several times with a fork, then place the joint in a roasting bag and secure the end loosely with an elastic band.

Cook the lamb on full power for 30 minutes, turning the joint around three times during cooking to prevent it from over cooking in any one area. Transfer the meat to a conventional roasting tin and sprinkle with salt, then cook in a hot oven (220 C, 425 F, gas 7) for a further 30 minutes. Spread the redcurrant jelly over the meat and cook for a further 5 to 10 minutes before serving.

Use the meat juices to make the gravy according to the instructions on page 204. If you wish to make a particularly delicious sauce, stir a few tablespoons of port into the gravy 5 minutes before it is completely cooked.

Minted Meatballs

———— SERVES 4 ————

These meatballs really do need the initial frying on the conventional cooker to give them a good flavour. If you own a microwave browning dish or skillet then you can cook the meatballs in that instead of on top of the cooker. Serve with rice or pasta.

450 g/1 lb minced lamb
salt and freshly ground
    black pepper
1 tablespoon chopped
    fresh mint
1 small onion, grated
2 tablespoons oil
1 egg
50 g/2 oz fresh
    breadcrumbs

1 lamb or beef stock cube
150 ml/¼ pint boiling
    water
1 (425-g/15-oz) can
    chopped tomatoes
1 bay leaf
mint sprigs to garnish

Mix the lamb with plenty of seasoning, the mint, onion, egg and breadcrumbs. Pound the mixture thoroughly so that it binds together well, then wet your hands and shape the meat into 16 meatballs.

Heat the oil in a frying pan on top of the cooker. The oil must be very hot before adding the meatballs, so that they brown quickly without losing any of their juices. Add the meatballs and turn them in the pan to brown all sides, then remove them with a slotted spoon and transfer them to a heatproof serving dish.

Dissolve the stock cube in the boiling water, then pour in the tomatoes and stir well. Pour this over the meatballs and add the bay leaf. Cover with cling film and cook on full power for 12 minutes, rearranging the meatballs once during cooking. Allow the meatballs to stand for 2–4 minutes, then garnish and serve.

Lamb and Spinach Loaf 🗒

———— SERVES 6 ————

Meatloaves cook very successfully in the microwave and they taste good if they are browned under the grill before serving. Serve this meatloaf hot.

675 g/1½ lb lean minced
    lamb
2 eggs, beaten
salt and freshly ground
    black pepper
freshly grated nutmeg
2 teaspoons dried basil
75 g/3 oz fresh
    breadcrumbs

1 (250-g/8.82-oz) packet
    frozen chopped spinach,
    defrosted (see below)
1 onion, chopped
2 cloves garlic, crushed
2 tablespoons oil

Place the lamb in a bowl. Add the eggs with plenty of seasoning and freshly grated nutmeg. Stir in the basil, breadcrumbs and spinach.

Mix the onion with the garlic and oil in a small basin, then cook on full power for 5 minutes. Stir this into the meat mixture, then press it into a greased loaf dish measuring about 28 × 11 cm/11 × 4½ in. The dish should hold about 1.4 litres/2½ pints. Cover with cling film, allowing a small gap for the steam to escape, then cook for 15 minutes, turning the dish round once during cooking. Allow the meatloaf to stand in the dish for 2 to 3 minutes, then turn it out on to a baking tray or Swiss roll tin. If you are using a tray, make sure it has a rim otherwise the meat juices will run off the edge.

Place the meatloaf under a moderately hot grill and cook until well browned – about 15 minutes. Transfer to a serving platter and garnish with watercress sprigs or arrange the vegetable accompaniments around the loaf.

Curried Lamb with Beans

———— SERVES 4 ————

Serve a cucumber raita (see page 132 for Spicy Raita) – a dish of chopped cucumber in chilled natural yogurt – and crisp popadums to accompany this spicy minced lamb combination. If you want to make the meal particularly filling offer Pullao Rice (see page 129) as well.

1 tablespoon grated fresh
    root ginger
2 cloves garlic, crushed
2 onions, chopped
4 green cardamoms
3 cloves
1 dried red chilli
½ teaspoon turmeric
2 teaspoons ground
    fenugreek

2 teaspoons cider vinegar
salt and freshly ground
    black pepper
675 g/1½ lb lean minced
    lamb
2 (425-g/15-oz) cans red
    kidney beans, drained
2 tablespoons chopped
    fresh mint
mint sprigs to garnish

Mix the ginger, garlic, onions, cardamoms, cloves, chilli, turmeric, fenugreek, cider vinegar and seasoning together in a liquidiser or food processor and blend to make a smooth paste. Stir in the minced lamb, breaking up the pieces and making sure that the spices are thoroughly incorporated. Cook on full power for 10 minutes, stirring once during cooking.

Lightly stir the beans into the meat, trying not to break them up as you do so. Continue to cook for a further 3 minutes. Stir the mint into the mince and allow to stand for a few minutes before serving. The mixture looks most attractive, if it is arranged in individual bowls, each one topped with a sprig of mint.

To defrost spinach in the microwave oven, place the packet on a plate and cook on full power for 3 minutes. Drain thoroughly before using.

Lamb and Leeks in Orange Sauce

—— SERVES 4 ——

2 medium leeks
675 g/1½ lb lamb fillet
2 oranges
1 lamb or beef stock cube
450 ml/¾ pint boiling
   water
salt and black pepper
1 tablespoon concentrated
   tomato purée
1 bay leaf
2 rosemary sprigs
2 tablespoons plain flour
25 g/1 oz butter
orange slices to garnish

Trim and thinly slice the leeks, then thoroughly wash them. Place them in a casserole or large bowl and cover with cling film, allowing a small gap for the steam to escape. Cook on full power for 2 minutes.

Trim the meat and cut it into small cubes. Grate the rind from one of the oranges and squeeze the juice from both. Dissolve the stock cube in the water, add seasoning and stir in the tomato purée.

Add the lamb to the leeks, then sprinkle the orange rind over and pour in the juice with the stock. Stir in the bay leaf and rosemary and re-cover the dish. Cook the casserole for 15 minutes, stirring once during cooking.

Beat the flour into the butter until smooth, then stir small knobs of this into the lamb one at a time, making sure they are completely melted before adding the next. Return the lamb to the microwave and cook for a further 3 minutes to thicken the sauce. Allow the casserole to stand for 2 to 3 minutes then garnish and serve.

Lamb-stuffed Aubergines

—— SERVES 4 ——

2 large aubergines (about
   350-g/12-oz each in
   weight)
salt and freshly ground
   black pepper
1 onion, chopped
1 clove garlic, crushed
1 tablespoon olive oil
450 g/1 lb minced lean
   lamb
2 tablespoons tahini
1–2 tablespoons sesame
   seeds

Cut the aubergines in half and cut a criss-cross pattern into the flesh, but be careful to avoid cutting through the skin at all. Using a teaspoon, carefully scoop out all the pieces of aubergine, then place them in a colander or sieve and sprinkle generously with salt. Set aside for 30 minutes.

Trim the shells neatly, place them in a roasting bag and secure the end loosely with an elastic band, then cook on full power for 5 minutes.

Meanwhile, mix the onion, garlic and oil together in a bowl and cover with cling film, allowing a small gap for the steam to escape. Cook the onion for 2 minutes, then stir in the lamb and cook for a further 5 minutes, stirring the meat once during cooking to break it up and rearrange it in the dish. Stir in the tahini.

Rinse and thoroughly dry the aubergine flesh, then add it to the meat, re-cover and cook for a further 5 minutes. Spoon this mixture into the aubergine shells and sprinkle the top with the sesame seeds. Place under a hot grill for a few minutes, then serve.

Moussaka

SERVES 4

The microwave oven really is fantastic for preparing dishes such as this one where more than one sauce is prepared and when cooked conventionally many pans would have to be scrubbed! Serve a crisp green salad with peppers and cucumber to complement the moussaka.

450–475 g/1–1¼ lb
   aubergines
salt and freshly ground
   black pepper
Meat Sauce:
1 large onion, chopped
2 cloves garlic, crushed
4 tablespoons olive oil
450 g/1 lb lean minced
   lamb

2 teaspoons marjoram
1 (425-g/15-oz) can
   chopped tomatoes
Topping:
25 g/1 oz butter
25 g/1 oz plain flour
300 ml/½ pint milk
2 eggs, beaten

Cut the ends off the aubergines, then thinly slice the rest. Place the slices in colander and sprinkle them generously with salt. Set aside for 30 minutes.

Meanwhile, prepare the meat sauce: place the onion and garlic in a basin (about 1.15-litre/2-pint capacity). Stir in half the oil and plenty of seasoning. Cook on full power for 4 minutes. Add the lamb to the onions, stirring well to break up the mince. Cook for 5 minutes, then stir in the marjoram and tomatoes and cook for a further 5 minutes.

Thoroughly rinse and dry the aubergines, then place the slices in a roasting bag, sprinkle in the oil remaining from the meat sauce and shake the bag well to coat all the slices evenly. Secure the end of the bag loosely with an elastic band, then cook for 4 minutes. Shake the bag and cook for a further 4 minutes.

Layer the aubergine with the meat sauce in a heatproof serving dish, starting and ending with a layer of aubergines. To make the topping, place the butter and flour in a basin. Add seasoning and gradually whisk in the milk. Cook for 4 minutes, then whisk thoroughly and whisk in the eggs. Pour this topping over the aubergines and place the dish under a hot grill until well browned and set on top. Serve at once.

Roast Pork with Sage and Onion Apples

SERVES 4 TO 6

Pork requires fairly lengthy, slow cooking in a conventional oven, so by using your microwave oven to pre-cook a large joint the overall cooking time can be reduced considerably and the result will be quite acceptable. I would not suggest that a pork roast is cooked completely in the microwave oven as the meat does not taste anything like as good as it should.

1.75-kg/3¾-lb joint of pork (on the bone)	1 large onion
	3 sprigs sage
salt and freshly ground black pepper	75 g/3 oz fresh breadcrumbs
4 cooking apples (about 675 g/1½ lb in weight)	a little milk
8 tablespoons demerara sugar	

Make sure the rind of the pork is thoroughly scored, and that the joint is tied neatly to retain its shape during cooking. Place the joint in a roasting bag and secure the end loosely with an elastic band, then cook on full power for 35 minutes. Turn the joint three times during cooking to prevent it from overcooking in any one area. Allow it to stand for 15 minutes before placing the pork in a roasting tin to finish cooking. Rub the rind all over with salt and transfer to a moderately hot oven (200 C, 400 F, gas 6) for 20 minutes, or until the rind is crisp and golden.

Meanwhile, prepare the sage and onion apples. Remove the cores from the apples and halve them widthways. Place the halves in a dish – a quiche dish is ideal, arrange them around the edge – then sprinkle the sugar over the cut surface. Prepare the stuffing by cooking the onion in a little fat from the pork. Place it in a small basin and cook on full power for 3 minutes, then stir in the sage, breadcrumbs and enough milk to bind the ingredients together. Add plenty of seasoning and pile the stuffing neatly on top of the apples, pressing it into the holes left by the cores.

Cook the apples for 8 minutes, then arrange them around the roast pork on a heated serving dish and keep hot while you prepare the gravy from the reserved meat juices (following the instructions on page 204).

You can use the microwave oven to shorten the cooking time for all roast meats. Allow at least one-third of the total cooking time in the conventional oven but give the joint up to 30 or 40 minutes in the microwave oven first. Keep the joint well covered while it is in the microwave to prevent it drying out.

Orchard Stew

SERVES 4

Tart cooking apples and sweet raisins are combined in a cider sauce to make an interesting pork casserole. Serve Potatoes Anna (see page 105) and Creamed Parsnips with Carrots (see page 106) to turn this casserole into a hearty autumn meal.

1 onion, chopped	50 g/2 oz raisins
2 tablespoons oil	salt and freshly ground black pepper
675 g/1½ lb lean boneless pork	225 g/8 oz cooking apples
2 tablespoons plain flour	2 tablespoons chopped parsley
1 chicken stock cube	
450 ml/¾ pint dry cider	
2 tablespoons demerara sugar	

Place the onion in a casserole with the oil, then cook on full power for 5 minutes.

Meanwhile, trim the pork of any fat and cut it across the grain into small fine slices. Stir the flour into the onion with the stock cube and cider. Add the sugar, raisins and seasoning to taste, then stir in the pork. Cover with cling film allowing a small gap for the steam to escape, then cook on full power for 10 minutes.

While the meat is cooking, peel, quarter and core the apples, then cut them into thick slices. Add these to the pork and continue to cook for a further 5 minutes. Allow the casserole to stand for 2 to 3 minutes before serving, then sprinkle the chopped parsley over the top.

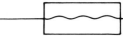

Frozen blocks of casseroles, soups or other similar foods can be put in their container into the microwave oven and cooked on full power for 2 minutes so that the sides have defrosted enough to slide the block out easily. Make sure that the containers are suitable for the microwave – don't use foil containers.

Pork with Red Cabbage

——— SERVES 4 ———

This tasty minced pork dish is ideal family fare but it is also interesting enough to serve for an informal supper party. Potato Cake (see page 104) tastes particularly good with this dish.

1 large onion, chopped
1 large clove garlic, crushed
3 tablespoons oil
175 g/6 oz red cabbage, shredded
450 g/1 lb minced pork
150 ml/¼ pint full-bodied red wine or beer
1 chicken stock cube
150 ml/¼ pint boiling water
1 bay leaf

Place the onion in a large bowl or suitable serving dish. Add the garlic and oil, then stir in the cabbage, making sure that all the ingredients are coated in oil. Cook on full power for 5 minutes.

Stir the pork into the cabbage mixture, making sure the meat is well broken up. Pour in the wine or beer, then dissolve the stock cube in the boiling water and pour that on top. Stir well, add the bay leaf and cook for a further 10 minutes, stirring once during cooking. Allow to stand for 2 to 3 minutes before serving.

Haricot Pork

——— SERVES 4 ———

This is a very simple, yet quite spicy dish which requires no accompaniment other than a fresh salad and perhaps some hot French bread for those who are particularly hungry. Serve the pork and bean mixture in individual bowls.

1 large onion, chopped
2 tablespoons olive oil
225 g/8 oz lean boneless pork
225 g/8 oz garlic sausage (in one piece)
2 (425-g/15-oz) cans white kidney beans, drained
plenty of chopped parsley

Place the onion in a bowl with the oil and cook on full power for 5 minutes. Trim and discard any fat off the pork and cut it across the grain into small fine slices. Cut the garlic sausage into small cubes.

Add the pork to the onion and continue to cook for a further 5 minutes. Stir in the garlic sausage and lightly toss in the beans without breaking them up at all. Cover with cling film and cook for 5 to 6 minutes, then toss in plenty of parsley and toss lightly before serving.

Note: the quality of this dish depends to a large extent on how good the canned beans are. Try various brands until you find a make which offers canned beans that have not disintegrated in the can. Sludgy beans are unpleasant both to look at and to eat!

Pork with Chick Peas

——— SERVES 4 ———

Canned chick peas are an incredibly useful ingredient to keep in the cupboard because their nutty flavour is complementary to many meats and vegetables. Serve this tasty pork dish with Orange Rice (see page 128) or Couscous (see page 164) and a crisp salad tossed with plenty of fried bread croûtons.

1 large onion, chopped
2 cloves garlic, crushed
4 tablespoons oil (olive oil is good if you like the flavour)
450 g/1 lb minced pork
2 teaspoons fennel seeds
50 g/2 oz sultanas
salt and freshly ground black pepper
225 g/8 oz ripe tomatoes
2 (400-g/14-oz) cans chick peas, drained
plenty of chopped parsley

Place the onion in a large bowl or casserole dish with the garlic and oil. Cook on full power for 5 minutes, then stir in the pork, breaking the meat up as you do so. Add the fennel seeds, sultanas and plenty of seasoning and continue to cook for 5 minutes.

While the meat is cooking peel the tomatoes (see page 123), then cut them in half and remove their seeds. Chop the flesh. Stir the chick peas into the meat and cook for a final 5 minutes.

Stir plenty of chopped parsley into the meat mixture, then arrange the chopped tomatoes in a neat row on top and serve at once.

Most cuts of pork are tender so this meat is particularly suitable for microwave cooking. However, as with all other meats, it is important that the pork is prepared properly before cooking. Select lean meat – loin, knuckle or leg meat can all be used – then trim off the fat and any sinews or membranes. Use a sharp knife to cut the meat across the grain into small thin slices rather than chunks as these will cook more successfully. Try to make the slices as even in size as possible.

Pork with Oregano and Olives

——— SERVES 4 ———

Lean, boneless pieces of pork cook very well in the microwave oven, particularly when they are braised in a well-seasoned sauce such as in this recipe. Without a sauce they tend to have a slightly unacceptable 'steamed' flavour. Serve buttered rice with this dish.

675 g / 1½ lbs lean boneless
  pork
1 teaspoon cider vinegar
2 teaspoons oregano
1 clove garlic, crushed
2 tablespoons olive oil
salt and freshly ground
  black pepper
2 tablespoons plain flour

2 teaspoons sugar
300 ml / ½ pint dry cider
50 g / 2 / oz black olives,
  stoned
100 g / 4 oz small button
  mushrooms
150 ml / ¼ pint natural
  yogurt to serve
  (optional)

Trim any fat off the pork, then cut it into small cubes. Place the meat in a bowl or casserole. Mix the cider vinegar with the oregano, garlic, olive oil and plenty of seasoning, then pour this mixture over the meat. Cover and leave in a cool place to marinate for at least 2 hours – the longer the better, if possible overnight.

Cover the marinated meat with cling film, allowing a small gap for the steam to escape, then cook on full power for 5 minutes, stirring once during this time. Stir in the flour and sugar, then pour in the cider, stirring to make a smooth sauce. Add the olives and mushrooms, stir well, then continue to cook for a further 12 minutes, stirring once to rearrange the meat in the dish.

Allow the pork to stand for 2 to 3 minutes before serving it and offer a small bowl of natural yogurt to accompany the dish if you like.

Use this recipe as a guide if you want to prepare a similar, simple pork casserole. As the flavouring ingredients – the garlic, herbs and olives – do not constitute a significant bulk if they are omitted the cooking time will not be significantly different. So, if you are preparing a simple dish of pork cooked in stock, with mushrooms and onion for example, then follow the instructions given in this recipe. Once you are accustomed to improvising in this way you will be able to adapt all your favourite recipes successfully for cooking in the microwave oven.

Spanish Pork

The way in which meat is cut before cooking affects the result achieved in the microwave oven. Cut across the grain into small slices rather than chopped into chunks, the finished dish will be tender and the pieces of meat cook more quickly. Serve this spicy pork dish with plenty of buttered rice or Couscous (see page 164).

1 onion, chopped	1 chicken stock cube
1 green pepper	2 tablespoons
2 large cloves garlic, crushed	concentrated tomato purée
3 tablespoons olive oil	12 stuffed olives
675 g/1½ lb lean boneless pork	1 tablespoon oregano
2 tablespoons plain flour	salt and freshly ground black pepper
450 ml/¾ pint full-bodied red wine	150 ml/¼ pint soured cream

Place the onion in a fairly large casserole or bowl. Cut the stalk end off the pepper and remove the seeds from inside, then chop the flesh and add it to the onion with the garlic and oil. Stir well to coat the ingredients in oil then cook on full power for 5 minutes.

Meanwhile, prepare the meat: cut off any fat and trim away any small bits of membrane or tough tissue. Cut the pork into thin slices, cutting across the grain. Stir the flour into the onion mixture. Pour in the wine, stirring continuously, then add the stock cube, tomato purée and olives. Stir in the oregano and seasoning to taste then mix in the pork.

Cover the casserole and cook for 15 minutes, stirring once during cooking. Allow to stand for 2 to 3 minutes, then swirl in the soured cream and serve at once.

Pork and Peach Terrine

———— SERVES 4 TO 6 ————

Serve this terrine with a selection of salads, new potatoes or baked potatoes, or some hot crusty bread.

I onion, chopped	50 g/2 oz fresh
2 cloves garlic, crushed	breadcrumbs
I tablespoon oil	225 g/8 oz lean streaky
salt and freshly ground	bacon
black pepper	2 bay leaves
450 g/I lb lean boneless	2 orange slices
pork	I (425-g/15-oz) can peach
grated rind of I orange	slices, drained
2 blades mace	
12 stuffed green olives,	
halved	

Place the onion, garlic, oil and seasoning in a bowl or large basin and cook on full power for 3 minutes.

Meanwhile, cut the pork into neat cubes, then add these to the onion with the orange rind and mace. Cook for 5 minutes. Stir well, then remove the mace and add the olives. Stir in the breadcrumbs, making sure all the ingredients are well mixed.

Cut the rinds off the bacon, then stretch the rashers out quite thin using the back of a knife. Arrange the bay leaves and orange slices in the base of a 1.15-litre/2-pint terrine (not a cast iron one, but one which is suitable for the microwave oven). Line the dish with the bacon rashers, making sure they overlap neatly and come right over the edge of the container. Alternatively you could use a loaf dish.

Press half of the meat mixture into the dish, then lay the peach slices on top. Press the remaining pork over the fruit and fold over the ends of the bacon rashers.

Cover the terrine with cling film, then cook for 4 minutes. Turn the dish and cook for a further 4 minutes. Weight the terrine and allow it to cool completely, then chill for several hours, preferably overnight.

To serve, turn the terrine out of the dish and cut into slices.

Drying Herbs – use the microwave oven to dry herbs which can be stored for winter. Thoroughly wash the herbs and pat them dry on a clean tea-towel. Lay them on absorbent kitchen paper (well spread out) and cook on full power for a few minutes. I find that sage, thyme and rosemary dry very well, allowing about 5 minutes for a handful.

Porky Pancakes

———— SERVES 4 ————

It is not possible to cook pancakes in the microwave oven but it is useful to be able to prepare the filling for stuffed pancakes simply by throwing all the ingredients into a bowl in the microwave, rather than frying them off at the same time as tossing pancakes.

Pancake Batter:	2 tablespoons plain flour
100 g/4 oz plain flour	½ chicken stock cube
2 eggs	150 ml/¼ pint boiling
300 ml/½ pint milk	water
Filling:	I quantity Apple Sauce
I onion, chopped	(page 205)
25 g/I oz butter	I quantity Mushroom
450 g/I lb minced pork	Sauce (page 200)
2 teaspoons chopped sage	*Garnish:*
salt and freshly ground	a little grated Parmesan
black pepper	cheese
	a little chopped parsley

Sift the flour for the batter into a bowl. Make a well in the middle and break in the eggs, then add a little of the milk. Beat the eggs and milk together, gradually working in the flour, until smooth. Pour in the milk a little at a time to keep the batter thin enough to beat. Beat thoroughly, then set aside for 30 minutes if you have sufficient time.

Place the onion in a large basin with the butter and cook on full power for 5 minutes. Stir in the pork, sage, seasoning and flour. Dissolve the stock cube in the boiling water, then pour the stock into the meat mixture and stir thoroughly. Cover with cling film and cook for 15 minutes. Stir once during cooking.

To make the pancakes, heat a large frying pan or omelette pan and grease it lightly with a little oil. Add enough batter to coat the bottom of the pan thinly, then cook until golden brown on the under side. Turn and cook the second side. Layer pieces of absorbent kitchen paper between the pancakes to prevent them from sticking after they have been cooked.

Spread each cooked pancake with a little apple sauce. Add some of the pork and roll up neatly. Lay the filled pancakes in a shallow serving dish and heat for 2 minutes in the microwave (the sauces should have been hot already, this is just a temperature boost). Pour the mushroom sauce over, then mix the Parmesan cheese with the parsley and sprinkle on top. Serve at once.

Gingered Pork

———— SERVES 4 ————

The microwave oven is very useful for cooking certain Chinese-style dishes. Because of the way in which many such dishes are prepared and marinated for rapid stir-frying they are also suitable for quick microwave cooking. Many Oriental steamed dishes can also be cooked in the microwave oven with equal success. Try this gingered pork dish either as an unusual first course or serve it with plenty of rice as a main course.

225 g/8 oz lean boneless pork	2 tablespoons soy sauce
50 g/2 oz fresh root ginger	1 (425-g/15-oz) can baby sweet corn
a few drops of sesame oil	4 spring onions to garnish

Cut the pork into fine shreds, discarding any fat as you do so. Peel the ginger, then thinly slice it and cut the slices into fine shreds. Mix this with the pork, add the sesame oil and soy sauce and make sure the ingredients are thoroughly mixed, then set aside to marinate for 30 minutes. Cook on full power for 5 minutes.

Drain the sweet corn and cut any slightly large cobs in half lengthways. Mix the corn into the pork and continue to cook for a further 3 minutes. Meanwhile, shred the spring onions into long strips and sprinkle these over the pork before serving.

Stuffed Vine Leaves

———— SERVES 4 ————

Packets of vine leaves are available from many good supermarkets or delicatessens. Unopened they will keep in the refrigerator for several weeks so they are worth buying when you happen to see them. To make them tender to eat, the leaves require cooking in boiling water and this is easiest done on top of the cooker while the filling is bubbling away in the microwave. Serve the filled leaves with a Greek salad and brown rice.

1 onion, chopped	150 ml/¼ pint full-bodied red wine
2 cloves garlic, crushed	
2 tablespoons olive oil	1 (425-g/15-oz) can chopped tomatoes
12 large vine leaves	
350 g/12 oz minced pork	1 bay leaf
2 tablespoons tahini	1 teaspoon oregano
salt and freshly ground black pepper	

Place the onion in a basin with the garlic and oil, then cook on full power for 3 minutes.

Bring a saucepan of salted water to the boil on the hob, then add the vine leaves and simmer for 10 minutes. At the end of the cooking time drain the leaves thoroughly.

Add the pork to the onion, with the tahini and seasoning to taste, then return the meat to the oven and cook for a further 5 minutes. Lay the vine leaves out flat and place a little of the minced pork mixture on each, then fold them up to make neat packages and place them close together in a dish – a fairly deep quiche or gratin dish will do, but remember that you are going to pour a sauce over in a few minutes.

Mix the wine with the tomatoes and bay leaf in a basin, then stir in the oregano and seasoning to taste. Heat for 3 minutes, then pour this sauce over the vine leaves and cook for 5 minutes. Serve at once.

Savoury Roly-poly

———— SERVES 4 TO 6 ————

This recipe is useful for using up all sorts of leftovers – cold roast meat; bits of cheese or bacon; cold cooked carrots or beans; or any other ingredients you happen to have in the refrigerator. Here I have used cooked ham to give you some idea as to what to buy if you want to make this for a particularly economical, warming meal. Serve a Tomato Sauce (see page 200) to finish the main dish.

1 large onion, chopped	2 tablespoons prepared mild mustard
2 tablespoons oil	
100 g/4 oz cooked ham, finely chopped	*Suet Pastry:*
	100 g/4 oz self-raising flour
2 tablespoons chopped parsley	50 g/2 oz shredded suet
100 g/4 oz button mushrooms, chopped	about 50 ml/2 fl oz cold water
salt and freshly ground black pepper	

Place the onion in a basin with the oil and cook on full power for 5 minutes. Stir in the ham, parsley and mushrooms with plenty of seasoning.

To make the pastry, sift the flour into a bowl and add a good pinch of salt. Stir in the suet then add water to make a soft but not sticky dough. Roll the pastry out on a floured surface to give an oblong of about 18 × 10 cm/7 × 4 in. Spread the mustard over the pastry leaving a small border around the edge. Spread the ham mixture over the middle of the pastry and dampen the edges, then roll up from the long side and lift the roll carefully on to a flat dish.

Cover the dish with cling film, allowing room for the pastry to rise. If this is not possible, then put the dish inside a roasting bag and secure the end loosely with an elastic band. Cook for 7 minutes, turning the dish round once during cooking. Serve at once.

Fruited Gammon Steaks

——— SERVES 2 ———

Choose gammon steaks without a great deal of fat on them to cook in the microwave oven.

2 (225-g/8-oz) gammon steaks
grated rind and juice of 1 orange
1 teaspoon horseradish mustard

100 g/4 oz dried apricots, chopped (use the sort which do not require pre-soaking)
orange slices to garnish

Trim the rind off the gammon and snip any fat to prevent the steaks from curling. Mix the orange rind and juice with the mustard and apricots. Arrange the gammon in a large shallow dish, ideally an oval dish but a quiche dish will do. Spoon the sauce and apricots evenly over the meat, then cook on full power for 10 minutes.

About half way through the cooking time turn the gammon steaks over and around in the dish so that any overlapping areas are moved towards the outside of the dish.

Garnish the gammon with orange slices and serve.

If you want to prepare four gammon steaks, then do them in two batches. Cook the first pair for 8 minutes, then reheat them for 2 minutes to serve.

Gammon Stew with Herb Dumplings

——— SERVES 4 ———

450 g/1 lb gammon pieces
1 onion, chopped
100 g/4 oz carrots, sliced
1 large green pepper
2 sticks celery, sliced
2 tablespoons oil
2 tablespoons plain flour
300 ml/½ pint ham stock or dry cider
salt and black pepper

Dumplings:
100 g/4 oz self-raising flour
50 g/2 oz shredded suet
2 tablespoons chopped fresh herbs, for example parsley, sage, thyme and rosemary
50 ml/2 fl oz cold water

Trim the gammon pieces, then cut them into small pieces. Place the onion and carrots in a large bowl. Cut the stalk end off the pepper, remove all the seeds and pith, then chop and add it to the onion. Stir in the celery and oil and cover with cling film, allowing a small gap for the steam to esape. Cook on full power for 10 minutes.

Stir the flour into the vegetables and add the stock or cider, stirring continuously. Add the gammon and re-cover the dish, then cook for a further 10 minutes.

Prepare the dumplings. Sift the flour into a bowl and mix in the suet with a good pinch of salt and the herbs. Mix in enough water to make a soft dough. Shape this into six dumplings. Taste and adjust the seasoning for the stew, then place the dumplings on the surface of the liquid. Cook for a further 4 minutes and serve at once.

Meat Loaf with Vegetables

──── SERVES 6 ────

This is a good way of making a pound of mince more interesting without being extravagant. The meatloaf tastes as good cold as it does hot, so it is ideal for taking on picnics or for light summer suppers.

450 g/1 lb minced pork
175 g/6 oz fresh
   breadcrumbs
2 tablespoons chopped
   fresh herbs
salt and black pepper
1 egg, beaten

350 g/12 oz frozen mixed
   vegetables
225 g/8 oz cream cheese
4 spring onions, chopped
Garnish (optional):
cucumber slices
radish slices

Mix the pork with half the breadcrumbs, the herbs, plenty of seasoning and the beaten egg. Mix thoroughly, then press just over two-thirds of the mixture into a greased loaf dish measuring about 28 × 11 cm/10 × 4½ in (about 1.4-litre/2½-pint capacity). Make sure the meat lines the base and sides of the dish as evenly as possible.

Place the frozen vegetables in a basin and cook on full power for 2 minutes, then drain off any water and stir in the remaining breadcrumbs, seasoning and cream cheese. Add the spring onions and make sure the ingredients are thoroughly mixed. Press this mixture into the middle of the meatloaf then place the remaining minced meat mixture on top, smoothing it over to enclose the cream cheese completely.

Cover with cling film, allowing a small gap for the steam to escape, then cook on full power for 15 minutes, turning the dish round once during cooking.

At the end of the cooking time, allow the meatloaf to stand in the dish for 5 minutes, then turn it out on to a baking tray or serving dish which can be put under the grill. Place under a hot grill for a few minutes to brown the meat, then serve hot or cold. Garnish if liked with slices of cucumber and radish arranged alternately along the top.

Absorbent kitchen paper is useful for covering any foods which are likely to splatter during cooking; for example, bacon rashers, meatloaves and chops. Remove the paper as soon as the food is cooked as it tends to stick as it cools.

Cider-glazed Meatloaf

——— SERVES 6 ———

Plainly cooked, rabbit can be slightly bland and un-interesting, but seasoned with herbs and spices it can be turned into many tasty meals. Rabbit cooks fairly quickly and, unlike the tougher cuts of meat, it does not require lengthy tenderising so it is ideal for preparing in a microwave oven.

This meatloaf can be served hot with a selection of vegetables or cold with salad; it is also ideal for taking on a picnic.

350 g/12 oz boneless rabbit, cubed	1 tablespoon chopped fresh sage
2 onions, chopped	dash of Worcestershire sauce
1 bay leaf	100 g/4 oz gooseberries
2 blades of mace	2 tablespoons brown sugar
salt and freshly ground black pepper	3 tablespoons dry cider
75 g/3 oz fresh breadcrumbs	*Garnish:*
225 g/8 oz pork sausagemeat	4 bay leaves
1 egg, beaten	a few juniper berries

Place the rabbit, onions, bay leaf and mace in a basin. Add seasoning to taste and toss the ingredients together. Cover with cling film, allowing a small gap for the steam to escape, and cook on full power for 7 minutes, stirring once during cooking. Allow the mixture to cool slightly, then coarsely mince the rabbit with the onions but remove the bay leaf and mace. Reserve all the cooking juices. If you have a food processor it is ideal for this.

Mix the breadcrumbs and sausagemeat into the minced meat, add all the cooking juices, the egg, sage and Worcestershire sauce. Sprinkle in seasoning to taste and make sure that all the ingredients are thoroughly com-bined. Top, tail and halve the gooseberries; if they are frozen then allow them to half thaw first. Stir the fruit into the meat mixture without breaking the pieces. Press the mixture into a 1.15-litre/2-pint loaf-shaped dish and cover the top loosely with absorbent kitchen paper. Cook for 14 minutes, turning the dish twice during cooking. Wrap the dish in cooking foil, placing the shiny side inwards, and leave the meatloaf to rest for 5 minutes.

Meanwhile, mix the sugar and cider together in a small basin or mug and heat it in the microwave for 2 minutes. Heat the grill. Unwrap the meatloaf and turn it out on to a small roasting tin or foil-lined baking tray. Brush all the cider glaze over the top and sides of the loaf and place it under the grill until golden brown, basting frequently with the cider.

To serve, brush a little of the glaze over the bay leaves and juniper berries and press them on top of the loaf, then lift it on to a serving plate.

Kidneys in Red Wine

——— SERVES 4 ———

These kidneys are ideal for a quick supper dish or for an economical but not dreary dinner. Serve them with buttered noodles or rice.

450 g/1 lb lambs' kidneys	1 bay leaf
1 onion, chopped	300 ml/½ pint red wine
25 g/1 oz butter	100 g/4 oz button mushrooms, halved
2 tablespoons plain flour	2 tablespoons chopped parsley
salt and freshly ground black pepper	

Cut the kidneys in half and snip out their cores. Place the onion in a bowl or casserole with the butter and cook on full power for 3 minutes.

Stir in the flour and plenty of seasoning, then add the bay leaf and pour in the wine, stirring to make a smooth sauce. Add the kidneys, then cover the bowl with cling film, allowing a small gap for the steam to escape. Cook for 8 minutes.

Stir in the button mushrooms and continue to cook for a further 2 minutes before serving, sprinkled with plenty of chopped parsley.

Cumberland Kidneys with Soured Cream

——— SERVES 4 ———

1 onion, chopped	2 tablespoons redcurrant jelly
25 g/1 oz butter	150 ml/¼ pint red wine
salt and freshly ground black pepper	150 ml/¼ pint soured cream
450 g/1 lb lambs' kidneys	*Garnish:* (optional)
2 tablespoons plain flour	orange slices
grated rind and juice of 1 orange	parsley sprigs

Place the onion and butter in a bowl or dish with plenty of black pepper. Cover with cling film and cook on full power for 3 minutes.

Meanwhile, halve the kidneys and remove their cores. Stir the flour, orange rind and juice and redcurrant jelly into the onion, then pour in the wine and add the kidneys. Stir well, adding seasoning to taste, then cover the dish and cook for 10 minutes, stirring once during cooking.

Swirl the soured cream into the kidneys and serve, garnished with orange slices and parsley sprigs if you like.

Chilli Liver

———— SERVES 4 ————

Serve this spicy liver dish with plenty of boiled rice and a good green salad, with plenty of unusual vegetables like endive, chicory, avocados and courgettes.

1 large onion, chopped	3 teaspoons ground
2 cloves garlic	coriander
3 tablespoons oil	1 (425-g/15-oz) can
1 green pepper	chopped tomatoes
450 g/1 lb lambs' liver	2 (425-g/15-oz) cans red
1 tablespoon chilli	kidney beans, drained
powder	2 tablespoons chopped
salt and freshly ground	parsley
black pepper	

Place the onion in a dish with the garlic and oil. Cut the stalk end off the pepper, then remove all the seeds and pith from inside. Chop the green part and add this to the onion. Cook on full power for 5 minutes.

Meanwhile, cut the liver into small cubes. Stir the chilli powder, seasoning and coriander into the onion mixture, then add the liver and pour in the tomatoes. Stir well and continue to cook for a further 5 minutes.

Add the kidney beans to the liver, stirring them in carefully so as not to break them up. Continue to cook for a final 5 minutes. Before serving, stir in the chopped parsley and taste, adjusting the seasoning if necessary.

Herbed Liver

———— SERVES 4 ————

Liver cooks very successfully in the microwave oven and it can be topped with croûtons or served on crisply fried bread to add interest to the texture. Here herbs are included to enliven the taste and garlic croûtons give extra crunch.

450 g/1 lb lambs' liver	2 tablespoons chopped
175 g/6 oz lean smoked	parsley
bacon	1 (425-g/15-oz) can
1 large onion, chopped	chopped tomatoes
salt and freshly ground	2 medium-thick slices
black pepper	fresh bread
sprig of sage	50 g/2 oz butter
1 bay leaf	2 tablespoons oil
sprig of thyme	2 cloves garlic, crushed

Cut the liver into thin slices. Remove and discard the rind off the bacon, then chop the rashers and place them in a dish with the onion. Cook on full power for 5 minutes.

Lay the prepared liver in the dish and sprinkle in plenty of seasoning. Add the herbs, including the parsley, then pour the tomatoes over and cover with cling film, allowing a small gap for the steam to escape. Continue to cook for 10 minutes, rearranging the liver once during this time.

While the liver is cooking, cut the crusts off the bread and cut the slices into small neat cubes. Heat the butter and oil together in a frying pan and add the garlic. Fry for a few minutes, then add the bread cubes and shake the pan well to coat them completely in the fat. Fry, turning the bread frequently, until the cubes are golden brown all over. Drain on absorbent kitchen paper.

When the liver is cooked, top with the croûtons and serve at once.

Mustard Rabbit Stew

———— SERVES 4 ————

Rabbit is a tender meat so it cooks well in the microwave. However, being rather bland, it benefits from a well-flavoured sauce and mustard is the traditional ingredient which is used to enliven rabbit. Serve the stew with creamed potatoes or dumplings, cooked on top of the stew for the last 4 minutes of the cooking time.

1 onion, chopped	1 tablespoon prepared
175 g/6 oz lean bacon	English mustard
2 tablespoons plain flour	300 ml/½ pint boiling
salt and freshly ground	water
black pepper	450 g/1 lb boneless rabbit
1 chicken stock cube	

Place the onion in a casserole or bowl. Cut off and discard the rinds from the bacon, then chop the rashers and add them to the onion. Cook on full power for 5 minutes.

Stir in the flour and seasoning to taste, then add the crumbled stock cube and stir in the mustard and water. Trim the rabbit and cut the meat into neat cubes, then add it to the sauce.

Cover with cling film, allowing a small gap for the steam to escape, then cook on full power for 15 minutes, stirring once during cooking. Allow to stand for a few minutes before serving.

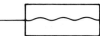

If you are having a barbecue with several different sorts of meats and other foods, chicken joints can be partly cooked in the microwave oven first to prevent them from burning over the charcoal before they are cooked through. The same goes for large pieces of meat. You can successfully barbecue whole legs of lamb, joints of beef or whole poultry in this way.

VEGETABLE DISHES

Most vegetables cook very well in the microwave oven and the results are often better than by conventional cooking methods. Instead of cooking in large quantities of water, the vegetables are usually put in a roasting bag or dish with a small amount of liquid or a knob of butter. Depending on the type of vegetable, the cooking time can be far quicker than by conventional methods – courgettes, for example, cook incredibly quickly and they have the best flavour possible. Salt should not be added to the vegetables before cooking as this tends to produce tiny dehydrated patches on the surface. Add any seasoning once the vegetables are cooked.

The recipes included here offer a complete range of ideas. The simple recipes give the basic cooking times for different types of vegetables but at the same time offer an interesting way of serving them. As with any other food the quantity affects the cooking time so where an unusual quantity of ingredients has been given in the recipe an alternative time is offered for different amounts. It is not difficult to judge cooking times once you are used to microwave cooking. Usually, if you prepare half the quantity of food, then the cooking time will be longer than half the time stated in the recipe. So, if you take the halved time as a starting point it will be easy to continue cooking for the remaining short period.

For baked potatoes there is a short chart giving cooking times for different quantities, with a guide to the size in weight. It is important to emphasise that even though it may be worth cooking four or six potatoes in the microwave, it is not a good idea to plan a baked potato party

round your microwave oven.

If you like stuffed vegetables, then you will find the microwave oven invaluable. Peppers, for example, can be cooked, stuffed and served all in the same dish and, when presented at the table, will still have an appetising appearance. Marrow is another vegetable which is cooked with comparative speed in the microwave oven and I include two recipes; one a vegetarian dish (or serve it as an accompaniment to a main dish) of stuffed marrow rings, the other a whole marrow stuffed with minced pork. Both dishes have an excellent full flavour and very good colour.

Old-fashioned boiled onions with butter are something which I hadn't eaten for years until I bought a microwave. Now I can prepare whole cooked onions without having to use a large saucepan and in far less time. Not only are they good on their own but they can be served with a variety of flavoured butters and there are suggestions for turning them into tasty supper dishes.

Asparagus is a vegetable which it is difficult to cook conventionally because of its length, so it too is a winner in the microwave. It can be prepared in a large oval serving dish or in a roasting bag.

As well as these simple suggestions, the recipes include old-favourites like Ratatouille and Mushrooms à la Grecque (see pages 123 and 124) with some new ideas; Runner Beans in Garlic and Walnut Sauce or Spiced Aubergines (see pages 113 and 121) for example. So, next time you want to make a chop special, or turn a couple of chicken joints into an interesting meal, try making the vegetable accompaniment more exciting.

Baked Potatoes

Whenever you ask anyone about microwave cooking they always seem to enthuse about baked potatoes! This must be one of the most popular reasons for many of the microwave sales. So what's so good about microwaved 'baked' potatoes? The answer is speed.

There is, however, rather more than that to say about baked potatoes. It is possible to cook one, two or four large potatoes in the microwave oven with comparative speed; that is, significantly faster than in a very hot conventional oven. If on the other hand you are planning to have a bonfire party, for example, and you need to cook baked potatoes for twenty people, then put them in your conventional oven and they will be cooked far quicker.

The whole point is that as the amount of food put into the microwave oven is increased, so the cooking time has to be increased. The confusing fact about microwave cooking is that the time increase is not necessarily proportional to the increase in quantities. The other thing to remember is that the larger the potatoes, the longer they will take to cook. Eventually, a cut-off point is reached at which it is more sensible to put the potatoes in a conventional oven.

Having outlined all the possible pitfalls of baking potatoes in the microwave oven, I would now like to tell you how good they are! If you are cooking a small to average number of baked potatoes then they are cooked very quickly, it takes a great deal to produce overcooked areas and they are delicious if the skin is quickly browned off under the conventional grill. Another useful advantage is that cooked, leftover baked potatoes can be reheated without spoiling. Here are cooking times for large baked potatoes, big enough to make a meal in themselves, and medium-sized baked potatoes which could be served as an accompaniment to a main dish. One of these would make an average portion, while two would be a really generous helping. The potatoes should be pricked with a fork before cooking otherwise they will burst.

COOKING TIMES

Large potatoes (350 g/12 oz each in weight)

1 potato	8 minutes
2 potatoes	15 minutes
4 potatoes	27 minutes

During cooking, there should be no need to turn one or two potatoes but the four potatoes would need re-arranging once or twice.

Medium-sized potatoes (about 150 g/5 oz each in weight)

1 potato	4 minutes
2 potatoes	5 to 6 minutes
4 potatoes	10 minutes
6 potatoes	18 to 19 minutes

During cooking the six potatoes would require re-arranging once during cooking, the others should not need moving round.

When the potatoes are cooked, brush them with a little oil or butter and put them under a hot grill for a few minutes, turning them once, to make the skin crisp and brown. This is not essential, but if you like crisp skins this is the way to achieve them. Serve the potatoes with butter or try any of the ideas given here.

TO TOP BAKED POTATOES:

Soured Cream and Chives Stir in 2 tablespoons chopped chives into 150 ml/¼ pint soured cream (enough for 4 medium-sized potatoes).

Blue Cheese Cream Mash 100 g/4 oz ripe Danish blue cheese into 150 ml/¼ pint soured cream (enough for 4 medium-sized potatoes).

Soured Cream with Anchovy Mash 1 (50-g/2-oz) can anchovy fillets with the oil from the can. Add seasoning to taste and 150 ml/¼ pint soured cream (enough for 4 medium-sized potatoes).

Soured Cream with Crispy Bacon Cook rindless bacon rashers according to the instructions on page 169 allowing a little extra cooking time for the bacon to become crisp. When cool, crumble or chop it and sprinkle over the cream-topped potatoes.

Cream Cheese with Herbs Mix 2 tablespoons chopped fresh herbs into 100 g/4 oz cream cheese (enough for 2 medium-sized potatoes).

Cream Cheese with Pineapple Mix 1 (340-g/12 oz) can pineapple pieces (drained of juice) into 225 g/8 oz cream cheese (enough for 4 medium-sized potatoes).

Cream Cheese with Ham and Onion Finely chop 100 g/4 oz cooked ham and 4 spring onions, then mix these ingredients into 225 g/8 oz cream cheese (enough for 4 medium-sized potatoes).

Cream Cheese and Salami Beat a little single cream into the cream cheese to make it thin enough to pipe. Fold sliced salami into cornets, then pipe a little cream cheese into each. Arrange two salami cornets on each slit potato with tomato wedges and parsley.

Lemon Prawns Cook 1 small chopped onion with 25 g/1 oz butter on full power for 5 minutes. Add 225 g/8 oz peeled cooked prawns and the grated rind of 1 lemon. Heat for 2 minutes, then spoon on to the potatoes (enough for 4 medium-sized potatoes).

Bacon and Pepper Cook 1 large chopped onion with 1 deseeded and chopped green pepper and 225 g/8 oz chopped rindless bacon for 8 minutes on full power. Spoon over the potatoes (enough for 4 medium-sized potatoes).

Bacon Rolls Roll up 2 rindless rashers lean bacon for each potato, thread these on to metal skewers and cook them under the conventional grill until crisp and golden. You can cook these at the same time as you brown the skin of the potatoes.

Chicken Sauce Make 300 ml/½ pint Béchamel Sauce (see page 200), then stir in 225 g/8 oz chopped cooked chicken and 2 tablespoons chopped parsley. Add a pinch of thyme and cook for 2 minutes. Spoon the chicken sauce over the cut baked potatoes (enough for 4 medium-sized potatoes).

Eggs Mornay Make 300 ml/½ pint Cheese Sauce (see page 200). Add 4 roughly chopped hard-boiled eggs and spoon the mixture into the cut potatoes. Top with chopped parsley (enough for 4 medium-sized potatoes).

Ham and Mushroom Make 300 ml/½ pint Mushroom Sauce (see page 200) and stir in 225 g/8 oz cubed cooked ham. Spoon into the cut potatoes (enough for 4 medium-sized potatoes).

TO STUFF BAKED POTATOES:

(**Note:** the reheating time for the stuffed baked potatoes will depend on the number that are put in the oven. The filling should still be quite hot and in some cases it may not require heating up at all, particularly if the top is to be grilled until brown.)

Cheese Potatoes Allow 50 g/2 oz grated cheese for each potato. Scoop the middle out of the cooked potato and mash it with butter, seasoning, a little milk and the cheese. Pile the mashed potato back into the skins and heat on full power, then grill until golden brown.

Savoury Stuffed Potatoes Allow 50 g/2 oz grated cheese for each potato and add 1 tablespoon grated onion for each. Mash the potato with butter, seasoning and milk, then mix in the cheese, onion, plenty of chopped parsley and 25 g/1 oz chopped cooked ham for each potato. Pile back into the skins and heat to serve.

Fisherman's Potatoes Thoroughly mash 1 (120-g/4¼-oz) can sardines in tomato sauce with seasoning to taste, 1 crushed clove garlic, a little lemon rind and a dash of Worcestershire sauce. Mix into the potato mashed with butter and spoon the filling into the skins. Top with grated cheese and grill until golden (enough sardine for 2 potatoes).

Porky Potatoes Finely chop 2 freshly cooked pork sausages for each potato. Mash the potato with butter, a pinch of rubbed sage and plenty of chopped parsley. Stir in the sausage and pile the potato back into the shells. Top with parsley or sage sprigs and serve.

Creamy Turkey Potatoes Finely chop 100 g/4 oz cooked turkey for each potato. Mash the potatoes with 25 g/1 oz cream cheese for each one, plenty of seasoning and a little cream or milk. Mix in the turkey and heat through, then serve topped with a little cranberry sauce. (This is a good idea for the post-Christmas turkey.)

TO FILL BAKED POTATOES:

For all the following ideas, you will need large potatoes. Cut the baked potatoes in half and scoop out the middle of the potatoes. Mash the potato with butter, milk and seasoning, then put it back into the skins, pressing it against the sides and piling it up round the edge. If you like the potato mixture can be piped back into the skins, but this is difficult if you are not used to handling very hot piping bags. The mashed potato case should be browned under a hot grill before the filling is added.

Potato Scrambles Prepare the potatoes, then, when they are under the grill browning, scramble the required number of eggs (about 2 to each potato). Use any of the scrambled egg ideas on page 152 if you like. Top with chopped parsley and a couple of slices of tomato to serve.

Sherried Chicken Liver Potatoes Prepare the Sherried Chicken Livers on page 161 while the potatoes are browning. Spoon the mixture into the potatoes and top with plenty of chopped parsley to serve.

Greek Salad Potatoes An unusual but delicious combination of creamy hot potato and very crunchy cold salad. Allow a little diced cucumber, a little chopped onion and green pepper, 1 small tomato peeled, deseeded and chopped and 50 g/2 oz crumbled feta cheese for each potato. Mix all these salad ingredients and dress them with a little olive oil. Pile them into the potato and add a few black olives.

Tuna Potatoes Make up 300 ml/½ pint Mushroom Sauce (see page 200), then stir in the liquid from 1 (198-g/7½-oz) can tuna in oil. Flake the fish into the sauce and add plenty of chopped parsley. Spoon this into the potato before it is grilled, then top the filling with a little grated cheese and grill until thoroughly browned.

Baked Beans and Sausages Grill 1 sausage for each potato as you brown the potato edge. Heat 1 (425-g/15-oz) can baked beans for each pair of potatoes. Allow 4 minutes on full power for the baked beans. Slice the sausages and mix them into the beans, then spoon the mixture into the potatoes. This is a useful snack for youngsters.

Eggs in Potatoes Allow 1 small egg for each potato half. Brown the potatoes first, then drop an egg into each half and prick the yolk with a cocktail stick. Cook for the following times:

2 potato halves	7 minutes
4 potato halves	10 minutes

(If you are preparing larger numbers do them in two batches.)

Minted New Potatoes

———— SERVES 4 ————

Although the equivalent of boiled old potatoes is not an outstanding success in the microwave oven, new potatoes are excellent when cooked in this way. Here they are served with butter and mint, but you can try any of the ideas suggested below if you want to make an unusual potato dish.

675 g/1½ lb new potatoes
2 tablespoons water
mint sprigs
a little salt

To serve:
generous knob of butter
a little chopped mint

Scrape or scrub the potatoes and place them in a roasting bag with the water. Add a couple of large sprigs of mint and secure the end of the bag loosely with an elastic band. Cook on full power for 10 to 12 minutes, depending on the size of the potatoes.

Season the cooked potatoes lightly, then serve them with butter and a little chopped mint.

New Potatoes with Almonds Brown 50 g/2 oz flaked almonds in 50 g/2 oz butter in a small basin or mug (covered with cling film) on full power for 4 minutes. Cook the potatoes as in the main recipe, but omitting the mint, then pour the almonds and butter over and serve.

New Potatoes with Bacon Lay 4 rashers rindless bacon on a double thickness of absorbent kitchen paper on a plate. Cover with another piece of absorbent paper and cook on full power for 7 minutes. Cook the new potatoes as in the main recipe, omitting the mint. Allow the bacon to cool, then crumble it and sprinkle it over the cooked potatoes with a handful of chopped parsley.

Potatoes Provençale Cook the potatoes as in the main recipe, omitting the mint. Crush 2 cloves garlic into a basin and add 50 g/2 oz butter. Stir in 225 g/8 oz chopped peeled tomatoes and 2 tablespoons chopped stoned black olives. Cook on full power for 4 minutes, then pour over the potatoes, toss well and serve.

Potato and Mushroom Mornay Make a Béchamel Sauce following the instructions on page 200. Cook the potatoes according to the instructions in the main recipe, omitting the mint. Stir them into the sauce with 100 g/4 oz button mushrooms and 50 g/2 oz finely crumbled Lancashire cheese. Cook on full power for 2 minutes, then serve.

Potatoes Lyonnaise

———— SERVES 4 ————

450 g/1 lb onions, finely chopped
50 g/2 oz butter
575 g/1¼ lb potatoes

4 tablespoons double cream
salt and freshly ground white pepper

Place the onions and butter in a basin, cover with cling film, allowing a small gap for the steam to escape, and cook on full power for 5 minutes.

Finely slice the potatoes (the peeled weight should be about 450 g/1 lb), then rinse and thoroughly dry them. Layer the potatoes and onions in a gratin dish, adding 2 tablespoons of the cream and plenty of pepper about halfway through, then the remaining cream and some pepper on top of the potatoes. Do not add any salt at this stage.

Cover with cling film and cook for 15 minutes. Sprinkle a little salt on top and cook under a hot grill until well browned. Serve at once.

This classic, yet simple, potato dish complements grilled meats, poultry and fish as well as roast joints. This recipe can also be used as a base for a tasty supper dish and a few ideas are included below.

VARIATION
Layer some finely chopped, rindless bacon in with the potatoes and onions. Top with grated Cheddar cheese and brown the dish under the grill.

Alternatively, chop some cooked ham, ham sausage or garlic sausage and mix in 2 tablespoons chopped fresh herbs. Layer this mixture with the potatoes, again top with cheese and grill until brown.

Onions are cooked far more successfully, in all sorts of dishes, if they are chopped rather than sliced. The result is a better flavour and onions which are soft in the finished dish.

Fantail Potatoes

——— SERVES 4 ———

These potatoes, also known as hasselback potatoes, are traditionally cooked in the oven. Because the bulk of the potato is broken up and separated slightly by slicing, they cook particularly quickly in the microwave oven – far better than whole, peeled raw potatoes. Browned and crisped under the grill, these make an excellent accompaniment to moist, saucy dishes.

8 medium-sized potatoes	50 g/2 oz Emmental or
2 tablespoons water	Gruyère cheese, finely
50 g/2 oz butter	grated

Cut the potatoes into fairly thin slices, leaving them attached at the base. Take great care not to slice straight through the potato and separate the pieces.

Place the potatoes in a shallow dish – a gratin or quiche dish – then sprinkle the water over them. Cover with cling film and cook on full power for 10 to 12 minutes. Turn the dish once during cooking. The potatoes which I timed were tender after 10 minutes, but the timing can vary with size and shape.

Carefully insert a knife between the slices, to ease them apart slightly, but do not break them up. Dot with the butter and sprinkle the cheese over, then cook under a hot grill until golden brown. Serve at once.

Stuffed Sweet Potatoes

——— SERVES 4 ———

2 large sweet potatoes	salt and freshly ground
(total weight about	black pepper
1.5 kg/3 lb)	2 tablespoons chopped
225 g/8 oz lean bacon	fresh coriander
2 cloves garlic, crushed	
1 large onion, finely	
chopped	

Prick the potatoes all over with a fork, then place them on a double thickness of absorbent kitchen paper as far apart as possible in the oven. Cook on full power for 20 minutes. The potatoes should still be firm in the middle.

Halve the potatoes and scoop out the flesh, leaving the skins whole with a thin lining of potato. Cut the rind off the bacon and chop the rashers. Place these in a large bowl with the garlic and onion. Add seasoning to taste and cook on full power for 5 minutes. Meanwhile, cube the sweet potato.

Add the sweet potato to the onion and bacon, then cook for 10 minutes. Stir in the coriander and replace the mixture in the shells to serve.

Potato Cake

——— SERVES 4 ———

This can be served as an accompaniment to a main dish or it can be topped with ham, salami, cheese or eggs and served as a delicious supper dish; try some of the suggestions below if you are stuck for ideas.

1 small onion, chopped	450 g/1 lb potatoes
25 g/1 oz butter	100 g/4 oz black olives,
1 clove garlic, crushed	stoned and chopped

Place the onion in a shallow 20-cm/8-in round dish with the butter and garlic. Cook on full power for 4 minutes.

Grate the potatoes on a coarse grater (or use a food processor), wash them thoroughly and dry them on absorbent kitchen paper. Prepare the potatoes while the onion is cooking, leave it in the oven if you are still grating when the timer stops. If you prepare the potatoes in advance, they will discolour and look horrid in the finished dish.

Add the potatoes, mixed with the olives, to the onion, then press the mixture down firmly and cover with cling film, allowing a small gap for the steam to escape. Cook for 10 minutes then transfer to a hot grill and cook until browned. Serve straight from the dish, cutting the potato into wedges at the table, or use it as a base for any of the topping ideas given below.

TOPPING IDEAS:

Salami and Gherkin Overlap 100 g/4 oz sliced salami and 4 sliced gherkins on top of the grilled potato cake and heat in the microwave for 2 minutes.

Ham and Tomato Roll up 8 small slices cooked ham and arrange them on top of the grilled potato cake, laying them from the centre outwards. Arrange 4 sliced tomatoes in between the ham rolls.

Tuna and Cheese Drain the oil from 1 (198-g/7-oz) can of tuna and use this to cook the onion instead of the butter. Flake the fish over the potato as soon as it is removed from the microwave. Top with 100 g/4 oz grated cheese and grill until golden.

Egg and Anchovy Mash 1 (50-g/2-oz) can of anchovy fillets with their oil and a little lemon juice. Stir in 150 ml/¼ pint mayonnaise. Hard boil 4 eggs on the conventional cooker while the potato cake is grilling so that they will be hot to serve with it. Roughly chop them, then arrange them neatly on top of the cake with plenty of chopped parsley and serve at once, with the anchovy dressing.

Spicy Sweet Potato

—— SERVES 4 ——

One large sweet potato, cooked with aromatic cinnamon and ginger can be served in small portions to four people as an interesting accompaniment to a meat or fish main dish.

1 large sweet potato (about 675–900 g/1½– 2 lb in weight)	150 ml/¼ pint soured cream
1 large onion, chopped	1 tablespoon grated fresh root ginger
75 g/3 oz butter	1 tablespoon grated lemon rind
1 teaspoon ground ginger	
½ teaspoon cinnamon	
salt and freshly ground black pepper	

Prick the potato several times with a fork, then place it on a double thickness of absorbent kitchen paper on a plate. Cook on full power for 12 to 15 minutes, turning the potato over and round once, or until tender right through but not too soft.

Place the onion in a basin with 25 g/1 oz of the butter and cook for 4 minutes. Stir in the ginger, cinnamon and seasoning and cook for 2 minutes.

Peel and cube the potato, then add it to the onion and cook for 3 minutes. Stir in the remaining butter and transfer to a warmed serving dish. Mix the soured cream with the root ginger and lemon rind and serve this with the spicy sweet potato.

Potatoes Anna □

—— SERVES 4 TO 6 ——

Using your microwave to cook the potatoes and a very hot oven to brown the outside gives a perfect result for this dish.

1.25 kg/2½ lb potatoes	freshly ground white pepper
100 g/4 oz butter	

Thinly slice the potatoes – a food processor or slicing and shredding machine is ideal for this. Melt the butter in a small basin for 1½ minutes. Wash and thoroughly dry the potato slices.

You need a dish with straight or slightly sloping sides: a 1.15-litre/2-pint ovenproof glass soufflé dish is suitable. Brush the dish with butter, then neatly layer the potatoes over the base and sides of the dish – if the dish is well greased with melted butter the slices will adhere to the sides. Brush the layer of potatoes with melted butter, then add a second layer, pressing them well against the dish. Continue until all the potatoes are used, remembering to butter each layer and adding white pepper between every third or fourth layer (not too much or the result will be very peppery).

Cover the potatoes with cling film, pressing them down well, then cook on full power for 15 minutes. Press the potatoes down again and transfer them to a very hot oven (240 C, 475 F, gas 9). Cook for a further 15 to 20 minutes.

Carefully slip a palette knife around the sides of the dish to loosen the potato cake. Press hard against the sides of the dish so as not to lose any of the slices which might be stuck. If the potatoes are not browned enough, then quickly flash them under a hot grill. (If the dish used to cook them is a good conductor of heat then they should be well browned.) Serve at once.

Purée of Celeriac with Pistachio Nuts

—— SERVES 4 ——

Celeriac is a large root vegetable which has the same flavour as celery but it is slightly more delicate. As well as being a useful ingredient for salads, this root cooks successfully to make a delicious accompaniment for hot meals. Puréed in this recipe, it is light, delicately flavoured and deliciously tinged with the taste of pistachio. Serve the celeriac with poultry dishes, fish or veal; alternatively, offer it as an unusual starter, with crisp melba toast.

1 large celeriac root (about 1 kg/2 lb in weight)	generous knob of butter
	salt and freshly ground white pepper
4 tablespoons water	4 tablespoons chopped pistachio nuts
75 ml/3 fl oz single cream	

Peel the celeriac root fairly thickly to reveal the creamy-white flesh below. Cut this into 1-cm/½ in cubes. Rinse and thoroughly drain the vegetable, then place the cubes in a roasting bag with the water. Secure the opening of the bag with an elastic band, allowing room for the steam to escape during cooking. Shake the bag to make sure all the pieces of celeriac are moistened, then cook on full power for 15 minutes. Using a tea-towel to protect your hand, shake the bag once during cooking so as to rearrange the pieces of vegetable.

Snip the very corner off the roasting bag and allow the liquid to drain off over a sink or bowl, then transfer the celeriac to a food processor or liquidiser. Process the vegetable until it is quite smooth, adding the cream, butter and seasoning to taste: you may have to do this in batches if you are using a liquidiser. Alternatively, mash the celeriac using a hand masher, then press it through a sieve to obtain a perfectly smooth purée. Stir in the pistachio nuts and transfer the celeriac to a serving dish.

Reheat in the microwave for 3 to 4 minutes and serve at once.

Beetroot with Soured Cream

─── SERVES 4 ───

450 g / 1 lb beetroot
2 tablespoons water
1 large onion, chopped
25 g / 1 oz butter
salt and freshly ground
  black pepper

a little freshly grated
  nutmeg
150 ml / ¼ pint soured
  cream
1 tablespoon chopped
  chives to garnish

Thoroughly wash the beetroot and place it in a roasting bag with the water. Secure the end loosely with an elastic band and cook on full power for 8 minutes. Allow to stand for 5 minutes, then rinse the beetroot under cold water and at the same time rub off their skins. Dice the beetroot and set it aside.

Put the onion in a serving bowl with the butter and cook on full power for 5 minutes. Stir in seasoning to taste, a little nutmeg and the beetroot. Pour in the cream and cook for 2 minutes, then serve garnished with the chives.

If you have cooked vegetables or other ingredients in a roasting bag with liquid which is no longer required, then drain them by holding the bag over the sink, or a basin, and snip off just the corner of the bag.

Creamed Parsnips

─── SERVES 4 ───

675 g / 1½ lb parsnips
3 tablespoons water
1 tablespoon lemon juice
50 g / 2 oz butter
4 tablespoons double
  cream

a little ground mace
salt and freshly ground
  black pepper
1 tablespoon chopped
  parsley to garnish

Peel and trim the parsnips, then cut them into cubes and place these in a roasting bag with the water and lemon juice. Shake the bag well, secure the end loosely with an elastic band and cook on full power for 15 minutes.

Allow the cooked vegetables to stand in the bag, with the end tightly sealed, for 3 or 4 minutes, then snip the corner off the bag to drain off any liquid and transfer the parsnips to a large bowl. Mash the vegetables with the butter and cream, adding the mace and seasoning to taste. Serve at once garnished with chopped parsley.

Creamed Parsnips with Carrots While the parsnips are cooking, chop 1 onion and coarsely grate 225 g / 8 oz carrots. Mix these in a bowl with 50 g / 2 oz butter and cover with cling film. When the parsnips are cooked, cook the onion and carrots on full power for 5 minutes. Mash the parsnips with the cream, but do not add the butter. Stir the carrot mixture into the parsnips and serve at once. This gives the vegetable a good colour and an interesting texture.

Stuffed Onions

SERVES 4

These stuffed onions make a delicious main dish for a vegetarian meal, or they can be served as an accompaniment to meat or fish dishes. Alternatively, you could add about 50 g/2 oz finely chopped smoked bacon to the filling for a tasty supper dish.

4 large onions (about 225 g/8 oz each)
2 tablespoons water
100 g/4 oz button mushrooms, finely chopped
50 g/2 oz fresh breadcrumbs
1 teaspoon chopped sage

50 g/2 oz sunflower seeds, ground
salt and freshly ground black pepper
2 tablespoons chopped parsley
100 g/4 oz matured Cheddar cheese, grated
watercress to garnish (optional)

Stand the onions as far apart as possible in a shallow dish – a quiche dish is ideal. Add the water, cover with cling film, allowing a small gap for the steam to escape, and cook on full power for 10 minutes.

Meanwhile, prepare the stuffing: mix the mushrooms with the breadcrumbs and sage. Stir in the ground sunflower seeds with plenty of seasoning and the parsley. At this stage the mixture may seem rather dry but don't worry – by the time the cooked chopped onion is added it will be quite moist.

When the onions are cooked allow them to stand for a few minutes, then remove their middles. This is not the easiest of tasks because the onions are very hot to handle. The best thing to do is protect your hand with a double thick piece of absorbent kitchen paper, then scoop out the middle of the onion with a small spoon. Once the middle is loosened it will come out fairly easily, but the problem is usually achieving this without breaking the outer shell at the same time trying to hook the spoon around the piece which is being removed. When the middle is removed you should have a shell which is two layers thick.

Finely chop the removed onion and add it to the stuffing. Mix thoroughly, then press this stuffing back into the onion shells. Replace them in the dish (rinse and wipe it dry first), then cook for 3 minutes. Sprinkle the cheese over the onions and grill them until browned. Serve at once garnished with watercress if liked.

Steamed Onions with Creamed Gruyère

————— SERVES 4 —————

The microwave oven is incredibly useful for cooking traditional boiled onions. Here they are served with a creamy Swiss cheese mixture, but if you would like to keep them very simple, then have the onions with a knob of butter and plenty of pepper. If you want to turn them into a more substantial dish, then try some of the ideas given below.

4 large onions (select
  even-sized ones, each
  about 450 g/1 lb in
  weight)
2 tablespoons water
Creamed Gruyère
75 g/3 oz butter

salt and freshly ground
  black pepper
75 g/3 oz Gruyère cheese,
  finely grated
1 teaspoon prepared
  English mustard

Place the onions as far apart as possible in a shallow dish – a quiche dish is ideal. Sprinkle in the water, then cover the vegetables with cling film, allowing a small gap for the steam to escape. Cook on full power for 8 to 9 minutes. The onions should be cooked after 8 minutes so check carefully. They should be tender but still firm when cooked.

    While the onions are cooking beat the butter with plenty of seasoning, the cheese and mustard until pale and creamy. Serve the onions with this mixture piled on top.

Gratin of Onions Cook the onions as in the main recipe. While they are cooking prepare the ingredients for a Cheese Sauce (see page 200). When the onions are ready cook the sauce according to the recipe instructions. Pour the sauce over the onions and top with a mixture of 25 g/ 1 oz grated cheese and 25 g/1 oz breadcrumbs. Brown under a hot grill, then serve at once.

Cheese-grilled Onions Cook the onions as in the main recipe. Top each one with a large slice of Cheddar cheese, then place under a hot grill until melted and lightly browned. Serve at once.

Onions with Bacon Cook the onions as in the main recipe. Lay 4 rindless bacon rashers on a double thickness of absorbent kitchen paper on a plate. Cook on full power for 2½ minutes. Chop the cooked bacon and sprinkle it over the cooked onions. Add a knob of butter to each and sprinkle with a little chopped parsley before serving.

Buttered Onion Ideas Serve the onions with plain, herb or garlic butter. Alternatively, beat canned anchovies, lemon rind, finely chopped ham, finely chopped tomatoes or ground coriander into butter and use generous knobs of it to top the cooked onions. For an unusual starter, serve the cooked onions with a variety of different flavoured butters, all chilled and sliced or served in small pots.

Glazed Onions

————— SERVES 2 TO 4 —————

Pickling onions, cooked with butter and a little sugar make a delicious vegetable accompaniment but remember to serve them only with those dishes which do not contain large quantities of vegetables in a sauce or stuffing.

450 g/1 lb pickling onions
2 tablespoons water

50 g/2 oz butter
1 teaspoon sugar

Place the onions in a 1.15-litre/2-pint basin or in a suitable serving dish. Add the water and butter and cover with cling film, allowing a small gap for the steam to escape. Cook on full power for 5 minutes, then stir in the sugar and continue to cook for a further 8 to 10 minutes, depending on how large the onions are. Serve at once.

Braised Celeriac with Bacon

————— SERVES 4 —————

1 small onion
100 g/4 oz lean bacon
1 celeriac root (about
  675 g/1½ lb in weight)
½ chicken stock cube

150 ml/¼ pint boiling
  water
2 tablespoons chopped
  fresh parsley

Finely chop the onion and place it in a large basin or bowl. Cut off and discard the rinds from the bacon, then chop the rashers. Mix the bacon with the onion and cover with cling film, allowing a small gap for the steam to escape. Cook on full power for 4 minutes.

    While the onion and bacon are cooking, thickly peel the celeriac and cut the vegetable into small cubes. Dissolve the halved stock cube in the boiling water and set aside.

    Stir the celeriac into the onion and bacon, then pour in the stock and stir thoroughly to moisten all the pieces of vegetable. Cover with cling film, allowing a small gap for the steam to escape, then cook for 10 to 12 minutes, stirring once during cooking.

    Sprinkle the chopped parsley over the celeriac and allow the braised vegetable to stand for 2 minutes before serving.

Creamed Spinach

———— SERVES 4 ————

2 (227-g/8-oz) packets
   frozen leaf spinach
25 g/1 oz butter
3 tablespoons plain flour

150 ml/¼ pint single cream
salt and freshly ground
   black pepper
freshly grated nutmeg

Place the frozen spinach in a large bowl with the butter. Cook on full power for 4 to 6 minutes, or until the spinach blocks have defrosted enough to be able to separate the leaves slightly. Do not continue to cook the spinach because there are still icy pieces as these will prevent the mixture from overcooking towards the end of the time.

Stir in the flour and cream and add plenty of seasoning. Continue to cook for a further 6 to 8 minutes, or until the mixture is thickened and creamy. Taste and adjust the seasoning, adding freshly ground nutmeg to taste. Serve at once.

Streaky Artichokes

———— SERVES 4 ————

Jerusalem artichokes can be cooked in the microwave oven with less chance of disintegrating than by conventional means. Their delicate flavour makes them an excellent accompaniment for fish and chicken dishes. Here they are combined with just a little chopped streaky bacon and plenty of chopped parsley.

450 g/1 lb Jerusalem
   artichokes
2 tablespoons water
a little lemon juice
100 g/4 oz lean streaky
   bacon

2 tablespoons chopped
   parsley
salt and freshly ground
   black pepper

Peel or thoroughly scrub the artichokes, then place them in a roasting bag with the water and lemon juice. Secure the end loosely with an elastic band and cook on full power for 10 minutes. Close the end of the bag tightly and set aside while the bacon cooks.

While the artichokes are cooking, the rinds from the bacon should be removed and discarded and the rashers chopped. Place the chopped bacon in a basin and cook for 6 minutes, stirring once. Add the parsley and drained artichokes and mix well, then serve at once, sprinkled with seasoning to taste.

Use your microwave oven to prepare small quantities of baby food. You can reheat or cook small quantities of puréed foods very quickly. Make sure the bowl is both suitable for the microwave oven and heatproof.

Julienne of Carrots

———— SERVES 4 ————

Traditional and simple, this way of cooking carrots is ideal for the microwave oven and a good accompaniment for most savoury dishes, roasts and grills.

450 g/1 lb carrots
25 g/1 oz butter
1 teaspoon sugar

2 tablespoons water
salt and freshly ground
   black pepper

Cut off and discard both ends from the carrots, then slice the vegetables thinly in a lengthways direction. Cut the slices in half if they are very long, then cut them into fine strips – julienne strips.

Place the carrots in a roasting bag with the butter, sugar and water, then cook on full power for 6 to 7 minutes. Give the bag a good shake, add seasoning to taste and serve at once.

To cook fresh spinach, thoroughly wash the leaves and shake off the excess water. Trim off the stalks, then place the leaves in a roasting bag and loosely secure the end with an elastic band. Cook on full power for 5 to 6 minutes, then drain thoroughly and use as required. For the above recipe, omit the first 4 to 6 minutes, then continue.

Root vegetables can be cut in many different ways for cooking in a microwave oven but try to ensure that all the pieces are evenly sized.

Broccoli with Bacon

———— SERVES 4 ————

450 g/1 lb broccoli
2 tablespoons water
175 g/6 oz lean streaky
  bacon
1 large onion, chopped
50 g/2 oz butter
2 tablespoons chopped
  parsley

Trim any long tough stalks off the broccoli, then place the spears in a roasting bag and add the water. Secure the end loosely with an elastic band and cook on full power for 7 to 8 minutes. Close the bag tightly and set aside until the bacon is cooked.

While the broccoli is cooking, cut off and discard the rinds from the bacon, then chop the rashers. Place the chopped bacon with the onion and butter in a basin. Cook for 7 minutes, then stir in the chopped parsley. Add seasoning to taste.

Arrange the broccoli in a serving dish, then pour the bacon mixture over and serve.

Cabbage with Apple

———— SERVES 4 ————

1 onion, finely chopped
2 teaspoons celery seeds
2 tablespoons oil
450 g/1 lb white cabbage
350 g/12 oz (2 medium-
  sized) cooking apples
a little lemon juice
1 tablespoon demerara
  sugar
salt and freshly ground
  black pepper
25 g/1 oz sultanas

Place the onion in a fairly large serving bowl with the celery seeds and oil. Cook on full power for 4 minutes.

Cut the hard core from the cabbage and shred the rest finely. Add this to the onion and continue to cook for a further 4 minutes. Meanwhile, peel, core and quarter the apples, then cut them into medium-thick slices. Sprinkle the slices with a little lemon juice to prevent them from discolouring. Add the apples to the cabbage with the sugar, seasoning and sultanas, then cook for a final 5 minutes. Give the mixture a good stir and serve.

Smoked Dutch sausages cook particularly well in the microwave. Prick the skin a few times, then lay the sausage on a plate and cook on full power for 4 minutes. For a delicious supper dish, thickly slice the sausage and mix it with the cooked cabbage and apples.

Cauliflower au Gratin

—— SERVES 4 TO 6 ——

1 cauliflower (about 450 g/ 1 lb in weight)	100 g/4 oz matured Cheddar cheese, grated
2 tablespoons water	1 tablespoon prepared English mustard
40 g/1½ oz plain flour	
salt and freshly ground black pepper	25 g/1 oz fresh breadcrumbs
600 ml/1 pint milk	halved grilled tomatoes to serve (optional)
25 g/1 oz butter	

Trim the tough outer leaves and any thick hard core from the cauliflower, then wash it thoroughly and place it in a large dish. An ovenproof glass casserole or fairly deep serving dish is ideal for this. Add the water then cover the cauliflower with cling film, allowing a small gap for the steam to escape, and cook on full power for 15 minutes.

Place the flour and plenty of seasoning in a basin – a 1.15-litre/2-pint basin is ideal. Whisk in the milk, then add the butter and cook for 10 minutes, whisking once during cooking. At the end of the cooking time, whisk in most of the cheese and continue to whisk until it has melted.

Stir the mustard into the sauce, then pour it over the cauliflower. Mix the remaining cheese with the bread-crumbs and sprinkle this mixture over the cauliflower. Brown and crisp the topping under a hot grill, then serve at once with the grilled tomatoes if liked.

Cauliflower au Gratin with Bacon Lay 4 lean rindless bacon rashers on a double thickness of absorbent kitchen paper on a plate. Cover with a piece of absorbent kitchen paper and cook on full power for 2½ minutes. Cook the bacon while you are whisking the cheese into the sauce. Chop the rashers, then sprinkle them over the sauce-topped cauliflower before adding the breadcrumb mixture. Brown as above.

Herb and Onion Gratin Cook the cauliflower as in the main recipe. Finely chop 1 onion, then cook it with the butter for the sauce. Allow 4 minutes on full power. Stir in the flour and whisk in the milk, then cook as above. When all the cheese is stirred into the sauce, add 2 tablespoons mixed chopped fresh herbs. Continue as above.

Vegetable Pie

—— SERVES 4 ——

I used to make this pie regularly when my weekly food allowance stretched no further than sausages, mince and cheese! With a good (cheap) local vegetable market the ingredients can be varied according to what is in season.

Layered with hard-boiled eggs and plenty of chopped fresh parsley, this is still one of my favourite supper dishes and using the microwave means that I don't have to mess around with one saucepan for the vegetables and yet another for the sauce. A medium-sized mixing bowl is all that is needed in addition to the pie dish.

350 g/12 oz potatoes,
  cubed
225 g/8 oz carrots, sliced
1 large onion, chopped
225 g/8 oz cauliflower
  florets
2 tablespoons water
25 g/1 oz butter or
  margarine
2 tablespoon plain flour
salt and freshly ground
  black pepper

300 ml/½ pint milk
175 g/6 oz Cheddar
  cheese, grated
2 tablespoons chopped
  parsley
1 quantity of shortcrust
  pastry (page 39) or 1
  (365 g/13 oz) puff
  pastry, defrosted if
  frozen
beaten egg to glaze

Place the potatoes, carrots, onion and cauliflower in a mixing bowl (not too large), add the water and cover with cling film, allowing a small gap for the steam to escape. Cook on full power for 15 minutes.

Transfer the vegetables to a 1.75-litre/3-pint pie dish. Place the butter or margarine, flour, seasoning and milk in the bowl in which the vegetables were cooked (no need to wash it out) and whisk thoroughly. Cook for 6 minutes, whisking thoroughly once during cooking and at the end of the cooking time. Whisk in the cheese, then stir in the parsley and pour the sauce over the vegetables in the pie dish.

For the lid, roll out the pastry to about 5 cm/2 in slightly larger than the top of the dish. Cut a 2.5-cm/1-in strip from the edge of the pastry. Dampen the rim of the dish and press the strip of pastry on to it. Dampen this pastry edge, lift the lid over the pie and press the edges well to seal in the filling. Trim the edges and use the trimming to make decorative leaves or shapes for the top of the pie. Cut a small hole in the top of the pie, glaze with beaten egg and stick on the pastry shapes. Glaze these too, then bake in a hot oven (230C, 450F, gas 8) for 15 to 20 minutes or until golden brown.

OTHER INGREDIENTS TO ADD:

Hard-boiled eggs These taste very good in the pie. Cut 4 eggs into quarters and mix them in the dish with the cooked vegetables. Continue as above.

Bacon Cut the rinds off 225 g/8 oz bacon, then chop the rashers and cook these in the bowl before the vegetables. Allow 3 minutes on full power. Transfer to the pie dish, then mix the bacon into the vegetables when they are cooked. Continue as in the main recipe.

Leeks Slice the leeks (about 100 g/4 oz) and wash them thoroughly. Drain the slices and add them to the vegetables instead of the onions. Cook as in the main recipe.

Courgettes Use only firm, small courgettes and lightly peel them. Cut the courgettes into thick chunks and add them to the vegetables after 12 minutes of the cooking time. Allow an extra minute. Continue as in the main recipe.

Sweet corn and peas These are useful if you are short of some of the other vegetables, or to add colour. Do not cook them with the other vegetables, but add them when the ingredients are turned into the pie dish.

French Beans in Cream

—— SERVES 4 ——

Use this recipe as a guide whenever you want to cook French beans. If you are going to serve the cooked beans without their cream dressing, but in a dish with a little butter, then allow an extra minute on the cooking time.

350 g/12 oz French beans
150 ml/¼ pint double
  cream

1 tablespoon celery seeds
salt and freshly ground
  black pepper

Trim and thoroughly wash the beans, then drain them, leaving a little moisture on the pods. Place the beans in a roasting bag and secure the end with an elastic band, allowing enough room for the steam to escape during cooking. Cook on full power for 5 minutes, then set aside for 1 minute.

Cut the corner off the bag and drain any liquid off the beans, then transfer them to a serving dish. Pour in the cream and sprinkle the celery seeds over. Cook for a further 4 minutes. Add seasoning and serve at once.

Broad Beans with Ham

—— SERVES 4 ——

1 large onion, chopped
50 g/2 oz butter
450 g/1 lb shelled broad
   beans

225 g/8 oz cooked ham,
   shredded
2 tablespoons chopped
   parsley

Place the onion in a basin or serving bowl with the butter and cook on full power for 6 minutes. Put the beans in a roasting bag with 2 tablespoons water and cook on full power for 9 to 10 minutes, then snip the corner off the bag and drain off the liquid. Add the beans to the onion with the ham and toss well. Cook for 1 minute, then serve, sprinkled with chopped parsley.

Runner Beans in Garlic and Walnut Sauce

—— SERVES 4 ——

If you're looking for a new way to treat the annual abundance of runner beans, then try this recipe for a change. This vegetable dish would go well with a dish such as Veal Rolls (see page 80).

450 g/1 lb runner beans
4 tablespoons water
1 large onion, chopped
2 cloves garlic, crushed
50 g/2 oz butter

salt and freshly ground
   black pepper
50 g/2 oz walnut pieces,
   chopped

Trim, string and diagonally slice the beans, then place them in a roasting bag with the water. Secure the end loosely with an elastic band and cook on full power for 5 to 7 minutes, depending on how old or tough the beans are.

Place the onion, garlic and butter in a large basin and cook on full power for 5 minutes. Stir in the seasoning and nuts, then cook for 1 minute. Toss in the beans and cook for a further minute before serving.

Follow the cooking time in this recipe to cook plain runner beans. Drain the beans and add seasoning and butter to taste, then serve.

Sprouts with Almonds

—— SERVES 4 ——

This is a simple, traditional recipe, good with roast turkey in particular.

450 g/1 lb sprouts
2 tablespoons water
100 g/4 oz blanched
   almonds

50 g/2 oz butter
salt and freshly ground
   black pepper

Place the trimmed sprouts in a roasting bag with the water and cook on full power for 10 minutes.

Put the nuts and butter in a mug or small basin and cook for 4 minutes. Turn the sprouts into a serving dish and pour over the nuts and butter. Add seasoning to taste, then serve.

Sprouts with Chestnuts

—— SERVES 4 ——

This is a traditional recipe for Brussels sprouts and it makes an excellent accompaniment for the Christmas turkey.

225 g/8 oz chestnuts
1 small onion, finely
   chopped
50 g/2 oz butter
450 g/1 lb sprouts

2 tablespoons water
a little lemon juice
salt and freshly ground
   black pepper

Wash the chestnuts and make a slit in each one to thoroughly pierce the shell and inner skin. Rinse the nuts, then put them, still damp, in a basin. Cover with cling film, allowing a small gap for the steam to escape, then cook on full power for 5 minutes.

Place the onion and butter in a microwave-proof serving bowl and cook for 5 minutes. While the onion is cooking peel the chestnuts and set them aside. Put the sprouts in a roasting bag with the water, secure the bag loosely with an elastic band and cook for 10 minutes. Snip the corner off the bag and drain the sprouts over a bowl or the sink.

Stir the sprouts and chestnuts into the cooked onion. Cook for 1 minute, then sprinkle with a little lemon juice and season to taste. Serve while still hot.

Cooking chestnuts in the microwave oven is far easier than boiling them. The peeled chestnuts can be chopped or puréed for use in stuffings or for sweet dishes.

Asparagus Hollandaise

SERVES 4

This makes a good accompaniment to fish and poultry dishes, or it can be served with thinly sliced bread and butter for a light first course.

450 g/1 lb asparagus
2 tablespoons water
salt and freshly ground
   black pepper
1 quantity Hollandaise
   Sauce (page 201)

Garnish:
coarsely grated lemon
   rind
chopped watercress sprigs

Trim any woody parts off the asparagus stalks, wash them and place in a roasting bag. Add the water and secure the end of the bag loosely with an elastic band.

At this stage, make sure all the ingredients are ready to prepare the sauce so that the cooked asparagus is not sitting on the side while you are weighing out butter and the other ingredients.

Cook the asparagus on full power for 5 to 7 minutes, then close the end of the bag tightly while you cook the sauce. Drain the asparagus, then arrange the spears on a warmed serving platter. Sprinkle with a little seasoning (not too much salt) then pour the sauce over and add a garnish of lemon rind and watercress. Do not put too much on the sauce, just enough to add a little colour and enhance the flavour.

This recipe gives the basic cooking time for asparagus. You can use fresh asparagus in the Chicken and Asparagus Jalousie (see page 59) if you like; following the cooking time in this recipe and omit the canned vegetable from the jalousie.

Artichokes Provençale

———— SERVES 4 ————

This is a simple way of serving artichokes either for a first course or with plenty of hot crusty Granary bread for a light lunch or late supper.

4 globe artichokes
2 tablespoons lemon juice
8 tablespoons water
450 g/1 lb firm tomatoes
1 onion, chopped
2 tablespoons olive oil

1 clove garlic, crushed
salt and freshly ground
  black pepper
4 tablespoons chopped
  parsley

Trim any long thick stalks off the artichokes, then wash them thoroughly and shake the excess water out of the leaves. Snip the tips off the leaves (use a pair of kitchen scissors), then place the artichokes in a roasting bag and sprinkle in the lemon juice and water. Secure the opening loosely with an elastic band, then cook on full power for 20 to 25 minutes. To make sure the artichokes are cooked, try pulling off one of the leaves: it should come away fairly easily.

While the artichokes are cooking, peel the tomatoes (see page 123) and cut them in half. Remove all the seeds from inside and chop the flesh. Place the onion in a large basin with the oil and garlic. Stir well, then cook for 6 minutes.

Trim the artichokes while the onion is cooking. Remove the very large outer leaves around the base to give a neat shape. Carefully separate the leaves and pull out the cluster which covers the choke in the middle of the vegetable. By pulling this out the hairy, inedible choke should be removed but carefully take out any remaining bits without damaging the prime part – the artichoke bottom. The artichokes should still be fairly hot when this preparation is finished.

Add the seasoning to the onion and mix well, then stir in the tomatoes and cook for 3 minutes. Lightly stir in the parsley. Place the artichokes on individual serving plates and spoon the tomatoes into the middle. Serve at once; the filling will be hot and the artichoke bottoms will be warm to bring out their delicate flavour to the full.

Artichokes cook very well in the microwave oven, without having to engage vast pans of boiling water. Use the cooking instructions in this recipe as the basic cooking time for globe artichokes. If you want to cook two artichokes, then reduce the cooking time to about 15 minutes. Serving ideas: the cooked artichokes can be served with Hollandaise Sauce (see page 201) or Egg Sauce (see page 200). They can also be allowed to cool, then trimmed and served with a simple French salad dressing.

Leek and Bacon Flan

———— SERVES 4 TO 6 ————

In this recipe the pastry flan case is cooked in the conventional oven for a perfect result, meanwhile the creamy filling is prepared in the microwave. Once assembled the flan is quickly browned under the grill, so there is no lengthy second cooking time in the conventional oven and the flan is on the table ready for lunch or supper in half the time normally required.

Pastry:
225 g/8 oz plain flour
generous pinch of salt
100 g/4 oz margarine *or*
　　50 g/2 oz lard and 50 g/
　　2 oz margarine
2–3 tablespoons cold
　　water
Filling:
175 g/6 oz lean bacon
100 g/4 oz leeks

25 g/1 oz butter
3 tablespoons plain flour
300 ml/½ pint milk
salt and freshly ground
　　black pepper
freshly grated nutmeg
25 g/1 oz fresh
　　breadcrumbs
50 g/2 oz Caerphilly
　　cheese, finely crumbled

First make the pastry: sift the flour and salt into a bowl, then add the fat cut into small pieces. Rub the fat into the flour until the mixture resembles fine breadcrumbs. Gradually stir in the water so the mixture just binds together. Gather up the pastry with your fingertips and press it lightly together.

Turn the pastry out on to a lightly floured surface, knead it very lightly so it forms in a smooth ball, then roll it out to give a circle large enough to line a 23-cm/9-in flan dish. Lift the pastry by rolling it over a rolling pin, then unroll it on to the flan dish. Press the pastry neatly into the base of the dish and trim off any excess by rolling the rolling pin over the top of the dish. Don't be tempted to cut the pastry right back inside the rim as it will shrink during cooking and leave the sides too shallow. Prick the base all over with a fork and chill for as long as possible. If you like, the flan case can be prepared and covered with cling film the day before it is required.

To cook the flan case, place a piece of greaseproof paper in it, then sprinkle in dried peas or baking beans to cover the base. Cook in a moderately hot oven (200 C, 400 F, gas 6) for 15 minutes. Remove the greaseproof paper and peas, return the flan to the oven and cook for a further 15 to 20 minutes.

While the pastry is cooking prepare the filling. Cut the rind off the bacon and chop the rashers evenly. Trim and finely slice, then thoroughly wash and drain the leeks. Add these to the bacon with the butter and cook on full power for 8 minutes. Stir in the flour and milk, add seasoning to taste, then cook for a further 4 minutes. Season with nutmeg.

Pour the leek and bacon into the freshly cooked flan case. Mix the breadcrumbs with the cheese and seasoning, then sprinkle this evenly over the flan filling and cook under a hot grill until golden brown. Serve at once.

Leeks in Cider

———— SERVES 4 ————

4 leeks (choose ones
　　which are even in
　　length and not too
　　bushy, weighing about
　　575 g/1¼ lb)
150 ml/¼ pint medium dry
　　cider

salt and freshly ground
　　black pepper
25 g/1 oz butter
1 teaspoon cornflour
2 tablespoons water

Trim the ends off the leeks and remove any loose or damaged outer leaves. Thoroughly wash the leeks and lay them in a shallow dish – a lasagne or oval gratin dish is suitable. Pour in the cider and sprinkle in seasoning to taste, then dot with butter and cover the dish with cling film. Cook on full power for 10 minutes, turning the leeks over once during this time.

Blend the cornflour with the water, then stir this solution into the liquid surrounding the vegetables and cook for a further 3 minutes. Allow to stand for 2 minutes, then serve the leeks from the cooking dish.

To cook leeks very simply, trim, wash and slice them. Wash them again to make sure there is no grit between the layers, then drain them and place in a roasting bag with a knob of butter (about 25 g/1 oz). For 450 g/1 lb leeks allow 7 minutes on full power. Shake the bag once during cooking.

Courgettes Niçoise

———— SERVES 4 ————

These courgettes can be served for a light first course or they can be served to accompany simple main dishes.

8 small courgettes
1 large clove garlic,
　　crushed
4 tablespoons olive or
　　sunflower oil

450 g/1 lb tomatoes,
　　peeled (page 123)
salt and freshly ground
　　black pepper
plenty of chopped parsley

Trim the ends off the courgettes, then peel them very thinly. Place them in a roasting bag. Add the garlic and oil, then quarter the tomatoes and place them in the bag with the courgettes.

Secure the end of the bag loosely with an elastic band, then cook the courgettes on full power for 4 minutes. Gently turn the vegetables in the bag, replace them in the microwave and cook for a further 3 to 4 minutes. Add seasoning to taste to the cooked vegetables before turning them out on to one serving dish or individual dishes. Serve topped with plenty of chopped parsley.

Courgette Parcels

—————— SERVES 4 ——————

The microwave oven cooks courgettes well however they are prepared, but these packages really are superb. The greaseproof paper wrapping keeps in all the flavour of the courgettes and, when opened, the vegetables are delicious.

450 g/1 lb small courgettes, sliced	freshly ground white pepper
50 g/2 oz butter	4 herb sprigs – mint, parsley, basil or dill

First prepare four squares of double-thickness greaseproof paper, each measuring about 28 cm/11 in. The easiest way to prepare these is to cut out four oblong sheets measuring 28 × 56 cm/11 × 22 in, then fold them in half.

Trim the ends off the courgettes, wash the skins and slice the vegetables fairly thinly. Divide the courgettes between the squares of greaseproof paper, top with butter, add some pepper then a sprig of your chosen herb to each package. Fold the paper over the courgettes, folding the top down several times to seal them neatly. Fold the open ends several times, taking them tightly up to the courgettes.

Place the packages, slightly staggered in position, on a large plate. Cook on full power for 4 to 5 minutes. After 4 minutes, the courgettes will be crunchy and cooked, but allow the extra time if you prefer the vegetables quite soft.

Place one package on each of four small plates and take them to the table unopened. This standing time will allow the courgettes to complete their cooking.

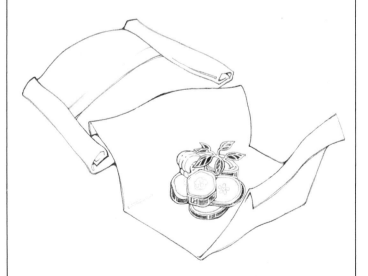

Stuffed Marrow

—————— SERVES 4 ——————

The microwave oven is truly amazing for cooking whole marrows! No longer do you have to put the stuffed vegetable in the oven for many hours, checking it, so many times in vain, to feel for the long awaited tenderness; now, in less than 20 minutes, you can cook a meat-stuffed marrow with greater flavour success than before. There is just one small, but very important, point to remember and that is the dimensions of your microwave oven. It's very easy to plan ahead a meal around this year's prize marrow but very disappointing when the wretched thing doesn't fit into the oven; so check first, particularly if you have a turntable in your microwave.

1 (2-kg/4¼-lb) marrow	1 teaspoon dried mixed herbs
2 large onions, chopped	freshly grated nutmeg
1 tablespoon oil	**Topping:** (optional)
675 g/1½ lb lean minced pork	50 g/2 oz fresh breadcrumbs
salt and freshly ground black pepper	50 g/2 oz Cheddar cheese, grated
1 (227-g 8-oz) packet frozen chopped spinach	
75 g/3 oz fresh breadcrumbs	

Slice a fairly thick cap off the marrow down its length to give a boat-shaped, deep portion ready for stuffing. Scoop out all the seeds and soft fibrous flesh around them.

Place the onions in a basin with the oil, then cook on full power for 5 minutes. Add the pork, breaking up the meat and stirring it with the onion. Stir in seasoning to taste and cook for 3 minutes.

Place the packet of frozen spinach on a plate and cook for 4 minutes. Snip a tiny hole in the corner of the packet and drain off the excess liquid, then add the spinach to the meat. Stir in the breadcrumbs and herbs, and add nutmeg to taste with a little extra seasoning.

Fill the marrow with the meat mixture, pressing it down well with the back of a spoon. Place the stuffed vegetable in a roasting bag and secure the end loosely with an elastic band. Cook for 10 to 12 minutes, turning the marrow round twice during cooking. The timing will vary slightly according to the shape of the marrow. The one I timed was evenly shaped and rounded at both ends and was cooked in 10 minutes.

If you like, mix the topping ingredients and place them on top of the filling, then brown the mixture under a hot grill. Serve at once.

Stuffed Marrow Rings

—— SERVES 4 ——

If you have a marrow that is too large to fit into your oven, then try cooking it in rings. These are filled with a delicious herby lentil and tomato mixture. When I set out to test a lentil filling I was not totally convinced but once I'd tasted it I decided that it was much more interesting than the usual mince.

4 (3.5-cm/1½-in) thick slices marrow (about 675 g/1½ lb in weight)
1 large onion, chopped
50 g/2 oz butter
225 g/8 oz lentils
300 ml/½ pint boiling water
salt and freshly ground black pepper
1 teaspoon dried mixed herbs
1 (400-g/14-oz) can chopped tomatoes
2 tablespoons creamed horseradish
Garnish:
lemon wedges and slices parsley sprigs

Peel the marrow rings and hollow out the seeds and soft fibrous flesh which surrounds them to leave neat rings.

Place the onion and half the butter in a basin (about 1.15-litre/2-pint capacity, but no smaller) and cook on full power for 3 minutes. Add the lentils and pour in the boiling water. Stir in seasoning to taste, the herbs and tomatoes, then cover with cling film, allowing a small gap for the steam to escape. Cook for 15 minutes by which time the lentils should be tender but still retain their shape.

Beat in the horseradish and remaining butter, taste and add more seasoning if necessary. Arrange the marrow rings as far apart as possible in a shallow dish (a gratin or quiche dish). Cover with cling film and cook for 7 to 8 minutes. Pile the lentil mixture into the rings, mounding it on top so that they are almost completely covered. Cook for 2 minutes, then garnish with lemon wedges and slices and parsley, arranged beside the marrow rings, and serve.

VARIATIONS

Additional ingredients can be stirred into the cooked lentil stuffing. For example, cook 4 to 6 rindless bacon rashers following the instructions on page 169. Chop the cooked bacon and stir it into the lentils with 50 g/2 oz grated Cheddar cheese. Top the stuffed marrow rings with a little grated cheese and cook them under a hot grill until browned.

Chicory and Ham Gratin

—— SERVES 4 ——

Chicory cooks very well in the microwave oven, I always find that by conventional cooking methods this vegetable requires lengthy cooking to tenderise the pieces to the middle, often leaving the outer leaves lacking in texture. So being able to microwave chicory will restore it to my repertoire of hot dishes and hopefully you will try it too.

4 pieces chicory (about 225 g/8 oz in weight)
1 tablespoon lemon juice
freshly ground black pepper
4 slices baked ham, trimmed of excess fat
50 g/2 oz fresh breadcrumbs
2 tablespoon chopped parsley
25 g/1 oz walnut pieces, chopped
about 25 g/1 oz butter

Wash and trim the chicory, then place the pieces in a shallow dish – a quiche dish is excellent. Sprinkle the lemon juice and pepper over, then cover with cling film, allowing a small gap for the steam to escape. Cook on full power for 4 minutes.

Roll each piece of chicory in a slice of ham, taking care not to burn your fingers. Arrange the rolls in the dish. Mix the breadcrumbs with the parsley and nuts, then spoon this topping down the middle of the rolls and dot with butter. Cook under a hot grill until browned and crisp, then serve at once.

When food is covered with cling film, the steam builds up and the cling film forms a vast 'balloon' which can burst, causing an alarming bang and defeating the object of covering the food in the first place. To prevent this happening a small gap is left in the top. However, if the food is to be cooked for only a short while, and if it is of a type which will not become very hot during that time, then there is no need to leave a gap, and often it is best not to do so.

Corn-on-the-cob

—— SERVES 2 ——

Served with butter, this corn can make a good first course as well as a vegetable accompaniment to grilled meats or barbecued foods.

2 cobs of corn, husks removed

2 tablespoons water
butter to serve

Place the corn in a roasting bag with the water and secure the end loosely with an elastic band. Cook on full power for 7 to 8 minutes. Allow to stand in the bag for 2 minutes, then serve with the butter.

Creamed Corn

—— SERVES 4 ——

This is a good way of turning simple sweet corn into a rather special side dish.

450 g/1 lb frozen sweet corn
2 tablespoons plain flour
salt and freshly ground black pepper

100 ml/4 fl oz milk
2 tablespoons dry sherry
50 g/2 oz butter

Place all the ingredients in a large bowl, stir thoroughly and cook on full power for 9 minutes, stirring once during cooking and again at the end of the cooking time. Allow to stand for 2 minutes before serving.

To cook from frozen, allow 10 minutes for the cobs of corn and do not put any water into the bag with them.

Aubergines with Tomatoes

—— SERVES 4 ——

These aubergines taste good hot, with meat or fish dishes, or, like ratatouille, they can be chilled before serving.

575 g/1¼ lb aubergines
salt and freshly ground black pepper
4 tablespoons olive oil
2 cloves garlic, crushed
1 (425-g/15-oz) can tomatoes

2 tablespoons lemon juice
2 tablespoons chopped fresh basin or
1 tablespoon dried basil

Trim the ends off the aubergines, then cut them into cubes. Place these in a colander and sprinkle liberally with salt, then set aside for 30 minutes. At the end of this time the vegetables must be thoroughly rinsed and dried on absorbent kitchen paper.

Place the aubergines in a casserole or suitable serving dish. Add the oil, garlic and tomatoes. Stir in the lemon juice with seasoning to taste. Add the dried basil if you cannot obtain fresh. Cover with cling film, allowing a small gap for the steam to escape, then cook on full power for 16 to 17 minutes, or until the aubergines are thoroughly cooked but not sludgy. If you intend serving the dish chilled, then allow only 15 minutes cooking time.

Stir the fresh basil into the aubergines and serve at once or cool and chill if preferred.

VARIATION
The cooked aubergines can be ladled into shallow individual serving dishes, then topped with grated cheese and grilled until brown.

Spiced Aubergines

———— SERVES 4 ————

These make a good accompaniment to curries and spiced main dishes.

675 g/1½ lb aubergines
salt and freshly ground
    black pepper
4 cloves garlic, crushed
2 tablespoons oil
2 tablespoons ground
    coriander

2 teaspoons curry powder
    (use a good-quality
    brand)
2 tablespoons lemon juice
Garnish:
lemon wedges
coriander sprigs

Trim the ends off the aubergines and cut the rest into chunks. Place these in a colander and sprinkle the pieces liberally with salt. Set aside in a sink, or over a large bowl, for 30 minutes.

Meanwhile, place the garlic, oil and spices in a large basin or bowl and cover with cling film. Cook on full power for 2 minutes. Stir in seasoning to taste and the lemon juice.

Drain, rinse and dry the aubergines, then add them to the spice mixture and mix well to coat all the pieces of vegetable. Re-cover the bowl and cook for 18 to 20 minutes. Stir the aubergines once during cooking.

Serve garnished with lemon wedges and fresh coriander sprigs.

Chorizos Flageolet

———— SERVES 4 ————

Serve this spicy bean and sausage mixture as a light supper or lunch dish, or have it with a main course instead of rice or pasta.

1 onion, chopped
1 tablespoon ground
    coriander
2 tablespoons oil

225 g/8 oz chorizo sausage
1 (425-g/15-oz) can
    flageolet beans

Place the onion in a bowl with the coriander and oil. Cut the chorizos into bite-shaped chunks and add these to the onion. Cover with cling film, allowing a small gap for the steam to escape, and cook on full power for 5 minutes.

Drain the beans and add them to the onion mixture, then cook for a further 4 minutes and serve. The sausage should be spicy enough to season the dish, so extra salt and pepper is unnecessary.

Note: you can use other canned beans in this dish—try red kidney beans or butter beans, or a combination of several different types.

Spicy Peas

———— SERVES 4 ————

This recipe turns boring old frozen peas into something rather exotic – a good vegetable accompaniment for curried fish or meat dishes, these peas are also useful for topping Pullao Rice (see page 129).

1 large onion, finely
    chopped
1 clove garlic, crushed
2 teaspoons mustard seeds
1 teaspoon ground
    coriander

1 teaspoon ground ginger
50 g/2 oz butter
350 g/12 oz frozen peas
salt and freshly ground
    black pepper

Place the onion in a basin (1.15-litre/2-pint capacity) or suitable serving dish. Add the garlic, mustard seeds, coriander and ginger. Top with the butter, cover with cling film and cook on full power for 4 minutes.

Stir in the peas and re-cover the dish, allowing a small gap for the steam to escape this time, then cook for a further 6 minutes. Stir thoroughly and add seasoning to taste then serve at once.

Creamed Lentils

———— SERVES 4 ————

These creamy, lightly spiced lentils are very good with curried dishes, or they can be served as part of a vegetarian menu.

1 onion, finely chopped
25 g/1 oz butter
salt and freshly ground
    black pepper
2 tablespoons ground
    coriander

225 g/8 oz red lentils
600 ml/1 pint water
150 ml/¼ pint single cream
2 tablespoons chopped
    fresh coriander

Place the onion in a large basin with the butter. Cook on full power for 3 minutes, then stir in the seasoning to taste and the coriander. Add the lentils and pour in the water. Stir well, then cover the basin with cling film and cook for 15 minutes.

Beat the lentils thoroughly and add the cream. Replace in the microwave for 2 minutes. Beat well and serve sprinkled with chopped fresh coriander.

Vegetable Curry

─── SERVES 4 TO 6 ───

You can use almost any type of vegetables you like in a curry, but do beware of creating an unidentifiable mixture of flavours. It is best to select a few vegetables which complement each other both in flavour and texture and try to include at least one type which will absorb the aroma of the spices – potatoes, aubergines or cauliflower for example.

The ones which I have used in the recipe below complement each other in flavour and texture, without being too mixed. If there are too many types included then the dish can seem like a vast pot of every leftover that could be found and the result can be a little off-putting! If you do decide to experiment with different vegetables, try to prepare the various types according to how they will cook in the microwave. For example, celery requires lengthy microwave cooking if it is not cut up into tiny pieces and courgettes could well become a purée if they are cooked for the same time as aubergines or onions. So give it a little thought and add the vegetables in different stages as necessary.

Serve the curry as the main dish for a vegetarian meal, with Creamed Lentils (see page 121) or as a side dish with spicy meat recipes.

1 small aubergine
salt and freshly ground
　black pepper
450 g/1 lb potatoes
225 g/8 oz carrots
2 sticks celery
25 g/1 oz fresh root
　ginger, grated
1 onion, finely chopped
2 green chillies, deseeded
　and finely chopped
2 cloves garlic, crushed
2 tablespoons ground
　coriander

2 teaspoons ground
　fenugreek
2 teaspoons ground cumin
4 cardamoms
2 tablespoons oil
225 g/8 oz cauliflower
　florets
1 (425-g/15-oz) can
　tomatoes
1 chicken or vegetable
　stock cube
150 ml/$\frac{1}{4}$ pint boiling
　water

Trim the ends off the aubergine, cut it into cubes and place these in a colander or sieve. Sprinkle liberally with salt, then set aside for 30 minutes. At the end of this standing time thoroughly rinse the aubergines, then dry the pieces on absorbent kitchen paper.

Cut the potatoes and carrots into cubes. Finely dice the celery. Mix the ginger, onion, chillies and garlic in a large bowl or large casserole. Add the spices and oil and mix thoroughly. Add the aubergines, potatoes, carrots and celery, tossing well to coat all the vegetables in the spice mixture. Cover the dish with cling film, allowing a small gap for the steam to escape, then cook on full power for 10 minutes, stirring once during cooking.

Add the cauliflower and tomatoes. Dissolve the stock cube in the boiling water and pour it over the vegetables, then mix well. Continue to cook for a further 15 minutes. Allow to stand for 2 to 3 minutes, mix together well, taste and adjust the seasoning then serve.

Ratatouille

Cooked in the microwave oven, ratatouille really is delicious; the flavour of each vegetable is brought out and the cooked dish certainly does not become an unidentifiable sludge. Serve the ratatouille hot or chilled, with the addition of chopped fresh garden herbs, like mint or rosemary, to suit the main dish. The ratatouille can also be served as a first course, with some warmed crusty bread.

450 g/1 lb aubergines
salt and freshly ground
   black pepper
1 red pepper
1 green pepper
1 large onion, chopped
2 large cloves garlic,
   crushed

150 ml/¼ pint olive oil, or
   sunflower oil if you
   prefer the flavour
450 g/1 lb firm ripe
   tomatoes
225 g/8 oz courgettes
plenty of chopped parsley
a little lemon juice

Trim the ends off the aubergines, then cut into chunks. Place these in a colander or sieve and sprinkle generously with salt. Set aside for 30 minutes, then rinse thoroughly and dry on absorbent kitchen paper.

While the aubergines are soaking in salt prepare the other ingredients. Trim the stalks off the peppers and remove all the seeds and pith from inside. Cut them into strips. Place the onion in a roasting bag with the peppers and garlic. Add the aubergines and pour in the oil, then secure the end of the bag loosely with an elastic band. Cook on full power for 5 minutes. Remove the bag from the oven, give it a good shake to rearrange all the ingredients, then replace it in the oven and cook for a further 6 to 7 minutes. A word of warning: the roasting bag will be *very* hot when you take it from the oven, so protect your hands with tea-towel while you are shaking up the ingredients.

While the aubergines are cooking, peel and quarter the tomatoes, then trim and slice the courgettes. Add these ingredients to the roasting bag – again take care when you open the bag as there will be an escape of very hot steam. Continue to cook for a further 5 minutes. Transfer the ratatouille to a serving dish and stir in the parsley with plenty of seasoning. Add a squeeze of lemon juice and serve at once, or cool then chill thoroughly.

To peel tomatoes: Place the tomatoes in a large bowl and pour in boiling water to cover them. Leave for 30 to 60 seconds depending on how ripe the fruit is, then drain and peel at once. Use a sharp knife to slit the skins and the rest should slide off easily.

Mushrooms à la Grecque

—— SERVES 4 ——

Serve these hot or cold, as a vegetable accompaniment or as a separate course to begin the meal.

450 g/1 lb button mushrooms
100 ml/4 fl oz olive oil
2 cloves garlic, crushed

salt and freshly ground black pepper
plenty of chopped parsley

Wipe and trim the mushrooms, then place them in a large bowl with the oil, garlic and plenty of seasoning. Cover and cook on full power for 5 minutes. Stir in the parsley and serve at once or cool and thoroughly chill the mushrooms before serving.

Stuffed Peppers

—— SERVES 4 ——

By cooking them in the microwave, the tender green or red peppers retain their bright colour and look particularly appetising. Serve these pork-stuffed peppers with Orange Rice (see page 128) and Creamed Spinach (see page 109); this combination makes a delicious meal.

1 onion, finely chopped
1 clove garlic, crushed
1 tablespoon oil
350 g/12 oz minced pork
salt and freshly ground black pepper

100 g/4 oz mushrooms, chopped
4 even-sized red or green peppers
50 g/2 oz fresh breadcrumbs

Place the onion, garlic and oil in a large basin and cook on full power for 3 minutes. Add the minced pork, breaking up the meat and mixing it with the onion, then stir in seasoning to taste and the mushrooms. Continue to cook for 5 minutes.

Cut the stalk ends off the peppers (reserve these), then scoop out all the seeds and pith from inside. Thoroughly wash and drain the shells.

Stir the breadcrumbs into the meat mixture, then spoon the filling into the prepared peppers. Stand the peppers in a dish – a medium-sized heatproof glass casserole dish is ideal as it should hold the peppers firmly in place a they cook. Replace the pepper tops and cover with cling film, allowing a small gap for the steam to escape. Cook for 10 minutes, then allow to stand for a few minutes before serving.

Ricotta Mushrooms with Green Sauce

—— SERVES 4 ——

Serve these stuffed mushrooms as the main course or as a starter, in which case they will serve six people rather than four. Alternatively you can always prepare fewer mushrooms – say 8 instead of 12 – and cook them for about 2 minutes less.

12 open mushrooms
350 g/12 oz ricotta cheese
4 teaspoons concentrated tomato purée
1 large clove garlic, crushed
freshly ground black pepper

Green Sauce:
2 ripe avocado pears
juice of 1 lemon
2 tablespoons chopped fresh basil
150 ml/¼ pint mayonnaise

Wipe and trim the stalks off the mushrooms, then arrange them on a large shallow serving dish.

Mix the ricotta with the tomato purée and the garlic. Add pepper and beat well until almost smooth. Pile this mixture into the mushrooms and cook on full power for 8 minutes, turning the dish round once.

For the sauce, halve, stone and peel the avocados, then remove the flesh. Mash the avocados with the lemon juice and remaining ingredients, then place the mixture in a small basin and cook for 6 minutes.

Serve the mushrooms, arrange on individual serving plates, with a little of the sauce poured over. Serve the remaining sauce separately.

Gratin of Creamed Mushrooms

———— SERVES 4 ————

Serve this creamy mushroom dish as an accompaniment to a main dish which has no sauce. Alternatively, offer the mushrooms as a first course, in which case hot crusty bread would go well with them.

50 g/2 oz butter
I small onion, very finely chopped
450 g/I lb small button mushrooms
salt and freshly ground black pepper
150 ml/¼ pint double cream

2 tablespoons chopped parsley
Topping:
50 g/2 oz fresh breadcrumbs
50 g/2 oz Lancashire cheese, finely crumbled or grated

Place the butter in a large basin or casserole with the onion and cook on full power for 6 minutes. Add the mushrooms, tossing them thoroughly, then cook for 3 minutes. Add seasoning to taste and pour in the cream, then cook for a further 5 minutes. Stir in the parsley at the end of the cooking time.

Mix the breadcrumbs and cheese for the topping, then sprinkle them over the mushrooms and put the dish under a hot grill until the crust is golden brown. Serve at once.

Sesame Vegetable Strips

———— SERVES 4 ————

Simply cooked, with a seasoning of soy sauce and sesame oil, these vegetables go well with any Chinese dish or they taste equally good with other simple main courses – grilled chicken or fish for example.

I large leek
2 celery sticks
I large carrot
a few drops of sesame oil
2 tablespoons corn oil

I (540-g/I-lb 3-oz) can bamboo shoots
2 tablespoons soy sauce
I tablespoon sesame seeds

Cut the leek into 5-cm/2-in lengths, then cut these in half. Place the pieces cut side down on a board and slice them lengthways into fine strips. Wash them thoroughly to remove any grit, then dry the leek and place it in a bowl. Cut the celery and carrot into similar strips and add these to the leek. Pour in the oils and toss well, then cook on full power for 5 minutes.

Meanwhile, drain the bamboo shoots and cut them into fine strips. Stir these into the other vegetables with the soy sauce. Sprinkle the sesame seeds over the vegetables and cook for a final 3 minutes. Do not stir the vegetables – this way the sesame seeds stay on top.

Simple Chop Suey

———— SERVES 4 ————

This is a light vegetable dish to serve with Chinese dishes or it goes well with grilled meats and poultry. Try using a combination of canned oriental vegetables and fresh ingredients to make a more interesting side dish if you like.

I small onion
2 sticks celery
2 carrots
50 g/2 oz button mushrooms
2 tablespoons oil

I clove garlic, crushed
a few drops of sesame oil
salt and freshly ground black pepper
225 g/8 oz bean sprouts
2 tablespoons dry sherry

Slice the onion very finely, then cut the slices in half and separate them into shreds. Place these in a bowl or suitable microwave proof serving dish. Finely shred the celery and carrots and add them to the onion. Finely slice the mushrooms and set these aside. Stir the oil and garlic into the onion mixture, cover the bowl with cling film, then cook on full power for 5 minutes.

Stir the mushrooms, sesame oil and seasoning to taste into the vegetables and cook for a further 2 minutes. Finally, add the bean sprouts and sherry, then cook for 4 minutes before serving.

Beef Chop Suey

———— SERVES 4 ————

Serve this oriental vegetable and beef dish with plain rice, Egg Fried Rice (see page 137) or as part of a more extensive Chinese meal.

350 g/12 oz frying steak
I teaspoon monosodium glutamate (optional)
I teaspoon sesame oil
2 tablespoon soy sauce
25 g/I oz fresh root ginger, finely shredded

I large carrot
I (227-g/8-oz) can water chestnuts, drained
I (227-g/8 oz) can bamboo shoots, drained
225 g/8 oz bean sprouts

Trim any fat off the steak and cut it across the grain into fine strips. Place these in a suitable casserole dish or large bowl and add the monosodium glutamate (if used), sesame oil and soy sauce. Cover and set aside to marinate for 2 to 3 hours, or longer if you have the time.

Trim the carrot, then cut it into fine strips. Slice the water chestnuts and bamboo shoots. Add the carrots to the meat, then cook on full power for 8 minutes, stirring once during cooking. Add the remaining ingredients and cook for a further 5 minutes. Toss well and serve at once.

RICE & PASTA

The advantages of cooking rice in the microwave oven centre not around speed but more on efficiency. All types of rice can be prepared in the microwave oven either on their own or as part of any number of dishes.

How often have you cooked rice in a saucepan of boiling water (not the super-processed, easy cook type of grain) taking great care about all the quantities and not to stir the grains as they cook, only to find that some of the wretched stuff has stuck to the bottom? Because the cooking vessel does not heat in the microwave oven there is no danger of the rice sticking to it or burning.

The best sort of container to use for average quantities of rice is a large basin or mixng bowl. If you are cooking enough rice for just one or two people, then you can cook it in a heatproof glass measuring jug. For a real saving on washing up, if you have a suitable serving dish or a large decorative bowl, then rice and many of the rice dishes in this chapter can be cooked and served in the one container.

So what about pasta? Well, unlike rice, it is not really worth cooking pasta in the microwave oven. As you have probably read so many times, large quantities of liquid take a long time to heat up in the microwave oven and pasta really does need to be cooked in a lot of water. You can, if you like, use a large mixing bowl full of water to cook the pasta, but it is slow, difficult to handle and a waste of your microwave.

However, while the pasta is bubbling away on top of the hob you can conjure up all sorts of clever sauces and accompaniments in the microwave. Do something really simple with melted butter and garlic, or olive oil and herbs, if you like, then toss in the drained pasta. Alternatively, try some of the sauces and combinations in this chapter; a Spaghetti Marinara (see page 139) made with fresh mussels, if you like, or Tuna Conchiglie that burst with flavour (see page 143). If you really are looking for an old favourite, then try Macaroni Cheese (see page 141) – you may even be persuaded to play a few tricks to enliven it a little.

For the popular pasta combination dishes – lasagnes and cannelloni creations – you will find that the microwave oven is a real help. The different sauces always seem to produce dozens (well, I exaggerate, two or three) of dirty saucepans when they are prepared conventionally. You will still have bowls to wash, but they are never quite as daunting. Once the pasta is assembled a quick flash under the grill is all it needs to finish off a mouthwatering dish.

With the selection of dishes in this chapter tucked firmly up your sleeve, you'll be able to cope with the most demanding of families, a host of guests at party time or the most sophisticated of simple supper parties.

Plain Cooked Rice

One of the main advantages of cooking rice in the microwave is that it can be cooked and served in the same dish. Generally, it is no quicker to cook rice in the microwave than on the hob, but there is less effort involved because there is no need to watch over it until it reaches boiling point.

225 g/8 oz long-grain rice (white)

600 ml/1 pint water
½ teaspoon salt

Place the rice in a large basin or bowl. Pour in the water (cold) and stir in the salt. Cover with cling film, allowing a small gap for the steam to escape, and cook on full power for 15 minutes. Leave the rice to stand for 5 minutes, then fluff up the grains with a fork before serving.

RICE IDEAS

Lemon or Orange Rice Add the grated rind of 1 large lemon or orange to the rice with the salt. Cook as above. Lemon-flavoured rice is good with fish dishes while orange rice goes very well with both lamb and pork.

Herb Rice Add chopped fresh herbs to the cooked rice. Use a herb to complement the main dish or simply use a mixture of several different herbs. As a rough guide, parsley and dill will go well with fish; sage and rosemary taste good with pork; mint or rosemary can be served with lamb; and chives are good with cheese or egg dishes. If you are using a selection of herbs balance the stronger ones with the more delicate flavours: for example, use smaller quantities of sage, thyme and rosemary than dill, marjoram (fresh) and parsley.

Rice with Almonds Cook the rice as in the main recipe. Put 50 g/2 oz flaked almonds in a small basin with 50 g/2 oz butter. Cover with cling film and allow 4 minutes on full power. Toss the browned almonds and the butter into the cooked rice.

Rice with Tomatoes Peel and halve 450 g/1 lb tomatoes, then remove all their seeds and chop the flesh. Stir the tomatoes into the rice 1 minute before the end of the cooking time.

Coconut Rice Soak 100 g/4 oz desiccated coconut in 600 ml/1 pint boiling water until cold, then strain the liquid and squeeze all the water out of the coconut. Use this coconut milk to cook the rice (measure it first to make sure there is a full pint and add more water if necessary). Coconut rice tastes excellent with curries.

Saffron Rice Pound ¼ teaspoon saffron strands with a pestle and mortar. Pour in a little boiling water, then make this liquid up to 600 ml/1 pint and use to cook the rice. Serve with curries, spicy dishes or fish and chicken.

Yellow Rice Add ½ teaspoon turmeric to the rice. This gives a strong colour and flavour to the rice.

Brown Rice

—— SERVES 4 ——

225 g/8 oz brown rice
750 ml/1¼ pints water

1 teaspoon salt (or to taste)

Place the rice in a bowl or large basin, then pour in the water and stir in the salt. Cover with cling film, allowing a small gap for the steam to escape, then cook on full power for 25 minutes. Allow the rice to stand for 3 to 4 minutes before serving.

Note: to cook 100 g/4 oz brown rice use 350 ml/12 fl oz water and ½ teaspoon salt and cook as above.

Sunflower Rice

—— SERVES 4 ——

This lively mixture of well-textured brown rice, fresh herbs and slightly crunchy, cooked sunflower seeds makes a particularly delicious accompaniment to moist main dishes. It also forms a base for a delicious rice salad to which you can add all sorts of fresh vegetables – cooked and raw – as well as fish, poultry or eggs.

50 g/2 oz sunflower seeds
50 g/2 oz butter
1 small onion, chopped
225 g/8 oz brown rice
750 ml/1¼ pints water
1 teaspoon salt (or to taste)

4 tablespoons chopped parsley
2 tablespoons chopped mixed fresh herbs – for example, thyme, basil, marjoram, sage, chives or lemon balm

Place the sunflower seeds in a mug and top them with half the butter, then cook on full power for 4 minutes. Remove from the oven and set the seeds aside.

Place the remaining butter in a bowl or large basin with the onion and cook on full power for 3 minutes. Add the rice and pour in the water, then stir in the salt and cover the bowl with cling film, allowing a small gap for the steam to escape. Cook for 25 minutes, or until the rice is tender.

Quickly stir the herbs into the rice and allow it to stand for a few minutes, so that their flavour will be absorbed with the moisture remaining on the grains. Stir in the sunflower seeds just as you are serving the rice, this way they will remain crunchy.

Basmati Rice

—— SERVES 4 ——

Basmati rice has a superb scent and flavour and it is the best rice to serve with curries and spiced dishes. The grains are first washed but it is important that they are not damaged at this stage, so they must not be ground against each other with your fingers or shaken violently in a colander.

225 g/8 oz basmati rice
600 ml/1 pint water
a little salt

Place the rice in a large basin or bowl and pour in plenty of cold water. Swirl the water round the rice, then drain it off and add more water to cover the grains. Carefully run your fingers through the grains to remove the excess starch, but do not handle the rice roughly. Drain the rice thoroughly in a sieve, then replace it in the bowl and pour in the measured water. Add a pinch of salt and cover with cling film, allowing a small gap for the steam to escape. Cook on full power for 23 to 25 minutes. Leave the covered rice to stand for 4 minutes, then carefully fluff up the grains to serve.

It is important to find the right cooking vessel for preparing rice in the microwave oven. Unlike on a conventional hob, the liquid froths up, so the dish you use must be large enough to contain the rice with its liquid, without boiling over at all. However, if the container is too broad, the rice will not be generously covered with liquid during cooking so the surface grains may dry out as the water is absorbed. Therefore, ideally, the vessel should be deep without being too broad. A measuring jug is ideal for small quantities of rice, but for average portions it does not contain the liquid as it froths up. So select a deep bowl which is not too wide – a mixing bowl or deep soufflé dish will do very well.

Pullao Rice

—— SERVES 4 ——

1 onion, chopped
1 cinnamon stick
1 bay leaf
4 cardamoms
50 g/2 oz ghee or butter
225 g/8 oz basmati rice
salt and freshly ground
  black pepper
600 ml/1 pint water
¼ teaspoon saffron strands
a little boiling water

Place the onion in a large basin or bowl with the cinnamon stick, bay leaf and cardamoms. Add the ghee (clarified butter, also available in the form of a vegetable fat) or butter and cook on full power for 4 minutes.
    Wash the rice thoroughly, without damaging the grains at all. Drain the rice and add it to the onion with seasoning to taste and the water. Cover with cling film and cook for 20 minutes.
    While the rice is cooking, pound the saffron strands in a pestle and mortar until they are reduced to a powder. Add a little boiling water, then sprinkle this solution over the rice, lightly forking it in, but not mixing the grains too much. Cook for a further 3 to 5 minutes, then allow to stand for 4 minutes before serving.

Rich Fruit Pullao

—— SERVES 4 ——

25 g/1 oz flaked almonds
50 g/2 oz raisins
50 g/2 oz dried apricots
  (the type which do not
  require pre-soaking)
50 g/2 oz butter
1 quantity Pullao Rice (see
  above)
2 tablespoons chopped
  fresh coriander leaves

Place the almonds and raisins in a small basin. Chop the apricots, then add them to the raisin and almond mixture. Top with the butter and cook on full power for 4 minutes. Remove from the oven and set aside.
    Prepare the pullao according to the recipe instructions. When it is cooked, pour the fruit and nut mixture over the rice and carefully fork it into the pullao. Sprinkle with the coriander and serve at once.

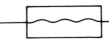

To cook 100 g/4 oz rice (either ordinary rice or basmati rice) allow half the quantities of water and salt but cook the rice for the same length of time. This quantity will serve two.

Paella

——— SERVES 4 ———

This traditional rice and seafood mixture cooks very well in the microwave oven. If you want to use fresh mussels when they are in season, follow the cooking instructions for Moules à la Marinière (see page 51) using water instead of wine. Cook the mussels before the paella, then strain their cooking juices and use this liquor with boiling water to make up the quantity of stock given in the recipe below.

1 red pepper	225 g/8 oz long-grain rice
225 g/8 oz carrots	2 chicken thighs
1 large onion	salt and freshly ground
4 tablespoons olive oil	black pepper
2 large cloves garlic,	225 g/8 oz peeled cooked
crushed	prawns
½ teaspoon saffron strands	100 g/4 oz frozen peas
450 ml/¾ pint plus 2	225 g/8 oz frozen mussels
tablespoons boiling	a few whole cooked
water	prawns to garnish
1 chicken stock cube	

Cut the stalk end off the pepper, then scoop out all the seeds and pith from inside. Cut the flesh into fine strips. Slice the carrots and chop the onion, then mix all these vegetables in a large bowl with the oil. Add the garlic and cook on full power for 5 minutes.

Meanwhile, pound the saffron strands in a pestle and mortar until they are completely crushed. Mix in the 2 tablespoons boiling water. Dissolve the stock cube in the larger quantity of water (use less water and the reserved mussel liquor to make up the amount if you have cooked fresh mussels).

Stir the rice into the vegetables and add the chicken. Stir in seasoning to taste, then pour in the saffron and stock. Cover and cook for 10 minutes.

Remove the chicken from the bowl and cut all the meat off the bones, then roughly chop it and return it to the bowl. Add the prawns, peas and frozen mussels and stir well to mix all the ingredients. If you are using fresh mussels, then add them about 2 minutes before the end of the cooking time. Cook the paella, covered, for a further 15 minutes, then allow to stand for 3 to 4 minutes before serving. Toss the whole prawns into the rice mixture as it is served.

Note: you can make a paella as elaborate as you wish, depending on how extravagant you feel in your use of seafood. Add, for example, prepared fresh scallops, cut into slices. Stir these with the prawns and frozen peas. If you like, preserved squid (available in jars) and cockles can also be included and these should be added about 3 minutes before the end of the cooking time.

The microwave is useful for heating all sorts of convenience foods – canned soup, pasta products, rice and sauces.

Chicken Risotto

SERVES 4

1 large onion, chopped	1 chicken stock cube
1 red pepper	salt and freshly ground
1 green pepper	black pepper
1 clove garlic, crushed	100 g/4 oz button
4 tablespoons oil	mushrooms, sliced
4 boneless chicken breasts	225 g/8 oz tomatoes
225 g/8 oz long-grain rice	plenty of chopped parsley
600 ml/1 pint boiling	freshly grated Parmesan
water	cheese to serve

Place the onion in a large serving dish or mixing bowl. Cut the stalk ends off the peppers and remove all the seeds and pith from inside. Chop the pepper shells and add them to the onion. Stir in the garlic and oil then cook on full power for 5 minutes.

Cut the chicken breasts into bite-sized pieces, then add these to the onion and pepper mixture and cook for a further 5 minutes. Stir in the rice and boiling water, then add the crumbled stock cube. Stir in seasoning to taste, but be careful not to add too much salt as stock cubes are normally quite salty. Cover with cling film, allowing a small gap for the steam to escape, then cook for 20 minutes.

While the risotto is cooking, peel the tomatoes (see page 123) and chop them roughly. Add these with the mushrooms to the risotto, re-cover and cook for a further 5 minutes. Fork up the rice and add the chopped parsley, then serve with plenty of Parmesan cheese.

Chicken and Cashew Risotto Stir 50 g/2 oz salted cashew nuts into the risotto just before it is served.

Chicken Risotto with Salami Buy 225 g/8 oz salami in one piece, then remove its skin and cut it into small cubes. Stir these into the risotto about 2 minutes before the end of the cooking time.

Chicken and Ricotta Risotto Break 225 g/8 oz ricotta cheese into chunks and add these to the risotto just before it is served. Sprinkle with plenty of freshly chopped basil — delicious!

Chicken Biriani

——— SERVES 4 ———

A biriani is a spiced rice dish cooked with meat or fish. It forms a meal in itself and is useful for a quick supper.

I large onion, chopped	2 tablespoons garam
2 tablespoons oil	masala
2 tablespoons grated fresh	225 g/8 oz basmati rice
root ginger	4 tablespoons chopped
2 cloves garlic, crushed	fresh coriander
4 boneless chicken breasts	750 ml/1¼ pints boiling
salt and freshly ground	water
black pepper	I chicken stock cube

Place the onion in a large bowl with the oil. Stir in the ginger and garlic, then cook on full power for 5 minutes.

Cut the chicken into bite-sized pieces, then add these to the onion mixture with the seasoning to taste and the garam masala. Cover with cling film, allowing a small gap for the steam to escape, then cook for 5 minutes.

Thoroughly wash the basmati rice, taking care not to damage the grains. Drain and add the rice to the chicken, stirring well. Stir in the coriander and pour in the boiling water. Crumble in the stock cube and cover as before with cling film. Cook for 25 to 27 minutes. At the end of the cooking time, fork up the grains and serve at once, with Spicy Raita (below).

Spicy Raita

I small cucumber	150 ml/¼ pint natural
I–2 green chillies	yogurt
I tablespoon chopped	
mint	

Peel and dice the cucumber, then place it in a colander and sprinkle generously with salt. Leave for 30 minutes before rinsing the salt off. Dry the pieces of cucumber on absorbent kitchen paper and place in a serving bowl.

Cut the stalk ends off the chillies, then remove all the seeds from inside and chop the green part very finely. Mix the chillies into the cucumber with the mint, then pour in the yogurt and chill lightly before serving.

Peanut Risotto

——— SERVES 4 ———

This was one of my favourite dishes when I was a student, mainly because it was particularly cheap to make and offered what I considered was a sensible amount of protein for very little cash!

I large onion, chopped	100 g/4 oz frozen peas
I red pepper	100 g/4 oz frozen sweet
2 tablespoons oil	corn
2 cloves garlic, crushed	100 g/4 oz roasted peanuts
225 g/8 oz long-grain rice	2 tablespoons chopped
600 ml/1 pint chicken	parsley
stock or water	
salt and freshly ground	
black pepper	

Place the onion in a large bowl. Cut the stalk end off the pepper, then remove the seeds and pith from inside and chop the pepper shell. Mix the pepper, oil and garlic into the onion and cook for 4 minutes on full power.

Stir in the rice and stock or water and add a little seasoning, then cover with cling film, allowing a small gap for the steam to escape. Cook for 15 minutes. Add the peas and sweet corn and cook for a further 10 minutes.

Add the peanuts and parsley and fork these ingredients into the rice, then serve in individual bowls.

Vegetable Risotto

——— SERVES 4 ———

I large onion, chopped	750 ml/1¼ pints water
I red pepper	I vegetable or chicken
2 carrots, diced	stock cube
50 g/2 oz butter	salt and freshly ground
I clove garlic, crushed	black pepper
225 g/8 oz cauliflower	plenty of chopped fresh
florets	parsley
225 g/8 oz frozen cut	freshly grated Parmesan
French beans	cheese to serve
225 g/8 oz brown rice	

Place the onion in a large bowl. Cut the stalk end off the pepper, then remove all the seeds and pith from inside and chop the red shell. Add this to the onion and stir in the carrots. Top with the butter and cover with cling film, allowing a gap for the steam to escape, and cook on full power for 5 minutes.

Add the garlic. Break the cauliflower into small pieces and add these to the onion mixture. Stir in the beans and rice, pour in the water and crumble in the stock cube. Add a little seasoning and re-cover with cling film, again allowing a gap for the steam to escape. Cook for 30 minutes.

To serve, allow the rice to stand for 3 to 4 minutes at the end of the cooking time, then fork in the parsley – add plenty – and serve with Parmesan cheese.

Mackerel Kedgeree

——— SERVES 4 ———

This is a very quick recipe for kedgeree – using smoked mackerel instead of haddock. Serve it for breakfast or as a lunch or supper dish.

I large onion, chopped	450 g/1 lb smoked
50 g/2 oz butter	mackerel fillets
grated rind of 1 lemon	4 tablespoons chopped
225 g/8 oz long-grain rice	parsley
½ teaspoon turmeric	4 eggs
600 ml/1 pint water	lemon wedges to garnish
I chicken stock cube	

Place the onion in a large bowl with the butter and lemon rind. Cook on full power for 4 minutes, then stir in the rice and turmeric. Pour in the water and crumble in the stock cube. Cover with cling film, allowing a small gap for the steam to escape, and cook on full power for 20 minutes.

While the rice is cooking, flake the fish off its skin and mix it with the parsley. Cook the eggs in a saucepan of boiling water on the hob for 10 minutes. Drain and plunge them into cold water. Stir the fish and parsley mixture into the rice and cook, covered, for a further 5 minutes. Allow to stand for 4 minutes. Shell and roughly chop the eggs, then stir them into the kedgeree. Serve garnished with lemon wedges.

Traditional Kedgeree Use 450 g/1 lb smoked haddock fillet. Skin the fish (see page 20) and cut the flesh into large chunks. Add the fish to the rice when it has had 5 minutes cooking time. Arrange the fish on top of the rice, in the liquid, but do not stir it in at this stage. Stir the fish into the rice when you add the eggs.

Nasi Goreng

——— SERVES 4 ———

This is an Indonesian fried rice dish, slightly hot with chillies and flavoured with dried shrimps. These are available from Indian or oriental food stores. Before use wash them thoroughly.

3 tablespoons dried	225 g/8 oz long-grain rice
shrimps	salt and freshly ground
I large onion, chopped	black pepper
2 cloves garlic, crushed	I chicken stock cube
3 green chillies	600 ml/1 pint boiling
4 tablespoons oil	water
350 g/12 oz lean boneless	25 g/1 oz butter
pork	2 eggs, beaten

Thoroughly wash and drain the shrimps, then place them in a basin and cover with hot water. Set aside to soak for 15 minutes. Place the onion and garlic in a large bowl. Cut the stalk end off the chillies, then remove all the seeds from inside and chop the green part. Add this to the onion and stir in the oil. Cook on full power for 3 minutes. Meanwhile, cut the pork into fine strips. Add this to the cooked onion with the rice and seasoning to taste, then cook for a further 5 minutes.

Dissolve the stock cube in the boiling water. Drain and chop the shrimps, then add them to the rice and pour in the stock. Stir well and cook, covered with cling film, for 20 minutes. Allow to stand for 5 minutes at the end of the cooking time.

During the standing time, melt the butter in a frying pan on the hob and pour in the eggs. Cook until golden on the underneath and turn over, then cook until golden on the second side. Cut this omelette into strips, then quickly toss them into the nasi goreng and serve at once.

Lamb Pilaff

——— SERVES 4 ———

I onion, chopped	salt and freshly ground
2 cloves garlic, crushed	black pepper
2 tablespoons oil	600 ml/1 pint water
450 g/1 lb minced lamb	2 tablespoons
I bay leaf	concentrated tomato
4 green cardamoms	purée
I cinnamon stick	**Garnish:**
2 tablespoons ground	4 hard-boiled eggs,
coriander	quartered
225 g/8 oz basmati rice	fresh coriander leaves

Place the onion in a large mixing bowl with the garlic and oil. Stir in the lamb, breaking up the mince. Add the bay leaf, cardamoms and cinnamon stick and cook on full power for 5 minutes. Stir in the coriander.

Wash the rice, treating the grains gently, then drain it thoroughly and add it to the onion. Add seasoning to taste and pour in the water. Stir in the tomato purée and cover with cling film, allowing a small gap for the steam to escape. Cook for 25 to 27 minutes, carefully stirring the rice and meat once.

Allow to stand for a few minutes, then serve garnished with the hard-boiled eggs and coriander.

Fruited Pork Risotto

—— SERVES 4 ——

The combination of full-flavoured Mediterranean herbs, tangy orange and sweet apricots work wonders for some minced pork and rice in this simple dish. Serve a garlic-dressed tomato salad with the risotto.

1 onion, chopped
450 g/1 lb lean minced
   pork
salt and freshly ground
   black pepper
1 green pepper
225 g/8 oz long-grain rice
100 g/4 oz dried apricots
   (the type which do not
   require pre-soaking)

grated rind of 1 orange
1 chicken stock cube
600 ml/1 pint boiling
   water
1 tablespoon oregano
orange slices to garnish

Place the onion in a large bowl with the pork. Add seasoning to taste, then break up the meat. Cut the stalk end off the pepper and remove all the seeds and pith from inside. Chop the pepper flesh and add it to the meat. Cook on full power for 10 minutes.

Add the rice to the pork and mix it in thoroughly. Roughly chop the apricots, or cut them up with scissors, and add them to the risotto. Stir in the orange rind. Dissolve the stock cube in the boiling water, then pour it into the bowl and add the oregano. Stir to make sure the ingredients are thoroughly mixed.

Cover the bowl with cling film, allowing a small gap for the steam to escape, then cook for 25 minutes, stirring once during cooking. Roughly fork the ingredients and serve garnished with orange slices.

Other fruit combinations which complement this risotto:

Pineapple and Raisin Use pineapple chunks canned in natural juice (drained) and seedless raisins (not too many or they will overpower the dish).

Mango and Lemon Rind Add drained, canned or fresh mango slices and grated lemon rind just before you serve the risotto.

Ham and Fennel Risotto

—— SERVES 4 ——

Fibrous vegetables like fennel and celery require lengthy cooking in the microwave oven unless they are cut finely before cooking. In this risotto the fennel is chopped and it cooks quickly to impart a delicious flavour to the combination of ham and rice. A simple green or tomato salad is the only accompaniment which is needed for this dish.

175 g/6 oz fennel
1 onion
1 small red pepper
3 tablespoons olive oil
450 g/1 lb cooked ham
2 chicken stock cubes
750 ml/1¼ pints boiling
   water

350 g/12 oz long-grain rice
salt and freshly ground
   black pepper
4 tablespoons chopped
   parsley
fennel sprigs to garnish

Trim and finely chop the fennel. Chop the onion. Halve the pepper, remove all the seeds and stalk, then cut it into small dice. Place these prepared ingredients in a large bowl with the oil. Cover with cling film, allowing a small gap for the steam to escape, and cook on full power for 5 minutes.

Meanwhile, cut the ham into small cubes. Dissolve the stock cubes in the boiling water. Stir the ham, stock and rice into the fennel mixture with plenty of freshly ground black pepper and a little salt. Cover the bowl with cling film, allowing a small gap for the steam to escape, then cook for 22 to 24 minutes, stirring once during cooking.

At the end of the cooking time gently fork the parsley into the rice which should be slightly moist, not completely dry. Allow to stand for 5 minutes before serving garnished with fennel sprigs.

Vegetable Risottos A risotto is an excellent dish for using up small quantities of fresh vegetables or leftover cooked ones. Try using celery (very finely chopped), carrots, French beans, broccoli, cauliflower, canned artichoke hearts and peppers. Cut all the ingredients up fairly finely and cook them with an onion and butter for about 5 minutes before you add the rice. Use a vegetable stock cube if you are preparing a vegetarian meal, otherwise use a chicken cube. You can use brown rice if you like. The addition of herbs is almost essential and cooked ham, bacon or nuts are also tasty ingredients to include.

Spanish Rice

——— SERVES 4 ———

This is a colourful rice accompaniment to serve with meat fish or poultry dishes. It goes particularly well with dishes which have a lot of sauce.

1 large red pepper	225 g/8 oz long-grain rice
1 large green pepper	salt and freshly ground
1 large onion, chopped	black pepper
2 cloves garlic, crushed	600 ml/1 pint water
4 tablespoons oil	50 g/2 oz stuffed green
100 g/4 oz black olives,	olives, sliced
stoned	

Cut the stalk ends off the peppers, then remove all the seeds and pith from inside. Rinse and dry the peppers, then cut the shells into dice. Mix the peppers, onion, garlic and oil in a large bowl and cook on full power for 5 minutes.

Meanwhile, roughly chop the black olives. Add these to the peppers with the rice and seasoning to taste. Pour in the water and cover the bowl with cling film, allowing a small gap for the steam to escape. Cook for 20 minutes. Add the stuffed green olives and re-cover the bowl, then cook for a final 5 minutes. Allow to stand for 5 minutes, then fork the rice to fluff up the grains. Serve at once.

Rice Ring This recipe for Spanish rice is also good served cold. Press the freshly cooked rice mixture firmly into a ring dish and cover it immediately with cling film. Leave the rice to cool, then chill it in the refrigerator. To serve, turn the rice out on to a flat platter and fill the middle with a main course salad – cooked chicken in a mayonnaise dressing, tuna fish salads or similar – or simply garnish the rice with watercress leaves. Serve at once.

Rice with Chinese Sausages

——— SERVES 4 ———

I am sure this recipe may sound very obscure if you are not familiar with Chinese food, and it may be a strange idea to include it in a general microwave cookbook; however, I offer it to anyone who is lucky enough to be able to find Chinese sausages because they cook so very well in the microwave oven.

This is a book about getting the best out of your microwave and if you like Chinese food, then you really can utilise the microwave oven for some rather exciting recipes. Chinese sausages are dried (*wind dried* is the term used) and quite spicy. Because they are dried these sausages need to be cooked over a steaming liquid, by moist heat, not in a conventional oven. They are available from Chinese supermarkets, often found tucked away in corners of large towns and cities.

Serve the cooked rice and sausages with Gingered Pork (see page 93) and Peking Duck (see page 72) for a real feast.

225 g/8 oz long-grain rice	4 spring onions, shredded
600 ml/1 pint water	2 eggs, beaten
4 dried Chinese sausages	a little soy sauce.

Put the rice in a large bowl with the water. Cover with cling film and cook on full power for 10 minutes. Lay the sausages on top and cook for a further 7 minutes. Sprinkle the spring onions over and set aside.

Heat a little oil in a frying pan on the hob, then pour in the eggs and cook until golden underneath; turn and cook the second side until golden. Remove the omelette from the pan and cut it into shreds. Remove the sausages from the rice and slice these diagonally. Fork the spring onions into the rice with a sprinkling of soy sauce (to taste). Mix the sausages and omelette and pile it on top of the rice to serve.

Note: because the sausages used in the above recipe are dried they can be stored quite successfully for several months in an airtight plastic bag in the bottom of the refrigerator. There are different types of wind-dried sausages and some contain a fair portion of offal. Price is usually a reasonable guide to quality.

Saucy Rice

——— SERVES 4 ———

This is a good supper dish which can be made from any leftovers you like. I have used cooked chicken, mushrooms and sweet corn in this version, but you could try cooked ham, peas, French beans, roughly chopped hard-boiled eggs, cooked pork or beef or any cold cooked vegetables. Add chopped herbs which are in season and serve with plenty of crusty bread.

1 large onion, chopped	225 g/8 oz cooked chicken
50 g/2 oz butter	100 g/4 oz button
225 g/8 oz long-grain rice	mushrooms, sliced
600 ml/1 pint water	100 g/4 oz sweet corn
1 chicken stock cube	2 tablespoons chopped
1 quantity Béchamel	fresh herbs (whatever is
Sauce (page 200)	in season)

Place the onion in a large bowl with the butter. Cook on full power for 4 minutes, then stir in the rice and the water. Crumble in the stock cube and cover the bowl with cling film, allowing a small gap for the steam to escape.

Make the béchamel sauce according to the recipe instructions. Chop the chicken and mix it into the sauce with the rice mixture and mushrooms. Stir in the sweet corn and herbs, then cook for a further 4 minutes. Ladle the moist rice mixture into a bowl and serve at once.

Rice and Ham Layer

——— SERVES 4 ———

This is a really tasty dish to serve for supper or lunch, with a salad or Cabbage with Apple (see page 110).

1 onion, chopped	1 quantity Cheese Sauce
25 g/1 oz butter	(page 200)
225 g/8 oz long-grain rice	225 g/8 oz cooked ham,
600 ml/1 pint boiling	sliced
water	salt and freshly ground
1 chicken stock cube	black pepper
4 tablespoons chopped	2 tomatoes, sliced, to
parsley	garnish

Place the onion in a large basin or bowl with the butter. Cook on full power for 3 minutes. Stir in the rice, pour in the water and crumble in the stock cube. Stir until the cube dissolves. Cover with cling film, allowing a small gap for the steam to escape, then cook on full power for 25 minutes. Stir in the parsley.

Make the cheese sauce according to the recipe instructions, pour it into the rice and mix well. Season to taste. Layer the ham and rice mixture in an ovenproof dish ending with a layer of the rice. Place under a hot grill until golden, then serve garnished with tomato slices.

Egg-fried Rice

——— SERVES 4 ———

This is particularly easy to make in the microwave compared to the effort involved by using a frying pan. I once ruined a frying pan by cooking egg-fried rice in it – the combination of sticking scrambled egg and starchy rice combined to form a permanent coating!

You can add all sorts of ingredients to this dish: bits of cooked chicken or pork, vegetables like bamboo shoots and water chestnuts, carrots and sweet corn, or nuts and fruits (try flaked almonds and pineapple bits). Even in its simple form below, fried rice makes a good supper dish, but with these more elaborate additions it can become quite substantial.

2 slices fresh root ginger,	1 chicken stock cube
finely chopped	600 ml/1 pint water
1 green chilli	4 spring onions, chopped
2 tablespoons oil	225 g/8 oz peeled cooked
a few drops of sesame oil	prawns
225 g/8 oz long-grain rice	2 eggs
salt and freshly ground	
black pepper	

Place the ginger in a large bowl. Cut the stalk end off the chilli, then slit the green part and scrape all the seeds from inside. Chop the shell and add it to the ginger. Stir in the oil and sesame oil, add the rice and seasoning then mix thoroughly. Cook on full power for 4 minutes.

Crumble the stock cube into the rice and pour in the water, then cover the bowl with cling film, allowing a small gap for the steam to escape. Cook on full power for 15 minutes.

Add the spring onions and the prawns to the rice, re-cover the bowl and cook for a further 5 minutes. Beat the eggs in a basin with a little seasoning, then cook them for 1 minute. Whisk the eggs once more then mix them into the hot rice and serve.

Note: this is an excellent recipe for using leftover cooked rice. Cooked rice freezes well for a couple of months. Cook some chopped onion, chopped green or red peppers, chopped chillies and grated fresh root ginger in a little oil with a few drops of sesame oil added. Allow about 5 to 10 minutes depending on the quantity of ingredients; they should be tender without being too soft. Stir in the cooked rice, cover the bowl and cook for about 5 minutes to reheat the grains. (The time will depend on the quantity.) When the rice is hot cook the beaten eggs as above and stir them into the rice. Cook for a further 1 minute before serving.

Rice Salad

——— SERVES 4 TO 6 ———

The great advantage of cooking this salad in the micro-wave is that it can be allowed to cool in the bowl and it can be chilled in the same container, even served from it if it is suitable.

You can vary the salad as you like, with other ingredients ranging from nuts and canned pineapple or chopped dessert apple to chopped salami or garlic sausage.

I large onion, chopped	100 g/4 oz shelled peas
I clove garlic, crushed	2 tablespoons chopped
2 tablespoons oil	mixed fresh herbs
225 g/8 oz long-grain rice	*Dressing:*
I chicken stock cube	4 tablespoons salad oil
600 ml/1 pint water	I tablespoons lemon juice
I red pepper	I tablespoon prepared
I green pepper	mustard
100 g/4 oz sweet corn	

Place the onion in a bowl with the garlic and oil, then cook on full power for 4 minutes. Add the rice and the crumbled stock cube. Pour in the water, then cover the bowl with cling film, allowing a small gap for the steam to escape. Cook on full power for 13 minutes.

Meanwhile, cut the stalk ends off the peppers and remove all the seeds and pith from inside. Chop the pepper shells. Mix the pepper with the sweet corn and peas, then add this ensemble to the rice and mix it in lightly. Re-cover the bowl and cook for a further 5 to 6 minutes.

Toss the herbs into the cooked rice. Put the dressing ingredients into a small screw-topped jar and shake well. Pour this dressing over the cooked rice and toss well, then cover and leave to cool. Chill lightly before serving.

Other ingredients to include in a rice salad:
Fish and Seafood Use canned tuna fish with peeled cooked prawns, mussels and cockles. Add lemon rind and plenty of chopped parsley to the salad.

Chicken or Turkey Cooked chicken and turkey, diced, make excellent additions to a rice salad. Add chopped spring onions to enliven these cooked ingredients.

Ham or Cooked Meats Lean cooked ham, diced, salami, garlic sausage or any other cold cooked meats can be included. Experiment with some of the continental sausages which are available. If they are fresh, then cook them under a hot grill until golden brown and drain the sausages on absorbent kitchen paper. When cold, slice the sausages to include in the salad.

Fruits Canned fruit, such as pineapple and peaches, can be included, or dried fruits – raisins and apricots – are also suitable.

Spaghetti Marinara

—— SERVES 4 ——

This is a recipe which is sure to appeal to lovers of seafood. You can include any seafood you like with the pasta and it goes without saying that it will taste better if it is fresh instead of canned or frozen. I have used prawns, mussels and smoked oysters because this gives a good flavour, but include a few scallops (sliced) and some smoked salmon pieces if you are feeling extravagant.

350 g/12 oz spaghetti
salt and freshly ground
   black pepper
1 onion, chopped
4 tablespoons olive oil
2 cloves garlic, crushed
2 white-skinned plaice
   fillets
225 g/8 oz peeled cooked
   prawns

225 g/8 oz cooked mussels
1 (105-g/3.66-oz) can
   smoked oysters,
   drained
2 tablespoons chopped
   fresh basil
2 tablespoons chopped
   parsley

Cook the spaghetti in boiling salted water for about 15 minutes, or until tender but not soft. Drain thoroughly.

Cook the seafood while the spaghetti is boiling. Place the onion in a large serving bowl (one which is microwave-proof, of course) and add the oil with the garlic. Stir well, then cook on full power for 5 minutes.

Cut the plaice into fine strips and add these to the onion, stirring well. Cook for 3 minutes, then add the prawns, mussels and oysters. Cook, covered with cling film for a further 5 minutes. Stir in the herbs and add the spaghetti, then toss well and serve at once.

Creamy Spaghetti Marinara For a rich sauce, stir 150 ml/¼ pint single cream into the fish with the prawns, mussels and oysters. You may have to allow an extra 1 to 2 minutes cooking time but taste the sauce to check if it is hot enough. Stir in the herbs and spaghetti as above.

Spaghetti Bolognese

—— SERVES 4 ——

1 large onion, chopped
1 large carrot, diced
1 large green pepper
2 large cloves garlic, crushed
4 tablespoons olive oil
salt and freshly ground black pepper
350 g/12 oz spaghetti
450 g/1 lb lean minced beef
2 tablespoons plain flour
1 beef stock cube
1 (795-g/1-lb 12-oz) can tomatoes
2 tablespoons concentrated tomato purée
2 teaspoons marjoram
300 ml/½ pint red wine
4 tablespoons chopped parsley
freshly grated Parmesan cheese to serve

Place the onion and carrot in a large basin. Cut the stalk end off the pepper and remove all the seeds and pith from inside. Chop the green part and add it to the onion and carrot. Stir in the garlic and 3 tablespoons of the oil. Add seasoning to taste and cook on full power for 6 minutes.

Meanwhile cook the spaghetti in plenty of boiling salted water with the remaining oil added. Allow about 15 minutes – the pasta should be tender but not soft. When it is cooked, drain the spaghetti thoroughly and turn it to a large warmed serving bowl or on to individual plates.

The meat sauce should be cooked while the pasta is boiling. Stir the beef into the cooked vegetables, add the flour, seasoning and crumbled stock cube then stir thoroughly. Pour in the tomatoes and stir in the tomato purée, marjoram and wine. Cook for 15 minutes, stirring once. Add the parsley, then pour the meat sauce over the spaghetti and serve with plenty of Parmesan cheese.

Wholewheat Spaghetti with Walnut Cream Sauce

—— SERVES 4 ——

This is ideal for a vegetarian meal. Serve a simple green salad as an accompaniment.

350 g/12 oz wholewheat spaghetti
salt and freshly ground black pepper
1 large onion, finely chopped
1 clove garlic, crushed
50 g/2 oz butter
1 teaspoon marjoram
225 g/8 oz walnut pieces, chopped
150 ml/¼ pint soured cream
2 tablespoons chopped parsley
freshly grated Parmesan cheese to serve

Cook the spaghetti in plenty of boiling salted water for about 20 minutes, or until tender but not soft. Drain thoroughly.

While the pasta is cooking prepare the sauce. Place the onion in a large bowl with the garlic and butter. Cook on full power for 6 minutes. Stir in the marjoram and walnuts and cook for a further 3 minutes. Pour in the soured cream and heat for 2 minutes.

Toss the hot spaghetti into the sauce and add the parsley. Sprinkle with plenty of pepper and serve with Parmesan cheese.

Spaghetti with Crab Sauce

—— SERVES 4 ——

You can use fresh or frozen crab in this recipe if you prefer either to the canned crab. Serve a crunchy cucumber salad with plenty of chopped fresh basil on top as an accompaniment. If you cannot obtain fresh basil then use chopped fresh chives instead.

450 g/1 lb spaghetti
1 small onion, finely chopped
25 g/1 oz butter
100 g/4 oz button mushrooms
4 tablespoons mayonnaise
4 tablespoons dry sherry
1 tablespoon concentrated tomato purée
salt and freshly ground black pepper
1 (169-g/7-oz) can crab meat in brine

First cook the spaghetti in plenty of boiling salted water for about 15 minutes, or until tender but not too soft. When the pasta is cooked drain it thoroughly.

While the spaghetti is cooking, prepare the crab sauce – if you work quickly you should be able to have the sauce ready just in time for serving with the pasta. Place the onion in a basin with the butter and cook on full power for 3 minutes.

While the onion is cooking, finely slice the mushrooms. Stir the mayonnaise, sherry, tomato purée and seasoning together until well mixed. Drain the crab and add it to the onion with the mushrooms and sauce. Stir well, then cook for a further 5 minutes.

To serve, transfer the freshly cooked spaghetti to a warmed serving bowl and pour in the sauce. Toss well to mix the pasta with the sauce, then serve immediately.

Pasta with Pine Nuts

—— SERVES 4 ——

Serve this simple pasta dish as a light supper, or to accompany a main dish. If you use fresh pasta it will taste particularly good.

225 g/8 oz pasta shapes
salt and freshly ground
   black pepper
5 tablespoons olive oil
1 clove garlic, crushed

1 small onion, finely
   chopped
50 g/2 oz pine nuts
2 tablespoons chopped
   fresh basil or parsley

Cook the pasta in boiling salted water, with a little of the oil added, for about 12 to 15 minutes, or until tender but not too soft. Drain thoroughly when cooked.

The sauce should be ready as soon as the pasta is tender – so prepare it while the pasta cooks. Pour the remaining olive oil into a large bowl. If you have a microwave-proof serving bowl, then it will be ideal for this dish. Add the garlic and onion and stir in the pine nuts. Cook on full power for 10 minutes, stirring once during cooking.

Toss the cooked pasta into the nut mixture and add the chopped basil or parsley. Season with black pepper and serve immediately.

Macaroni Cheese

—— SERVES 4 ——

225 g/8 oz macaroni
salt and freshly ground
   black pepper

1 quantity Cheese Sauce
   (page 200)

Cook the macaroni in plenty of boiling salted water for about 15 minutes, or until tender but not soft. Drain thoroughly, shaking the colander or sieve to get rid of all the water.

Make the cheese sauce while the pasta is cooking. Use most of the cheese in the sauce but reserve a little for topping the dish.

Stir the macaroni into the sauce and turn it into an ovenproof serving dish. Spinkle the reserved cheese over the top and cook under a hot grill until golden and bubbling. Serve at once.

MAKING MORE OF MACARONI CHEESE

Onion Cook 1 finely chopped onion in 25 g/1 oz butter for 5 minutes on full power. Stir in the flour for the sauce, then whisk in the other ingredients and continue as above.

Bacon Rolls Roll up two or four rashers of rindless bacon per person and skewer them to cook under the grill before you brown the macaroni cheese. Arrange these bacon rolls on top just before you serve the macaroni.

Mushrooms Add 100 g/4 oz sliced mushrooms with the macaroni. Grill as above.

Minced Lamb with Macaroni

—— SERVES 4 ——

This is an idea which comes from a rather strange Greek dish which tasted very good. Serve a tomato salad on plenty of crisp Iceberg or Cos lettuce to contrast with the soft texture of the meat and pasta.

225 g/8 oz macaroni
salt and freshly ground
   black pepper
1 large onion, chopped
2 cloves garlic, crushed
2 tablespoons olive oil
450 g/1 lb minced lamb
1 tablespoon marjoram

1 bay leaf
1 (425-g/15 oz) can
   chopped tomatoes
50 g/2 oz fresh
   breadcrumbs
2 tablespoons grated
   Parmesan cheese

Cook the macaroni in plenty of boiling salted water for about 15 minutes, or until tender but not soft.

Meanwhile, put the onion in a large bowl with the garlic and oil. Cook on full power for 5 minutes. Stir in the lamb and the marjoram, breaking up the meat thoroughly. Add the bay leaf and cover with cling film, allowing a small gap for the steam to escape. Cook for 5 minutes. Break up the lamb again, then stir in the tomatoes and plenty of seasoning. Cook, uncovered, for a further 5 minutes.

Add the drained pasta to the meat and mix thoroughly, then cook for 3 minutes. Ladle the mixture into individual ovenproof dishes. Mix the breadcrumbs with the Parmesan cheese and sprinkle over the meat and pasta, then put under a hot grill until golden brown. Serve at once.

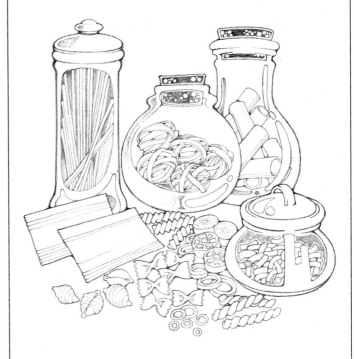

Macaroni with Mushrooms and Garlic

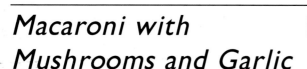

——— SERVES 4 ———

This is a delicious supper dish, good to serve with a moist main dish or ideal for a vegetarian lunch. Serve with a good mixed salad if you like.

225 g/8 oz macaroni
salt and freshly ground
    black pepper
50 g/2 oz butter
2 tablespoons olive oil
3 cloves garlic, crushed
350 g/12 oz button
    mushrooms, sliced

2 tablespoons chopped
    parsley
2 tablespoons chopped
    fresh basil *or*
    1 tablespoon dried basil
freshly grated Parmesan
    cheese to serve

Cook the macaroni in plenty of boiling salted water for about 15 minutes, or until tender but not soft. Drain thoroughly.

While the pasta is cooking, place the butter and oil in a basin with the garlic and cook for 1 minute on full power. Toss in the mushrooms and mix well, then cover with cling film, allowing a small gap for the steam to escape. Cook for 5 minutes.

Immediately the pasta is cooked, mix it with the mushroom mixture and the herbs. Add plenty of black pepper and a little salt then sprinkle with Parmesan cheese and serve.

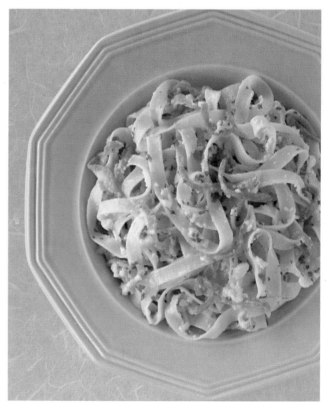

Tagliatelle Carbonara

——— SERVES 4 ———

This is a delicious, quick supper dish which basically consists of scrambled eggs with bacon and pasta. You can use any pasta shapes instead of the noodles, but it is always best to cook the pasta on the hob.

350 g/12 oz tagliatelle
salt and freshly ground
    black pepper
225 g/8 oz lean bacon
4 large eggs
4 tablespoons single
    cream

2 tablespoons grated
    Parmesan cheese
2 tablespoons chopped
    parsley

Cook the noodles in plenty of boiling salted water for 12 to 15 minutes, or until tender but not soft.

Meanwhile, cut the rinds off the bacon and cut the rashers into fine strips. Place the bacon in a large bowl – a serving bowl or a mixing bowl if you do not have a suitable serving dish – and cook on full power for 4 minutes.

While the bacon is cooking whisk the eggs with the cream and seasoning to taste – use plenty of black pepper but avoid too much salt if the bacon is salty.

Add the eggs to the bacon and cook for 4 minutes, whisking the eggs once during cooking. At the end of this time the eggs should be just setting and of a creamy consistency. Drain the pasta and add it to the eggs with the Parmesan cheese and parsley. Toss thoroughly and serve at once.

Tuna Conchiglie

——— SERVES 4 ———

Conchiglie are pasta shells and large ones can be filled with a sweet or savoury stuffing then cooked like lasagne or cannelloni. While the pasta shells are boiling on the hob you can quickly make the filling in the microwave oven, saving both on time and washing up. To finish the dish, the stuffed shells are browned under a hot grill. Serve with a fresh green salad for a light main course.

12 conchiglie shells
salt and freshly ground
   black pepper
1 (198-g/7-oz) can tuna in
   oil
1 onion, chopped
1 clove garlic, crushed
1 teaspoon marjoram
1 (400-g/14-oz) can
   chopped tomatoes
1 bay leaf
blade of mace

1 tablespoon concentrated
   tomato purée
2 tablespoons dry sherry
75 g/3 oz full fat cream
   cheese (for example
   Philadelphia cheese)
1 (213-g/7½-oz) can
   creamed mushrooms
25 g/1 oz fresh
   breadcrumbs
1 tablespoon grated
   Parmesan cheese

Cook the pasta shells in plenty of boiling salted water for about 10 minutes, or until tender but not soft. Meanwhile, drain the oil from the tuna into a basin (about 1.15-litre/ 2-pint capacity), add the onion, garlic and marjoram and stir in seasoning to taste. Cook on full power for 3 minutes.

Mix the tomatoes, bay leaf and mace in a jug, then stir in the tomato purée, sherry and seasoning to taste. Cook for 5 minutes. Drain the pasta shells and rinse them under cold running water, then set aside to drain completely.

Mix the cream cheese into the hot onion and add the tuna, breaking it up with a fork. Stir in the creamed mushrooms and breadcrumbs and beat the mixture to combine all the ingredients. Taste and adjust the seasoning if necessary. Using a teaspoon, fill the pasta shells with this tuna mixture, without piling it up too high at this stage.

Pour the tomato sauce into a shallow, ovenproof serving dish, then arrange the shells in it, standing them up as neatly as possible. Top the shells with any remaining fish mixture and heat through in the microwave for 5 minutes.

Meanwhile, heat the grill to the hottest setting. Sprinkle the Parmesan cheese over the top of the shells and place them under the grill until lightly browned on top. Serve immediately.

Tagliatelle with Chicken Livers

——— SERVES 4 ———

Serve a green salad to accompany this full-flavoured pasta dish.

350 g/12 oz tagliatelle
salt and freshly ground
  black pepper
1 small onion, chopped
2 cloves garlic, crushed
50 g/2 oz butter
450 g/1 lb chicken livers,
  chopped

2 tablespoons
  concentrated tomato
  purée
1 teaspoon marjoram
150 ml/¼ pint red wine
plenty of chopped parsley

Cook the tagliatelle in plenty of boiling salted water for about 15 minutes, or until tender but not soft. Drain thoroughly.

While the pasta is cooking, prepare the chicken liver sauce. Place the onion in a basin with the garlic and butter, then cook on full power for 5 minutes. Stir in the livers and the tomato purée. Add the marjoram and pour in the wine. Stir well, then cover with cling film and cook for 9 minutes, stirring once during this time. Season to taste.

When the pasta is cooked, transfer it to a serving bowl and pour the chicken livers on top. Add plenty of chopped parsley and serve at once.

Turkey Tagliatelle

——— SERVES 4 ———

Serve a very fresh, crisp salad to bring out the best in this full-flavoured turkey and pasta creation. If you like, you can adapt the recipe to use up leftover cooked turkey, but it won't taste quite as good.

1 onion, chopped
450 g/1 lb boneless turkey
  fillets
2 cloves garlic, crushed
2 tablespoons oil
225 g/8 oz tagliatelle
salt and freshly ground
  black pepper
1 (425-g/15-oz) can
  chopped tomatoes

175 g/6 oz button
  mushrooms
1 tablespoon fennel seeds
25 g/1 oz butter
50 g/2 oz black olives,
  stoned and chopped
2 tablespoons chopped
  parsley

Place the onion in a large bowl. Cut the turkey into fine strips and add these to the onion with the garlic and oil. Stir well to coat all the ingredients in oil, then cook on full power for 4 minutes.

Meanwhile, cook the pasta in plenty of boiling salted water. Add the tomatoes to the turkey and cook for 10 minutes. While the turkey is cooking slice the mushrooms. Stir the turkey once during the 10 minutes, then add the mushrooms and cook for a further 3 minutes.

Thoroughly drain the pasta and arrange it in a warmed serving dish. Remove the turkey mixture from the microwave. Place the fennel seeds in a mug or small basin and add the butter. Cook for 3 minutes. Spoon the turkey over the tagliatelle, then top with the fennel seeds, olives and parsley. Serve at once.

Creamy Chicken Cannelloni

——— SERVES 4 ———

This really is mouthwatering – the pasta tubes are filled with a purée of chicken and are topped with a very simple sauce. Before serving, a crispy crust of cheese and breadcrumbs completes the dish. Serve with a dish of hot vegetables – such as courgettes or French beans – or a crisp salad.

450 g/1 lb boneless
  chicken breasts
1 large onion, chopped
1 tablespoon corn oil
8 cannelloni tubes
salt and freshly ground
  black pepper
Simple Wine Sauce:
3 tablespoons plain flour

1 chicken stock cube
300 ml/½ pint milk
300 ml/½ pint dry white
  wine
Topping:
50 g/2 oz Caerphilly
  cheese, crumbled
50 g/2 oz fresh
  breadcrumbs

Cut the chicken into chunks – about 5 cm/2 in in size. Place these in a basin with the onion and oil. Toss well to coat the pieces with the oil, then cook on full power for 10 minutes, stirring once during cooking.

Meanwhile, cook the cannelloni in boiling salted water for 12 minutes, or until tender but not soft. Drain thoroughly and rinse under cold water, then drain again.

Finely mince the cooked chicken or process it in a food processor or liquidiser. Add seasoning to taste and press the chicken into the pasta tubes to fill them without breaking them. Arrange these in a fairly large, shallow serving dish.

For the sauce, place the flour in a basin, then crumble in the stock cube and gradually whisk in the milk. Cook on full power for 5 minutes. Whisk the thick sauce thoroughly before adding and whisking in the wine. Taste and add seasoning if necessary.

Pour the sauce over the filled cannelloni, then cook for 5 minutes. Meanwhile, mix the cheese with the breadcrumbs and sprinkle this mixture over the pasta. Cook under a hot grill for a few minutes, until golden brown and crisp on top. Serve at once.

Chicken Chow Mein

—— SERVES 4 ——

It is easier to cook the noodles quickly on top of the cooker than it is to find a large dish to cook them in the microwave.

I onion, halved and very thinly sliced	2 tablespoons soy sauce
I large carrot, cut into fine strips	225 g/8 oz Chinese egg noodles
2 tablespoons oil	I teaspoon cornflour
a few drops of sesame oil	100 ml/4 fl oz water
350 g/12 oz boneless chicken breast	I chicken stock cube
I (227-g/8-oz) can water chestnuts	2 spring onions, shredded, to garnish

Place the onion, carrot, oil and sesame oil in a large bowl. Cook on full power for 3 minutes.

Meanwhile, cut the chicken meat into fine strips and slice the water chestnuts, then add both to the vegetables and stir in the soy sauce. Cook for a further 5 minutes.

While the chicken is cooking, cook the noodles in plenty of boiling water for about 2 minutes, then drain them thoroughly and stir them into the chow mein. Blend the cornflour with the water and stir in the crumbled stock cube, then mix this into the chow mein. Cook for a final 4 minutes. Serve the chicken chow mein sprinkled with the spring onions.

Spinach-stuffed Cannelloni

—— SERVES 4 ——

This stuffed cannelloni makes a good vegetarian meal, or it can be served as a first course.

8 cannelloni tubes	225 g/8 oz cottage cheese
salt and freshly ground black pepper	freshly grated nutmeg
Filling:	I quantity Cheese Sauce (page 200)
I large onion, finely chopped	*Topping:*
50 g/2 oz butter	50 g/2 oz fresh breadcrumbs
I clove garlic, crushed	2 tablespoons grated Parmesan cheese
2 (227-g/8-oz) packets frozen spinach, defrosted	

Cook the cannelloni in plenty of boiling salted water for about 15 minutes, or until tender but not soft. Drain thoroughly.

For the filling, place the onion and butter in a large basin with the garlic and cook on full power for 5 minutes.

Thoroughly drain all the liquid from the spinach, then add it to the onion and cook for 3 minutes. Stir in the cottage cheese, add seasoning to taste and the nutmeg, then mix well, breaking up the cottage cheese. Cook for 3 minutes.

Stuff the cannelloni with this mixture and place them in a shallow dish. Make the cheese sauce using the smaller quantity of cheese, then pour it over the cannelloni and cook for 3 minutes.

Mix the ingredients for the topping, sprinkle these over the stuffed pasta and cook under a hot grill until thoroughly browned and crisp on top. Serve at once.

Chinese Mushroom Chow Mein

—— SERVES 4 ——

Chinese dried mushrooms are very dark in colour with a lighter underside on the caps. They are available from oriental supermarkets but they are rather expensive; however to balance out their cost, their flavour is quite strong so they are used only in small quantities for dishes such as this one. A mixture of both fresh and dried mushrooms, flavoured with garlic and spring onions, serve this chow mein with elaborate, moist main dishes.

4 large dried Chinese mushrooms	a few drops of sesame oil
225 g/8 oz Chinese egg noodles	I bunch of spring onions
2 large cloves garlic, crushed	225 g/8 oz button mushrooms
2 tablespoons oil	2 tablespoons soy sauce
	2 tablespoons dry sherry

Place the mushrooms in a mug or small basin and pour in enough boiling water to cover them. Put a saucer on top to keep the mushrooms in the water, then leave to soak for 10 minutes. Cook the noodles in boiling water for 2 minutes, then drain thoroughly and set them aside.

Place the garlic in a basin or bowl with the oil and sesame oil. Drain and slice the dried mushrooms, then add them to the oil and stir well. Finely shred the spring onions and add the white part to the basin. Stir well then cook on full power for 2 minutes. Meanwhile, slice the button mushrooms and add these to the other ingredients in the basin. Cook for a further 3 minutes before adding the noodles. Toss in the soy sauce and sherry and turn the noodles in the sauce to make sure they are well coated. Cook for a final 5 minutes before adding the green part of the spring onions. Toss well and serve at once.

Salmon Shell Savoury

SERVES 4

This is a really tasty, moist and filling supper dish. It is good enough to serve for an informal supper party too. Hot buttered toast adds interest in texture.

225 g/8 oz pasta shells (medium-sized)	600 ml/1 pint milk
salt and freshly ground black pepper	1 (439-g/15½-oz) can salmon
1 large onion, chopped	100 g/4 oz button mushrooms, sliced
50 g/2 oz butter	50 g/2 oz Emmental cheese, grated
40 g/1½ oz plain flour	

Cook the pasta in plenty of boiling salted water for about 15 minutes, or until tender but not soft. Drain thoroughly.

While the pasta is cooking prepare the sauce. Place the onion in a bowl with the butter and cook on full power for 5 minutes. Stir in the flour and seasoning, then gradually pour in the milk. Cook for 10 minutes, whisking the sauce once during cooking and again at the end of the cooking time.

Drain the liquid from the salmon into the sauce, then remove all the skin and bones from the fish and flake the flesh. Stir the flaked salmon into the sauce with the mushrooms and the cooked pasta. Taste and adjust the seasoning, then transfer to a serving dish and heat for 2 minutes. Sprinkle the cheese over and brown the top under a hot grill, then serve at once.

If you freeze prepared recipes in their cooking dishes, for example casseroles, then find that you need the dish for another purpose while the food is still in the freezer, then simply cook the food for about 1 to 2 minutes in the microwave so as to loosen the frozen block. The food can be re-packed and put back in the freezer and the dish can be washed for immediate use. However, remember that the dish must not be of the metal type.

Pork 'n' Bows

——— SERVES 4 ———

225 g/8 oz pasta bows
salt and freshly ground
　black pepper
1 large onion, chopped
2 cloves garlic, crushed
1 red pepper
2 tablespoons oil
2 tablespoons plain flour

1 chicken stock cube
300 ml/½ pint tomato juice
1 tablespoon dried mixed
　herbs
450 g/1 lb lean minced
　pork
grated rind of 1 orange
plenty of chopped parsley

Cook the pasta bows in plenty of boiling salted water for about 15 minutes, or until tender but not soft.

Place the onion and garlic in a large bowl – a serving bowl which is microwave-proof is ideal. Cut the stalk end off the pepper, then scoop out all the seeds from inside and chop the pepper flesh. Add this to the onion with the oil and cook on full power for 6 minutes.

Stir the flour and crumbled stock cube into the onion mixture, then pour in the tomato juice and add the herbs. Stir in the pork, breaking it up into small pieces. Cover the bowl with cling film, allowing a small gap for the steam to escape, then cook for 18 minutes. Stir the pork once during cooking.

At the end of the cooking time, stir in the orange rind and parsley. Taste and add seasoning, then throw in the pasta bows and mix well without breaking them up. Serve at once.

VARIATIONS

This is a very simple meat and pasta recipe which can be varied in any number of ways. For example, minced beef or lamb can be used instead of the pork. Substitute beef or lamb stock cubes and boiling water for the tomato juice. Vary the herbs – try thyme, sage, parsley or marjoram – and omit the orange rind and juice. You can use different pasta shapes instead of the bows and sliced mushrooms or chopped carrots can also be added to the meat.

It is quite possible to cook pasta in the microwave but you will need a very large bowl, plenty of boiling water and you will have to allow as long a cooking time as you would on the hob. All in all it's not worth it. Instead, aim to cook a sauce or accompaniment in the microwave while the pasta bubbles on the conventional cooker.

Lasagne al Forno

—— SERVES 4 TO 6 ——

Serve a large quantity of green salad with the lasagne – plenty of very crunchy lettuce (Iceberg), a green pepper, spring onions, cucumber, watercress leaves, courgettes, avocado pear and chopped fresh basil.

225 g/8 oz lasagne sheets
salt and freshly ground
 black pepper
Meat Sauce:
450 g/1 lb good minced
 beef
225 g/8 oz minced pork
1 large onion, chopped
2 tablespoons olive oil
2 cloves garlic, crushed
1 green pepper
675 g/1½ lb tomatoes
2 teaspoons marjoram

1 tablespoon concentrated
 tomato purée
300 ml/½ pint full-bodied
 red wine
1 beef stock cube
Topping:
50 g/2 oz butter
40 g/1½ oz plain flour
600 ml/1 pint milk
1 bay leaf
100 g/4 oz Cheddar
 cheese, grated
1 egg, beaten

For this you will need a large lasagne dish. If you have a turntable which cannot be stopped during the cooking process, then the dish may not fit into your oven, so, check first and use two smaller dishes if this is the case.

First cook the pasta by conventional means: in plenty of boiling salted water on top of the hob for about 15 minutes, so that it is *al dente*: that is tender with a bit of bite and not soft. Drain it into a colander and rinse the sheets under cold running water, then separate them and lay them on a clean tea-towel or double thickness of absorbent kitchen paper.

While the pasta is cooking you can prepare the other sauces in the microwave oven. Mix the meats together, making sure they are thoroughly combined. Place the onion in a large basin with the oil and garlic. Cut the stalk end off the pepper and remove all the seed from inside. Chop the green part finely, then add it to the onion and cook on full power for 5 minutes.

Meanwhile, peel the tomatoes following the instructions on page 123. Cut them in half, remove their seeds, then chop the flesh. Stir the tomatoes, marjoram and tomato purée into the onion, then pour in the wine and crumble in the stock cube. Add the mixed meat, breaking up the mince as you do so. Stir in plenty of seasoning and cover with cling film, allowing a small gap for the steam to escape. Cook for 18 minutes, stirring the meat once during cooking.

For the topping, place the butter and flour in a basin and whisk in the milk. Add the bay leaf and seasoning to taste, then cover with cling film and cook for 10 minutes, whisking once during cooking, then again at the end of the time. Whisk in two-thirds of the cheese after removing the bay leaf then whisk in the egg.

Layer the cooked pasta and meat in the dish and pour the sauce over the top. Cook for 4 minutes. Sprinkle the reserved cheese over the sauce and cook under a hot grill until golden and bubbling. Serve at once.

Ham and Broccoli Layer

—— SERVES 4 ——

Lasagne certainly isn't the only pasta which can be layered up in saucy dishes. You can use any of the pasta shapes or even cooked rice if you so wish. For this dish, use small shapes, preferably ones like bows which have pointed corners that will become very brown and crisp under the grill.

225 g/8 oz pasta shapes
salt and freshly ground
 black pepper
Broccoli Layer:
1 onion, chopped
25 g/1 oz butter
1 tablespoon plain flour
300 ml/½ pint milk
225 g/8 oz broccoli
Ham Layer:
275 g/10 oz cooked ham
2 tablespoons plain flour

2 tablespoons wholegrain
 mustard
1 tablespoon concentrated
 tomato purée
300 ml/½ pint dry white
 wine
Topping:
150 ml/¼ pint double
 cream
100 g/4 oz mild cheese,
 grated

First cook the pasta in plenty of boiling salted water for about 12 to 15 minutes, or until it is tender but not soft. Drain thoroughly and rinse under cold water, then drain again.

For the broccoli layer, place the onion in a large basin or casserole dish with the butter and cook on full power for 5 minutes. Stir in the flour and milk, adding the liquid slowly. Finely chop the broccoli and add it to the sauce, stirring well. Cook for a further 10 minutes, stirring once during cooking, then add plenty of seasoning.

Meanwhile, mince the ham for the second layer and put it in a basin with the flour. Stir in the mustard, wine and tomato purée, then cook on full power for 10 minutes, stirring once during cooking. Add seasoning to taste.

Pour the broccoli into a serving dish – choose a fairly deep one which can be put into the microwave oven and under the grill. Next add half the cooked pasta. Top this with the ham sauce, then a final layer of the remaining pasta. Cook in the microwave oven for 4 minutes.

Meanwhile, mix the cream with the cheese and spread this evenly over the pasta. Place under a moderately hot grill until the top of the pasta is golden brown and bubbling hot. Serve at once.

Seafood Lasagne

—— SERVES 4 TO 6 ——

225 g/8 oz lasagne verdi	225 g/8 oz shelled cooked
salt and freshly ground	mussels
black pepper	4 tablespoons chopped
Filling:	parsley
1 onion, chopped	**Topping:**
2 cloves garlic, crushed	40 g/1½ oz plain flour
50 g/2 oz butter	300 ml/½ pint milk
450 ml/¾ pint red wine	25 g/1 oz butter
1 fish stock cube	1 bay leaf
2 frozen preformed cod	300 ml/½ pint single cream
steaks, partly defrosted	2 egg yolks
225 g/8 oz peeled cooked	2 tablespoons grated
prawns	Parmesan cheese

Cook the lasagne in plenty of boiling salted water for about 15 minutes, until tender but not soft. Drain thoroughly, rinse under cold water and lay the slices on a clean tea-towel or absorbent kitchen paper to dry.

For the filling, place the onion and garlic in a large basin or bowl with the butter. Cook on full power for 5 minutes. Stir in the wine and crumbled stock cube. Cut the fish into small squares, then add to the sauce and cook for 10 minutes, stirring once. Add the prawns and mussels and cook for 2 minutes, then stir in the parsley.

Place the flour for the topping in a basin, then whisk in the milk. Add the butter and bay leaf and cook for 7 minutes, whisking once during cooking and thoroughly at the end of the cooking time. Whisk in the cream to thin the sauce, then whisk in the egg yolks to enrich it.

Layer the lasagne with the seafood mixture and pour the cream sauce on top. Cook for 5 minutes, turning the dish once. Sprinkle the Parmesan over and place under a hot grill to brown the top. Serve at once.

Lasagne Pie

—— SERVES 4 TO 6 ——

This is an unusual but very successful way of preparing lasagne. Used to line a quiche dish, the pasta provides an excellent encasement for a meaty filling.

225 g/8 oz lasagne	2 teaspoons tarragon
salt and freshly ground	450 g/1 lb boneless
black pepper	chicken breasts
3 tablespoons plain flour	225 g/8 oz mushrooms
1 chicken stock cube	50 g/2 oz cheese, grated
300 ml/½ pint boiling	
water	

Cook the lasagne in plenty of boiling, salted water until tender but not too soft – about 12 minutes. Drain thoroughly, then rinse under cold water and drain again.

While the pasta is cooking make the sauce: place the flour in a basin and crumble in the stock cube. Gradually

whisk in the boiling water and the tarragon, then cook on full power for 5 minutes. Remove and whisk thoroughly.

Line a 25 cm/10-in quiche dish with the pasta, reserving enough to cover the top too. Overlap the pieces so that they form a complete lining. Slice the chicken horizontally into thin pieces and lay these slices over the pasta. Slice the mushrooms and sprinkle them in an even layer over the chicken. Pour most of the sauce over the mushrooms – the pasta case should be almost filled; too much sauce will create a messy result and too little will leave the pasta dry. Fold the edges of the pasta lining over the filling, then top with the remaining lasagne, tucking the ends neatly down inside the dish.

Cover completely with cling film – you will probably have to use a double width to form a total cover. Do not pull it too tight and do not leave a gap. Cook on full power for 14 minutes. Remove from the oven, uncover and spread the reserve sauce over. Sprinkle the cheese on top, then cook under a hot grill until golden brown and crisp. Serve at once.

Vegetable Lasagne

—— SERVES 4 TO 6 ——

225 g/8 oz lasagne sheets	450 g/1 lb courgettes
(use wholewheat, verdi	225 g/8 oz mushrooms
or white)	2 tablespoons chopped
salt and freshly ground	fresh basil or 1
black pepper	tablespoon dried basil
Filling:	1 quantity Cheese Sauce
2 onions, chopped	(page 200)
2 cloves garlic, crushed	**Topping:**
1 green pepper	50 g/2 oz walnut pieces,
1 red pepper	chopped
4 tablespoons olive oil	50 g/2 oz cheese, grated

First cook the lasagne in a large saucepan of boiling salted water on top of the hob. It should be cooked for about 15 minutes, until tender but not soft. Drain thoroughly and rinse under cold water, then dry the sheets on a clean tea-towel or a double thickness of absorbent kitchen paper.

Place the onions in a large bowl with the garlic. Cut the stalk ends off the peppers, then remove all the seeds and pith from inside. Chop the pepper shells and add them to the onions. Stir in the oil and cover the dish with cling film, allowing a small gap for the steam to escape. Cook on full power for 10 minutes, stirring once during cooking.

Trim the courgettes and peel them very thinly if you like. Chop them into small cubes. Slice the mushrooms and add them to the onion mixture with the courgettes. Stir well and add the basil. Re-cover and continue to cook for a further 5 minutes. Add seasoning to taste.

Layer the cooked lasagne with the vegetable mixture in a large lasagne dish or two smaller ones if the oven will not hold a big dish. Make the cheese sauce according to the recipe instructions, then pour it over the lasagne and cook for 5 minutes, turning the dish once.

Mix the walnuts with the cheese for the topping, then sprinkle it evenly over the sauce. Brown under a hot grill and serve at once.

Supper Dishes & Snacks

When people venture out to buy a microwave oven, there is often a certain feeling that, even if it never does cook the thousands of daily meals we require, it will be the most valuable appliance around for preparing all those suppertime snacks, or for giving the children a quick tea.

So, here you are – all those hasty meals in a chapter. Included here you will find some ideas for eggs – scrambled and poached – which may well see you through a few busy mornings. There are recipes for substantial family suppers as well as interesting light meals. There are also suggestions for making canned foods more interesting.

If you do want to reheat canned beans, ravioli or similar snacks they can be arranged on the freshly buttered toast and put on a plate, then quickly heated through for serving. The microwave oven is ideal for reheating frozen foods of all types, bought or prepared at home. Follow a few basic, common-sense rules and you can't go wrong.

Never heat food in foil containers. If you have something wrapped in foil, then ease it out and transfer it to a serving dish. Cover with cling film and cook on defrost power or, if you are in a hurry, on full power. Check the food frequently to make sure that it is reheating evenly.

If you want to freeze prepared meals, then arrange them in divided containers – these can be purchased specially for the microwave oven – and pack them in a roasting bag tied securely with a microwave-proof clip (these come with some roasting bags) or with an elastic band. Remember to loosen the fastening when the meal is transferred to the microwave oven. Reheat the food on full power, turning the container fairly frequently. You could add a freshly made sauce or gravy if you like. Although this may sound rather unappetising and a bit like second-rate frozen T.V. dinners, there really is no reason why they should be. For example, you could prepare a larger quantity of Steak Bourguignonne (see page 80) and freeze a portion with Spanish Rice (see page 136) and some fresh sliced courgettes. When reheated, this would present a colourful, delicious and nutritious meal. Using this idea you could also prepare a range of different dinners which would be useful for occasions when you were unable to cook for an elderly relative, for example. Make sure the diner knows how to use the microwave or they really are forsaken!

Whatever your reasons for wanting to make a quick meal or tempting snack, then I hope you will find some of the ideas in this chapter useful.

Scrambled Eggs

Opinion seems to be very divided about whether scrambled eggs cooked in the microwave are successful or not. There are those who rave about them and those who seem to detest them, some people rejoice in the ease of washing up and others who swear by their non-stick saucepans. I confess that I am one of the ravers – so to speak – and I think microwaved scrambled eggs (the way I cook them) are really very good. I have also tasted some rather nasty, leathery yellow stuff that tried hard to be scrambled egg but failed miserably.

So why is it worth scrambling your eggs in the microwave oven? Cooking scrambled eggs on the top of the hob means standing over the pan every second if you want a creamy result; however you cannot go away and leave the eggs to cook in the microwave oven either because they do need regular whisking, *but* you can actually be buttering the toast or making the tea during the 2 minute intervals that you are not whisking the eggs. So don't let anyone put you off by saying it's more work cooking eggs in the microwave, it's not *but* you've got to get used to the frequent whisking.

Unless you do have a very good non-stick saucepan that has not suffered the ravages of time and a scouring pad, then you will find that washing up a basin in which the eggs were cooked is far easier than cleaning a dirty saucepan.

The other advantage that I find very useful is that as the eggs are cooking you can stop the process if needs be. For example, you can leave the eggs at the stage when they just need another half a minute or so, make and butter your toast, answer the telephone, cope with a screaming baby or any other interruption and still go back to finish cooking them without having a ruined supper. Obviously this would not be the case if the eggs were virtually cooked, but at the half-set stage they can be left for a while. The timing is fairly crucial and 30 seconds can mean rubbery eggs, so until you know your own particular oven, keep an eye on the eggs to see how they are setting. Once you have cooked your usual two or four eggs you will become used to the time it takes and know how careless you can be with them. I find that, now that I know my own oven very well, it is far easier to overcook the four eggs which I normally scramble by conventional means than in the microwave. It really is all down to practice.

Follow the instructions and times below, keeping a close eye on the eggs until you know *exactly* how long it takes to scramble a certain number of eggs in your oven.

COOKING INSTRUCTIONS

2 eggs —— whisk the eggs thoroughly with 1 tablespoon milk and seasoning to taste. Add about 15 g/ ½ oz (a good knob) of butter and cook on full power for 1 minute. Whisk thoroughly, then cook for another minute and whisk again. Cook for a final 30 seconds and whisk before serving.

4 eggs —— whisk the eggs thoroughly with 2 tablespoons milk, seasoning to taste and 25 g/1 oz butter. Cook on full power for 2 minutes, then whisk the eggs thoroughly. Cook for a further 1 minute and whisk again; cook for a final 1 minute, then whisk before serving.

6 eggs —— whisk the eggs thoroughly with 3 tablespoons milk and seasoning to taste. Add 1 large knob of butter (don't be mean, unless you are on a diet, because the butter gives the eggs a good flavour) and cook on full power for 2 minutes. Whisk the eggs thoroughly, cook for a further 2 minutes and whisk again. Cook for a final 2 to 2½ minutes, then whisk the eggs until smooth and serve.

WAYS WITH SCRAMBLED EGGS

Creamy Eggs Scrambled eggs are delicious made with single or double cream instead of milk. Cook them as in the instructions, using cream in place of the suggested quantities of milk.

Scrambled Eggs with Cheese Allow 50 g/2 oz finely grated cheese to every 2 eggs. Add the cheese to the eggs when they are half set and stir in a pinch of mustard powder if you like. Continue cooking until the eggs are set, then serve on toast or use to fill a baked potato. The addition of cheese makes the eggs more substantial.

Scrambled Eggs with Herbs A pinch of thyme, lots of chopped parsley and chives go very well with scrambled eggs. This is particularly tasty if you are serving the eggs with grilled sausages.

Eggs with Prawns A rather special supper dish, add 100 g/ 4 oz peeled cooked prawns to every 2 eggs when they are half set. Serve in small bowls with hot French bread. This also makes a good starter.

Smoked Salmon Special A good one for a very special breakfast treat (try serving this on Christmas morning with a bottle of champagne or buck's fizz). Add 25–50 g/1– 2 oz chopped smoked salmon to every 2 eggs (depending on how many you are cooking; if it is only two then use the greater quantity). Stir the smoked salmon into the eggs when they are almost set – the salmon should be warmed through but not cooked. This recipe can also be served as an elegant starter, on small circles of toast buttered or with very thin brown bread and butter.

Bacon Eggs Finely chop 50 g/2 oz lean rindless bacon for every 2 eggs and cook it in the basin for 2 minutes before adding the eggs. Add chopped spring onions to the cooked eggs if you like.

Eggs with Tomatoes Peel, deseed and chop 2 ripe but firm tomatoes for every 2 eggs. Add these to the half set eggs and continue cooking until the eggs are set. Stir the eggs rather than whisking them, but do make sure you thoroughly break up the set bits otherwise they will become leathery.

Spinach Scramble Place 1 (227-g/8-oz) packet frozen chopped spinach on a plate or dish. Cook on full power for 3 minutes. Thoroughly drain the spinach, then add it to 4 eggs and cook as in the main recipe. Season with a little grated nutmeg and top with grated Parmesan cheese. This is good served with buttered rice or pasta.

Hams and Eggs Add 50 g/2 oz chopped cooked ham to every 2 eggs. Stir the ham in when the eggs are almost set, then continue cooking.

Spicy Scrambled Eggs Cook 1 tablespoon grated fresh root ginger, 1 crushed clove garlic and 1 tablespoon chopped onion in a little butter for 3 minutes. Add 2 eggs to this quantity of spices, double these quantities for 4 or 6 eggs. Stir ½ teaspoon ground coriander into the cooked ginger and onion, then add and beat the eggs, and cook as in the main recipe. Sprinkle chopped fresh coriander leaves over the cooked eggs and serve them with basmati rice.

The microwave is very useful for defrosting frozen butter. Remove any foil wrapping and place the butter on a plate or in a dish. Cook on full power for 45 seconds.

If the butter is taken from the refrigerator and is too hard to spread on the bread, then give it 15 seconds on full power.

It is essential to prick the yolk of eggs very gently with a cocktail stick or similar implement before 'poaching' them in the microwave oven.

Poached Eggs

Whichever way eggs are cooked, they are not the easiest of ingredients to present as perfect. Individual tastes vary enormously, so it is difficult to advise people how best to poach eggs.

The way in which microwave ovens cook food means that the eggs do not cook in quite the same way as normal. Usually, as the eggs simmer in, or over, the water they are cooked from the white inwards. In the microwave oven the yolks cook at the same rate as the whites, if not slightly faster. So if you like eggs with firm whites and soft yolks then you are unlikely to achieve this in the microwave.

If you are not too fussy about small areas of floppy egg white, then microwaved poached eggs are fine. I find them easy to prepare when I am in a dreadful hurry.

A bun dish (or muffin dish) specially designed for the microwave oven is the best container to use, otherwise the eggs can be cooked in individual ramekin dishes. Crack the eggs into the containers and prick the yolk of each one with a small cocktail stick. Top each egg with a small knob of butter and cover with cling film, then cook for the times given below.

2 eggs	1 to 1¼ minutes
3 eggs	1½ to 1¾ minutes
4 eggs	1¾ to 2 minutes

SERVING IDEAS

On toast Most common and quickest; the eggs can be scooped out of their cooking containers and served on hot buttered toast.

Oeuf Hollandaise For a light first course; serve the poached eggs coated with Hollandaise Sauce (see page 201) and add a garnish of fennel sprigs. Offer melba toast or fine bread and butter as an accompaniment.

Eggs Florentine Serve the eggs on a bed of Creamed Spinach (see page 109). Have hot crusty bread as an accompaniment.

Sunshine Eggs the poached eggs can be served on Creamed Corn (see page 120). Hot Granary bread or bread rolls make a good accompaniment if this is a starter, otherwise cooked rice or pasta can be served to make the meal more substantial.

Smoked Haddock with Poached Eggs The cooked eggs can be served on cooked smoked haddock; this is a traditional breakfast dish.

Spanish Supper The poached eggs can be served to turn Spanish Rice (see page 136) into a satisfying supper dish.

Buck Rarebit Prepare Traditional Welsh Rarebit (see page 159). Spread this on the required number of slices of toast and grill the top until golden while the eggs are cooked. Serve the poached eggs on the rarebit.

Eggs Macaroni Serve the poached eggs with buttered cooked macaroni and plenty of Parmesan cheese. Season with freshly ground black pepper and top with chopped parsley.

Eggs Mornay

———— SERVES 4 ————

This is a good old favourite, made even easier with a microwave oven. Serve the eggs with their cheese sauce coating on a bed of cooked rice or pasta. A salad (of anything in season) will make this dish into a hearty supper.

8 large eggs
40 g/1½ oz plain flour
salt and freshly ground
    black pepper
600 ml/1 pint milk
25 g/1 oz butter

175 g/6 oz Cheddar
    cheese, grated
25 g/1 oz fresh
    breadcrumbs
chopped parsley to
    garnish

Cook the eggs in a saucepan of boiling water for 10 minutes, then drain and shell them.

While the eggs are cooking make the sauce: place the flour and plenty of seasoning in a large basin, then gradually whisk in the milk and add the butter. Cook on full power for 10 minutes, whisking twice during cooking. Whisk in 100 g/4 oz of the cheese.

Arrange the cooked eggs on rice or pasta if wished, or in an ovenproof dish. Pour over the sauce. Mix the breadcrumbs with the remaining cheese, then sprinkle this over the sauce grill until golden. Sprinkle chopped parsley on top and serve at once.

Devilled Eggs

———— SERVES 4 ————

8 eggs
1 onion, chopped
1 red pepper
100 g/4 oz lean bacon
1 clove garlic, crushed
2 tablespoons plain flour
2 tablespoons
    concentrated tomato
    purée

1 tablespoon prepared
    mustard
dash of Worcestershire
    sauce
½ chicken stock cube
300 ml/½ pint boiling
    water
chopped parsley to
    garnish

Cook the eggs in a saucepan of boiling water for 10 minutes, then drain and rinse them under cold water.

While the eggs are cooking, prepare the sauce. Place the onion in a large basin (1.15-litre/6-pint capacity). Cut the stalk end off the pepper, then remove all the seeds and pith from inside. Chop the pepper shell and put it into the basin with the onion. Cut off and discard the rinds from the bacon, then chop the rashers and add them to the onion and pepper. Stir in the garlic and cook on full power for 5 minutes.

Stir in the flour, tomato purée, mustard and Worcestershire sauce. Crumble in the stock cube into the basin, then gradually pour in the boiling water, stirring all the time. Return the sauce to the microwave and cook for a further 8 minutes, whisking the sauce once during cooking.

Shell the cooked eggs – they should still be hot – and cut them in half. Arrange the halves in individual dishes and spoon the sauce over them. Add a garnish of chopped parsley and serve at once.

Curried Eggs with Prawns

─── SERVES 4 ───

The addition of prawns to a simple boiled-egg curry makes this a slightly special dish. If you would prefer to make the curry without the prawns, then it will taste good on its own. Serve with Basmati Rice (see page 129).

1 large onion, chopped
2 cloves garlic, crushed
50 g/2 oz fresh root
 ginger, grated
4 green cardamoms
4 tablespoons oil
salt and black pepper
2 tablespoons ground
 coriander

1 chicken stock cube
300 ml/½ pint boiling
 water
8 eggs
225 g/8 oz peeled cooked
 prawns
2 tablespoons chopped
 fresh coriander

Place the onion in a basin with the garlic, ginger and cardamoms. Stir in the oil and add seasoning, then cook on full power for 4 minutes. Blend this mixture in a liquidiser or food processor to make a smooth paste. Return the paste to the basin and stir in the coriander, crumbled stock cube and water. Cook this sauce for a further 5 minutes.

While the sauce is cooking boil the eggs in a saucepan of boiling water for 10 minutes, then rinse them under cold water and remove their shells. Stir the prawns into the sauce and cook for 1 minute. Arrange the eggs in a serving dish and pour the prawns in sauce over them. Top with chopped coriander and serve at once.

This curry sauce can be served with poached eggs. Make the sauce first, then poach the eggs according to the instructions on page 153. Reheat the sauce for 1 minute while the eggs are standing. Pour the sauce into a serving dish and carefully scoop the eggs into it.

Breakfast Cocottes

———— SERVES 4 ————

Although this recipe is intended to be served for breakfast, these savoury bacon and egg pots taste good for any light meal. Serve with hot buttered toast.

100 g/4 oz mushrooms, sliced
4 tablespoons milk
salt and freshly ground black pepper

4 large eggs
4 lean rashers bacon
a little chopped parsley to garnish

Divide the mushrooms between four individual cocottes or casserole dishes. Make sure they are suitable for the microwave oven. Pour 1 tablespoon of the milk into each and add seasoning to taste. Crack an egg into each of the dishes. Cut off and discard the rinds from the bacon, then chop the rashers. Sprinkle the bacon over the eggs and pierce each yolk with just the point of a cocktail stick.

Cover the cocottes with cling film and cook on full power for 4 minutes. Allow to stand for 2 minutes, then sprinkle each with a little chopped parsley and serve at once.

Bacon and Tomato Breakfast

———— SERVES 2 TO 4 ————

The number of servings you will get out of this dish depends very much on individual requirements. If you are serving the dish on its own, with just some crunchy toast, then for a hearty breakfast it will serve two. For a light breakfast it could serve four. If the tomatoes and bacon are served with eggs or to accompany smoked haddock, they will serve four.

8 tomatoes
freshly ground black pepper

175 g/6 oz lean bacon, smoked or unsmoked as you prefer

Peel the tomatoes if you like, following the instructions on page 123, then cut them into quarters and arrange them in a dish – a soufflé dish or similar is ideal. Sprinkle plenty of black pepper over the tomatoes.

Cut the rinds off the bacon, then cut the rashers into very fine strips – you may find that a pair of kitchen scissors is the best implement for this. Sprinkle the bacon over the tomatoes and cook on full power for 7 minutes. Serve at once.

Porridge

———— SERVES 1 ————

This is a useful recipe for busy mornings – so teach the family to prepare their own winter breakfasts. The best container to use is a deep individual bowl which can be used to serve the cereal too. The porridge can be made with half milk and half water if you prefer.

50 g/2 oz quick porridge oats
300 ml/½ pint water

½ teaspoon salt
milk and sugar to serve

Put the oats in a bowl with the water and stir well. Add the salt and cook on full power for 4½ minutes, stirring once after 3½ minutes, then again when the porridge is cooked.

Pour milk into the porridge and serve with sugar to taste.

Smoked Mackerel Oaty

———— SERVES 4 TO 6 ————

This interesting combination of smoked fish and porridge oats actually tastes quite delicious! It is fairly rich, so depending on how hungry you are you may prefer to serve quite small portions. If you favour savoury breakfast dishes – particularly smoked fish ones – then why not try this one morning? Personally, I find it delicious for lunch or supper but a little overpowering for the beginning of the day.

1 small onion, chopped
50 g/2 oz butter
100 g/4 oz porridge oats
100 g/4 oz mild cheese, finely grated
675 g/1½ lb smoked

mackerel fillets (about 4 large ones)
150 ml/¼ pint soured cream
2 tablespoons creamed horseradish

Place the onion in a fairly large bowl and add the butter. Cook on full power for 3 minutes. Stir in the oats and cook for a further 5 minutes. Stir thoroughly and add the cheese, then mix well.

Remove all the skin from the mackerel fillets, then flake the fish in a microwave-proof dish removing any bones. Stir in the soured cream and horseradish. Top this fish mixture with the oats and cook for a further 7 minutes.

Place the casserole under a hot grill to brown and crisp the oats and cheese, then serve at once.

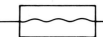

Cheese can be brought to room temperature quickly in the microwave oven. It should be unwrapped and placed on a plate. Cook on full power for just a few seconds to take the chill off the food.

Three Fondues

Fondues are fun to eat and easy to prepare – particularly if you can put the dish full of cheese in the microwave without fear of burning the bottom. For a light hearted dinner party a fondue is ideal and it can be as filling or as simple as you like depending on which accompaniments you serve.

Here are three fondue recipes, all quite different, but each delicious. The traditional Swiss fondue is made from white wine and Swiss cheese; the blue cheese fondue is good for a family supper, cheap and well flavoured; the Caerphilly fondue is very light and creamy with the slight tang of Caerphilly cheese.

Swiss Fondue

150 ml/¼ pint dry white wine
1 clove garlic, crushed
450 g/1 lb Gruyère cheese, grated

4 tablespoons plain flour
2 tablespoons sherry

Place the wine and garlic in a large fondue pot – not a metal one or one which has a metal trim. The great thing about making fondue in the microwave is that the bowl does not have to stand up to the heat of the hob. So, if you like, you can use an attractive microwaveproof serving bowl of any type. Cook on full power for 3 minutes.

Meanwhile, mix the cheese with the flour, making sure all the shreds are well coated. Beat half the cheese into the hot wine and cook for a further 2 minutes, then beat in the remaining cheese. Cook for a further 2 minutes. Add the sherry and give the fondue a good beating, then cook for a final 4 minutes.

Place the bowl over a fondue burner or candle plate warmer and keep hot so that everybody can help themselves from the bowl.

Caerphilly Fondue

150 ml/¼ pint dry cider
450 g/1 lb Caerphilly cheese, grated or finely crumbled

2 tablespoons plain flour
1 tablespoon prepared English mustard
freshly grated nutmeg

Pour the cider into the pot and cook on full power for 3 minutes.

Meanwhile, mix the cheese with the flour, then add it to the hot cider and beat thoroughly. Cook on full power for 3 minutes. Beat in the mustard and nutmeg to taste, then cook for a further 3 minutes.

Stand the pot over a burner or warmer and serve at once.

Blue Cheese Fondue

150 ml/¼ pint pale ale
225 g/8 oz Cheddar cheese
225 g/8 oz Danish blue

cheese, finely crumbled or grated
2 tablespoons plain flour

Pour the beer into the chosen fondue pot (see tip). Cook on full power for 3 minutes.

Meanwhile, mix the cheeses with the flour, then beat them all at once into the hot ale. Return the pot to the microwave and cook for 3 minutes. Remove and beat thoroughly, then cook for a final 2 to 3 minutes.

Stand the pot over a burner or warmer and serve at once.

WHAT TO HAVE WITH FONDUE

Bread Cut some crusty fresh bread into bite-sized cubes. French bread is ideal because it is so crisp.

Cauliflower Separate a cauliflower into small florets, removing any thick stalk.

Celery Cut scrubbed celery sticks into bite-sized lengths. Reserve any celery leaves to garnish the bowl of vegetables.

Apples Choose crisp, fairly tart dessert apples. Cut them into quarters and remove their cores, then cut the unpeeled apples into chunks. Toss the pieces in lemon juice to prevent discoloration.

Ham Cut neat cubes of cooked ham. You can also use garlic sausage or salami.

Sausages Grill some cocktail sausages until they are very crisp and brown. Drain on absorbent kitchen paper and serve. These can be reheated in the microwave for a few minutes if necessary.

Salads Salads which can be eaten with a fork always go down well with fondue. Make a tomato salad, cucumber salad or any seasonal salad. Cut all the ingredients up very small so that the salad can be eaten with a fork. If you are likely to have very hungry guests, then make a Rice Salad (see page 138) too.

Savoury Cheesecake

—— SERVES 6 ——

This is very simple to make and absolutely delicious! It is ideal for serving as part of a cold buffet, or it can be complemented by baked potatoes and a crisp green salad. If the idea sounds a little strange, try it first, then decide what you think, hopefully you'll be as pleased with the result as I was when I first made it.

100 g/4 oz butter
50 g/2 oz water biscuits
1 (150-g/5-oz) packet
  ready salted crisps
Topping:
25 g/1 oz butter
25 g/1 oz plain flour
300 ml/½ pint milk

1 chicken stock cube
450 g/1 lb cream cheese
100 g/4 oz garlic sausage,
  chopped
4 spring onions, chopped
sliced tomatoes to
  garnish

Melt the butter in a large basin on full power for 1½ minutes. Crush the biscuits and crisps finely, then add them to the melted butter and mix well. Press into the base of a 25-cm/10-in quiche dish and refrigerate until firm.

Place the butter, flour and milk in a basin, then gradually whisk in the crumbled stock cube. Cook for 5 minutes, whisking once during cooking. Whisk thoroughly at the end of the cooking time, then beat in the cream cheese, garlic sausage and spring onions. Spread the mixture evenly over the crisp base and chill until firm.

Garnish the cheesecake with a ring of tomato slices. Cut into wedges to serve.

ALTERNATIVE GARNISHING INGREDIENTS:
Grilled bacon rolls with tomatoes cut into wedges.
Whole cooked prawns with lemon wedges.
Thin slices of smoked salmon, rolled into neat slices, with lemon twists.
Cucumber slices and radish slices.
Sliced green stuffed olives with fine strips of red pepper.
Rolls of cooked ham with halved canned pineapple rings and parsley sprigs.
Toasted split almonds and diced cooked chicken with chopped parsley.
Whole cooked prawns and fine wedges of lemon.
Piped cream cheese (add a little milk to give a piping consistency) with tiny whole red chillies and sprigs of parsley.
Stoned black olives, each filled with a piece of walnut, and neat rolls of salami.
Quartered hard-boiled eggs and tomato wedges with sprigs of watercress.
Neat rows of chopped peeled tomatoes, without their seeds, and finely chopped green pepper.

Traditional Welsh Rarebit

—— SERVES 4 ——

This delicious quick snack can be made and stored in a covered basin in the refrigerator for a few days, then spread on toast and grilled to serve.

50 ml/2 fl oz pale ale
1 teaspoon prepared English mustard
225 g/8 oz Caerphilly cheese, grated or finely crumbled

toast to serve
Garnishes: (optional)
onion rings
watercress sprigs
parsley sprigs
tomato wedges

Pour the ale into a basin and heat for 2 minutes. Stir in the mustard and cheese and cook on full power for 3 minutes. Beat thoroughly, then spread on hot toast and grill until browned. Serve at once. Alternatively, allow the cheese mixture to cool and chill it until it is to be used.

Whisky Rarebit This tastes excellent; stir 1 tablespoon whisky into enough milk to give 50 ml/2 fl oz and use instead of the ale in the above recipe.

Herbed Rarebit Stir 2 tablespoons chopped fresh herbs into the prepared rarebit before spreading it on the toast.

Buck Rarebit Top each portion with a poached egg just before serving (see page 153).

Ham Rarebit Lay a slice of cooked ham on the toast before spreading and grilling the cheese.

Breakfast Rarebit Top the rarebit with a poached egg (see page 153) and a couple of cooked bacon rashers (see page 169).

Continental Rarebit Top each portion with garlic sausage and fine green or red pepper rings.

Sausage Rarebit Top each portion with grilled sausages and tomato wedges.

Smokey Rarebit Top each portion with a little flaked smoked mackerel. Add chopped fresh parsley and a squeeze of lemon juice.

Sardine Rarebit Top the bread with sardines, then spread a little rarebit over each portion and grill until brown.

Gnocchi

———— SERVES 4 ————

Gnocchi is a type of pasta which is prepared fresh from semolina, potatoes or flour. Here is a recipe for semolina gnocchi, adjusted to cook in the microwave oven.

The semolina is first cooked in water to make a paste, as for a sweet pudding but very much thicker. The paste is then poured into a tin to set and cut into squares, or shapes and these are cooked in boiling water then grilled, baked or served with a sauce. In the microwave oven the basic paste should not be as thick as for boiling; the cut gnocchi can then be cooked in a dish covered with cling film, topped with cheese and grilled for a crisp, golden crust.

If you like, serve the plain gnocchi (not grilled) with a Tomato Sauce (see page 200) poured over the squares, or with a Bolognese sauce (see Spaghetti Bolognese, page 140). Alternatively, for a really delicious result, offer a Pesto Sauce (see below) to accompany the crusty grilled gnocchi. A fresh crisp green salad is by far the best accompaniment for gnocchi.

600 ml/1 pint boiling water	75 g/3 oz butter
200 g/7 oz semolina	*Topping:*
8 tablespoons grated Parmesan cheese	100 g/4 oz mozzarella cheese, grated
1 large egg, beaten	2 tablespoons grated Parmesan cheese
salt and freshly ground black pepper	1 tablespoon oregano

Pour the boiling water into a large mixing bowl and gradually whisk in the semolina. Cook on full power for 4 minutes, then beat the mixture thoroughly.

Beat in the Parmesan cheese, then when it is thoroughly incorporated beat in the egg, plenty of seasoning and the butter. Turn the mixture into a shallow tin – about 30 × 18 cm/12 × 7 in – then smooth the top with a palette knife or spatula and cover with cling film. Set aside to cool, then chill the gnocchi for several hours or overnight.

To complete the cooking, cut the gnocchi into squares. Grease a shallow dish with butter (one which is suitable for the microwave oven and for putting under the grill to brown the gnocchi) and lay the squares of gnocchi, slightly overlapping, in it. You will need a fairly large dish – about 23–25 cm/9–10 in. in diameter. Cover the dish with cling film and cook for 12 minutes.

Meanwhile, mix the cheeses and oregano for the topping. Heat the grill. Sprinkle the topping evenly over the gnocchi and place it under the grill until well browned and bubbling. Serve at once, on its own or with a pesto sauce.

To cook half the quantity of gnocchi, allow 3 minutes cooking time for the semolina in water, then 7 to 10 for the gnocchi shapes. Top and grill as in the main recipe.

Pesto Sauce

2 tablespoons pine nuts	150 ml/¼ pint olive oil
2 cloves garlic, crushed	salt and freshly ground black pepper
large handful fresh basil	
4 tablespoons freshly grated Parmesan cheese	

Grind the pine nuts with the garlic – a liquidiser or food processor is useful for this. Chop the basil including the thinner stalks – discard only the very thick ones as the others will contribute to the flavour. Add the basil and Parmesan cheese to the nuts and blend the mixture to a purée. Gradually work in the oil and add seasoning to taste, then serve with gnocchi, with Ham and Fennel Risotto (see page 134), with Stuffed Peppers (see page 124) or with a bowl of plain cooked rice (see page 128) for a very simple supper.

Salmon and Celery Gratin

———— SERVES 4 ————

1 onion, chopped	*Topping:*
2 tablespoons oil	100 g/4 oz Cheddar cheese, grated
1 (425-g/15-oz) can chopped tomatoes	50 g/2 oz fresh breadcrumbs
1 (213-g/7½-oz) can salmon	*Garnish:*
salt and freshly ground black pepper	chopped parsley
1 (540-g/1.19-g) can celery hearts, drained	coarsely grated lemon rind

Place the onion in a bowl with the oil and cook on full power for 4 minutes. Pour in the tomatoes. Drain the liquid from the salmon into the onion and tomato mixture, then flake the fish, removing any skin and bones, and add it to the mixture. Stir in the seasoning to taste. Pour this into a gratin dish and arrange the celery hearts on top. Cook for 7 minutes.

Meanwhile, mix the cheese with the breadcrumbs and sprinkle the topping mixture in an even layer over the celery. Place under a hot grill until well browned and very crisp. Garnish with chopped parsley and lemon rind then serve.

Sherried Chicken Livers

SERVES 2 TO 4

For a light, very quick snack these creamed chicken livers are good served on hot buttered toast or on croûtes of bread. For a slightly more substantial lunch or supper dish, serve them with rice or pasta, or with a baked potato.

1 onion, chopped	150 ml/¼ pint single cream
25 g/1 oz butter	salt and freshly ground
2 tablespoons plain flour	black pepper
2 tablespoons dry sherry	2 tablespoons chopped
450 g/1 lb chicken livers,	parsley
chopped	

Place the onion and butter in a large basin and cook on full power for 3 minutes. Stir in the flour, sherry and livers and cook for a further 6 minutes, stirring once during this time.

Pour in the cream and add seasoning to taste, then cook for 3 minutes. Stir lightly and serve at once, sprinkled with chopped parsley.

Corned Beef Hash

SERVES 4

The cooking time for this allows for chilled vegetables which have been in the refrigerator for several hours.

450–675 g/1–1½ lb cooked	450 g/1 lb corned beef, cut
mixed vegetables (to	into cubes
include potatoes with	salt and freshly ground
cabbage, carrots, beans	black pepper
or any others)	50 g/2 oz butter

Roughly chop the vegetables and mix them with the corned beef, adding plenty of seasoning. Press the mixture into a 20-cm/8-in shallow dish (a quiche or gratin dish) and dot with butter.

Cook on full power for 6 to 8 minutes. Brown the hash under a hot grill if you like, but it tastes good even if it isn't grilled. Serve from the dish, cutting it into wedges.

Avocado Savoury

SERVES 4

This is delicious for lunch or supper; serve a tomato salad with a good garlic dressing and plenty of hot French bread as accompaniments.

1 onion, chopped	6 stuffed green olives,
50 g/2 oz butter	chopped
salt and freshly ground	25 g/1 oz fresh
black pepper	breadcrumbs
2 large ripe, firm avocado	2 tablespoons grated
pears	Parmesan cheese
a little lemon juice	
100 g/4 oz cooked ham,	
roughly chopped	

Place the onion and half the butter in a gratin dish and stir in seasoning to taste. Cook on full power for 4 minutes.

Meanwhile, halve the avocado pears and remove their stones. Peel and roughly chop them, then sprinkle lemon juice over the pieces. Add the avocado to the onion and sprinkle the chopped ham and olives on top. Mix the breadcrumbs and Parmesan cheese, sprinkle over the ham and dot with the remaining butter. Cook for 4 minutes.

Place the gratin under a hot grill until golden brown on top, then serve at once.

Pizza

———— SERVES 2 TO 4 ————

Quick pizzas using bought prepared bases can be quite tasty, depending on how good the topping is. If you would prefer to use your own home-made bread base, then make several when you have your conventional oven on and cook them until they are just set but not browned. Freeze these to top and reheat in the microwave.

25-cm/10-in pizza base
I large onion, chopped
I or 2 cloves garlic, crushed
3 tablespoons olive oil
salt and black pepper
2 tablespoons concentrated tomato purée
2 teaspoon marjoram
pinch of thyme
225 g/8 oz mushrooms, sliced
100 g/4 oz mozzarella cheese, shredded
I (50-g/2 oz) can anchovy fillets
a few black olives, stoned

Place the pizza base on a large plate or in a shallow dish. Place the onion, garlic and oil in a basin and cook on full power for 4 minutes. Stir in the seasoning to taste, the tomato purée, herbs and mushrooms. Spread this mixture over the pizza base, then top it with cheese, the anchovy fillets arranged in a lattice and their oil, drizzled evenly over the whole area, and the olives, decoratively arranged.

Cook the pizza on full power for 4½ to 5 minutes, then allow to stand for 2 minutes before serving.

ALTERNATIVE TOPPINGS

Fresh Tomato and Salami Peel (see page 123) and slice 350 g/12 oz ripe tomatoes. Arrange these on top of the cooked onion and garlic on the pizza (there is no need to add the concentrated tomato purée to the onion). Add the herbs and lay 100 g/4 oz sliced salami on top. Sprinkle the cheese over and cook as above.

Seafood Pizza Cook the onion as in the main recipe and mix in the other ingredients apart from the mushrooms. Top with 100 g/4 oz peeled cooked prawns, 100 g/4 oz cooked mussels and I (200-g/7-oz) can tuna fish, drained and flaked. Add the cheese, anchovies and olives and cook as in the main recipe.

No-cheese Pizza For some people who are allergic to cheese, traditional pizza has to be avoided. Omit the cheese from the recipe but add extra mushrooms or other meat toppings, such as salami. Sprinkle a little olive oil over the pizza to prevent the ingredients from drying out during cooking.

Ham and Cream Cheese Pizza Omit the mozzarella cheese, anchovies and black olives from the above recipe. Top the pizza with 225 g/8 oz cooked ham slices, arranged in neat rolls. Add 225 g/8 oz Philadelphia cheese, cut into chunks, and a few chopped stuffed green olives. Cook as in the main recipe.

Garlic Sausage Pizza Top the pizza with 100 g/4 oz thinly sliced garlic sausage and very thinly sliced Gruyère cheese. Arrange the anchovies and olives on top and cook as in the main recipe.

Special Florentine Supper

———— SERVES 4 ————

This is a tasty, economical supper dish to serve with hot buttered rice, freshly made toast or plenty of warm crusty bread.

2 (227-g/8-oz) packets frozen chopped spinach
I onion, chopped
50 g/2 oz butter
salt and freshly ground black pepper
freshly grated nutmeg
8 slices good cooked ham (the better the ham the nicer the dish)
a little prepared mustard (try mustard with chives or wholegrain mustard)
4 eggs
2 tablespoons double cream
4 large ripe tomatoes, chopped, to garnish

Defrost the spinach, if necessary, by placing the packets individually on a large plate and cooking separately for 3 minutes each. Set aside.

Place the onion in a basin with half the butter and cook on full power for 6 minutes. Drain the spinach and add it to the onion with seasoning to taste and a little nutmeg. Mix thoroughly, then transfer the spinach to a shallow dish so that it forms a fairly thick layer on the base.

Spread a little mustard over the slices of ham and roll them up neatly. Arrange these on top of the spinach allowing room for the eggs to go in between when they are cooked. Cover with cling film and set aside for a while.

Rinse out the basin which was used to cook the onion, then put the eggs in it and whisk them with seasoning to taste plus the cream. Add the remaining butter to the eggs and cook for 2 minutes. Whisk the eggs thoroughly, then cook for a further I minute.

Cook the ham and spinach for 5 minutes, then remove from the oven. Replace the eggs in the oven and cook for a further I minute. Whisk them thoroughly. Uncover the ham and spinach and arrange spoonfuls of the scrambled egg in between the slices of ham. Top with the chopped tomato and serve at once.

If you have a browning dish, follow the manufacturer's instructions for heating it up, then cook the pizza on it for a crunchy base. This is particularly useful if you are using home-made, par-cooked bases instead of the bought type.

Couscous

——— SERVES 4 ———

In North African countries couscous is a dish consisting of a spicy mutton or chicken stew, served with a steamed semolina preparation; it is this semolina product that we commonly tend to think of as couscous.

The small grains of semolina are already cooked and they require carefully steaming – usually in a special steamer without a lid and known as a couscousière – to prevent them from becoming a firm lump of unpalateable stodge. The microwave oven is ideal for this cooking process – the grains are rinsed in water, then cooked damp for just 5 minutes.

If you like you can serve the couscous to accompany the Pork with Oregano and Olives (see page 90) or Fish Plaki (see page 45). Alternatively, you can complete the recipe below and serve the couscous with the vegetables and nuts, and offer a bowl of crumbled feta cheese as an accompaniment.

I large onion, chopped	225 g/8 oz couscous
4 tablespoons olive oil	salt and freshly ground
I red pepper	black pepper
50 g/2 oz blanched	*To serve:*
almonds, chopped	225 g/8 oz feta cheese,
2 cloves garlic, crushed	finely crumbled
50 g/2 oz black olives,	½ Iceberg lettuce,
pitted and roughly	shredded
chopped	

Place the onion in a large bowl with the oil. Cut the stalk end off the pepper, then remove all the seeds and pith from inside. Chop the shell and add it to the onion. Stir in the almonds, garlic and olives and cook on full power for 5 minutes.

To cook the couscous, put it in a bowl and pour in cold water to cover. Gently run your fingers through the grains swirling them in the water without damaging them. Drain off the water, leaving the couscous moist. Cover with cling film, allowing a small gap for the steam to escape, and cook on full power for 5 minutes. Remove from the oven and leave covered while the vegetables are heated.

Return the onion mixture to the oven and cook for a further 2 minutes. Stir in seasoning to taste. Scoop the couscous into a ring on a serving dish, then ladle the vegetables into the middle. Top with the lettuce and cheese and serve at once, before the hot ingredients have time to become cold. The contrast between the hot and cold is very pleasing, but serve the cold mixture separately if you prefer.

Quick Creamy Tuna

——— SERVES 2 TO 4 ———

This really is a quick out-of-a-can meal to serve with rice or pasta and it tastes far better than any of the commercially prepared supper foods. Serve it for two persons on a dish of cooked rice or pour the fish mixture over plenty of cooked pasta and toss it all together well to make a hearty supper for four.

I large onion, chopped	4 tablespoons dry sherry
I red pepper	4 tablespoons chopped
I (198-g/7-oz) can tuna in	fresh parsley
oil	salt and freshly ground
I (295-g/10.4-oz) can	black pepper
condensed mushroom	
soup	

Place the onion in a basin. Cut the stalk end off the pepper, then remove all the seeds and pith from inside. Chop the pepper shell and add it to the onion. Drain all the oil from the can of tuna and pour over the onion and pepper mixture, then stir well. Cover with cling film, allowing a small gap for the steam to escape, then cook on full power for 7 minutes.

Add the tuna to the basin, breaking it into flakes with a fork. Stir in the soup and sherry, then re-cover the basin and cook for a further 4 minutes. Stir in the parsley and seasoning to taste before serving.

Note: this saucy fish mixture can be transformed into any number of delicious dishes; for example try turning it into a pie dish and adding a puff pastry crust. It can be topped with creamed potatoes if you prefer, or it can be used as a filling for a lasagne or savoury pancakes.

Sausagemeat Savoury

——— SERVES 4 ———

Although I would not suggest that you cook sausages in the microwave oven, sausagemeat can be cooked successfully in this type of recipe, where it is broken up and served in a sauce. Ladle the cooked sausagemeat over a dish of rice or pasta or into a ring of piped mashed potatoes. It can also be used as a filling for a pie.

I onion, chopped	salt and freshly ground
I large green pepper	black pepper
I teaspoon thyme	4 tablespoons chopped
450 g/I lb good quality	fresh parsley
pork sausagemeat	croûtons (page 53) to
I (425-g/15-oz) can	garnish
chopped tomatoes	

Place the onion in a microwave-proof casserole dish or bowl. Cut the stalk end off the pepper, then remove all the seeds and pith from inside and chop the green shell. Add this to the onion with the thyme and sausagemeat. Break the meat up using a wooden spoon, then cook, uncovered, on full power for 10 minutes. Break the meat up once during cooking and give it a good stir.

At the end of the cooking time stir in the tomatoes and seasoning to taste, then cook for a final 3 minutes. Lightly stir in the parsley, then serve the sausagemeat topped with crunchy croûtons.

Red Bean Bake

——— SERVES 4 ———

This savoury bean crumble is delicious with a fresh mixed salad for lunch or supper, or it can be served as an accompaniment to grilled meats. It is also ideal for serving as the main dish for a vegetarian meal.

1 large onion, chopped
2 cloves garlic, crushed
salt and freshly ground
    black pepper
50 g/2 oz butter
1 (425-g/15-oz) can red
    kidney beans, drained
1 (425-g/15-oz) can
    chopped tomatoes
300 ml/½ pint red wine,
    cider or stock

large bunch of fresh
    herbs, for example
    sage, parsley, rosemary
    and thyme
4 thick slices bread, made
    into crumbs
75 g/3 oz Cheddar cheese,
    grated

Place the onion and garlic together in a casserole, add seasoning to taste and half the butter. Cook on full power for 4 minutes, stirring once. Add the kidney beans and tomatoes, then stir in the wine (or cider or stock if you prefer) and cook for 5 minutes.

Meanwhile, wash and trim the herbs: for the best flavour use a fairly large bunch of parsley, a large sprig each of sage and rosemary, and several sprigs of thyme. If you do not have a wide selection of fresh herbs try using a combination of fresh and dried. Finely chop the herbs you have chosen and mix them into the breadcrumbs. Stir in the cheese and add seasoning to taste, then spoon this mixture lightly over the top of the beans; do not press the topping down. Cook for 4 minutes.

Meanwhile, heat up the grill, then dot the remaining butter over the top of the crumble and place it under the hot grill until golden. Serve immediately.

Ratatouille Chick Peas

——— SERVES 4 ———

This makes a good lunch or supper dish. The recipe uses canned ratatouille but if you have any leftover ratatouille then it will taste even better. Serve with hot crusty bread.

2 (375-g/13.2-oz) cans
    ratatouille (or home-
    made ratatouille)
1 (400-g/14-oz) can chick
    peas, drained
100 g/4 oz cheese, grated

25 g/1 oz fresh
    breadcrumbs
salt and freshly ground
    black pepper
1 teaspoon dried mixed
    herbs

Mix the ratatouille with the chick peas and divide the mixture between four individual dishes – casserole dishes or small ovenproof dishes are ideal. Cover each one with cling film and cook on full power for 7 minutes, turning each dish once.

Meanwhile, mix the cheese with the breadcrumbs, seasoning and herbs. Sprinkle this topping over the ratatouille and cook under a hot grill until golden brown. Serve at once.

Ravioli Snack

——— SERVES 2 ———

Canned ravioli can be heated very successfully in the microwave oven to be served on toast, or in any of the ways suggested below.

1 (425-g/15-oz) can ravioli
2 or 4 slices hot buttered
    toast

Pour the ravioli with all the sauce from the can into a bowl or basin and cook on full power for 4 minutes.

Make the toast and butter it while the ravioli is heating, then spoon the ravioli on to the toast and serve at once.

RAVIOLI IDEAS

Grilled Ravioli Heat the ravioli as above, then sprinkle a good pinch of oregano over the top and add plenty of grated cheese, or a generous sprinkling of grated Parmesan cheese. Cook under a hot grill until golden and bubbling.

Special Ravioli Finely chop 1 onion and cook it with 1 crushed clove of garlic and 50 g/2 oz butter for 4 minutes. Pour in the ravioli and add a teaspoon of dried mixed herbs. Heat as above, then serve with plenty of warmed crusty bread.

Ravioli with Ham and Tomato Roughly chop 100 g/4 oz cooked ham. Peel and chop 225 g/8 oz ripe tomatoes, then mix them with the ravioli, adding the ham and plenty of seasoning and some chopped parsley. Heat for 6 minutes, then serve on or with hot buttered toast.

Suppertime Kebabs

———— SERVES 2 TO 4 ————

Arrange these kebabs on a bed of cooked rice – why not try Tomato Rice or Herb Rice (both on page 128) – or on a dish of Macaroni Cheese (see page 141).

1 (241-g/8½-oz) smoked   2 carrots, sliced
  pork sausage   1 green pepper
225 g/8 oz cauliflower

Cut the sausage into slices – they should not be too thick. Break the cauliflower into small florets and slice the carrots (medium-thick slices are best so that they cook easily). Cut the stalk end off the pepper, remove all the seeds and pith from inside, then cut the flesh into squares.

Thread all the prepared ingredients on to four wooden skewers and place them in a roasting bag. Secure the end of the bag loosely with an elastic band, then cook on full power for 5 to 6 minutes. At the end of the cooking time the vegetables should still be crunchy. Allow to stand for 2 minutes in the bag, then remove and serve as required.

Sardine Baps

———— SERVES 2 TO 4 ————

This is a quick and easy hot snack, and they actually taste rather good! If you want to dress these baps up with an elaborate garnish you could serve them as a really cheap hot first course, but it is not the sort of thing you would expect to find at an elegant dinner party!

1 (124-g/4⅜-oz) can   2 baps
  sardines in oil   2 tablespoons Parmesan
grated rind of 1 lemon   cheese grated
a little lemon juice   *Garnish:* (optional)
salt and freshly ground   2 small tomatoes, cut into
  black pepper   small wedges
1 small clove garlic,   halved lemon slices
  crushed (optional)   watercress sprigs

Mash the sardines with the oil from the can, then beat in the lemon rind and juice, seasoning to taste and the garlic (if used). Split the baps and spread the sardine mixture evenly over them. Sprinkle the cheese on top and arrange the baps on a large plate. Cook on full power, turning the plate once. Serve, topped with the garnishing ingredients if you like.

Tostada Snack

SERVES 4

Crisp tostadas – Mexican corn pancakes – are available in packets from most supermarkets and they make a very good base for many a quick snack. Here are some ideas to try, add any other ingredients you like.

4 tostadas
1 (298-g/10½-oz) can cream-style corn
100 g/4 oz button mushrooms, sliced

2 pickled jalapeño chillies, chopped
salt and freshly ground black pepper
100 g/4 oz cheese, grated

Place the tostadas on a large plate, then spread the corn over them. Top with the mushrooms and chillies, then add plenty of seasoning. Sprinkle the cheese very evenly over the tostadas and cook on full power for 5 to 6 minutes, turning the plate round once during cooking. The tostadas will be very hot so allow about 2 minutes standing time before they are eaten.

MORE TOPPING IDEAS

The cream corn makes a good, moist base on which to build up the topping, but you can substitute canned creamed mushrooms instead if you like.

Corn and Hot Bean Make up the Hot Bean Dip according to the instructions on page 33. Mound this on top of the creamed corn and cook the tostadas on full power for 4 to 5 minutes. While they are cooking, halve, stone and peel 2 ripe avocado pears. Slice these and arrange them on top of the bean dip. Serve at once.

Chorizo Tostadas Arrange 100 g/4 oz sliced chorizo sausage on top of the creamed corn, adding the chillies if you like hot food. Cook for 5 to 6 minutes on full power. Meanwhile, halve, stone and peel 1 ripe avocado pear. Mash this with a little lemon juice and 1 crushed clove of garlic. Spoon a little avocado on each tostada and serve.

Chicken Tostada Chop 225 g/8 oz cooked chicken meat and pile it on top of the corn. Add 2 tablespoons mayonnaise and plenty of seasoning to each, spreading it to cover most of the chicken. Cook for 5 to 6 minutes on full power. Add chopped parsley and serve.

Prawn Tostadas Mix 225 g/8 oz peeled cooked pawns with a little paprika, the grated rind of 1 small lemon and 2 tablespoons chopped parsley. Spoon these on top of the corn and heat on full power for 5 minutes. Serve at once.

Anchovy Bread

—— SERVES 4 TO 6 ——

This hot anchovy bread makes a good alternative to a first course if you are planning an informal supper party. It is also good buffet fare, so hand round to those who are not inclined to indulge in a full meal.

I tablespoon anchovy essence	freshly ground black pepper
grated rind of $\frac{1}{2}$ lemon	50 g/2 oz butter
a few drops of lemon juice	I short French loaf

Beat the anchovy essence, lemon rind and juice and plenty of pepper into the butter. Cut through the French bread almost to the base to give slices which are all attached.

Spread the butter between the slices and over the top of the loaf, then re-shape it and place it on an oval plate. If the loaf is too long for any of your plates, then cut it in half and place the two pieces side by side.

Cook on full power for I minute. Cut between the slices, then arrange them on a napkin-lined basket to serve.

HOT BREAD IDEAS

Herb Bread Mix 4 tablespoons chopped fresh herbs into the butter instead of the anchovy mixture. Continue as above.

Garlic Bread Beat 2 crushed cloves garlic into the butter and continue as above.

Lemon Bread Beat the grated rind of I large lemon and 2 tablespoons chopped parsley into the butter and continue as above. This is very good with fish or seafood.

Absorbent kitchen paper is very useful for covering foods such as bacon which splatter when cooking in the microwave oven. It is also useful for putting underneath food such as hot dogs.

Hamburgers

If you are going to make your own hamburgers, then I wouldn't suggest that you cook them in the microwave oven because they will taste very much better grilled or barbecued. However, if you buy frozen hamburgers then they can be cooked quite successfully in the microwave and I was quite surprised at just how tasty the results were.

I used all-beef hamburgers, each weighing 100 g/4 oz and they were cooked straight from the freezer. If you are going to serve the hamburgers in buns, then have ready the required number, split and toasted on the cut side. Offer relishes (there is a good Sweet Corn Relish on page 210), mustard and salad ingredients with the hamburgers.

Place the hamburgers on a plate and cover them with absorbent kitchen paper, then cook for the times given below.

COOKING TIMES

2 hamburgers	$5\frac{1}{2}$ minutes
4 hamburgers	9 minutes

Stuffed Pitta Bread

—— SERVES 4 ——

4 slices pitta bread	4 large crisp lettuce leaves
I (298-g/10½-oz) can cream style corn	8 spring onions, trimmed
8 slices garlic sausage	

Split the pitta bread down one side and through the middle to make a neat pocket. Spread some of the corn in each piece and carefully place 2 garlic sausage slices in each pocket. Heat the stuffed pitta two at a time, on a large plate, allowing 2 minutes on full power for each pair.

As soon as the pitta is hot, slip a lettuce leaf and a couple of spring onions into each. Serve at once.

Toasted Sandwiches

The microwave oven can be used to make delicious toasted sandwiches. Toast the required number of slices of bread on both sides. Sandwich these together with the filling – try cheese, ham, tuna fish, cooked chicken or a combination of ingredients – then place the sandwiches on a piece of absorbent kitchen paper on a plate and cook on full power for I to 2 minutes, or long enough to heat the filling. The result is a piping hot sandwich with a crisp toasted crust. The time taken to heat the sandwiches will depend on the type of filling and the number of sandwiches. It is best to cook only two or three sandwiches together at a time and prepare any more in a second batch.

Hot Dogs

I large onion, chopped	prepared mustard to taste
25 g/I oz butter	I–4 frankfurters
salt and black pepper	I–4 long bread rolls, split

Place the onion in a basin with the butter and seasoning to taste. Cook on full power for 5 minutes.

Spread mustard to taste into the required number of rolls and place a frankfurter in each. Place the hot dogs on a piece of absorbent kitchen paper, or on a folded paper napkin, then cook them on full power for the time given below. Spoon a little cooked onion on to each hot dog, then fold the paper or napkin round the roll to serve.

COOKING TIMES

I hot dog	$\frac{3}{4}$–I minute
2 hot dogs	I$\frac{1}{2}$ minutes
3 hot dogs	I$\frac{3}{4}$ minutes
4 hot dogs	2 minutes

Hot Bacon Sandwiches

My idea of a really quick, delicious snack is a hot bacon sandwich made with bread which has been toasted on the outside only – yum! You can choose whether to make the sandwiches with untoasted bread or otherwise, or to put the cooked bacon into rolls instead of sandwiches.

I allow two rashers of bacon for each sandwich. Have the bread buttered, spread with mustard or pickle, or any relish you like. Cook the bacon on a special microwave roasting rack if you have one (but it is not necessary) or lay them on a large plate. Cover the rashers with absorbent kitchen paper and cook them for the times given below.

Make sure the bread is ready before you cook the bacon, so that the rashers can be sandwiched straight away, that way the heat from the bacon warms the bread and in I minute the sandwiches are ready.

COOKING TIMES

2 bacon rashers	I$\frac{1}{2}$–2 minutes
4 bacon rashers	2$\frac{1}{2}$ minutes
6 bacon rashers	4$\frac{1}{2}$ minutes
8 bacon rashers	5 minutes

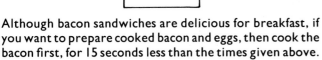

Although bacon sandwiches are delicious for breakfast, if you want to prepare cooked bacon and eggs, then cook the bacon first, for 15 seconds less than the times given above. Cook the eggs next, according to the instructions given on page 153, then when they are standing for serving, finish cooking the bacon for $\frac{1}{2}$ to I minute. Serve at once.

Beans on Toast

—— SERVES I OR 2 ——

The advantage of heating up beans on toast in the microwave is that it saves using a saucepan! An ultra-lazy snack.

I (227-g/8-oz) can baked
  beans
2 slices hot buttered toast

Make the toast under your conventional grill or in an electric toaster, then place the slices on one or two plates and pile the beans on top. Heat on full power for 3 minutes. Serve at once.

Hot Ham and Cheese Muffins

This is a good quick snack for when you are in a hurry but really do want something quite satisfying to eat. Use either wholemeal or plain muffins – both types heat very well in the microwave oven.

Split each muffin and place a folded slice of ham and a slice of cheese inside. Arrange the muffins as far apart as possible on a plate and cook for the following times:

2 muffins	2$\frac{1}{2}$ minutes
4 muffins	4 minutes

FILLING IDEAS

Cheese and Onion Use cheese cut into slices and onion rings.

Cream Cheese and Mushroom Fill an open mushroom generously with Philadephia cheese (or similar, because a very soft cream cheese is unsuitable as it will melt) then sandwich this in the muffin.

Pork and Apple Arrange a slice of dessert apple and a generous slice of roast pork in each muffin.

Corned Beef and Mustard Spread each muffin generously with the mustard of your choice, then add a thick slice of corned beef.

PUDDINGS & DESSERTS

Not only is the microwave oven ideal for cooking perfect poached fruits and simple crumbles or crisps, but it can be useful for turning out a splendid cheesecake, a sophisticated savarin or a light chiffon flan.

Fruits cook particularly well in the microwave: whole or sliced, they can be turned into any number of exciting desserts as well as being served with some luscious clotted cream or a homely custard sauce.

Other traditional puddings that take on a new cooking slant include rice pudding. Now, with a microwave in the kitchen, you can prepare creamy rice pudding in minutes rather than hours. Along with the basic recipe there are some serving suggestions in this chapter. Hot or cold it's bound to be a winner.

Unfortunately, success with other milk puddings is not always guaranteed. However, semolina cooks easily and really is a good, nutritious pudding to serve when the main course is not too substantial. It's not a good idea to present these sorts of hearty puddings after a vast stew and dumplings (I'm sure that's why so many people get put off traditional puddings) but if the main dish is light they will probably go down a treat.

Apart from those occasions when you think out a menu well in advance and plan to serve a particular dessert, most mid-week meals often lack a closing course. Often this is a conscious decision to avoid calorie-ridden recipes or those foods which are not too good to eat everyday but for many people the dessert means more planning, more shopping and the need to think ahead, so it just doesn't materialise on the table!

As well as being invaluable for quickly defrosting and reheating ready-prepared frozen desserts – fruit pies, crumbles and sponge puddings – your microwave oven is the gadget to turn to when you want to stew fruit in a hurry, poach some pears or 'bake' a few apples. In fact, there really is no excuse for presenting the family with an unfinished meal when you have a microwave oven in the kitchen.

For instance, take a couple of ingredients from the refrigerator – eggs and milk – add a little sugar and in under 10 minutes you will have individual baked custards. Served with fresh or poached fruits, these little wonders make a well-balanced pudding. Still on the traditional front, steamed puddings can be prepared very quickly but you will have to accept the fact that small amounts have to be prepared in large basins. So, even though they taste just as good as ever before, traditional steamed puddings don't look quite as attractive as they could.

Fruits cook very successfully in the microwave oven – whether they are to be turned into an elaborate dessert, like mousse or ice cream, or served simply poached with some whipped cream, it's always worth turning to the microwave to cook fresh or frozen fruit. Dried fruits can also be cooked quicker than by conventional means, without the need for lengthy pre-soaking.

If you have already discovered the delights of quick microwaved desserts then you may well have to keep an eye on the calories. So try making simple unsweetened fruit compotes, adding a low-calorie sweetener just before serving the fruit. There are lots of sweet ideas to try and I hope you will enjoy them.

Sponge Pudding

—— SERVES 4 ——

Steamed sponge pudding cooked in the microwave tastes good but it looks pretty awful! The problem is that the mixture rises quite a lot (with less raising agent the problem is not quite as bad, but the result is not as good) so the basin has to be large. When cooked the mixture falls back to give a light sponge. So only a small amount of mixture can be cooked in a 1.15-litre/2-pint basin for it to be successful. Serve it into individual dishes in the kitchen and no-one will ever know that the pudding didn't look like the usual masterpiece, but they will be sure to praise its flavour and texture.

50 g/2 oz butter, softened	1 egg, lightly beaten
50 g/2 oz sugar	100 g/4 oz jam
50 g/2 oz self-raising flour	

Mix the butter, sugar, flour and egg in a bowl and beat thoroughly until pale, soft and light. Grease a 1.15-litre/2-pint pudding basin, then spoon the jam into it. Spread the creamed mixture on top and cook on full power for 4 minutes.

Leave the pudding to stand in the basin for 4 to 5 minutes, then turn it out and cut it into individual portions to serve.

Chocolate Pudding Sift 2 tablespoons cocoa into the flour and continue as in the main recipe, omitting the jam. Serve the pudding with a quick Chocolate Toffee Sauce (see page 206).

Fruit Pudding Omit the jam. Gently stir 50 g/2 oz dried mixed fruit into the pudding mixture, then cook it as for the main recipe. Serve with Custard Sauce (see page 208).

Marmalade Pudding Prepare the pudding mixture as for the main recipe, beating the grated rind of 1 lemon into the mixture. Use marmalade instead of the jam and cook as in the main recipe.

Jam Roly-poly

—— SERVES 4 TO 6 ——

This is an old-fashioned pudding that is good to serve on winter days. Custard Sauce (see page 208) is almost an essential accompaniment!

100 g/4 oz self-raising flour	grated rind of ½ orange
50 g/2 oz shredded suet	225 g/8 oz jam

Place the flour in a bowl with the suet and orange rind, then mix thoroughly. Stir in just enough water to make a soft but not sticky dough. Knead it lightly, then roll it out on a floured surface to give an oblong shape measuring about 18 × 10 cm/7 × 4 in, keeping the corners as square as possible.

Lift the pastry on to a large shallow dish, then spread the jam in the middle, leaving a border around the edge. Roll it up from the long side and slide it into the middle of the dish. Cover with cling film, there should be enough room for the pastry to rise, so if the covering sits too tightly on the roly-poly use a roasting bag instead.

Cook on full power for 7 to 8 minutes, turning the dish round once during cooking. Serve cut into slices.

VARIATIONS
The roly-poly can be filled with a mixture of dried fruits, first cooked in apple juice in the microwave oven, then drained and mixed with finely chopped nuts – roasted almonds or hazelnuts are good. Alternatively, chopped canned fruits can be mixed with a little jam and used to fill the roll – try chopped peaches with a little raspberry jam or pears with ginger marmalade.

Orange Rhubarb Crumble

—— SERVES 4 ——

The microwave oven is useful for cooking the fruit for the crumble but the topping is not as crisp and crumbly as if it were cooked in a conventional oven. However the top can be browned under the grill and the result is incredibly speedy.

675 g/1½ lb rhubarb, sliced	40 g/1½ oz butter
grated rind and juice of	25 g/1 oz sugar
1 large orange	50 g/2 oz chopped walnuts
175 g/6 oz sugar	
Topping:	
50 g/2 oz plain flour	

Place the rhubarb in a deep dish – a pie or soufflé dish. Sprinkle the orange rind over and pour in the juice. Sprinkle the sugar over the fruit. Cook on full power for 6 minutes.

Meanwhile, sift the flour for the topping into a bowl and rub in the butter. Stir in the sugar and nuts, then sprinkle this topping over the fruit. Do not press it down, but simply sprinkle it over so that it covers the fruit completely.

Cook the crumble for 4 minutes, then place the dish under a hot grill and cook until evenly browned on top. Serve at once, with Custard Sauce (see page 208) or whipped cream

Christmas Pudding

—— SERVES 4 ——

Small Christmas puddings cook quickly and successfully in the microwave oven but it is best not to extend this to large ones which are very solid. The dense mixture only cooks through if the basin is small enough for the microwaves to penetrate towards the middle.

There is just one other thing to remember – don't put a lucky shilling in your pudding, it could be most unlucky!

25 g/1 oz shredded suet	1 egg, beaten
75 g/3 oz currants	1 tablespoon black treacle
75 g/3 oz raisins	pinch of cinnamon
75 g/3 oz sultanas	pinch of ground mixed
25 g/1 oz blanched	spice
almonds, chopped	1 tablespoon brandy or
50 g/2 oz dates, chopped	rum
small piece preserved	75 g/3 oz fresh
ginger, finely chopped	breadcrumbs
grated rind of ½ orange	
40 g/1½ oz dark brown	
sugar	

The method is simple – just mix all the ingredients together in a bowl and make sure they are well combined. Grease a 600-ml/1-pint basin and put the mixture into it, smoothing the top down evenly. Cover with cling film and cook on full power for 5 minutes.

Remove the covering, cover immediately with fresh cling film, stretching it over the basin and cook for 15 seconds. Allow to cool and the covering will form an airtight seal. It is best to use the thicker freezer film for this. Wrap the basin in foil and store for at least a month to mature. Best after 6 to 8 weeks.

To reheat the pudding, cook for 2 to 3 minutes, then serve with brandy butter or Brandy Sauce (see page 208).

Almond Pudding

—— SERVES 4 ——

Like other steamed puddings, this is not an attractive looking dessert, but it tastes very good. So serve it for a family meal and put it on the plates in the kitchen, topped with Custard Sauce (see page 208) or whipped cream.

50 g/2 oz butter or	50 g/2 oz ground almonds
margarine	grated rind of 1 orange
50 g/2 oz demerara sugar	1 egg, beaten
50 g/2 oz self-raising flour	

Place the butter and sugar in a basin and melt for 2 minutes on full power. Beat in the flour, almonds, orange rind and egg. Turn the mixture into a greased 900-ml/1½ pint pudding basin and cook for 2 to 2½ minutes.

Allow to stand for 2 minutes, then turn out and serve at once.

VARIATION
Use ground hazelnuts or walnuts in this pudding instead of the almonds. Grind the nuts in a food processor or liquidiser, or pass them through a fine mouli grater.

Apricot and Almond Amber

—— SERVES 4 ——

This is a sponge-topped fruit pudding which should be served hot. Custard Sauce (see page 208), Jam Sauce (see page 206) or cream go well with the pudding and ice cream can also be served if you want to create a marked contrast between the the hot and cold.

1 (425-g/15-oz) can	50 g/2 oz ground almonds
apricot halves	1 large egg
50 g/2 oz butter	50 g/2 oz flaked almonds,
50 g/2 oz caster sugar	toasted
50 g/2 oz self-raising flour	

Drain the apricot halves and use the juice to make a jam sauce if you like. Place the butter and sugar in a bowl, sift in the flour and add the ground almonds, then break in the egg. Beat all the ingredients thoroughly until they are pale in colour and very creamy in consistency. Use an electric food mixer for this if you have one (or a food processor).

Place the fruit in a 1.15-litre/2-pint deep dish. Spread the creamed mixture over the top and sprinkle the flaked almonds over. Cook on full power for 5 minutes. Allow to stand for 3 minutes before serving.

Gooseberry Crunch

——— SERVES 4 ———

Although at first glance this may seem like nothing more than a recipe for a dessert which the children can prepare, it does, in fact, taste very good. The addition of ginger to the crunchy cornflake mixture peps it up wonderfully!

450 g/1 lb gooseberries	2 tablespoons clear honey
100 g/4 oz sugar	2 teaspoons ground ginger
50 g/2 oz butter	50 g/2 oz cornflakes

Place the gooseberries in a deep 1.15-litre/2-pint dish. Sprinkle the sugar over the fruit and cover with cling film, allowing a small gap for the steam to escape. Cook on full power for 6 minutes, stirring the fruit once during cooking.

Place the butter and honey in a large basin and cook for 2 minutes. Stir in the ginger and cornflakes, then press this mixture all over the top of the fruit and cook for 1 minute. Serve at once.

VARIATIONS
You can use almost any other fruits in this crunchy dessert. Try fresh or frozen soft fruits (raspberries, strawberries, blackberries or mulberries), blackcurrants, apples, pears, rhubarb or a mixture of fruits. Canned fruits – peaches or apricots – can be mixed with fresh or frozen fruits. Dried fruits like apricots, figs, raisins, apples, peaches and pears, can be cooked in apple juice in the microwave oven for about 15 minutes before being used as the base for the crunchy topping. Hopefully these ideas will trigger off a few thoughts of your own for a simple, economical pudding.

It takes about 3 to 4 minutes to defrost 450 g/1 lb gooseberries in the microwave. Remove any metal ties from the bag, or take the lid off a container. Place the fruit on a plate if necessary, then cook on full power.

Savarin

——— SERVES 4 TO 6 ———

This is quite an impressive dessert, particularly if the middle is filled with a colourful fruit salad, with strawberries, grapes and pineapple included for an exotic flavour.

175 g/6 oz strong white flour	1 small ripe pineapple
25 g/1 oz sugar	50 g/2 oz black grapes
1½ teaspoons dried yeast	2 kiwi fruit
250 ml/8 fl oz lukewarm milk	1 orange
1 egg, beaten	*Syrup:*
Fruit Salad:	50 g/2 oz sugar
100 g/4 oz strawberries	100 ml/4 fl oz water
	4 tablespoons rum

Sift the flour into a bowl and mix in the sugar. Sprinkle the yeast over the milk, then set it aside for about 10 minutes or until the yeast has dissolved and the liquid is frothy. Make a well in the flour, pour in the yeast liquid and beaten egg, then gradually beat in the flour to make a batter. Beat until the batter is very smooth and elastic. Grease a 900-ml/1½ pint ring dish and pour in the batter, then leave it in a warm place until risen almost to the top of the dish.

Cook the savarin on full power for 3½ minutes, then allow it to stand in the dish for 2 minutes before turning out on to a wire rack to cook completely.

Prepare the fruit for the salad according to their type. Hull the strawberries; trim, peel and core the pineapple, then cut the flesh into cubes; halve the grapes and remove the seeds. Peel the kiwi fruit and cut into slices. Cut the skin and all the pith off the orange. Holding the orange over a plate remove the fruit segments from between the membranes using a small serrated knife. Squeeze the juice from the unwanted core and add this to the salad. Mix all the fruit. You can include any fruit which is in season.

Place the sugar and water for the syrup into a basin and cook for 3 minutes. Stir to dissolve the sugar completely, then stir in the rum. Stand the savarin on a serving platter then pierce it all over with a skewer; spoon some of the rum syrup over and set both aside to cool.

To serve, pile the fruit salad in the middle of the ring and pour the syrup over. Serve any extra salad and syrup to accompany the dessert.

If you do not have a special ring dish for the microwave, then use a plain round fairly deep-sided dish – a soufflé dish is ideal. Stand an upturned jam jar in the middle of the dish. Make sure the dish and the jar are thoroughly greased before putting in the mixture which is to be cooked.

Rhubarb and Apple Charlotte

———— SERVES 4 TO 6 ————

This pudding tastes good served either hot or cold, with Custard Sauce (see page 208), cream or ice cream.

100 g/4 oz fresh breadcrumbs	100 g/4 oz butter
1 teaspoon ground ginger	450 g/1 lb rhubarb
$\frac{1}{2}$ teaspoon cinnamon	225 g/8 oz cooking apples
50 g/2 oz demerara sugar	175 g/6 oz sugar

Mix the breadcrumbs in a mixing bowl with the ginger, cinnamon and sugar. Melt the butter for 1½ minutes on full power, then pour it over the breadcrumb mixture and cook for 4 minutes, stirring once during cooking.

Meanwhile, prepare the fruit. Wash and trim the rhubarb and cut the stalks into slices. Peel, core and slice the apples and mix them with the rhubarb. Add the sugar. Cook the fruit for 8 minutes, then stir well.

Layer the breadcrumb and fruit mixtures in a heatproof bowl, ending with a layer of breadcrumbs on top. Serve hot, or cool then chill thoroughly before serving.

Note: other fruits can be used in this recipe; try plums, pears, peaches, raspberries or blackcurrants for example.

Spiced Apple Toasties

———— SERVES 4 ————

This is another really quick pudding, or it can make a good snack for those with a taste for sweet foods. At firt glance at the ingredients you may think that it is rather an unappetising idea to combine fruit, sugar and those packeted crisp toasted bread rounds, but do try this recipe because the result is both fast and enjoyable.

4 Dutch Crispbakes	$\frac{1}{2}$ teaspoon cinnamon
1 large cooking apple	50 g/2 oz butter
50 g/2 oz sugar	

Place the toasted bread rounds as far apart as possible on a shallow dish – a quiche dish is ideal. Core, peel and cut the apple into four thick slices. Place one on each round. Mix the sugar and cinnamon, then sprinkle it over the apples and dot with the butter.

Cook on full power for 4 minutes and serve at once – the middle of the toasted base will have softened, but the edges should still be crisp.

Chocolate Banana Flans

———— SERVES 4 ————

This is a good children's pudding – bought flan cases spread with chocolate hazelnut paste and filled with bananas.

4 individual sponge flan cases	2 tablespoons redcurrant jelly
4 tablespoons chocolate hazelnut spread	2 small bananas, sliced
	a little lemon juice

Place the flan cases as far apart as possible in a shallow dish or flat plate. Spread the inside of each one with chocolate hazelnut spread. Warm the redcurrant jelly in a small basin or mug for 30 seconds on full power.

Dip the bananas in lemon juice, then arrange them in the flan cases and brush a little redcurrant jelly over the top. Cook for 2 minutes, then serve at once.

Stuffed Apples

———— SERVES 4 ————

An old favourite, this pudding can be cooked in the microwave oven in a fraction of the time required in the conventional cooker.

4 medium cooking apples	2 tablespoons water
75 g/3 oz demerara sugar	50 g/2 oz butter
50 g/2 oz raisins	
50 g/2 oz walnut pieces, chopped	

Core the apples, then score the skin all around the outside to prevent the fruit from bursting during cooking. Place the apples as far apart as possible in a shallow dish.

Mix the sugar, raisins and walnuts and use a teaspoon to press this stuffing into the holes left by the cores. Sprinkle the water over and dot each apple with butter. Cook on full power for 6 to 6½ minutes. Allow to stand for 2 minutes, then serve with all the juices from the dish poured over the fruit.

ALTERNATIVE FILLINGS

Date and Orange Substitute chopped dried dates for the raisins and add the grated rind of 1 orange. Use chopped blanched almonds instead of the walnuts and pour the juice from the orange over instead of the water. Cook as above.

Mincemeat Use 225 g/8 oz mincemeat instead of the filling ingredients. Sprinkle 2 tablespoons rum or brandy over the apples instead of the water but do not dot with butter. Cook as above.

Apricot and Hazelnut Substitute dried apricots for the raisins (use the sort which do not require pre-soaking) and use hazelnuts instead of the walnuts.

St Clement's Apples

──────── SERVES 4 ────────

This is a slightly different idea for stewed apples. Served the cooked fruit hot with a custard sauce or cold with ice cream.

675 g/1½ lb cooking apples	100–175 g/4–6 oz sugar
grated rind and juice of 1 orange and ½ lemon	4 cloves

Peel and quarter the apples, then remove their cores and cut them into eighths.

Place the fruit into a bowl or large basin with the orange and lemon rind and juice. Sprinkle the sugar on top and stir in the cloves. Cover with cling film, allowing a small gap for the steam to escape, then cook on full power for 7 minutes. Allow to stand for 2 minutes before serving.

STEWED APPLE IDEAS

Many people think of stewed apples as being the apple pulp which is in fact an apple sauce. Stewed fruits should be tender but still retain their shape and the microwave oven is excellent for achieving this.

Apples with Raisins Add 50 g/2 oz raisins to the apples. Break a cinnamon stick into the dish and add 2 cloves. Pour in about 150 ml/¼ pint dry cider and add a little lemon juice, then cook as in the main recipe.

Apples with Almonds Cook the apples in dry white wine or cider, omitting the orange rind and juice. Toast 50 g/2 oz slivered almonds and sprinkle them over the fruit before serving it hot or chilled.

Apple Pudding

──────── SERVES 4 ────────

This is a dark, rich apple pudding which is quick and economical to prepare. By browning off the bread topping under the grill the whole pudding takes on a better appearance and flavour. Serve it with Custard Sauce (see page 208) or whipped cream.

about 9–10 medium-thick slices bread	½ teaspoon ground mixed spice
about 75 g/3 oz butter	675 g/1½ lb cooking apples
100 g/4 oz dark muscovado sugar	2 teaspoons granulated sugar

Cut the crusts off the bread. Lightly butter a 900-ml/1½-pint dish – a soufflé dish is best. Sprinkle a little muscovado sugar all round the inside of the dish. Butter the bread slices and use them to line the dish, placing the buttered side outwards. Mix the remaining sugar with the spice.

Peel, core and slice the apples, then press these into the dish, sprinkling the layers with the sugar and spice mixture. Cut the remaining buttered bread slices diagon-

ally in half to make triangles. Press these on top of the apples, arranging them neatly and making sure the whole pudding is covered. Press down well.

Cover the top of the pudding with cling film, pulling it tightly across the bread to keep the slices in place. Make sure the cling film is drawn tightly over the edges of the dish, then pierce a small hole right in the middle.

Cook on full power for 10 minutes, turning the dish round once during cooking. At the end of the cooking time test to see if the apples are cooked by piercing the pudding with a pointed knife: you will be able to feel if the apples are soft or still hard.

Sprinkle the granulated sugar over the top of the pudding and dot it with extra butter if it seems dry, then cook under a hot grill until golden. Serve at once.

Poached Blackcurrants

──────── SERVES 4 ────────

These simple, full-flavoured fruits are delicious served either warm or cold with clotted cream. Alternatively you can use them in a variety of dishes as suggested below.

450 g/1 lb blackcurrants	4 tablespoons orange liqueur
175 g/6 oz sugar	

Top and tail the currants, then place them in a bowl with the sugar. Cover with cling film, allowing a small gap for the steam to escape, and cook on full power for 10 minutes, stirring once during cooking.

Allow the fruit to stand for 2 minutes, then stir in the liqueur and serve when hot or warm. Alternatively, allow the currants to cool completely, chill thoroughly and serve with cream or ice cream.

The cooked blackcurrants can be used for any of the following puddings:

Blackcurrant Charlotte Prepare the breadcrumb mixture as for the Rhubarb and Apple Charlotte (see page 176), omitting the ginger from the mixture and adding the grated rind of 1 orange. Layer this with the cooked blackcurrants and heat for 2 minutes before serving. Alternatively the dessert can be served cold.

Blackcurrant Fool Purée the cooked currants in a liquidiser then press the purée through a sieve. Make up a Custard Sauce (see page 208) and gradually stir the fruit purée into it. Cool and pour into glasses, then chill thoroughly.

Blackcurrant Crumble Use the blackcurrants as the base for the Orange Rhubarb Crumble on page 172. Cook the fruit for just 8 minutes before adding the topping, then continue as for the crumble recipe.

Gingered Rhubarb Compote

—————— SERVES 4 ——————

A microwave oven is so useful for conjuring up quick puddings that there is no excuse for leaving the rhubarb to grow tough in the garden. Serve this compote hot with Custard Sauce (see page 208) or cream or leave it to cool then serve with clotted cream or ice cream.

450 g/1 lb young rhubarb
grated rind and juice of
  1 orange
100 g/4 oz sugar
50 g/2 oz crystallised
  ginger, sliced

150 ml/¼ pint medium
  sweet cider
orange slices to decorate
  (optional)

Cut the rhubarb into 5-cm/2-in lengths and place them in a bowl with the orange rind and juice, the sugar and ginger. Pour over the cider and stir well. Cover with cling film and cook on full power for 8 minutes, stirring twice during cooking.

Allow the fruit to stand for 2 to 3 minutes before serving. If it is to be served cold, the rhubarb looks attractive poured into individual glass dishes, with orange slices balanced on the rim of each glass.

Cherry Compote

—————— SERVES 4 ——————

100 g/4 oz sugar
pared rind of 1 lemon
150 ml/¼ pint water

150 ml/¼ pint port
675 g/1½ lb cherries,
  stoned

Place the sugar, lemon rind and water in a large bowl and cook on full power for 5 minutes, stirring once.

Add the port and cherries and cook for a further 5 minutes. Remove the lemon rind and serve the compote hot or chill it and serve cold.

Mixed Fruit Compote Instead of a simple cherry dessert, why not include other fruits? Try peeling peaches, halving and stoning them, then cut them into quarters. Use peeled, cored and quartered pears and include a few quartered fresh figs just before serving the compote. If you like, substitute a light red or white wine instead of the port and trickle a little liqueur over the compote just as it is served. Grand Marnier, Kirsch, cherry or apricot brandy would all be suitable.

Pear and Strawberry Compote

———— SERVES 4 ————

Other fruits can be combined with the pears in this simple fruit dessert. For example try plums, peeled peaches or stoned cherries instead of the strawberries. Serve clotted cream and crisp, light dessert biscuits to accompany the compote.

4 firm pears	300 ml/½ pint sweet white
juice of ½ lemon	wine
50 g/2 oz sugar	2 teaspoons arrowroot
pared rind of 1 orange,	2 tablespoons water
cut into fine strips	225 g/8 oz strawberries

Peel the pears and remove their cores from the base, leaving the stalks intact and the fruit whole. Sprinkle them with lemon juice to prevent them from discolouring. Stand the pears in a dish or bowl and sprinkle in the sugar. Add the orange rind and pour in the wine. Cover with cling film, allowing a small gap for the steam to escape, then cook on full power for 8 minutes, turning the fruit over once during cooking.

Meanwhile, blend the arrowroot to a smooth cream with the water. Remove the stalks and cores from the strawberries and cut any large ones in half. Stir the arrowroot solution into the syrup and cook for a further 4 to 5 minutes. Lastly stir in the strawberries and stand for 2 to 3 minutes before spooning the fruit, with the juices, into individual dishes to serve.

Stuffed Poached Pears If you like, the cored pears can be stuffed with a mixture of ground nuts and fruit juice before they are cooked. Try, for example, mixing ground hazelnuts, walnuts or almonds with a little fresh orange juice (enough to just bind the nuts together). Add grated orange rind if you like, then press the mixture into the cavity left by the cores, Poach the pears in the same way as for the main recipe, but omit the strawberries. Serve hot, with a Chocolate Sauce (see page 206).

Tropical Bananas

——— SERVES 4 ———

These bananas in a sweet coconut and ginger flavoured sauce are delicious. Serve them with plenty of whipped cream for a special dessert.

4 firm bananas
a little lemon juice
150 ml/¼ pint ginger wine
4 tablespoons sweetened
   cream of coconut

Decoration:
orange slices
kiwi slices

Peel the bananas and dip them in a little lemon juice to keep them white. Place them in a shallow dish – a gratin or quiche dish is suitable.

Mix the ginger wine with the cream of coconut and pour it evenly over the fruit – use a spoon to make sure that each banana is covered. Cook on full power for 5 minutes.

Have the decoration ready and add the slices of orange and kiwi to the banana at once. Serve straightaway.

Stuffed Peaches

——— SERVES 4 ———

This is simple, a good stand-by for when you have to think up a pudding in a hurry and it really does taste rather good! If you like, stuff fresh peaches in this way, remembering to peel them first. Serve with Chocolate Sauce (see page 206).

1 (794-g/1¾ lb) can peach
   halves
100 g/4 oz ground almonds
2 tablespoons caster sugar
2 tablespoons ginger wine
   (preferably **Crabbies**
   green ginger wine as
   this gives a good
   flavour)

Decoration:
2 pieces preserved stem
   ginger
a few strips of angelica,
   cut into leaves

Drain the peaches and arrange them in a circle in a large round dish. Mix the almonds with the sugar and wine to make a sticky paste. Place a ball of this paste in each half, then cook on full power for 5 minutes. There is no need to cover the peaches during cooking.

Meanwhile, slice the preserved ginger thinly and use these slices to decorate the hot peaches. Add angelica leaves and serve at once.

Note: canned pear halves or lightly poached fresh pears can also be stuffed in this way.

Mincemeat Bananas

——— SERVES 4 ———

This really is a very quick dessert and it is wickedly mouthwatering. The quality of the mincemeat is important, so add a little brandy to shop-bought varieties. Serve with clotted cream for real luxury.

pared rind of 1 orange
4 small bananas
225 g/8 oz mincemeat

50 g/2 oz flaked almonds,
   browned

Cut the orange rind into fine strips, then place it in a small basin with enough water to cover the pieces and cook on full power for 15 minutes. Set aside while you prepare the bananas.

Peel the bananas and arrange them neatly in a fairly large dish – a quiche dish or similar. Spoon the mincemeat neatly over the fruit, then cook for 4 minutes.

While the bananas are cooking, drain and dry the orange strips on absorbent kitchen paper. Sprinkle the rind and the flaked almonds neatly over the mincemeat and serve at once. If the bananas are left to stand, they will tend to discolour.

Almonds can be browned quite successfully in butter in the microwave. Place 50 g/2 oz flaked almonds in a mug and add 50 g/2 oz butter. Cover with cling film, allowing a small gap for the steam to escape, then cook on full power for 4 minutes. Shake well and use as required for sweet or savoury dishes.

Dried Fruit Salad

—— SERVES 4 ——

Serve this fruit salad hot or leave it to cool, then chill it thoroughly before serving. It is a good breakfast dish – make it the night before and put it in the refrigerator ready for the next day.

225 g/8 oz dried fruits, for
    example apricots,
    apples, pears, peaches,
    prunes and raisins
grated rind and juice of
    1 large orange

1 cinnamon stick
450 ml/¾ pint medium
    sweet cider

Place the fruits in a large basin, then sprinkle in the orange rind and juice and add the cinnamon stick. Pour in the cider and cover with cling film, allowing a small gap for the steam to escape.

Cook on full power for 15 minutes, pressing the fruit into the juice twice during cooking. Allow to stand for 5 minutes before serving.

Note: for a slightly more exotic salad, add 4 green cardamoms and 50 g/2 oz blanched almonds to the fruits before cooking. Stir in 2 tablespoons rum just before serving.

Spiced Figs

—— SERVES 4 ——

A slightly unusual, simple dessert which is quite good to serve after an Indian menu. Offer it only as one of two puddings to guests unless you know that they like figs, because this fruit is not to everyone's taste.

12 dried figs
6 green cardamoms
½ teaspoon cinnamon
pared rind and juice of
    1 orange

100 ml/4 fl oz ginger wine
175 ml/6 fl oz water
3 tablespoons demerara
    sugar

Place the figs and cardamoms in a large basin or bowl. Sprinkle in the cinnamon. Finely shred the orange rind, then add it to the fruit with the juice, ginger wine and water. Stir in the sugar.

Cover with cling film, allowing a small gap for the steam to escape, then cook on full power for 10 minutes. Allow to stand for 2 to 3 minutes before serving. Alternatively allow the fruit to cool, then chill thoroughly before serving.

Drunken Apricots

—— SERVES 4 ——

Serve clotted cream or good, home-made vanilla ice cream to complement these apricots in a rich wine and brandy syrup. They can be prepared up to two days in advance and stored in an airtight container in the refrigerator.

225 g/8 oz dried apricots
300 ml/½ pint rosé wine
4 tablespoons brandy

3 tablespoons honey
50 g/2 oz blanched
    almonds

Place the apricots in a large basin or casserole dish. Pour the wine and brandy over them, then stir in the honey. Split each almond and add them to the apricots.

Cover with cling film, allowing a gap for the steam to escape, then cook on full power for 15 minutes. Stir the fruit thoroughly at the end of the cooking time. Set aside to cool, then chill lightly before serving.

Apple Flan

—— SERVES 4 TO 6 ——

This is a simple flan to prepare and it makes a light dessert to follow a rich meal – it complements a traditional roast dinner, for example.

1 (200-g/7-oz) bag coconut
    cookies
100 g/4 oz butter
450 g/1 lb cooking apples

1 tablespoon caster sugar
100 g/4 oz marmalade
150 ml/¼ pint double
    cream, to serve

Finely crush the biscuits – do this in a food processor if you have one, otherwise put the biscuits in a strong polythene bag and pound them with a rolling pin. Place the butter in a large basin and melt it on full power for 2 minutes. Stir in the biscuit crumbs, then, when all the crumbs are thoroughly coated, press the mixture into the base of a 20-cm/8-in flan dish. Smooth the top with the back of a metal spoon.

Peel, core and thickly slice the cooking apples, then arrange them neatly on top of the biscuit crust. Sprinkle the sugar over the apples, then cover the dish with cling film, allowing a small gap for the steam to escape. Cook for 4 minutes, by which time the apples should be tender but not mushy.

Put the marmalade in a small basin or mug and heat it for 2 minutes. Press it through a fine sieve, then brush the marmalade all over the apples. Allow to cool and chill lightly.

Whip the cream until it stands in soft peaks, then pipe it round the flan or swirl it evenly all over the top and serve cut into wedges.

Spiced Peaches

—— SERVES 4 ——

This is a good way of turning fresh peaches into a special hot pudding. Serve whipped cream with them.

4 large, firm peaches
150 ml/¼ pint rosé wine
75 g/3 oz sugar

2 cinnamon sticks
6 cloves

Place the peaches in a large bowl and pour on enough freshly boiling water to cover them. Leave them for 30 to 60 seconds then drain and peel them. Cut the peeled fruit in half and remove the stones.

Mix the wine with the sugar and spices in a bowl, then heat for 2 minutes on full power. Stir well and add the peaches. Cover with cling film, allowing a small gap for the steam to escape, and cook for 4 to 5 minutes, depending on how firm the peaches are. Spoon the fruit into individual heatproof dishes and serve at once.

Creating a Dessert from Canned Peaches Drain the syrup from the peaches and pour it into a basin. Add a cinnamon stick and the finely shredded, pared rind from 1 small orange. Lightly toast 50 g/2 oz split almonds and stir them into the syrup, then cook on full power for 5 minutes. Stir in 150 ml/¼ pint brandy and replace the peaches in the syrup. Allow the fruit to stand for 5 minutes, then heat through for 5 minutes, or chill thoroughly before serving.

Pears in Cider

—— SERVES 4 ——

This is an inexpensive dessert which is quite impressive enough to serve at a dinner party. Select firm pears which have a good flavour. The early autumn is a good time for this dessert.

4 firm pears
a little lemon juice
pared rind of 1 orange

150 ml/¼ pint dry cider
100 g/4 oz sugar
50 g/2 oz sultanas

Peel the pears, leaving their stalks intact. Dip the fruit in lemon juice to prevent them discolouring, then place them in a dish.

Cut the orange rind into fine strips, then add these to the pears and pour in the cider. Stir in the sugar and add the sultanas. Stir well, cover with cling film and cook on full power for 10 minutes.

Stir the syrup once during this time, then again at the end of the cooking time. Depending on how firm the pears are, they may require a further 2 minutes cooking. Serve hot or allow the fruit to cool then chill thoroughly.

Caramelised Oranges

——— SERVES 4 ———

These simple caramelised fruits make an excellent dinner party dessert. They can be (and are best) prepared the day before and chilled thoroughly before serving. Offer clotted cream to accompany them.

4 large oranges
175 g/6 oz sugar
6 tablespoons water

Pare the rind thinly from one of the oranges, then cut it into fine strips and set aside. Cut all the peel and pith off the fruit, then slice the oranges and remove all the seeds. Reshape the fruit in a heatproof dish.

Place the sugar and water in a 1.15-litre/2-pint basin and stir thoroughly. Cook on full power for 12 minutes.

Stir the caramel after 2 minutes to make sure the sugar has dissolved, then continue cooking without stirring. Keep a close eye on the caramel after 10 minutes, in case your oven cooks it quickly. At 12 minutes the caramel should be light golden, for this recipe it should be quite rich in colour and a further 30 seconds should be long enough. (At 13 minutes the caramel will be very dark and possibly overcooked.) When the caramel is a rich brown remove it from the oven and pour it over the oranges, making sure they are evenly coated. Allow to cool, then chill thoroughly. The caramel will melt on the fruit when it has stood for several hours. They should be left overnight for best results.

If you want to make the caramelised oranges and serve them soon afterwards, then *very carefully* trickle 4 tablespoons boiling water into the freshly cooked caramel allowing it to stand for a few minutes before pouring it over the fruit. The added water will prevent it from hardening. However, do be extremely careful as the water will make the caramel spit violently. Protect your hand with an oven glove and stand at arm's length.

To decorate the fruit, cook the reserved strips of orange rind, in enough hot water to cover, on full power for 5 minutes. Drain thoroughly and sprinkle over the oranges just before serving.

Creamed Rice

——— SERVES 4 ———

This is by no means an economical way of making rice pudding, but it is incredibly quick and quite delicious. Served hot, just as it is, the pudding tastes fine or it can be sprinkled with nutmeg and grilled to give a brown skin, alternatively it can be used for any of the ideas given below.

50 g/2 oz pudding rice
40–50 g/1½–2 oz sugar
600 ml/1 pint water

300 /½ pint single or
  double cream
freshly grated nutmeg

Place the rice in a large basin with the sugar to taste and water. Cover with cling film, allowing a small gap for the steam to escape, then cook on full power for 25 minutes.

Stir the rice well at the end of the cooking time, then stir in the cream. Single cream gives a good result, but double cream really does make the pudding quite luxurious.

Heat through for 1 minute before serving. The pudding can be transferred to a heatproof serving dish, sprinkled with a little freshly grated nutmeg and browned under the grill; or it can be spooned into individual dishes and served without a brown skin.

RICE IDEAS

Creamed Rice Brûlée Use only 25 g/1 oz sugar with the rice when you are cooking it. Beat 2 egg yolks into the rice immediately it is cooked, then stir in the cream. Pour the rice straight into a heatproof serving dish and allow it to cool, then chill thoroughly. Cover the top of the rice with an even layer of brown sugar and place it in the freezer to chill for 30 minutes.

Have a very hot grill ready to cook the rice. Place the dish under the grill and cook until the sugar melts and caramelises. Serve at once.

Raisin Nut Rice Stir 50 g/2 oz raisins into the cooked rice, then add the cream and heat as above. Divide the pudding between individual dishes and top each portion with toasted chopped hazelnuts. Serve at once.

Almond and Orange Rice Mix 50 g/2 oz finely chopped blanched almonds and the grated rind of ½ orange into the rice when you add the water. Cook as above, then sprinkle the surface of the cooked rice with 25 g/1 oz toasted flaked almonds just before it is served.

Apple Rice Make up 1 quantity of Apple Sauce (see page 205) before cooking the rice. Set this aside and cook the rice as above. Reheat the apple sauce for 3 minutes, then serve it to accompany the pudding.

Scandinavian Rice Use double cream to make the rice. Stir 25 g/1 oz raisins and 25 g/1 oz toasted flaked almonds into the freshly cooked rice, then allow it to cool. Stir in 50 g/ 2 oz chopped crystallised ginger, 50 g/2 oz chopped glacé cherries and 2 tablespoons chopped angelica. Add 2 tablespoons rum and chill the rice thoroughly in individual glass dishes. Serve with light crisp biscuits.

Blackberry Mousse

——— SERVES 4 TO 6 ———

You can use frozen fruit to prepare this mousse, but remember to allow about 3 to 4 minutes extra on the initial cooking time so as to give the berries time to defrost.

450 g/1 lb blackberries
100 g/4 oz sugar
2 tablespoons cornflour
2 eggs, separated

2 tablespoons water
150 ml/¼ pint double
  cream

Place the blackberries in a large basin with the sugar and cook on full power for 7 to 8 minutes. Purée the fruit in a liquidiser or food processor or by pressing it through a fine sieve. If you make the purée in a liquidiser or food processor then press it through a sieve afterwards to remove all the seeds.

Blend the cornflour with the egg yolks and water until smooth, then stir the solution into the blackberry purée. Cook for 5 minutes, then thoroughly whisk the thickened fruit sauce, scraping it from the sides of the bowl. Whisk in the cream, then set the sauce aside to cool and chill lightly until set.

Whisk the egg whites until they stand in stiff peaks but do not over-whisk or they will become very dry and difficult to fold into the fruit. Whisk a couple of spoonfuls of the egg white into the blackberry purée, then carefully fold in the remainder using a metal spoon.

Transfer the mousse to glasses or glass dishes and chill lightly before serving. Do not leave the mousse in the refrigerator for more than a couple of hours or the egg whites will begin to separate out.

The microwave is great for making praline. Split 100 g/ 4 oz blanched almonds and place them in a well-oiled shallow baking tin. Make the caramel as for the above recipe, then pour it over the nuts and set aside to cool. Crush the hardened caramel and nuts with a steak mallet or heavy rolling pin. This can be used for decorating cakes, to top ice creams or other light desserts, or to be included in a box of mixed sweets.

Semolina Pudding

SERVES 4

600 ml/1 pint milk
50 g/2 oz sugar
40 g/1½ oz semolina

Place the milk and sugar in a large basin or mixing bowl. Heat on full power for 5 minutes. Whisking the milk continuously, slowly pour in the semolina. Whisk thoroughly, then cook for 3 minutes. Remove from the oven and whisk again, then return the bowl to the oven and cook for 2 minutes. Remove from the oven, whisk thoroughly and allow to stand for 2 minutes.

The semolina can be served swirled into dishes, with cream to pour over it or with jam.

Chocolate Semolina Mould Make the semolina as above. Break a 5-oz/150-g bar plain dessert chocolate into small squares, then whisk the chocolate into the freshly made semolina. Continue whisking until the chocolate has dissolved completely, then pour the mixture into a 1.15-litre/2-pint mould and chill until set. Turn out to serve.

Hot Chocolate Trifle

SERVES 6

This makes a good quick pudding and it's more suitable for cold days than a chilled trifle. It can of course be chilled before serving if preferred.

1 chocolate sponge cake
  (home-made or bought)
4 tablespoons sweet
  sherry
1 (385-g/14-oz) can
  apricot pie filling
2 tablespoons custard
  powder
2 egg yolks
2 tablespoons sugar
600 ml/1 pint milk
Decoration:
coarsely grated chocolate
25 g/1 oz flaked almonds,
  toasted
50 g/2 oz maraschino
  cherries, chopped

Roughly crumble the cake into a heatproof serving bowl. Sprinkle the sherry over, then spread the pie filling evenly over the cake. Cook on full power for 4 minutes.

Place the custard powder in a 1.15-litre/2-pint basin, then gradually whisk in the egg yolks, sugar and a little of the milk. Heat the remaining milk for 4 minutes, then pour it into the yolk mixture, whisking all the time. Cook this custard on full power for 2½ to 3 minutes.

Pour the custard over the sponge and fruit base. Mix the ingredients for decoration, then sprinkle them over the top of the trifle and serve at once.

Chocolate Pots

SERVES 4

These are chocolate-flavoured custards. They are quite rich, so do not offer them after a very filling main course dish. They are, in fact, an excellent and economical pudding to serve youngsters.

2 tablespoons cocoa
350 ml/12 fl oz milk
2 small eggs
3 tablespoons caster sugar
150 ml/¼ pint single cream

Place the cocoa in a heatproof measuring jug with the milk and heat on full power for 5 minutes.

Meanwhile, beat the eggs with the sugar, then strain the chocolate flavoured milk over them, whisking all the time. Strain this custard into four individual ramekin dishes and place them in a shallow dish: a large quiche or lasagne dish is ideal. Place the dish in the microwave, then pour in enough boiling water to come up to the edge of the outer dish. Cook on full power for 6 to 8 minutes, check the custard frequently during cooking as the time will vary according to how big the outer dish is and the amount of water which it holds.

Leave the custards to cool completely, then chill them thoroughly. Pour a thin layer of cream over each pot just before serving.

Gooseberry Fool

———— SERVES 4 TO 6 ————

675 g / 1½ lb gooseberries   wafer biscuits to serve
225 g / 8 oz sugar
300 ml / ¾ pint double cream

Top and tail the gooseberries and place them in a bowl with the sugar. Cover with cling film, allowing a small gap for the steam to escape, then cook on full power for 10 minutes. Set aside to cool slightly.

Purée the warm fruit in a liquidiser or food processor until smooth, then press through a sieve. Thoroughly chill the purée. If you like the purée can be coloured slightly with green food colouring to produce a more palatable appearance. Whip the cream until it stands in soft peaks, then fold it into the gooseberry purée and spoon the fool into glasses to serve. Add a wafer biscuit to each.

If you want to freeze gooseberries for making a fool in the winter months, then cook the purée as above and allow it to cool before putting it in a suitable freezer container, allowing a little head room for the purée to expand.

Crème Caramel

———— SERVES 4 ————

Individual crème caramels cook successfully and incredibly quickly in the microwave oven. This is one of the recipes for which you can use a lower power setting; however, I have great success by cooking them in this way – by standing the ramekins in a dish of water. The water attracts a certain amount of the microwave energy, so reducing the amount which reaches the custards and preventing them from curdling.

100 g / 4 oz sugar   5 teaspoons sugar
4 tablespoons water   350 ml / 12 fl oz milk
2 small eggs   drop of vanilla essence

Place the sugar and water for the caramel in a 1.15-litre/ 2-pint basin and cook on full power for 10 to 11 minutes, stirring once during cooking. The caramel should be golden. Divide the caramel between four ramekin dishes, swirling them round to coat the base and sides.

Beat the eggs with the sugar, then pour in the milk and vanilla essence. Strain this custard into the caramel coated dishes and stand them in a quiche or gratin dish. Place the dish in the microwave oven and pour in boiling water to come to the top of the outer dish. Cook for 3 to 3½ minutes. Turn the dishes once during cooking. Remove and chill for several hours before turning the caramels out to serve.

Tropical Cheesecake

──── SERVES 6 ────

This is a rich cheesecake based on a fruit cornflour sauce and it resembles baked cheesecakes more than the light gelatine mixtures which are similar to mousses.

1 (200-g/7-oz) bag coconut cookies
100 g/4 oz butter
1 (376-g/13¼-oz) can crushed pineapple
4 tablespoons ginger wine
50 g/2 oz cornflour

50 g/2 oz sugar
450 g/1 lb cream cheese
Decoration: (optional)
150 ml/¼ pint double cream
2 kiwi fruits, sliced
crystallised ginger

Crush the biscuits to fine even crumbs – this is easy if you own a food processor, otherwise place the biscuits in a plastic bag and crush them with a rolling pin. Take care not to split the bag – I have often found myself with crumbs all over the kitchen!

Melt the butter in a basin on full power for 1½ minutes. Stir in the biscuit crumbs, then press the mixture into the base of a 23-cm/9-in loose-bottomed quiche tin or dish. Chill thoroughly until set.

Mix the crushed pineapple with the ginger wine in a measuring jug, then make it up to 600 ml/1 pint with water. Place the cornflour in a large bowl, then gradually stir in some of the pineapple mixture, making sure the cornflour does not form lumps. Stir in all the fruit and the sugar, then cook for 8 minutes, whisking once during cooking. The sauce should be quite thick. Whisk it thoroughly, then start beating in the cream cheese, adding it in small portions and beating until it melts completely. Pour the cream cheese mixture over the biscuit base and chill thoroughly until set and very cold.

If you wish to decorate the cheesecake, whip the cream until it stands in soft peaks, then spoon it into a piping bag fitted with a star nozzle. Pipe a border of cream around the cheesecake and decorate it with halved kiwi fruit slices and some crystallised ginger.

Satsuma Swirl

—— SERVES 4 ——

This is a rich creamy, full-flavoured dessert. Serve it very cold, with crisp dessert biscuits like brandy snaps or shortbread fingers.

450 g/1 lb seedless satsumas
100 g/4 oz sugar
150 ml/¼ pint cream sherry

2 tablespoons cornflour
2 tablespoons water
150 ml/¼ pint double cream

Thoroughly wash the fruit and remove the stalk end, but do not peel. Place the satsumas in a large bowl or casserole, then add the sugar and pour in the sherry. Cover with cling film, allowing a small gap for the steam to escape, and cook on full power for 15 minutes. Turn the fruit over once during this cooking time.

Blend the cornflour with the water, then stir it into the syrup surrounding the satsumas and cook for a further 3 minutes, or until the liquid has boiled and thickened.

Allow the fruit to cool slightly, then lift it out of the syrup and blend it to a smooth purée in a liquidiser or food processor. Press the purée through a fine sieve to remove any bits of unprocessed peel and whisk it into the sauce. Set aside to cool, then chill lightly.

Whip the cream until it stands in soft peaks, then swirl it through the fruit purée and transfer the dessert to individual glasses or dishes. Chill thoroughly before serving.

SOME WAYS TO SERVE SATSUMA SWIRL

Satsuma Meringues Spoon the swirl into meringue nests and decorate them with strips of orange peel.

Satsuma Flan Use the fruit swirl to fill a pastry or sponge flan case.

Satsuma Ice Cream Thoroughly whisk the cream into the satsuma purée, then freeze it in a shallow container until half frozen. Whisk thoroughly to remove any ice crystals, then freeze again until firm. Serve scooped into glass dishes and offer chocolate sauce as an accompaniment.

The microwave is invaluable for melting chocolate. Break it into small squares and put it in a basin. Allow about 2 to 3 minutes for a 225-g/8-oz bar.

Chocolate Apricot Cheesecake

—— SERVES 6 ——

1 (300-g/11-oz) packet chocolate digestive biscuits
175 g/6 oz butter
2 (425-g/15-oz) cans apricot halves in syrup
50 g/2 oz cornflour

grated rind of 1 large orange
450 g/1 lb cream cheese
Decoration (optional)
orange slices
chocolate curls

Crush the digestive biscuits in a food processor or by placing them in a plastic bag and crushing them with a rolling pin. Melt the butter in a large bowl for 1 minute on full power. Stir in the biscuits and cook for a further 1 minute, then press the mixture into a 23-cm/9-in flan dish or loose-bottomed flan tin. Chill until firm.

Thoroughly drain the apricots and dry the halves on absorbent kitchen paper. Make the syrup up to 600 ml/1 pint with water. Place the cornflour in a large bowl with the orange rind. Gradually stir in the syrup, making sure that the cornflour does not form any lumps. Cook for 7 to 8 minutes, whisking thoroughly once during cooking and again at the end of the cooking time. The sauce should be smooth and very thick.

Gradually beat the cream cheese into the hot sauce, adding it in small amounts and beating each addition until it has melted completely. Arrange the apricot halves on the biscuit base, then spoon the cheesecake mixture on top. Smooth the surface and chill thoroughly until set.

Decorate the cheesecake, if you like, with orange slices and chocolate curls.

Banana and Walnut Flan

—— SERVES 4 TO 6 ——

This is a rich flan filled with caramelised walnuts mixed with sliced bananas. Decorate the edge with piped whipped cream or serve the flan with clotted cream.

Sweet Pastry:
175 g/6 oz plain flour
100 g/4 oz butter
50 g/2 oz caster sugar
1 egg yolk
1–2 tablespoons water

Filling:
225 g/8 oz walnut pieces
100 g/4 oz demerara sugar
50 g/2 oz butter
4 medium bananas

First make the flan case: sift the flour into a bowl and rub in the butter until the mixture resembles fine breadcrumbs. Stir in the sugar, then add the yolk and enough water to mix the ingredients to a smooth dough. On a well-floured surface, lightly roll out the pastry to fit the base of a 20-cm/ 8-in flan dish or tin. Carefully lift the pastry into the dish and press it into the base and up around the sides of the dish, making a neat edge at the top. Alternatively, chill the pastry for about 20 to 30 minutes, then roll it out to a circle large enough to line the base and sides of the dish. Prick the base of the pastry all over with a fork.

Line the flan case with greaseproof paper and fill it with dried peas or baking beans. Bake in a moderately hot oven (200C, 400F, gas 6) for 15 minutes, then remove the greaseproof paper and peas and cook for a further 5 to 10 minutes, or until the pastry is cooked through.

Meanwhile, make the filling. Place the walnuts and sugar in a basin or bowl and mix thoroughly. Add the butter, then cook on full power for 8 minutes, stirring once during cooking. Try to time the cooking of the filling to more or less coincide with the end of the flan case cooking time.

Peel and slice the bananas and stir them into the nut mixture as soon as it is removed from the microwave. The mixture will sizzle slightly, but make sure it is well mixed. Spoon the filling into the flan case and serve warm not cold.

St Clement's Chiffon

—————— SERVES 6 ——————

In the same way as this light flan is prepared in the microwave oven you can cook the filling for a lemon meringue pie. You can use a bought sponge flan case instead of a home-baked pastry case and the meringue can be browned under a moderately hot grill.

100 g/4 oz butter	grated rind and juice of
225 g/8 oz digestive	2 lemons
biscuits, crushed	25 g/1 oz cornflour
grated rind and juice of	175 g/6 oz sugar
2 oranges	2 egg whites

Place the butter in a fairly large bowl, then cook in the microwave on full power for 1½ minutes, or until melted. Pour in the biscuits and mix thoroughly. Press this mixture into a 25-cm/10-in flan dish or loose-bottomed tin. Chill until firmly set.

To make the filling, stir the fruit rind and juice into the cornflour in a measuring jug. Make up to 600 ml/1 pint with water, then pour into a bowl and stir in the sugar. Cook for 10 minutes, whisking thoroughly once during cooking and at the end of the cooking time. Set the sauce aside to cool until it is lukewarm, whisking it occasionally to prevent a skin from forming.

Whisk the egg whites until they stand in stiff peaks. Stir about 2 tablespoons of the stiff whites into the fruit sauce, then carefully fold in the rest without knocking any of the air out of the mixture; use a metal spoon for this. Swirl the chiffon mixture into the flan case and chill for 2 to 3 hours before serving. The flan is best eaten on the same day as it is made or no later than the following day or the eggs tend to separate from the fruit sauce.

Chocolate Crunch Pie

—————— SERVES 6 ——————

This cold dessert is economical and easy to make without even having to wash up a saucepan from preparing the sauce! For a rich dessert, use half the quantity of milk and substitute double cream for the remaining portion.

175 g/6 oz unsalted butter	450 ml/¾ pint milk
100 g/4 oz muesli	225 g/8 oz plain dessert
50 g/2 oz digestive biscuits	chocolate
25 g/1 oz cornflour	**Decoration:**
50 g/2 oz sugar	150 ml/¼ pint double
2 tablespoons ginger wine	cream
or sherry	crystallised ginger

Place the butter in a basin and melt it in the microwave on full power for 1½ minutes. Stir in the muesli and cook for 3 minutes, stirring once. Crush the digestive biscuits, then add them to the muesli and stir thoroughly. Press this mixture into the base of a 24-cm/9½-in springform tin or loose-bottomed cake tin. Chill for at least 30 minutes, or until thoroughly set.

To make the chocolate topping, blend the cornflour and sugar with the ginger wine, then gradually pour in the milk, stirring continuously. Cook on full power for 8 minutes, whisking thoroughly after 4 minutes. At the end of this time the sauce should have boiled and thickened. Break the chocolate into squares and whisk these into the sauce, then continue whisking until they have completely dissolved.

Pour the chocolate sauce over the chilled base and chill until set. To decorate the dessert, remove it from the tin, leaving the base in place, and place it on a serving platter. Whip the cream until it stands in soft peaks, then spoon it into a piping bag fitted with a star nozzle. Pipe a border of cream around the dessert and top with pieces of crystallised ginger. Serve within a couple of hours of decorating and store in the refrigerator until then.

BAKING

It is with great care that I would like to present a very limited number of so-called 'baking' recipes for microwave ovens.

I have spent hours making cakes, teabreads, yeast mixtures and doughs for the microwave oven and I am afraid I am not convinced that there are many recipes which I could present in a book aimed at getting the best out of your microwave rather than cooking every possible dish in it.

The microwave oven basically steams food. Bearing this in mind, think about your favourite traditional baking recipes cooked in a steamer rather than in the oven. What would you think of that idea if it were presented in a cookbook? Not much, most probably.

However, that is not all there is to say about breads and cakes. Forget about making dough and kneading it for many hours but, instead, take a fairly thick batter and beat it until it forms a smooth yeast mixture. Allow it to rise as per usual, then pour it into a jug or basin rather than a loaf tin and cook it in the microwave. You will achieve a light, home-baked loaf with a good flavour and spongy texture. It is ideal for serving

with the first course of a special dinner party even if it's not a practical idea for day-to-day toast and sandwiches.

Melted cake mixtures can be cooked with success too. Gingerbread, made in small quantities, is very successful, so too is a sticky mixture for chocolate brownies. If you want to make a cake in a hurry, then the microwave is ideal. A chocolate cake mixture can be cooked in a ring mould, then decorated to give an impressive result.

One important thing to remember is that the shape of the cooking container for baking mixtures is most important. Ring dishes are by far the best for cakes, and jugs take the lead when it comes to cooking bread batters.

Bearing this in mind, try some of the recipes in this chapter; I hope you will be pleasantly surprised having read the introduction. I find the bread idea the best – it's useful for when you've run out of bread, a good talking point at dinner parties and at least it is likely to taste more interesting than many of the shop-bought alternatives.

Quick Jug and Basin Bread

—— MAKES 2 SMALL LOAVES ——

Bread mix cooks very successfully in the microwave oven if it is made up with more water than is suggested on the packet. The mixture should be a stiff batter and not a dough which can be kneaded. The jug bread is particularly useful sliced to serve with a starter, as the small round slices are quite attractive and, unlike conventionally baked bread, they do not have a heavy crust. Serve the basin bread cut into wedges.

1 (280-g/10-oz) packet bread mix	oil for greasing
300 ml/$\frac{1}{2}$ pint hand-hot water	3–4 tablespoons sesame seeds or dark poppy seeds

Empty the bread mix into a bowl, make a well in the middle and pour in the water, then gradually beat it in to make a very thick, smooth batter. Beat thoroughly until the mixture is smooth and quite elastic. If you have a food processor or food mixer then use it for this otherwise tiring task.

Grease a 1.15-litre/2-pint basin and a 600-ml/1-pint heatproof glass measuring jug. Sprinkle the inside of both with either sesame seeds or poppy seeds to coat them completely. Pour batter into the measuring jug up as far as the 175-ml/6-fl oz mark; pour the rest of the batter into the basin. As you are pouring the mixture into the containers, aim it right in the middle because if it touches the sides as it falls, then it will take with it some of the seed coating from the sides.

Cover with cling film and leave in a warm place until the mixture in the jug has reached the 350-ml/12-fl oz mark. Cook the two separately: cook the jug mixture first, on full power, for 4 minutes. Allow the bread to stand in the container for 2 minutes, then turn it out on to a wire rack to cool.

Cook the basin bread for 6 minutes. Again leave the bread to stand for 2 minutes, then turn it out on to the wire rack to cool. Serve either warm or cold.

DIFFERENT FLAVOURED BREADS

This quick bread-mix recipe can be flavoured with all sorts of ingredients to make interesting sandwiches or the bread will make a starter more interesting if it is served sliced and buttered.

Herb Bread Add 3 tablespoons chopped fresh mixed herbs or one particular herb depending on how you want to serve the bread.

Nutty Bread Add finely chopped walnuts (about 100 g/ 4 oz) to the bread mix.

Caraway Bread Add 1 tablespoon caraway seeds to the bread mix and sprinkle the inside of the jug and basin with caraway seeds before pouring in the batter.

Onion Bread Finely chop 2 large onions and cook them with 25 g/1 oz butter in a basin. Cook for 8 minutes on full power. Allow the cooked onion to cool slightly then beat it into the bread mix.

Cheese Bread Finely grate 75 g/3 oz matured English Cheddar and beat it into the bread mix.

Bacon Bread Finely chop 225 g/8 oz lean, rindless bacon and cook it in the microwave for 5 minutes. Drain off the fat and add it to the bread mix with 2 tablespoons grated onion.

Note: these above variations can also be applied to the recipe for Wholemeal Jug Bread.

Wholewheat Jug Bread

—— MAKES 2 SMALL LOAVES——

I would not suggest that anyone should decide to make all their own bread in the microwave, but it is useful to have the facility for making some home-made bread quickly for a dinner party or if you just happen to have run out of bread when the shops are closed. These loaves are made from a yeast batter which requires only one proving.

175 g/6 oz wholewheat flour	175 ml/6 fl oz lukewarm water
$\frac{1}{2}$ teaspoon salt	a little oil for greasing
1$\frac{1}{2}$ teaspoons dried yeast	4 tablespoons poppy seeds
$\frac{1}{4}$ teaspoon sugar	

Put the flour and salt into a bowl. In a different bowl sprinkle the yeast and sugar over the water, then set aside in a warm place for about 10 minutes until dissolved and frothy.

Make a well in the flour, pour in the yeast liquid and gradually mix in the flour to make a thick batter. Beat this thoroughly until it is very smooth and elastic. Grease two 600-ml/1-pint measuring jugs with the oil, or one jug and a 1.15-litre/2-pint basin, then coat the inside with poppy seeds. Pour the batter into the prepared containers and cover the tops with cling film. Leave in a warm place until the batter has risen to the 350-ml/12 fl oz mark or higher.

Cook on full power for 3$\frac{1}{2}$ minutes. Leave in the jug for 2 minutes, then turn out to cool on a wire rack.

Use plain mugs to make individual-sized loaves. Make sure the mugs are well greased and fill them only one-third full of batter, thus allowing room for it to rise.

Bread Rolls

MAKES 8

The best container for cooking rolls is a special bun dish for microwave ovens, these are usually circular. The rolls can also be cooked in ramekin dishes, mugs or flower pots (with a small piece of greaseproof paper placed over the holes to prevent the batter from running out).

1½ teaspoons dried yeast
½ teaspoon sugar
175 ml/6 fl oz lukewarm
  water
175 g/6 oz strong white or
  wholewheat flour

½ teaspoon salt
a little oil for greasing
sesame seeds or poppy
  seeds for topping

Sprinkle the yeast and sugar over the water and set aside in a warm place for about 10 minutes or until frothy. Sift the white flour into a bowl or pour the wholewheat flour straight in. Add the salt, then make a well in the middle. Give the yeast liquid a good stir to make sure all the yeast has dissolved, then pour it into the flour and gradually beat in the flour to make a smooth batter. Beat thoroughly for about 6 to 10 minutes, so that the batter is smooth and elastic. If you have a food mixer or food processor, then it is ideal for this.

Thoroughly grease eight bun holes or six bun and two ramekin dishes. Divide the dough between the prepared containers and leave to stand in a warm place until risen almost to the edge of the dishes. Sprinkle with sesame seeds or poppy seeds.

Cook the six rolls for 2½ minutes on full power. If you are cooking two on their own then cook them for 2 minutes. If you have a container which takes all eight rolls, then cook them for 2½ to 3 minutes.

Allow the rolls to stand in the dishes for 2 minutes, then turn them out on to a wire rack to cool completely.

Fruit Ring

Serve this teabread ring sliced and buttered.

50 g/2 oz butter
50 g/2 oz sugar
50 g/2 oz black treacle
150 g/5 oz self-raising flour
½ teaspoon mixed spice

50 g/2 oz sultanas
25 g/1 oz chopped mixed
  peel
1 egg, beaten

Grease a 900-ml/1½-pint ring dish. Put the butter, sugar and treacle in a basin and heat on full power for 2 minutes.

Sift the flour and spice into a bowl. Add the sultanas and peel and mix thoroughly. Make a well in the dry ingredients and pour in the melted mixture, then beat in the egg and gradually mix in the dry ingredients to make a soft mixture. Turn this into the prepared dish and cook for 3½ minutes.

Allow the ring to cool in the dish for 2 to 3 minutes, then turn it out on to a wire rack to cool completely.

Malted Ring

Serve this plain malted cake buttered, like a teabread.

100 g/4 oz self-raising flour
3 tablespoons powdered
  malted drink
¼ teaspoon baking powder

50 g/2 oz butter
50 g/2 oz golden syrup
1 tablespoon milk

Grease a 900-ml/1½-pint ring dish. Sift the flour, malted drink and baking powder into a bowl. Melt the butter with the syrup on full power for 2 minutes. Make a well in the dry ingredients then gradually beat in the melted mixture and the milk until smooth.

Pour the mixture into the prepared dish and cook for 3½ minutes. Allow to cool in the dish for 2 minutes, then turn out to cool completely on a wire rack. Wrap in cling film while just warm. Serve sliced.

Containers for cooking bread in the microwave.

Battenburg Cake

This cake works quite well in the microwave because once the basic mixture is cooked it has to be trimmed and sandwiched together, so the end result does not look inferior for having been made in a microwave.

100 g/4 oz butter or margarine	pink food colouring
100 g/4 oz caster sugar	strawberry jam
2 eggs	450 g/1 lb marzipan
100 g/4 oz self-raising flour	caster sugar for sprinkling

Cream the butter or margarine with the sugar until the mixture is pale and soft. Beat in the eggs and use a metal spoon to fold in the flour.

Grease two (13 × 19-cm/5 × 7½-in) loaf dishes (these slope to slightly smaller dimensions towards the base). Put half the mixture into one of the dishes and spread it out evenly. Cook on full power for 2½ to 3 minutes, turning the dish round after 2 minutes.

Colour the remaining mixture with a little pink food colouring, then turn it into the other dish and spread it out evenly. Cook for the same length of time as the first cake.

Allow the cakes to cool in their dishes for about 5 minutes, then turn them out on to a clean tea-towel on a wire rack. Allow to cool completely.

To assemble the Battenburg cake, spread one layer of cake with jam, then place the other piece on top. Cut the cake in half down its length, then turn one piece upside down to give a chequered effect. Spread a little jam down the cut side and sandwich the pieces of cake together.

Trim all the edges neatly.

Reserve about a quarter of the marzipan, then lightly knead the remainder, and roll it out on a clean surface dusted with icing sugar. The rolled-out marzipan should form an oblong shape large enough to wrap around the cake: about 18 × 28 cm/7 × 11 in. Brush a little jam over the marzipan, then lift the cake into the middle. Carefully fold the marzipan round the cake, pressing the join together well. Trim off any excess at the ends and add the trimmings to the reserved marzipan.

Turn the cake over so that the join is underneath and place it on a serving platter. Knead the trimmings into the reserved marzipan and divide this into three equal portions. Roll these with your fingers into long strips, then plait them together and press this on top of the cake. Pinch the edges of the marzipan between your fingers, then sprinkle a little caster sugar over the cake and serve it cut into slices.

If you have a packet of marzipan, or some leftover home-made marzipan, which has become slightly hard, then heat it in the microwave for a few seconds to help soften it before kneading and rolling.

Chocolate Ring Cake

If you want to make a very special cake then the microwave is certainly not the cooker to use! However, so often it would be nice to offer unexpected guests a slice of cake with their coffee, or knock up a special treat for Sunday tea. And that's when the microwave comes to the fore – a simple chocolate cake can be cooked in less than 5 minutes. This is quite a shallow cake so if you want to make something which looks a little more impressive then make two cakes of this size and sandwich them together with whipped cream.

50 g/2 oz butter, softened
50 g/2 oz caster sugar
50 g/2 oz self-raising flour
2 tablespoons cocoa
1 egg

Grease a 900-ml/1½-pint ring dish. Place all the ingredients in a basin and beat thoroughly with a wooden spoon or using an electric mixer. When the mixture is soft and light turn it into the prepared dish and smooth the surface with a knife.

Cook on full power for 3½ minutes. Leave the cake in the dish for 2 minutes, then turn it out on to a wire rack to cool. Top with any of the suggestions below when cold.

Chocolate and Nuts Melt 175 g/6 oz plain chocolate in a basin on full power for 2 minutes. Pour over the cake (just the one layer or two, sandwiched with whipped cream), then top with 50 g/2 oz toasted chopped hazelnuts.

Iced Rum Ring Sandwich two cakes together with whipped cream. Make a smooth icing with 225 g/8 oz sifted icing sugar and 2 to 3 tablespoons rum. Coat the cake completely with the rum icing and decorate it with chocolate curls or coarsely grated chocolate.

Black Forest Ring Make two ring cakes. Drain 1 (425-g/15-oz) can black cherries and reserve a few for decoration. Sandwich the cakes together with the cherries and whipped cream, then cover the outside thinly with more of the cream. Press finely grated chocolate all over the cake and add swirls of cream with the reserved cherries as decoration.

If you are sandwiching a cake together with jam, then warm the jam in the pot first (remove any metal lid) for about 30 seconds and it will spread evenly over the cake without breaking the surface.

Sticky Brownies

──── MAKES 8 ────

These are very sweet, rich and sticky; real diet-killers!

50 g/2 oz butter or
    margarine
100 g/4 oz demerara sugar

75 g/3 oz self-raising flour
40 g/1½ oz cocoa powder
1 egg, beaten

Place the butter or margarine and sugar in a basin (1.15-litre/2-pint capacity). Sift the flour and cocoa powder together and grease a large loaf dish (1.75-litre/3-pint capacity).

Melt the butter and sugar for 2 minutes on full power. Working quickly, beat in the dry ingredients and the egg, in that order. Transfer the mixture to the prepared loaf dish – it does not need the depth, but during cooking the mixture will rise and fall. The dimensions of the dish will give the right depth of cake.

Cook for 2 minutes. Remove from the oven and allow to cool completely in the dish. When cold, cut the mixture into eight squares and carefully remove them from the dish.

Chocolate Crunch Cups

──── MAKES 14 ────

The microwave is ideal for preparing quick treats such as these. This is also a good recipe for the younger members of the family to make in a microwave oven.

50 g/2 oz cornflakes
50 g/2 oz raisins
2 tablespoons chopped
    mixed peel

175 g/6 oz plain chocolate
50 g/2 oz butter

Mix the cornflakes with the raisins and mixed peel in a bowl. Put the chocolate, broken into squares, and butter in a basin and melt on full power for 2 minutes, stirring lightly after 1 minute.

Pour the chocolate on to the cornflake mixture and mix thoroughly. Pile spoonfuls of this mixture into 14 paper cake cases and chill lightly until set.

Note: you can vary the breakfast cereal and use other fruits in the mixture. Try chopped glacé cherries, chopped walnuts or hazelnuts, chopped dates or a few chopped apricots.

Gingerbread Ring

This does work well in the microwave and is ideal for a quick tea-time treat. The cooked gingerbread stores well in a closed polythene bag or airtight container.

100 g/4 oz self-raising flour
1 tablespoon ground
    ginger
50 g/2 oz demerara sugar
50 g/2 oz black treacle
50 g/2 oz butter

¼ teaspoon bicarbonate of
    soda
1 tablespoon cold milk
grated rind of 1 lemon
1 egg, beaten

Thoroughly grease a 900-ml/1½-pint ring mould dish. Sift the flour and ginger into a mixing bowl. Place the sugar, treacle and butter in a basin and melt on full power for 2 minutes.

Meanwhile, stir the bicarbonate of soda into the milk and add the lemon rind to the flour. Stir the melted ingredients into the flour mixure, then beat in the egg and dissolved bicarbonate of soda. When the ingredients are all thoroughly combined, pour the mixture into the ring mould and cook for 3 minutes.

Allow the cooked gingerbread to stand in the dish for 4 to 5 minutes, then turn it out on to a wire rack to cool. Wrap in cling film while still warm. Slice and serve when cold.

Coconut Mallow Squares

──── MAKES ABOUT 25 ────

1 (200-g/7-oz) packet
    white marshmallows
75 g/3 oz butter
225 g/8 oz gingernut
    biscuits

50 g/2 oz desiccated
    coconut

Place the marshmallows and butter in a large bowl, then cook on full power for 3 minutes stirring once. Grease a 23-cm/9-in square shallow tin.

Crush the biscuits to fine crumbs, add these to the melted mixture with the coconut and stir thoroughly. Press the mixture into the prepared tin and cool, then chill until firm. Cut into squares and serve.

If you have some butter cream or similar icing in the refrigerator ready to ice a cake, warm it on full power in the microwave oven for 15 to 30 seconds to make it easy to spread.

Toffee Bran Bars

——— MAKES 16 ———

450 g/1 lb creamy toffees
50 g/2 oz butter
grated rind and juice of
1 small orange
100 g/4 oz All Bran

100 g/4 oz mixed dried
fruit
50 g/2 oz glacé cherries,
chopped

Place the toffees, butter, orange rind and juice in a large bowl and cook on full power for 3 minutes.

Stir the melted toffee mixture to mix it thoroughly to make sure the ingredients are all well coated in toffee. Turn the mixture into a 30 × 18-cm/12 × 7-in tin. Smooth the top, then allow to cool and chill until firm. Cut the mixture into 16 fingers to serve.

Muesli Fingers

——— MAKES 8 ———

These munchy muesli bars are quite good lunch-box fillers or to have with mid-morning coffee.

50 g/2 oz butter
50 g/2 oz golden syrup
175 g/6 oz muesli (with
plenty of fruit and nuts)

2 tablespoons wholemeal
flour

Grease a large loaf or oblong dish measuring about 13 × 19 cm/5 × 7½ in. Place the butter and syrup in a bowl and melt these ingredients on full power for 1½ minutes. Stir in the muesli and flour and mix all the ingredients thoroughly. Press the mixture into the dish and cook for 3 minutes.

Allow the muesli mixture to cool in the dish. When it is just warm cut it into eight fingers, then lift these out of the dish when completely cold.

If you are making boiled cakes to cook in your conventional oven, then the ingredients which are to be boiled can be cooked on full power in the microwave oven instead of in a saucepan.

Nutty Scottish Fingers

——— MAKES 12 ———

These chocolate and oat fingers are quite more-ish! Made from toasted hazelnuts and ground almonds, they are crunchy and satisfying. Top them with melted chocolate if you like.

100 g/4 oz porridge oats
100 g/4 oz ground almonds
50 g/2 oz demerara sugar
100 g/4 oz butter
50 g/2 oz hazelnuts,
chopped and toasted

100-g/4-oz packet plain
chocolate drops
2 tablespoons milk

Place the porridge oats in a microwave-proof mixing bowl with the almonds, sugar and butter. Cook on full power for 6 minutes, or until the sugar has melted. Stir thoroughly once during the cooking time.

Immediately the mixture is removed from the oven, add the hazelnuts and chocolate drops, then stir thoroughly until all the chocolate melts. Stir in just enough of the milk to bind the ingredients together, then press the mixture into a 15-cm/6-in square shallow tin. Allow to cool completely, then chill until firm and cut into fingers to serve.

SAUCES & PRESERVES

I include preserves in this chapter title with my tongue firmly in my cheek! Really, the microwave oven is not the cooking medium to use if you want to turn this year's crop of cooking apples into pounds of chutney, or if you're planning to make the annual supply of Seville marmalade. Stick to the old preserving pan because it's by far the best method.

However, if you want to make a little chutney to bring out the best in one of your curries, or if you think a pot or two of tangy lemon curd would be a nice treat for tea, then this is where your microwave oven really will come in useful. For preparing small quantities of chutneys or sweet preserves it is a great help.

When it comes to making sauces and gravies, forget about your saucepans and turn to bowls. Your microwave oven is going to revolutionise your approach to sauces; or at least it may do if you give it a good trial run!

For most sauces you can throw all the ingredients into a large basin and give them a good whisk. You can't actually go away and leave them unattended, but you can do other things while the sauce is cooking. Even the notoriously

difficult Hollandaise Sauce (see page 201) can be prepared with almost ensured success and no time wasted. So, there's no real excuse for serving a dry meal anymore!

It is not too difficult to adapt your own recipes for chutneys and pickles for microwave cooking. If you want to make a small quantity of preserve, then reduce the recipe portions accordingly and place all the ingredients which are cooked together in a large bowl or casserole. Do not cover the dish but allow the steam to escape so as to thicken the preserve. Cook on full power, watching the mixture as it cooks, until the chutney has thickened or until the ingredients in a pickle are tender but not too mushy. For sweet preserves, microwave cooking is suitable only for very small quantities as it is easier to overcook a jam or overset a preserve if you are unfamiliar with the precise timing needed for your oven. The best advice I can offer is to follow your manufacturer's instructions. Sweet butters – thick, very sweet fruit purées – are good to try in the microwave as these have a tendency to burn and stick to a saucepan when cooked by conventional methods.

Béchamel Sauce

———— SERVES 4 TO 6 ————

This is a basic savoury white sauce which can be varied easily in many ways. It can be served under many guises with fish, poultry and meat, vegetables, rice and pasta.

40 g/1½ oz plain flour
1 bay leaf
blade of mace
600 ml/1 pint milk
salt and freshly ground
  white pepper
25 g/1 oz butter

Place the flour in a large basin with the bay leaf and mace. Gradually pour in the milk, whisking all the time to prevent the flour from forming lumps. Add seasoning to taste and the butter, then cook on full power for 10 minutes, whisking twice during cooking and again thoroughly at the end of the cooking time. Remove the bay leaf and mace, taste and adjust the seasoning before serving.

SAUCES BASED ON BÉCHAMEL:

Butter Sauce To the cooked sauce add 100 g/4 oz butter and whisk thoroughly until it has completely dissolved. This gives a rich sauce which can be served with plain poached fish or simple pasta.

Parsley Sauce Chop a large handful of fresh parsley and add it to the sauce, then stir well and serve.

Mustard Sauce Stir 2 tablespoons prepared English mustard into the sauce.

Cheese Sauce Add 100–175 g/4–6 oz grated Cheddar cheese to the sauce and whisk thoroughly until it melts. Heat for 1 minute before serving.

Mushroom Sauce Add 225 g/8 oz finely sliced button mushrooms to the sauce and cook for 2 minutes.

Egg Sauce Finely chop 4 hard-boiled eggs and add them to the sauce with a little grated nutmeg.

Onion Sauce Finely chop 1 large onion or 2 small onions and cook these in 25 g/1 oz butter for 5 minutes on full power before adding the flour and milk. Stir in the bay leaf and mace and cook as in the main recipe.

To prepare 300 ml/½ pint of Béchamel Sauce, use 3 tablespoons plain flour instead of the 40 g/1½ oz. Use half the quantity of milk, but retain the same quantities of flavourings and butter. The method is exactly the same but the sauce should be cooked on full power for 6 minutes, whisking once during cooking and again at the end of the cooking time.

Sherried Mushroom Sauce

———— SERVES 4 ————

Serve this sauce with grilled pork or lamb chops and steaks or it goes particularly well with chicken. It can also be poured over hard-boiled eggs for a quick supper dish or starter.

2 tablespoons plain flour
50 g/2 oz butter
salt and freshly ground
  black pepper
250 ml/8 fl oz milk
150 ml/¼ dry sherry
225 g/8 oz button
  mushrooms, sliced

Place the flour, butter and seasoning in a basin. Whisk in the milk and sherry, then cook on full power for 6 minutes, whisking thoroughly once during cooking and again at the end of this cooking time. Make sure there are no lumps in the sauce before you add the mushrooms and scrape the whisk against the sides of the bowl to remove any flour which may be stuck to it.
  Stir in the mushrooms, return the sauce to the oven and cook for a further 2 to 3 minutes. Stir well, then pour the sauce into a serving boat, or over the food.

Tomato Sauce

———— SERVES 4 TO 6 ————

This is one of the most versatile of savoury sauces. It can be served as an accompaniment to meatloaves, hamburgers, chops, poultry or fish. Made with lots of garlic, it will turn some simple boiled pasta into a quick meal (particularly delicious with fresh pasta and freshly grated Parmesan cheese) or it can be used in any number of layered pasta dishes. Tomato sauce can also form the cooking medium for many foods: for example meatballs, chicken portions or slim slices of meat can be simmered in the sauce for a full, rich flavour.

2 celery sticks, finely
  chopped
1 large onion, chopped
1–3 cloves garlic, crushed
50 g/2 oz butter
1 bay leaf
2 tablespoons
  concentrated tomato
  purée
1 tablespoon plain flour
2 (425-g/15-oz) cans
  chopped tomatoes
150 ml/¼ pint full-bodied
  red wine
salt and freshly ground
  black pepper

Place the celery, onion and garlic in a 1.15-litre/2-pint basin. The amount of garlic used will depend on your own taste and on what the sauce is to be served with. Add the butter and cover the basin with cling film, allowing a small gap for the steam to escape. Cook on full power for 6 minutes.

Stir in the bay leaf, tomato purée and flour, then pour in the tomatoes and wine. Stir to make sure all the ingredients are mixed, then cook for 10 minutes, stirring once during cooking.

Remove the bay leaf from the sauce, then blend it in a liquidiser until smooth. Taste the sauce and add seasoning. Heat for 2 minutes and serve as required These quantities will make about 600 ml/1 pint of sauce.

Hollandaise Sauce

─────── SERVES 4 ───────

Hollandaise sauce is a smooth, rich sauce consisting of eggs and butter. It is usually served with fish, vegetables or egg dishes.

I was amazed that it could be cooked successfully in the microwave oven and positively delighted to discover a quick way of making this delicious but otherwise rather tiresome sauce.

2 tablespoons lemon juice	100 g/4 oz butter
1 tablespoon water	2 large egg yolks
salt and freshly ground	
white pepper	

Pour the lemon juice and water into a 1.15-litre/2-pint basin (you need one this size for room to whisk vigorously later). Add a little seasoning and cook on full power for 6 minutes.

Meanwhile place the butter in a heatproof measuring jug or small basin. When the lemon juice is removed from the oven whisk in the egg yolks immediately. Heat the butter for 2½ minutes, then slowly pour it on to the egg yolks whisking continuously.

Cook the hollandaise sauce for 30 seconds, give it a good stir and serve at once.

For even greater speed, this sauce can be made in a liquidiser. Put the egg yolks in the liquidiser. Heat the lemon juice as in the main recipe, then pour it into the working liquidiser and process for 1 minute. Heat the butter for 3½ minutes, so that it is really hot. While the liquidiser is working pour in the butter in a slow trickle. The very hot butter will cook and thicken the eggs in one go, ready for serving straight from the liquidiser.

Bread Sauce

─────── SERVES 4 ───────

Bread sauce is an old-fashioned English accompaniment to boiled ham and roast chicken or turkey. Correctly prepared it should be a delicate, creamy sauce, not too thick and surprisingly complementary with the traditional main dishes.

There is, in fact, one enormous advantage of cooking the sauce in the microwave oven, and that is all down to the revolutionary way in which the microwaves cook food. Because microwave-cooked food is heated to a certain extent from the inside out, the whole onion in the bread sauce gives its flavour more readily in this method than by conventional boiling. So there is no need to stand around for hours while the onion is infusing in the milk and the end result is better flavoured than ever!

6 cloves	salt and freshly ground
1 large onion, peeled	white pepper
1 bay leaf	a little freshly grated
600 ml/1 pint milk	nutmeg
100 g/4 oz fine fresh white	
breadcrumbs	

Stick the cloves into the onion and stand it in a 1.15-litre/2-pint basin. Cover with cling film and cook on full power for 2 minutes. Add the bay leaf and pour in the milk, then cook (again covered with cling film, allowing a small gap for steam to escape), for a further 6 to 6½ minutes.

Stir in the breadcrumbs, seasoning to taste and a little nutmeg, then cook for a further 2 minutes. There is no need to cover the basin for this final cooking period. Carefully scoop the onion and bay leaf out of the sauce and give it a good whisk. Taste and adjust the seasoning before serving.

Whisking sauces ensures an even mixing of the ingredients which prevents lumps forming. It is especially important when eggs are included in the sauce, as in the Hollandaise Sauce.

Sweet and Sour Sauce

———— SERVES 4 TO 6 ————

Serve this sauce with fish, meat or poultry. To make traditional sweet and sour pork coat pieces of pork (lean boneless cubes) in a batter and deep fry them until crisp and golden brown. Pile them in a large dish and pour this sauce over.

1 large onion, roughly chopped	2 tablespoons soy sauce
1 large carrot, cut into strips	3 tablespoons tomato ketchup
1 green pepper	1 tablespoon vinegar
2 tablespoons oil	1 (340-g/12-oz) can pineapple pieces in syrup
a few drops of sesame oil	
1 tablespoon cornflour	

Place the onion in a large basin with the carrot. Cut the stalk end off the pepper and remove all the seeds and pith from inside. Cut the pepper shell into short fine strips and add them to the onion mixture. Stir in the oil and sesame oil, then cook on full power for 5 minutes.

   Meanwhile, blend the cornflour with the soy sauce, ketchup and vinegar. Pour in the syrup from the fruit and stir well. Pour this liquid into the sauce then stir in the pineapple pieces. Cook for a further 5 minutes, stir well and serve as required.

Simple Sweet and Sour Marinade

———— SERVES 4 ————

This sweet and sour recipe is good for brushing over chops, gammon steaks or pieces of chicken before they are cooked. It makes an excellent marinade for fish or poultry and it can also be used to give barbecued food a lively tang. Prepare it in advance if you like and store it in a screw-top jar in the refrigerator.

2 tablespoons red wine vinegar	150 ml/$\frac{1}{4}$ pint red wine
4 tablespoons soft brown sugar	1 tablespoon concentrated tomato purée
1 tablespoon mild mustard	

Mix all the ingredients in a basin or measuring jug and cook on full power for 4 minutes. The sauce should boil for about 1 minute. Stir thoroughly, then use the sauce as required, to brush over meats, fish and poultry.

Wooden spoons can be left in the microwave oven if they are used for stirring a sauce or similar, but only for 5 minutes maximum.

Barbecue Sauce

——— SERVES 4 ———

This is a full-flavoured slightly sweet, piquant sauce, almost strong enough to class as a relish. It is delicious with hamburgers, chops, sausages, steaks, chicken or whole fish. It is intended as an accompaniment for charcoal grilled foods, but it can be served with simple chicken joints, cooked in the microwave oven, or whole mackerel cooked in the same way.

4 tablespoons concentrated tomato purée
1 tablespoon prepared English mustard
1 tablespoon Worcestershire sauce
1 tablespoon cider vinegar
4 tablespoons water
2 large cloves garlic, crushed
salt and black pepper

Place all the ingredients in a small basin or heatproof measuring jug, then cook on full power for 3 minutes. Stir thoroughly and serve as required, or spread the sauce over foods to be grilled. Remember this is a strongly flavoured sauce and should be eaten in small quantities, like a ketchup.

Pepper Sauce

——— SERVES 4 ———

Good to serve with meat, poultry or fish, this is a colourful sauce which is well flavoured with the tang of slightly sweet peppers.

1 red pepper
1 green pepper
1 yellow pepper
1 onion, finely chopped
25 g/1 oz butter
salt and freshly ground black pepper
2 tablespoons plain flour
1 chicken stock cube
30 ml/½ pint boiling water

Cut the tops off the peppers, then remove and discard the seeds and pith from inside each one. Chop the pepper shells and place them in a basin with the onion and butter. Cook on full power for 10 minutes.

Stir in the seasoning to taste and the flour. Dissolve the stock cube in the boiling water, then pour it into the peppers, stirring continuously. Cook for 5 minutes, then stir thoroughly and serve as required.

Gravy

——— SERVES 4 TO 6 ———

A full-flavoured gravy can only be made from good meat juices, so save all the cooking liquid from the meat. However, a perfectly tasty gravy sauce can be prepared even if you do not have any meat juices and this can be served with grilled sausages, meat patties or meat pies.

meat or poultry cooking juices
40 g/1½ oz plain flour
600 ml/1 pint boiling water or hot liquid drained from boiling vegetables
1 beef, lamb or chicken stock cube
salt and freshly ground black pepper

The meat juices can be from roasting joints of meat, chicken, turkey or duck. Cooking sediment from either steaks or chops can also be used to give a good gravy. It is important to drain away excess fat otherwise the gravy will be greasy. The most convenient container to use for cooking the gravy is a large basin (about 1.15-litre/2-pint capacity) but if you have completed the roasting time for meat in the conventional cooker and if the joint is in a dish which is suitable for microwave cooking, then this is the best vessel to use as any cooked-on flavour from the meat will be simmered off into the gravy.

Transfer the meat juices into the basin, if necessary, scraping all the meat sediment out of the roasting tin. Do not discard the tin to the washing up at this stage, rather pour in the boiling liquid which is to make the gravy and stir it round to obtain the most flavour.

Stir the flour into the juices, making sure there are no lumps, then gradually pour in the liquid, whisking all the time. Crumble in the stock cube – use beef or lamb ones for these meats, a chicken cube for pork or poultry of any kind. Whisk well, then cook on full power for 10 minutes. Whisk the gravy once during cooking, then thoroughly at the end of the cooking time. Taste and add seasoning and a little gravy browning if necessary. Pour into a sauceboat to serve.

TO ENRICH GOOD GRAVY

Wine Substitute 300 ml/½ pint red wine for half the liquid, but do not halve the stock cube. This makes a good gravy for beef, pork or lamb.

Sherry Add 4 tablespoons dry sherry with the liquid. Cook as above. This gravy goes particularly well with chicken or other poultry, but it can also be served successfully with any meat.

Port Add 4 tablespoons port with the liquid. Cook as above. Port-flavoured gravy is good with pork, lamb and duck. If you want to make a very rich sauce, substitute 150 ml/¼ pint port for an equal quantity of the liquid.

Horseradish or mustard A tablespoon of prepared English mustard or horseradish sauce peps up gravy to serve with beef

Wine Sauces

A good wine sauce can turn a simple main dish of grilled poultry or chops into an elegant entrée; a bad wine sauce will completely kill the food. A mistake which is frequently made is to buy the cheapest bottle of wine available on the supermarket shelf in the belief that it will not give itself away in the finished dish – unfortunately this is not the case. A wine that gets you in the back of the throat when you drink it will have the same effect when it is cooked. I am not suggesting that you spend a small fortune on a superior quality vintage bottle, but take one of the average-priced bottles which is quite drinkable. Remember that any small amounts of wine leftover in a bottle can be stored in an airtight container in the refrigerator or frozen for some time for future use in sauces.

As a general rule, rich, red wine sauces are served with red meats and game while white wines are used in sauces for fish and poultry. The obvious exception to this rule is coq au vin, chicken cooked in a rich red wine sauce. So the sauce to use will depend on the other ingredients in the dish and the accompaniments which are to be served.

White Wine Sauce

——— SERVES 4 TO 6 ———

1 small onion, very finely chopped
50 g/2 oz butter
50 g/2 oz white button mushrooms, chopped
40 g/1½ oz plain flour
600 ml/1 pint dry white wine
salt and freshly ground black pepper
1 chicken, fish or ham stock cube (depending on with what the sauce is to be served)
Bouquet Garni:
1 bay leaf
4 sprigs parsley
sprig of thyme

Place the onion in a large basin with the butter and cook on full power for 4 minutes. Stir in the mushrooms and flour, then gradually pour in the wine, stirring all the time. Add a little seasoning and the crumbled stock cube.

Use the bay leaf to wrap around the other ingredients for the bouquet garni, then tie it securely and add it to the sauce. Cook on full power for 10 minutes, whisking once during cooking and again thoroughly at the end of the cooking time. Remove the bouquet garni, taste and adjust the seasoning before serving the sauce. Add any meat juices to the sauce if they are available.

Red Wine Sauce

——— SERVES 4 TO 6 ———

50 g/2 oz butter
1 clove garlic, crushed
1 large onion or 100 g/4 oz
  small pickling onions
40 g/1½ oz plain flour
2 tablespoons mushroom
  ketchup
1 tablespoon concentrated
  tomato purée
1 beef stock cube or meat
  juices

600 ml/1 pint full-bodied
  red wine
salt and freshly ground
  black pepper
Bouquet Garni:
1 bay leaf
4 sprigs parsley
2 sprigs thyme

Place the butter in a large basin with the garlic and onion. Cook on full power for 5 minutes, then stir in the flour, mushroom ketchup, tomato purée and crumbled stock cube or meat juices. Gradually pour in the wine, stirring all the time, then add a little seasoning.

Tie the bay leaf securely around the other ingredients for the bouquet garni, then add it to the sauce. Cook on full power for 10 minutes, whisking the sauce thoroughly once during the cooking time and again when it is cooked. Remove the bouquet garni, taste and adjust the seasoning before serving the sauce.

Apple Sauce

——— SERVES 4 ———

Serve apple sauce with roast pork, baked ham or roast goose. Otherwise try some of the variations and serve the sauce with various other foods.

450 g/1 lb cooking apples
100 g/4 oz sugar
25 g/1 oz butter

Peel, core and quarter the apples, then cut them into slices and place these in a large basin with the sugar. Cover and cook on full power for 7 minutes.

Beat the soft apples, thoroughly, adding the butter, then set aside to cool. Transfer to a small dish to serve.

Lemon Apple Sauce Add the grated rind of 1 lemon to the apples when they are cooked. Serve this sauce with baked mackerel or veal.

Herbed Apple Sauce Stir 2 tablespoons chopped fresh herbs into the sauce. Try sage, parsley, thyme, rosemary and tarragon. These herbs can be mixed together or used separately to serve with roast chicken, pork, lamb, ham or certain simple fish dishes.

Spiced Apple Sauce Add 1 teaspoon mixed spice to the sauce and serve as for the main recipe.

Cumberland Sauce

——— SERVES 4 ———

This sauce is a traditional accompaniment for boiled or baked ham and roast lamb. It also tastes very good with roast pork and makes an unusual accompaniment for chicken or duck.

1 teaspoon cornflour
grated rind and juice of
  1 large orange
4 tablespoons redcurrant
  jelly

150 ml/¼ pint red wine
2 tablespoons port

Put the cornflour into a basin, then stir in the orange rind and juice. Add the redcurrant jelly and the wine, then stir in the port. Cook on full power for 6 minutes whisking once during cooking and again at the end of the cooking time. Serve at once.

Gooseberry Sauce

——— SERVES 4 ———

This is a savoury sauce which is usually served with mackerel, either grilled, fried or baked. This tart fruit can also be used to complement the richer meats – pork, for example, will benefit from a condiment of this type.

1 onion, finely chopped
25 g/1 oz butter
450 g/1 lb gooseberries,
  topped and tailed

75 g/3 oz sugar
salt and freshly ground
  black pepper

Place the onion in a bowl with the butter and cook on full power for 4 minutes. Add the gooseberries and sugar and cover the bowl with cling film, allowing a small gap for the steam to escape. Cook for a further 8 minutes, then stir in seasoning to taste and serve as required.

Cranberry Sauce

——— SERVES 4 ———

100 g/4 oz cranberries
100 g/4 oz sugar
2 tablespoons port

Place the cranberries in a large basin with the sugar and cover with cling film, allowing a small gap for the steam to escape. Cook on full power for 3 minutes, then stir thoroughly adding the port. Set aside, covered, until cool, then serve.

Orange Sauce

—— SERVES 4 ——

This is a sweet fruity sauce to serve with ice cream, sponge puddings and layered puff pastry with cream.

grated rind and juice of 2 large oranges
50 g/2 oz sugar

2 tablespoons cornflour
25 g/1 oz butter

Pour the orange rind and juice into a measuring jug and make it up to 300 ml/½ pint with water. Put the sugar and cornflour in a 1.15-litre/2-pint basin. Gradually pour in a little of the liquid, stirring all the time to make a smooth solution. Pour in the remaining liquid, stirring, then cook on full power for 3 minutes.

Whisk the sauce thoroughly and add the butter. Cook for a further 2 minutes, then whisk again and serve.

Lemon Sauce A sweet lemon sauce can be made in the same way as the orange sauce, using the juice of just 1 lemon and add a little extra sugar if necessary.

Jam Sauce

—— SERVES 4 ——

This sauce always revives pictures of lumpy school semolina with a dollop of something red in the middle!

However, in defence of this poor mis-judged recipe, it can be very good with all sorts of puddings – even with semolina! Made by conventional means, in a saucepan over the hob, it is all to easy to overcook and burn the jam, but in the microwave you really don't have to worry about such things.

The quality of the jam obviously determines the quality of the sauce and home-made is best. However, that's a nice ideal: I'm sure that home-made jam will be reserved for scones and jam, so select a good brand and try all sorts of flavours: black cherry, plum, pineapple or even marmalade can be used. Served with sponge puddings, rice pudding, semolina, stewed fruit, ice cream, fruit pies or Bakewell tart, this is a good store-cupboard standby.

225 g/8 oz good-quality seedless jam
2 tablespons water

Mix the jam with the water in a basin or suitable serving jug and cook on full power for 1 to 1½ minutes. Stir well and serve.

Chocolate Sauce

—— SERVES 4 ——

Serve this sweet sauce with ice cream, poached pears, profiteroles and creamy moulds

1 (150-g/5-oz) bar plain dessert chocolate
25 g/1 oz butter

4 tablespoons golden syrup

Break the chocolate into squares and place them into a basin with the butter and syrup. Cook on full power for 3 to 3½ minutes. Stir well and serve.

Chocolate Toffee Sauce

—— SERVES 4 ——

Almost every other cookery book and give-away leaflet has given the idea for melting chocolate toffee bars to make a quick sauce for ice cream, and it really is very good and it is even easier than usual when there's a microwave oven to hand. As well as tasting good with ice cream, this sauce can be poured over cheesecakes, Semolina Pudding (see page 185) and Pears in Cider (see page 182).

2 Mars Bars
2 tablespoons milk

Break the bars into a basin and cook on full power for 2 minutes. Beat well and stir in the milk, then serve at once.

Coconut Chocolate Sauce Use 2 Bounty Bars instead of the Mars Bars.

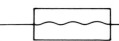

If you have a suitable jug – a heatproof, fairly large jug with no metal trimmings – then many sauces can be prepared straight in their serving container. Problems tend to occur when the sauce needs to be whisked, but if the vessel is large enough then this problem can be overcome.

Custard Sauce

———— SERVES 4 TO 6 ————

Serve custard sauce with hot puddings, or to form the top layer of a trifle.

2 tablespoons custard
  powder
2 egg yolks

2 tablespoons sugar
600 ml/1 pint milk

Place the custard powder in a 1.15-litre/2-pint basin. Add the egg yolks and sugar and whisk in a little of the milk. Heat the remaining milk on full power for 4 minutes.

Whisking all the time, pour the milk into the basin. Cook for 2½ to 3 minutes, whisking once during cooking then again at the end of the time.

Serve at once or cover the surface with a piece of greaseproof paper and allow to cool. When the custard is cool, the paper can be lifted off the surface (use a knife to scrape off the custard as you do so) and the custard will not have a skin.

Sweet Rum and Raisin Sauce

———— SERVES 4 TO 6 ————

This sauce is good to serve with baked or steamed sponge puddings. It also tastes very good poured over profiteroles which are filled with fresh cream. Alternatively use it to make a simple apple tart or pie taste rather special.

150 ml/¼ pint rum
50 g/2 oz raisins
2 tablespoons cornflour

3 tablespoons sugar
450 ml/¾ pint milk

Pour the rum over the raisins and leave them to macerate for as long as possible. They are best covered and left overnight.

Place the cornflour in a 1.15-litre/2-pint basin with the sugar, then whisk in a little of the milk. Heat the remaining milk for 3 minutes on full power. Whisking continuously, gradually pour the milk into the basin. Cook for 4 minutes, whisking once during cooking and again thoroughly at the end of the cooking time.

The sauce will be very thick and very hot, but this is as it should be. Gradually pour in the rum and raisins, stirring them in evenly. Do not whisk at this stage or you will break the raisins and thoroughly discolour the sauce. Heat for 30 seconds and serve at once.

Lemon Curd

———— MAKES ABOUT 1 kg/2 lb ————

3 eggs
grated rind and juice of
  3 large lemons

100 g/4 oz butter
325 g/12 oz sugar

Beat the eggs in a large bowl with the lemon rind. Pour the lemon juice into a basin with the butter and sugar. Cook this mixture on full power for 6 minutes.

Whisking the eggs continuously, gradually pour in the butter mixture. Place the bowl in the microwave and cook for 13 to 14 minutes. Whisk the curd after the first 2 and 4 minutes cooking, then every minute thereafter to prevent any small areas from overcooking.

Have a couple of scalded, warmed pots ready, then strain the curd and pour it into the pots. Cover at once with waxed paper discs and leave to cool. Top with lids and add labels before storing the curd. It can be kept in the refrigerator for up to 1 month.

Brandy Sauce

———— SERVES 4 TO 6 ————

Serve this sauce with Christmas Pudding (see page 173), fruit pies, poached or stewed fruit, or steamed sponge puddings.

2 tablespoons cornflour
3 tablespoons sugar
600 ml/1 pint milk
4 tablespoons brandy

Place the cornflour in a 1.15-litre/2-pint basin. Add the sugar, then whisk in a little of the milk. Heat the remaining milk on full power for 4 minutes.

Whisking all the time, gradually pour the milk on to the cornflour solution, then return the sauce to the oven and cook for a further 4 minutes. Whisk thoroughly at the end of the cooking time, adding the brandy as you do so. Serve at once.

Pear and Apricot Pickle

———— MAKES ABOUT 1.5 kg/3 lb ————

This is a bright, spicy pickle with a distinct tang. When cooked, the fruit should be soft but still in whole pieces in a small amount of sauce.

225 g/8 oz dried apricots	$\frac{1}{4}$ teaspoon turmeric
225 g/8 oz onions	200 ml/7 fl oz vinegar
450 g/1 lb firm pears	
1 tablespoon ground ginger	

Use a pair of kitchen scissors to cut the apricots into thin strips, then place them in a bowl or large casserole dish. Chop the onions – they should be fairly fine but not tiny pieces – and add them to the apricots. Peel the pears, remove their stalks and cores and cut the fruit into chunks; add these to the mixture in the bowl and mix well. Stir in the ginger, turmeric and vinegar and cook the pickle, uncovered, on full power for 15 minutes.

Stir the mixture once during this cooking time, then continue to cook for about 5 to 6 minutes, or until the fruit is soft. Transfer the pickle to warmed, clean pots and cover immediately with air-tight lids. Store in a cool place for 3 months, but make sure that it is covered properly or it may dry out on the surface. The preserve should be allowed to mature for about 2 weeks before it is eaten.

Spiced Onion Pickle

———— MAKES ABOUT 1.5 kg/3 lb ————

This is a very rich dark preserve made with pickling onions and muscovado sugar. Serve with cheese and cold meats.

675 g/1½ lb pickling onions	3 cloves garlic, crushed
225 g/8 oz muscovado sugar	150 ml/¼ pint vinegar
2 tablespoons ground coriander	1.25 kg/2½ lb cooking apples

Place the pickling onions in a bowl and add the sugar, then stir in the coriander and garlic. Pour in the vinegar, then cover the bowl with cling film, allowing a small gap for the steam to escape. Cook on full power for 10 minutes.

While the pickle is cooking, peel, core and slice the apples. Add them to the pickle and mix well, then press the slices down into the juices and continue to cook, uncovered, for a further 5 to 7 minutes. Stir once during this cooking time and again at the end of the cooking. The apples should thicken the juices and become quite pulpy.

Spoon the preserve into warmed, clean jars and cover it immediately with airtight lids. Allow to mature for a couple of weeks before eating. The pickle can be stored in a cool place for about 3 months.

Fresh Onion Relish

———— SERVES 4 ————

Fresh chutneys and relishes feature mainly in oriental cuisine, in the form of sambals, and side dishes. Unlike our traditional preserves, these chutneys and relishes are freshly prepared for each meal, although many of them can be kept successfully in the refrigerator for about a week. Serve this side dish, not only with Indian meals but as a complement to boiled ham or with grilled steaks and chops. It yields only a small quantity so you are unlikely to have any spare but if you do it can be kept in a covered container in the refrigerator for one or two days.

2 large onions	3 tablespoons lemon juice
2 green chillies	salt and freshly ground
4 large cloves garlic	black pepper
2 tablespoons oil	chilli powder
1 teaspoon cumin seeds	

Finely chop the onions and place them in a basin. Cut the stalk end off the chillies, then split them and remove all their seeds. Rinse the chillies under cold running water and dry them thoroughly. Cut them into fine slices and add these to the onion. Finely chop the garlic and stir it into the onion with the oil. Add the cumin seeds, then cook on full power, without covering the basin, for 5 minutes.

Stir in the lemon juice and seasoning to taste, then allow the relish to cool. Serve in a small bowl, sprinkled with a little chilli powder if you like.

Coconut Relish

———— SERVES 8 ————

This is another side dish which will go very well with curries of all types. It will also complement roasted meats and grills.

100 g/4 oz fresh coconut grated (about one-third of a small coconut)	4 tablespoons oil
	salt and freshly ground
1 large onion, finely chopped	black pepper
	4 tablespoons lemon juice
40 g/1½ oz fresh root ginger	2 tablespoons chopped fresh coriander leaves
4 teaspoons ground coriander	

Place the coconut in a large basin with the onion. Thinly peel, then finely chop the ginger and add it to the coconut. Stir in the coriander and oil, cover the basin with cling film and cook on full power for 10 minutes.

Stir in the seasoning to taste with the lemon juice and fresh coriander leaves. Allow to cool before serving. Any leftover relish can be stored in a covered container in the refrigerator for a couple of weeks.

Sweet Corn Relish

——— MAKES ABOUT 1.5 kg/3 lb ———

Serve this relish with hamburgers, hot dogs, barbecued foods or cold roast meats, ham and cheese.

1 large onion, chopped	3 tablespoons prepared
4 cloves garlic, crushed	English mustard
225 g/8 oz carrots, diced	generous pinch of
1 green pepper	turmeric
4 tablespoons oil	300 ml/½ pint white wine
salt and freshly ground	vinegar
black pepper	100 g/4 oz sugar
2 tablespoons cornflour	450 g/1 lb frozen sweet
2 tablespoons water	corn

Place the onion in a large mixing bowl with the garlic and carrots. Cut the top off the green pepper, then cut out all the seeds and pith from inside. Chop the green shell and add this to the onion with the oil. Stir to mix well, then add seasoning to taste. Cook on full power for 5 minutes.

Meanwhile, blend the cornflour with the water, mustard, turmeric and vinegar. Add the sugar to the onion mixture, then pour in the liquid and stir well. Cook for a further 5 minutes.

Stir in the sweet corn and mix thoroughly, then cook for 15 minutes, stirring three times during cooking. Ladle the relish into three thoroughly cleaned and scalded pots, then cover immediately and label with the name of the relish and the date on which it was made. Allow the preserve to mature for at least a week before eating it. It will keep for up to 3 months.

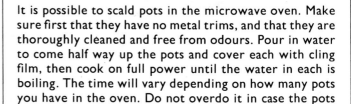

It is possible to scald pots in the microwave oven. Make sure first that they have no metal trims, and that they are thoroughly cleaned and free from odours. Pour in water to come half way up the pots and cover each with cling film, then cook on full power until the water in each is boiling. The time will vary depending on how many pots you have in the oven. Do not overdo it in case the pots break. When the water has boiled, leave the jars covered until you are ready to pot the preserve.

Protect your hands with an oven glove or tea-towel, then remove the cling film (it will have shrunk into the pots) and pour away the water. If the jars have been standing a long time, then reheat them, this way the water is very hot and the clean, hot pots barely need drying.

Cranberry Relish

──── MAKES ABOUT 1 kg/2 lb ────

This is a good relish to serve with hamburgers, baked ham and cold roast meats or poultry (particularly turkey!) or it also goes well with full-flavoured farmhouse Cheddar cheese.

450 g/1 lb cranberries
2 onions, finely chopped
3 cloves garlic, crushed
225 g/8 oz sugar

1 tablespoon wholegrain mustard
100 ml/4 fl oz red wine vinegar

Place the cranberries in a large bowl with the onions and garlic. Add the sugar, mustard and vinegar and stir well. Cover with cling film, allowing a small gap for the steam to escape, and cook on full power for 10 minutes. Uncover and give the relish a good stir, then cook for a further 5 minutes.

   Have ready two 450-g/1-lb pots, clean and thoroughly scalded. Stir the relish, then ladle it into the pots and cover tightly. Store in a cool place for up to 3 months.

Mango Chutney

──── MAKES ABOUT 675 g/1½ lb ────

675 g/1½ lb small green mangos
1 large onion, chopped
1–2 hot green chillies
1 tablespoon salt
2 tablespoons ground coriander

4 cloves garlic, crushed
100 g/4 oz sugar
150 ml/¼ pint cider vinegar

Peel the mangos and cut the fruit off the stones in chunks. Place the pieces in a large bowl with the onion. Cut the stalk end off the chilli(es) then scrape out the seeds and chop the green part. Add this to the mangos with all the remaining ingredients.

   Cover the bowl, allowing a small gap for the steam to escape, then cook on full power for 7 minutes. Uncover, and give the chutney a good stir to mix all the ingredients. Continue to cook without a cover, for a further 8 minutes, then ladle the chutney into clean, scalded pots and cover tightly. Allow the chutney to mature for at least a week before serving it.

DRINKS

Here are a few drink ideas to serve for different occasions – for when you have a horrid cold brewing deep inside, for a quick mid-morning break or for a warming welcome-home brew. If you're looking for a lively party punch, then that's here too.

The microwave oven is ideal for preparing single cups of drinks or for reheating any that have cooled down. If you are preparing a party punch, then keep it hot on defrost or a very low power in the microwave oven.

There are all-plastic coffee filter sets and percolators available for the microwave. I find that if I make a pot of coffee in advance it can be heated up in the microwave with far less fuss than making it at the end of the meal. However, do not use pots with a long thin spout as the coffee may spurt up the spout during heating.

Instant Coffee

I find the microwave oven useful for heating just one cup of coffee when I am on my own. It is also very handy for reheating ready-made coffee, either by the cup or in a jug.

To make a quick cup of instant coffee, place the coffee in the cup and pour in cold water as required. Heat for 2 to $2\frac{1}{2}$ minutes, depending on whether you like your coffee black or white. Add milk and sugar to taste.

Quick Mocha Mugs

This makes a sustaining drink for when you're feeling like more than coffee but not a snack.

$\frac{1}{2}$ teaspoon instant coffee
2 teaspoons cocoa powder
sugar to taste
milk

Put the coffee, cocoa and sugar in a mug and top up with milk allowing a little room for the liquid to froth up. Cook on full power for $1\frac{1}{2}$ minutes, then stir thoroughly before heating for a final 30 to 40 seconds.

Spiced Chocolate

——— SERVES 2 TO 3 ———

4 tablespoons cocoa powder
sugar to taste
$\frac{1}{2}$ teaspoon ground cinnamon

generous pinch of mixed spice
600 ml/1 pint milk

Place the cocoa in a basin or large (1.15-litre/2-pint) heatproof measuring jug. Add the sugar as you wish and the cinnamon. Put in the spice, then whisk in the milk.

Cook on full power for 4 to $4\frac{1}{2}$ minutes, then whisk thoroughly and pour into mugs to serve.

Red wine can be brought to room temperature quickly in the microwave oven. Put the open bottle in the oven for about 1 to $1\frac{1}{2}$ minutes. Make sure there are no lead wrappings left from the cork.

Hot Coffee Punch

SERVES 4 TO 6

Serve this warming winter drink to welcome guests on a cold night or as an opening drink to a weekend brunch party. Pour the spicey coffee into warmed punch cups or short, stout tumblers instead of mugs.

1.15 litres/2 pints freshly made coffee	25–50-g/1–2-oz sugar
	150 ml/¼ pint brandy
6 green cardamoms	150 ml/¼ pint single cream
2 cinnamon sticks	(optional)

Pour the coffee into a bowl and add the cardamoms. Break the cinnamon sticks and add them to the coffee, then set it aside to stand for 30 minutes.

Stir the sugar to taste into the coffee, then heat through for 10 minutes. Stir thoroughly, remove the spices and pour in the brandy. Heat for 2 minutes, then pour the spiced coffee into glasses to serve. Offer a jug of single cream with the coffee.

Hot Honey and Lemon

This is a good drink for relieving the symptoms of a miserable cold. It soothes the throat and warms a tired body.

2 tablespoons honey
juice of ½ lemon
strip of lemon peel
water

Put the honey in a mug and stir in the lemon juice. Add the lemon peel, then top up with water and cook on full power for 2 minutes. Stir well.

Warming Apple Cup

SERVES 6

1 (1-litre/35.2-fl oz) carton apple juice	2 pieces preserved ginger, sliced
6 cloves	1 tablespoon ginger syrup
10 juniper berries, coarsely crushed	

Pour the apple juice into a large bowl and add the other ingredients, then cook on full power for 10 minutes. Allow to stand for 5 minutes, then ladle the drink into glasses to serve.

Whisky Toddy

This is usually the drink everyone consumes when they feel the first depressing symptoms of winter flu approaching. Whether it does any good or not is open to debate, but this consoling toddy will ease any adult cold.

2 tablespoons whisky
2 tablespoons honey
a little lemon juice
water

Place the whisky and honey in a mug, then stir in the lemon juice and pour in water to almost fill the mug. Cook for 2 minutes on full power, stir well and drink.

Mulled Ale

SERVES 6

This really is very good – the idea did not immediately appeal to me but once I had tasted the result I was convinced. The mulled ale is quite a heavy drink, but it is heart warming and ideal for very cold winter evenings.

1.15 litres/2 pints ale (bitter, strong beers or pale ale)	8 tablespoons rum
	1 cinnamon stick, broken
50 g/2 oz sugar	½ teaspoon freshly grated nutmeg

Pour the ale into a large bowl, then stir in the sugar, rum and cinnamon stick. Add the nutmeg and cook on full power for 7 minutes.

Ladle the ale into strong glasses and serve at once. Any leftovers can be reheated for 1 to 2 minutes in the microwave.

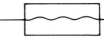

This recipe, and other drinks, can be made very simply if your oven has a temperature probe. Simply set the probe to turn the oven off at the required setting (70 C/158 F) and sit back to wait.

Mulled Wine

—— SERVES 4 TO 6 ——

l large orange	a little sugar
l6 cloves	4 tablespoons brandy
l cinnamon stick, broken	(optional)
l bottle red wine	

Stud the orange with the cloves, then place it in a large bowl. Cover with cling film and cook on full power for 2 minutes.

Add the cinnamon stick and pour in the wine, then heat for 5 minutes. Stir in a little sugar to taste and the brandy if used, then ladle into glasses.

The mulled wine can be reheated for l minute in the microwave, or individual glasses can be heated for 30 to 60 seconds.

Spiced Cider Punch

—— SERVES 4 TO 6 ——

l (1-litre/35.2-fl oz) bottle medium sweet cider	6 cloves
grated rind and juice of l orange	150 ml/¼ pint brandy (optional)
l dessert apple, cored and sliced	

Pour the cider into a large bowl and add the orange rind and juice. Stir in the apple slices and cloves, then cook on full power for 7 minutes.

Stir the brandy into the cider cup and ladle the drink into glasses to serve. If any drink is left, then it can be reheated for 1 to 2 minutes before serving.

Rum Cider Substitute an orange for the apple in the above recipe and add 2 cinnamon sticks. Add dark rum instead of the brandy; the result is excellent.

Peach Tea Punch

SERVES 6

There are many different flavoured tea bags available and they can be used to make delicately flavoured drinks. Try any other tea bags in this punch, if you cannot find any which are fruit flavoured then use Earl Grey tea bags or another fine blend.

3 peach-flavoured tea bags
1 (1-litre/35.2-fl oz) bottle sweet cider
1 cinnamon stick
sugar to taste

Place the tea bags in a bowl, then pour in the cider. Add the cinnamon stick and cook on full power for 10 minutes. Squeeze the tea bags with the back of a spoon about four times during cooking.

Remove the tea bags from the punch and add sugar to taste. Allow to stand for 5 minutes, then ladle the drink into glasses to serve.

Christmas Rum Punch

SERVES 4 TO 6

1 orange, sliced
1 lemon, sliced
50 g/2 oz raisins
50 g/2 oz blanched almonds, split
1 cinnamon stick, broken
1 bottle red wine
150 ml/¼ pint dark rum
2 tablespoons demerara sugar

Place the fruit in a bowl with the nuts and cinnamon stick. Pour in the wine and add the rum, then stir in the sugar. Heat on full power for 7 minutes. Pour the wine into glasses to serve.

The microwave oven can be used to soften fruit for making home-made wine. This is particularly useful for hard fruits like crab apples. Allow a few minutes, so that the fruits are tender but not cooked.

MENU PLANNING

The microwave oven is ideal for cooking one dish or for preparing meals for one or two people. If you want to cook a meal for four or more people using the microwave oven as the main appliance, then you will have to give the menu a little thought and plan the order in which you are going to cook the dishes. Remember, that unlike a conventional oven, your microwave oven affords a limited amount of space.

Once you are accustomed to using the microwave you will automatically be able to make the most of it for preparing family meals or for dinner parties, but until then you may like some guidance.

Bearing in mind the fact that the microwave oven will reheat foods quickly without causing any deterioration in flavour, texture or appearance, plan to cook some of the dishes in advance. If the vegetables are precooked, then arranged in their serving dishes and topped with butter, they can be reheated while the first course is being eaten. Cover the dishes with cling film to keep the moisture in. If you are well prepared in advance you can leave any dishes which require a very short cooking time until the last minute. Make pâtés or desserts which need chilling several hours in advance or on the day before. Make any soups in advance ready for reheating just before they are to be served. If you are planning to make a stew or dish by conventional cooking methods then you can utilise the microwave oven to reheat it before serving.

Even if the menu suggestions given here do not appeal, do read through the preparation instructions as they may give you ideas about how best to plan your own menus. Until you are used to the way in which your microwave oven copes with cooking whole meals you are best advised not to plan a large menu solely around this appliance. When I first bought my microwave oven I made the silly mistake of launching into action cooking a large meal in it. I was preparing a meat main dish and in addition I was catering for a vegetarian – a menu consisting of about six dishes for the main course, all left until the last minute to cook! We sat down to the meal eventually but I realised that my planning really had left a lot to be desired.

MENU I

Here is a tasty vegetarian menu which is also suitable for non-vegetarians. I like these dishes for their flavour and texture compared with any food, not just no-meat recipes. Make the salad as interesting as you can with as many vegetables as are in season.

Lentil Pâté

Wholewheat Spaghetti
with
Walnut Cream Sauce
Salad

Spiced Peaches

Preparation Plan
1 Make the lentil pâté in advance and chill it thoroughly.
2 Prepare the salad first.
3 Prepare the ingredients for the walnut cream sauce and the peaches.
4 Cook the spaghetti conventionally, drain it and transfer it to a microwave-proof serving dish. Make the walnut sauce and pour it over the pasta. Cover and set aside to heat before serving.
5 Cook the peaches and set them aside to heat through while the main course is being eaten.
6 Serve the pâté and put the spaghetti in the microwave oven to heat through.
7 Heat the peaches while the main course is being eaten.

MENU 2

Cheap and informal, this menu can be served as supper for two as well as an informal meal for friends.

Hot Garlic Bread

Chilli con Carne

Plain Cooked Rice

Salad

Gooseberry Fool

Preparation Plan
1 Make the gooseberry fool and chill it thoroughly.
2 Prepare the garlic bread, wrap it in a roasting bag and set it aside. You can make this the day before and keep it closely wrapped in several layers of cling film if you like.
3 Prepare and cook the chilli. While it is cooking make the salad. Leave the chilli covered once it is cooked.
4 Heat and serve the garlic bread. While the bread is served the microwave oven will cook the rice.
5 Heat the chilli con carne briefly before serving with the rice.

MENU 3

This is a light meal which is not too expensive as trout are now among the cheapest fish you can buy and they cook superbly in the microwave oven.

Chicken and Almond Soup

Spinach-stuffed Trout

Mushrooms à la Grecque

New Potatoes with Bacon

Chocolate Crunch Pie

Preparation Plan
1 Make the chocolate pie well in advance and chill it thoroughly.
2 Prepare the soup in advance to be reheated just before serving.
3 Prepare and stuff the trout but cook the potatoes first.
4 While the potatoes are cooking prepare the mushrooms. Half cook these for reheating later.
5 Reheat and serve the soup. Put the trout in to cook while the first course is being eaten.
6 Heat first the potatoes, then the mushrooms and serve with the trout.

MENU 4

This is an inexpensive, yet quite exciting menu. It's useful for a mid-week dinner or ideal for an informal supper party.

Hot Bean Dip

Mexican Drumsticks

Runner Beans in Garlic and Walnut Sauce

Baked Potatoes

Tropical Bananas

Preparation Plan
1 Make the bean dip in advance and put it into a suitable microwave-proof dish for reheating and serving.
2 Cook the runner beans to reheat them at the last minute.
3 Prepare the ingredients for the Mexican drumsticks and assemble them in the dish.
4 Cook the baked potatoes.
5 Heat the bean dip. Put the chicken in the microwave to cook while the dip is being served.
6 Heat the potatoes briefly, then transfer them to a hot grill to brown. Heat the runner beans.
7 Prepare and serve bananas at the last minute or they will discolour.

MENU 5

This is a simple two course meal, suited to family dinners.

Roast Chicken with Apple and Orange Stuffing

Fantail Potatoes
Julienne of Carrot
Creamed Parsnips

Creamed Rice Pudding

Preparation Plan
1 Prepare the stuffing. Stuff and truss the chicken. This can be done a few hours in advance and the bird can be chilled.
2 Prepare the potatoes and cook them in the microwave oven ready for browning in the conventional oven with the chicken. Once they are taken out of the microwave, leave the potatoes tightly covered with cling film.
3 Cook and cream the parsnips, then transfer them to a serving dish (one which you can put in the microwave) ready for reheating just before serving.
4 Cook the chicken in the microwave oven. While it is cooking, turn the conventional oven on to heat up and put the potatoes in the oven, on a top shelf, as soon as it is on.
5 Transfer the chicken to the conventional oven and cook the carrots in the microwave.
6 Reheat the creamed parsnips and prepare the rice pudding for cooking.
7 Take the chicken out of the oven and transfer it to a serving plate to keep hot. (Put it back into the conventional oven but turn the heat off.) Make gravy in the microwave.
8 Once the main course is ready to serve put the rice in the microwave to cook. Stir the cream into the rice and heat it through as you are about to serve it.

MENU 6

If you offer an alternative first course for this menu it will, in fact, serve as a vegetarian meal. It is intended as a full-flavoured menu which is easy to prepare in advance, even the day before if you so wish. The only part that needs to be prepared at the last minute is the starter.

Prawn-stuffed Mushrooms

Spinach-stuffed Cannelloni
Ratatouille
Hot Crusty Bread

Savarin

Preparation Plan
1 Make the savarin well in advance and prepare the fruit salad.
2 Prepare the spinach-stuffed cannelloni in advance to be heated through before serving.
3 Make the ratatouille in advance and heat that through before serving too.
4 Prepare and cook the stuffed mushrooms, then serve them for the first course.
5 While the first course is being eaten put the cannelloni in the microwave to heat through.
6 Brown the cannelloni under the grill and heat the ratatouille in the microwave.
7 Heat the bread very briefly while you are taking the cannelloni and ratatouille to the table.
8 Pile the fruit salad into the savarin and serve it to close the meal.

MENU 7

This is a slightly more sophisticated but quite traditional meal which can be served at a dinner party.

Baked Avocado with Cucumber

Beef Olives
New Potatoes
Courgette Parcels

Caramelised Oranges

Preparation Plan
1 Prepare the caramelised oranges several hours in advance and chill them thoroughly. They are best made the day before and kept covered in the refrigerator.
2 Prepare the beef olives ready for cooking and arrange them in a suitable dish. Set aside, covered.
3 Cook the new potatoes and transfer them to a serving dish ready for reheating in the microwave oven later.
4 Make the courgette parcels and cook the beef olives. While the beef is cooking prepare the avocado pears.
5 Cook and serve the avocado pears. Put the potatoes in the microwave to heat while the first course is being eaten.
6 Heat the beef very briefly – it should still be quite hot – then put the courgettes in to cook as the beef and potatoes are taken to the table.

MENU 8

This is a fairly inexpensive menu which is quite interesting enough to serve for a supper party so long as you know that the guests like fish.

Turkey Pâté

Haddock Italienne
Lemon Rice
Creamed Corn

Pears in Cider

Preparation Plan
1 Make the turkey pâté well in advance so that it has time to chill thoroughly. It is best made the day before and stored, covered closely, in the refrigerator.
2 Prepare the pears in cider first. These can be chilled to serve as a cold dessert, or reheated before serving.
3 Prepare the creamed corn and transfer it to a microwave-proof serving dish for reheating at the last minute.
4 Cook the rice. While the rice is cooking prepare all the ingredients for the fish and arrange it in its dish.
5 When the rice is cooked leave it tightly covered. Cook the fish, then add the topping and transfer it to the grill to brown.
6 While the fish is browning reheat the corn, then reheat the rice (it should still be fairly hot but a minute or so will bring it back to full heat).
7 When the main course is served reheat the pears ready for dessert if you like.

INDEX